INSIDE THE MIND OF TOYOTA

INSIDE THE MIND OF TOYOTA

Management Principles for Enduring Growth

Satoshi Hino

Foreword by Jeffrey K. Liker

Translated by Andrew Dillon

Productivity *Press*

New York

Original Japanese book edition published by Diamond, Inc., Tokyo, Japan as
Toyota Keiei Shisutemu no Kenkyū. Copyright © 2002 by Satoshi Hino.

English edition copyright © 2006 by Productivity Press, a division of The Kraus
Organization Limited.

All rights reserved. No part of this book may be reproduced or utilized in any
form or by any means, electronic or mechanical, including photocopying,
recording, or by any information storage and retrieval system, without permission in writing from the publisher.

Most Productivity Press books are available at quantity discounts when purchased in bulk. For more information contact our Customer Service Department
(888-319-5852). Address all other inquiries to:

Productivity Press
444 Park Avenue South, 7th Floor
New York, NY 10016
United States of America
Telephone 212-686-5900
Fax: 212-686-5411
E-mail: info@productivitypress.com
www.productivitypress.com

Library of Congress Cataloging-in-Publication Data

Hino, Satoshi, 1945-
    [Toyota keiei shisutemu no kenkyū. English]
    Inside the mind of Toyota : management principles for enduring growth /
Satoshi Hino ; foreword by Jeffrey K. Liker ; translated by Andrew Dillon.
            p.   cm.
    "Original Japanese book edition published by Diamond, Inc., Tokyo, Japan
as Toyota Keiei Shisutemu no Kenkyū. ©2002"—T.p. verso.
    Includes index.
    ISBN 1-56327-300-4 (alk. paper)
    1. Toyota Jidosha Kabushiki Kaisha—Management.   2. Automobile
industry and trade—Japan—Management—Case studies.   I. Title.
HD9710.J34T6363313   2006
658—dc22
                                                        2005030271

09 08 07 06   5 4 3 2

Contents

Foreword

When I wrote *The Toyota Way*, the purpose was clear: to stand apart from the many books on specific elements of the Toyota Production System (TPS) that merely emphasize "lean tools." You cannot pull out a piece of a system and expect it to perform. More importantly, Toyota has a much broader management approach, which makes TPS work. Without it, TPS is a lifeless drawing of a house.

The Toyota Way was intended to correct this misunderstanding through a set of management principles, stories bringing the principles to life, and easy reading to make the point crystal clear. It is obvious that Satoshi Hino has a different and complementary purpose. Hino-san draws on years of experience as an engineer in a Japanese auto company and presents a very detailed and information-rich picture of Toyota's management system. He did not work for Toyota, but was a long-standing fan of Toyota and followed the company intensively. Unfortunately for those of us who do not read Japanese, there is a rich base of articles, books, and documents about Toyota in Japanese that have not been translated or are difficult to obtain. Fortunately, Productivity Press decided to translate Hino's book into English. I say "fortunately" because this book is the real thing. It is filled with documentation and provides a deep account of many aspects of Toyota's management system.

If we estimate that *The Toyota Way* is 90 percent prose and 10 percent facts and diagrams, I would guess that Hino's work is made up of 60 percent facts and diagrams. Without even reading the book, anyone deeply interested in Toyota's management system could get a tremendous amount by just looking at the figures. Many of these I personally had never seen before, despite twenty years of visiting and studying Toyota. They helped fill in some holes in my knowledge.

One might expect a detailed, factual book to focus on the formal systems of Toyota's structure and miss the philosophy. That is certainly not the case with Hino's book. Hino is well aware of the importance of Toyota's philosophy and traces the DNA of Toyota management both in biographical terms, looking at the history of leaders in the company, and in philosophical terms, looking at the evolution of management thinking.

I have had many requests asking how Toyota excels at quality. The question is usually framed in terms of Toyota's quality control system. My standard answer is to say that quality is part of every function, and every person is an inspector checking the work passed to them and continuously improving processes. Hino goes a step further. He presents and dissects Total Quality Control as part of Toyota's functional management system, a system that is not well understood but is a key to their success. As in most parts of the book, Chapter 3 gives a very detailed and factual account of this simple and powerful system of management. We learn how Toyota's planning, quality management, cost management, finance and accounting, labor management, and more are organized and managed.

In Chapter 6, we get a glimpse of Toyota in the 21st century. Again, this is more a factual account than a crystal ball projection of where Toyota is heading. And again, we get an inside view that has been invisible to most of us who do not read Japanese. For example, we get insight into how Okuda shook up management of the company, dragging it into the 21st century sometimes in direct conflict with Toyoda family members—something very rare with previous leaders. We get some detail of the inner workings that are leading Toyota to grow as a company from a family business to a global company, but one that still maintains the Toyota DNA—without which it would be just like any other automotive company. We also get insights into Toyota's passion for reforming itself. Eiji Toyoda repeatedly emphasized the main threat to the company—complacency. He preached that the company must continually reflect deeply and reshape itself aggressively to fit the changing environment. Certainly Okuda and Cho continued this message in the modern age.

For me, this is a book that I will read through again and again, using it as a reference for specific facts and in-depth analysis. It is a great companion to *The Toyota Way*. The messages of both books are the same: To understand Toyota's success you must delve deeply into the underlying management principles and culture. If you want facts, figures, charts, and graphs that give you a detailed analysis and factual accounting, this is a must-read.

> Jeffrey K. Liker, Ph.D.
> Professor, Industrial and Operations Engineering
> University of Michigan

Translator's Foreword

Barely twenty-five years ago, the Toyota Production System was largely opaque to the Western world. With a few exceptions—Yasuhiro Monden's work comes to mind—the few available books on the subject were rough going, and almost none of them were in English. In North America and Europe, it was a visionary few who seized on and studied the first translations that I and others made of works by pivotal figures such as Shigeo Shingo and Taiichi Ohno. As Toyota ideas spread, the subsequent successes of these "early adopters" became a testament to the sustained effort and resources they devoted to absorbing Toyota's lessons and applying them to their own organizations.

Things have changed quite a bit since the early 1980s, although not always in predictable ways. That first wave of translations into English and the conspicuous successes of the early adopters and ex-Toyota Group consultants did not, oddly enough, seem to increase the demand for information directly from Japan. Instead, these and other influences ushered in a first generation of homegrown explicators, interpreters, promoters, and students of Toyota thinking and practice. The Toyota Production System (now sometimes called "lean production") became domesticated, popularized. It was reinterpreted as a collection of tools and techniques and repackaged in simple, digestible language.

The good news in all this is that Toyota is infinitely more approachable today than it was a quarter century ago. The bad news is that the flow of information from Japan is still sluggish and still impeded by obstacles of language, culture, and perhaps even our own impatience. We have learned a great deal about Toyota in recent years, but the paucity of information in English and other Western languages still conceals from us the breadth and dynamism of Toyota's achievements. And all the while, the widely noted gap between knowledge and hard results—both in Japan and in the rest of the world—seems to have grown wider.

So what should we do? How can we best absorb and profit from what Toyota has to teach? Clearly, familiarity with words, tools, and techniques is not enough. Nor is it enough to move equipment around or "raise awareness." These things are necessary, but they are far from sufficient, and Satoshi Hino tells us why: The success of the Toyota Production System can be separated neither from the painstaking action required to build and sustain it, nor from the managerial structures and practices of which it is a part. Hino's implication is clear: Build a strong managerial infrastructure, learn relentlessly, and practice, practice, practice.

A long-time and meticulous observer of Toyota, Hino reminds us that Toyota today is a triumph of humility over hype, of hard work and discipline over rigid formulas and facile "solutions." It is the embodiment of a way of thinking about the world. And it is a moving target, too. Even as it takes up new challenges in the new millennium—environmental friendliness, breakthrough fuel efficiencies, and systems integration, for example—Toyota distinguishes itself by its distinctive worldview and by its refusal to be complacent.

Hino's book, originally published in Japan in 2002, sought to encourage a revival in Japanese industry by drawing the attention of Japanese managers back to the sources of Toyota's achievement. It was a call to action, backed by hard evidence and considered conviction.

Our aim is not dissimilar. In publishing this English-language edition, Productivity Press, the translator, and the author hope to take this message beyond the Japanese manufacturing world and make it accessible to managers in organizations around the globe. Globalization and intensifying competition make the book particularly timely. Hino's subject matter is specific, but his implications are general: Theory and principles matter. Documentation is critical. An organization's success is intimately linked to how its leaders think about work, people, and society.

These are powerful lessons, and Hino has them clearly in mind as he guides us through the broader Management System that is the critical underpinning of Toyota's rise to prominence. The key to Toyota's strength, he says, is what lies beneath the surface of casual scrutiny: discipline, information management, unshakable principles, and coherent vision. And he gives details.

Unlike most Toyota watchers, Hino urges us to set our sights not on replicating Toyota's success, but on surpassing it. This point is crucial, because it moves our attention away from slavish imitation of what is visible on the surface and challenges us to tap into deeper and more powerful mechanisms of excellence.

This is not a cookbook and it is not "Toyota Lite." It deserves serious study, application, and experimentation. Learn how Toyota thinks, Hino is telling us. Learn Toyota's strengths, make them your own and then exceed them.

Andrew Dillon
September 2005

Preface to the English-Language Edition

The Toyota Production System has been called a revolutionary successor to Taylorism and the Ford system, and it is the subject of a great number of fine explanatory books. Few companies, however, seem to have adopted the Toyota Production System with success. Business process benchmarking demands that a company develop best practices that surpass its competitors. Even if a company becomes more profitable by introducing the Toyota Production System, we cannot assume that it has adopted the System successfully. For that, the company needs to go beyond Toyota and build its own unique production system. Until it does, it is merely following in Toyota's footsteps and will be unable to surpass its teacher.

Why is it that companies are unable to adopt the Toyota Production System very well? The Toyota Production System is difficult to introduce successfully without adopting the comprehensive Toyota Management System, of which TPS is only one part, a management system that encompasses matters such as corporate culture, management policies, and business methods.

I worked at a Japanese automotive manufacturing company until 1999. About 25 years ago, I became interested in the Toyota Production System and began studying it in order to surpass the Toyota Motor Corporation, the leader of the Japanese automotive industry. I could understand the effectiveness of techniques such as *kanban* systems or *andon* systems, but I couldn't understand the thinking of the Toyota people who worked out these unique methods. Their thinking—the structure of their minds—seemed essentially different from that of ordinary people like us. Unless we could grasp the structure of their minds, then even though we might be able to copy the Toyota Production System, we wouldn't be able to work out methods for going beyond it and we would never prevail. I concluded that I had to unravel how it was that their way of thinking came about.

At that point, I began to collect all sorts of information about Toyota, not merely about the Toyota Production System. What interested me in particular was the Toyota Management System, but unfortunately I came across no books that analyzed and explained the Toyota Management System in a systematic fashion. This was the start of my research into the Toyota Management System. I have studied Toyota in the intervening twenty years or so, and the present book is a compilation of those studies.

General Motors Corporation and the Ford Motor Company, the U.S. automakers that once held sway over the world's automotive industry, have now fallen into an extreme managerial slump. Their current fortunes show that their 20th-century management systems, complete with the waste, or *muda*, of mass production, are no longer appropriate for the 21st century. A company with *muda* can be profitable in an age when demand exceeds supply, but we are no longer in such an age. Moreover, waste in industry—for example, the waste of overproduction or the waste of having people do work that adds no value—eventually stresses the earth. The pessimistic estimate that the earth may become uninhabitable by the end of the 21st century is not necessarily unrealistic. Industry, which stresses the planet more than anything else, needs to pay careful attention to the establishment of management systems that eliminate all waste. A living example of this is the Toyota Management System, a fundamental system that will make it possible to ensure profits and protect the earth in the 21st century. I hope all companies continue to grow and develop in the 21st century. Learn the Toyota Management System from this book and use it as a basis to build your own best practices.

This English edition comes some three and a half years after the book's publication in Japan in June 2002. Certain circumstances have changed, and we have updated some obsolete data accordingly. As a basic principle, however, the translated English edition has not been updated. This is not the sort of book that needs to be rewritten every few years, since its goal is to view the future from the perspective of a historical analysis. If anything, I think the last three years have shown the "principles of enduring growth" described in this book to be correct.

Four chief developments have taken place at Toyota during these past three years: the completion of CCC21 (Construction of Cost Competitiveness for the 21st Century); the renewal of the company's product information system; the founding of the Toyota Institute; and the settling of the company's 2010 Global Vision.

As I mention in Chapter 6, CCC21 consists of activities to root out costs from the planning stage in every department and every process, including those of suppliers. CCC21 began in July 2000 and achieved its original goal of ¥1 trillion total cost reductions within three years. Since improved parts are introduced during model changes, moreover, a massive cost reduction effect has automatically rolled over into model changes for the globally strategic *Vitz*, *Corolla*, and *Camry* models. It is axiomatic that kaizen at Toyota never stops, so in the wake of CCC21, Toyota is taking on VI (Value Innovation) activities that fundamentally rethink design methods, including the appropriateness of materials.

Renewal of Toyota's product information system involves the integration that I touch on in Chapter 6. In January 2002, Toyota unified the management of all design information by taking part of the TIS (Total Information System for Vehicle Development), shown in Fig. 3.14, and restructuring it as E-BOMs (Bills of Material for Engineering) for design development aspects that deal with product function information. The company also took part of its SMS (Specification Management System), restructured it as M-BOMs (Bills of Material for Manufacturing) compatible with the newly constructed E-BOMs, and began using the M-BOMS for new models. The use of the new M-BOMs, extended to all models at the end of 2003, has developed into a system of "Global Integrated Parts Lists" that is uniform throughout the world. This has made it possible to apply "knowledge management" to design, something that for many years had been an area of concern. It has also made it possible to standardize M-BOMs that had differed somewhat in factories worldwide, thereby improving products, lowering costs, and shortening development lead times. It also assures a basis for rapidly advancing global expansion. Total investment in this initiative is reported to have been ¥200 billion, and this will not be recovered soon even if the initiative is successful. If it fails, then it cannot help but shake the foundations of management. Toyota is probably alone in the world in taking on such a bold system restructuring. Now Toyota is trying to improve its competitiveness by being the first automaker in the world to build a system of PLM (Product Lifestyle Management).

The Toyota Institute was founded in January 2001 for the purpose of transmitting the Toyota Way (booklets summarizing the Toyota management philosophy) to interested parties throughout the world. (The Toyota Way is introduced in Chapter 6.) Each year, several thousand students from all parts of the world come to the Toyota Institute to study the essence of the Toyota Way while staying at the Toyota Institute. Beginning with the company's entry into China around 1995 and followed by its aggressive expansion into France and Eastern Europe, Toyota found itself plunging headlong into global expansion and was deeply concerned that a lagging extension of its internal logistical base might start to bankrupt the company. For this reason, it was judged necessary that Toyota men and women of differing cultures and customs share and empathize with Toyota values and exercise disciplined Toyota-style management in their home countries. The result was the Toyota Institute. Toyota today is still stretched to the limit, still walking a tightrope. The Toyota Institute was launched at the last minute, and its effects will probably become apparent only slowly.

Toyota's "2010 Global Vision," announced in April 2002, evolved from the "2005 Vision," also introduced in Chapter 6. Resting on an assumption of a growing emphasis on recycling, the spread of advanced road and traffic systems and motorization on a global scale, the 2010 Global Vision calls for internal reform of engineering and product development, management systems, and profit structures. Toyota has set for itself the aim of achieving a total global share of 15 percent by as early as 2010. At the time the 2010 Global Vision was announced, GM held a 15 percent share and Toyota's share was around 11 percent. For Toyota to achieve a 15 percent share would mean kicking GM out of its position as the world's largest automotive company, a goal that no one would readily believe. Yet Toyota pulled ahead of Ford in 2003 and is positioned to pass GM in 2006, four years earlier than it planned. At the end of the 20th century, GM and Ford were making a killing in a pickup truck market that Japanese companies had not even entered. Perhaps this led the American manufacturers to commit the strategic error of losing a sense of crisis with respect to Japanese manufacturers, but even so, Toyota is catching up faster than predicted. Toyota's hot pursuit of its rivals can be extrapolated from the company's 21st-century business strategy (covered in Chapter 6), including the completion of the CCC21 initiative, the renewal of the company's product information management system, and the founding of the Toyota Institute. These developments validate the prediction that Toyota will surely continue to grow in the 21st century.

Translations of this book were published in 2003 in Korea and Taiwan. In Korea, Jaeyong Lee, managing director of Samsung Electronics, the son and heir apparent of Samsung Group chairman Kunhee Lee, gave copies of the book to over 100 Group executives with this note: "This is the most impressive book I've read recently. I'd like you to read it." SS Kim, the vice-chairman and CEO of LG Electronics, registered this book as No. 1 on the "CEO's Bookshelf" section of his personal homepage. Samsung and LG are rapidly growing global manufacturers of electric and electronics products and they are avidly reading this book with the goal of growing even faster. I hope readers in the English-speaking world will use this book to learn the principles of enduring growth, so that in the 21st century their companies both increase profitability and ease their impact on the earth's environment.

Satoshi Hino
Fall 2005

Introduction

WHY STUDY TOYOTA?

The Japanese economy rushed into the 21st century on the heels of a "lost decade," and a way out is not yet in sight. Corporate reorganizations have reversed course, and each year the number of Japanese companies declines. Layoffs caused by restructuring have become commonplace, and unemployment continues to rise to record levels. With the rise of China as the "world's factory," Japan's place in the world is in peril.

Microsoft's president Bill Gates's keynote address to COMDEX in Las Vegas on November 12, 2000, included the following observation:

> I keep near at hand a copy of My Years with General Motors by Alfred Sloan, the great leader who made GM the world's largest automaker. The important thing here is how to make organizations endure once the genius entrepreneurs who built them have passed on. In Japan there are two companies that serve as suitable examples of this: Toyota Motor and Sony. I'm not surprised when a company grows rapidly in the space of five years, but I'm extremely interested in companies that consistently generate superlative results over a twenty- or thirty-year period. Do they have embedded in them some mechanism for permanence? If they do, then a generational handoff won't wipe out their talent and their vitality.

Former General Electric CEO Jack Welch, in a November 6, 2001, interview with the *Nikkei Sangyo Shimbun*, addressed the question of Japanese firms reeling from poor performance and seeking management models in the West. Welch commented: "First of all, you have to learn the terms of winning from the management techniques of companies like Toyota. Japan has first-rate companies like Toyota and Sony. Firms like Ricoh and Canon, too, have now pulled ahead of Xerox in the U.S. Japan can find a way to break through the sluggish economy [by studying the innovative methods of its domestic winning teams]."

As Bill Gates and Jack Welch observed, companies structured for enduring growth lie right at our doorstep. By studying their examples, 21st-century Japan can once again become a model of prosperity in the world.

On January 1, 2002, the *Nikkei Sangyo Shimbun* published a ranking of companies according to their capacity for survival. "Survival potential" in this instance took the form of an index expressing whether a company's profits were sufficient to guard against the risk of income fluctuations after tax and other obligations had been satisfied. Reproduced below is the formula used for this purpose:

Survival potential = actual business profits before interest payments − survivability profits

Survivability profits = dividends + officers' bonuses + corporate taxes + interest costs and discount charges + risk charges

Risk charges = Standard deviation of the previous 10 years' business profits before interest payments on total capital × total capital (average of initial and final capital)

The companies ranked highest in survival potential were:

Rank	Company	Survival potential	Survivability Profits
1	Toyota Motor Corporation	¥378 billion	¥207 billion
2	Take Fuji	¥193.1 billion	¥27 billion
3	Takeda Pharmaceutical	¥183 billion	¥45 billion

Toyota, which leads in survival potential and survivability profits, was also in first place ten years ago. The results suggest just how enduring Toyota's business and profit bases really are.

Figure 0.1 is a map of strategic control in the automotive industry. Put together by McKinsey & Company, it shows trends in the financial positions of automobile manufacturers in the period from 1994 to 2000.

The performance measure on the vertical axis (Price Book Ratio or PBR) reflects the value of company shares in capital markets. Total current value can be expressed by the curve defined by the product of PBR and equity, shown on the horizontal axis.

As we see from this figure, Toyota is the industry leader, far surpassing other firms. Ford raised its PBR and edged toward leadership at one point, but its position is unclear since the Firestone episode in 2001. Although General Motors and DaimlerChrysler have clearly grown in scale, their results and strategic effectiveness remain questionable. As "integrators," they compare poorly with Toyota.

The secret of Toyota's stubbornly persistent growth in diverse environments has been ascribed to difficult-to-imitate "core competencies." But in the current crisis, where the rise of China threatens to scuttle Japan, reproducing Toyota's core competencies and making them broadly accessible to all Japanese companies has become a matter of critical need.

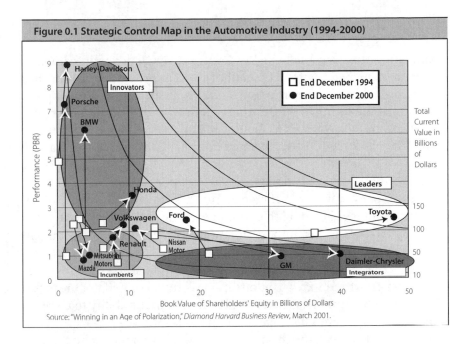

Figure 0.1 Strategic Control Map in the Automotive Industry (1994-2000)

Source: "Winning in an Age of Polarization," *Diamond Harvard Business Review*, March 2001.

Toyota itself recognizes that it cannot survive alone while the rest of Japan founders. Thus, through initiatives such as the Central Japan Industries Association[1] and the Japan Organization for Innovation in Manufacturing, Human Development and Quality,[2] Toyota is working to standardize and spread its management system. (See Chapter 6.)

It is difficult, however, for insiders to objectively evaluate an organization. Toyota does not see firms at the "bottom of the bottom." Its appraisal begins at the "bottom of the middle." For this reason, methods advocated by Toyota are too far removed from the realities of most companies and, at least initially, simply too difficult to follow.

In this book, we will be looking at Toyota from the outside, distilling and explaining the essence of Toyota's enduring growth in terms that relate to other companies. The book is structured with the aim of making it possible for other companies to perform on a par with Toyota.

The book is not aimed at companies in any particular industry, nor at companies of any particular scale or history. As long as they have a desire for managerial innovation, managers of any generation can build the mechanisms of enduring growth into their own companies. The principles discussed in this work can be applied to any company in any industry. Note that management functions do not vary according to scale either; how big or small your company is does not matter.

AN OUTLINE OF TOYOTA'S GROWTH

Wanting to introduce Total Quality Control (TQC), a certain company, Company A, invited a noted TQC authority, K, to provide guidance. Each time K visited, he mercilessly pointed out problems within the company. Members of the company's TQC office assumed that K's criticisms represented an objective view from the outside and felt obligated to listen to them. They absorbed his fragmentary comments, collected them as the "Sayings of K," and distributed them throughout the organization. Figure 0.2 shows those "sayings" in the form of a relational diagram.

The company manager in charge of TQC lashed out at his staff. "What were you thinking? Handing this stuff out will suck the energy out of the company." Ironically, his outburst followed on the heels of K's comment that the company suffers from narrow vision!

TQC activities at the company became ceremonial. Before long, they slowed to a crawl and were abandoned. The company could not break free of the diagram of problems that K had pointed out. Its ability to compete took a dive, and it eventually had to resort to layoffs.

Even now, I suspect, the company in this story does not really comprehend what caused it to slip and fall. It may not understand that K's fragmentary and negatively charged comments made it impossible for the company to see how to resolve any of its problems.

For a revised perspective, let's take K's remarks and turn them around (see Figure 0.3).

A close look at Figure 0.3 reveals something nearly identical to an outline of Toyota's growth. K was intimately familiar with the situation at Toyota; as a consultant, he must have unconsciously applied the Toyota construct.

The scheme in Figure 0.3 shows cause-and-effect relationships and can pretty much be read as an outline of what needs to be done to create a "company where sales lead to profits." What isn't clear, however, is how to go about creating the "causes" in the lower half of the diagram. It won't do any good to look for causes in limited observations, such as "benefits from rural location (simple and honest)." Only when a company examines the management situation at Toyota as a universal framework will the rules and principles needed to shift to the sort of growth illustrated in Figure 0.3 become evident.

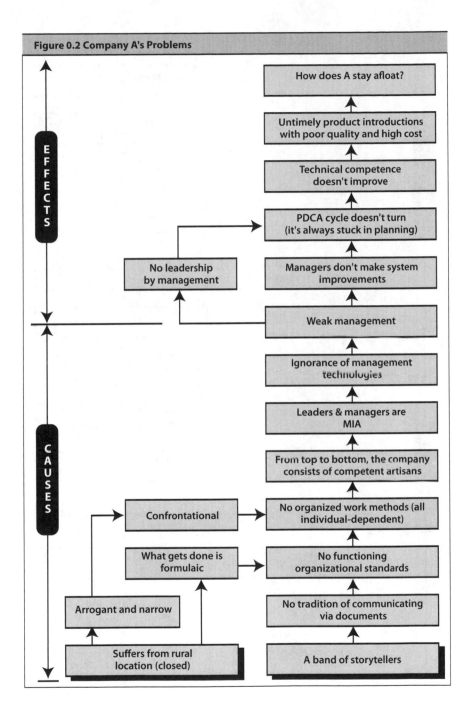

Figure 0.2 Company A's Problems

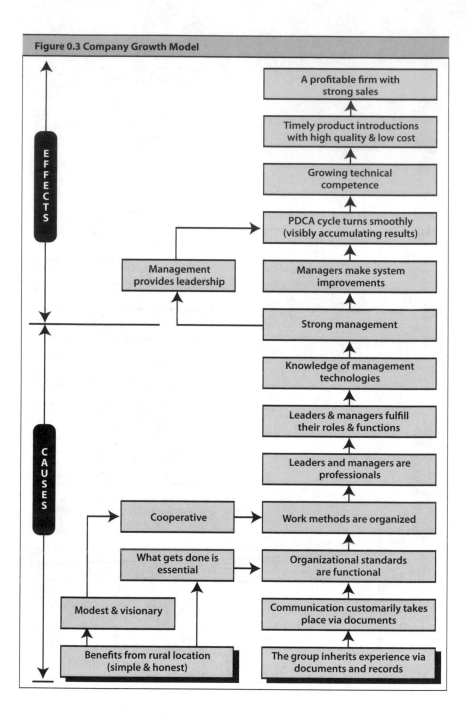

Figure 0.3 Company Growth Model

AN ANALYTIC PERSPECTIVE ON COMPANIES

Many books and documents have been devoted to the Toyota Production System, but very few companies have adopted the system with success. Parts are meaningful only in the context of a whole, and transplanting a part tends to result in less-than-perfect functioning. Companies need to adopt the system in its entirety.

Management is often compared to an iceberg. What is visible above the water consists of a company's output: the sales performance of its products and popular judgments on the strength of its brands. What determines all that, however, is what lies below the surface—the infrastructure. One objective of this book is to break down the infrastructure further and analyze Toyota's management system as an integrated corporate model.

By applying the model illustrated in Figure 0.4 to all companies, it is possible to see the strengths and weaknesses in each element of the structure. Strength refers to the degree of growth potential.

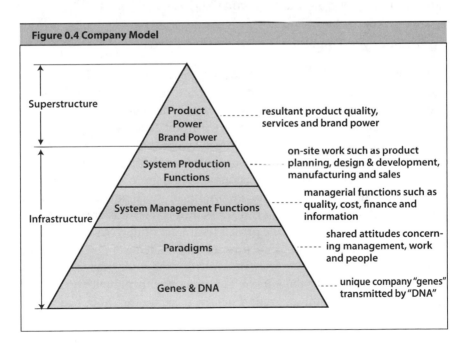

Figure 0.4 Company Model

Figure 0.4 reveals the densities, or strengths, of each element of a company's structure. Companies with strong superstructures and weak infrastructures can be viewed as the "five-year growth" companies mentioned by Bill Gates. They might ride a wave of good fortune or sell their products based on the example of a smaller pioneer's efforts, but are quite likely to fail within ten or twenty years. Companies like these were once the darlings of the public and have now gone under.

Conversely, companies whose superstructure is weak and whose infrastructure is strong (like Toyota in the early years) are likely to generate continuously superior results for twenty or thirty years.

Company A, cited above, is a company that grew by selling its technological prowess. It put all its effort into its superstructure and neglected its infrastructure, subsequently weakening both. Companies (like present-day Toyota) that are strong throughout are unshakably dominant. Historically, Toyota began managing by filling in its infrastructure, thereby building a company where strength extends all the way up to the superstructure.

Companies with weak infrastructures are no more substantial than Styrofoam pellets and will be blown about by the slightest breeze. Companies with solid infrastructures, on the other hand, are like icebergs. Strong winds may blow, but they won't budge.

CHAPTER SUMMARIES

In Chapter 1, *Toyota's Genes and DNA*, we analyze Toyota with a focus on "genes" and "DNA," as illustrated at the bottom of the company model presented in Figure 0.4. DNA is not the same as genes. It is, rather, the medium of genes. Without DNA, even the finest genes would perish after a single generation. The laws of biological evolution stipulate that recessive genes are weeded out. If we extrapolate and apply this theory to a company model, only growth genes can accumulate and evolve, as long as DNA is present. We will examine the origins of the Toyota genes and the process by which the DNA that transmits those genes was created. At the same time, we will illustrate the principles for creating DNA that mediate genes and for discovering and nurturing human talent capable of creating growth genes.

In Chapter 2, *The Toyota Paradigm*, we analyze Toyota with a focus on "paradigms," situated on the second tier from the bottom of our company model. Corporate paradigms are influenced by the genes passed down from previous generations and, via a path from a system of management functions to a system of production functions, determine the highest order power of the company's products and brands. Without clear company paradigms, the energies of managers and all employees cancel each other within the company and are not directed outside. Sooner or later, management collapses. In the presence of paradigms, the energies of all employees are aligned, and management can draw on strength beyond its own resources. We will explore the principles of paradigm formation and untangle Toyota's ethos, culture, and views on management, work, and people—all of which were formed under the influence of the company's growth genes.

In Chapter 3, *Toyota's System of Management Functions*, we analyze Toyota from the perspective of the "management function systems" located at the center of our company model. What we call management function systems are the systems that govern basic management functions shared throughout the corporate organization, such as quality, cost, technology, standards, personnel, information, and business. Quality improvements, cost reductions, human resource development, and the effective use of information all become possible via the creation of management function systems that transmit top management's intentions swiftly and accurately throughout the company and that draw out system-improvement efforts from middle managers and shopfloor-improvement efforts from employees. At Toyota, top management exerts leadership based on Toyota paradigms, middle managers develop systems in accordance with top management's aims, and all employees quietly engage in shopfloor improvement (*kaizen*). This chapter explains how Toyota created systems that function in this way and reveals the principles of building "functioning" management function systems.

In Chapter 4, *Toyota's System of Production Functions*, we analyze Toyota from the perspective of the "production function system" that exerts direct sway over the "product power" and "brand power" situated at the very top of the model. What we call the "production system" here refers to the chain of actual operational functions (from product design to manufacturing to sales) that take place in accordance with objectives set by the management function system. If the production function system is the warp, then the management function system is the weft that governs each production function. Many excellent studies of the Toyota Production System have already appeared, and for the most part, we will not venture into this territory. We will, instead, analyze Toyota's production function system by focusing on the areas of product planning and design and present the principles for building an effective production function system.

Chapter 5, *Product Power and Brand Power*, tells the story of the results of all the activities we will have previously discussed: Toyota product quality, service levels, and brand strength. In this chapter, we introduce several evaluations that authoritative third parties have made of Toyota's accomplishments in these areas and confirm once again the effectiveness of a corporate substructure that links "genes" and "DNA" with a "production function system."

The final chapter, *Toyota Management in the 21st Century*, takes a broad look at the sorts of strategies Toyota is adopting as it endeavors to manage in the 21st century. With the conviction that Toyota will undoubtedly keep growing in the new century, we provide evidence for the soundness of Toyota's principles of enduring growth.

---

1. Chubu Sangyo Renmei
2. Nihon Monozukuri Hitozukuri Shitsu Kakushin Kiko

--- 1 ---

Toyota's Genes and DNA

THE MEN WHO CREATED THE TOYOTA GENES

Who created the Toyota genes, and what kind of genes did they create? To answer this question, we need to examine the words and actions of past Toyota leaders. Figure 1.1 gives an overview of the company's leadership up to the present.[1]

Figure 1.1 A Succession of Leaders at Toyota

Decade	1930s	1940s	1950s	1960s	1970s	1980s	1990s	2000
Sakichi Toyoda								
Risaburo Toyoda								
Kiichiro Toyoda								
TMS Era — Shotaro Kamiya								
Seishi Kato								
Teizo Yamamoto								
Shoichiro Toyoda								
TMC Era — Taizo Ishida								
Taiichi Ohno								
Fukio Nakagawa								
Eiji Toyoda								
Masaya Hanai								
Shoichiro Toyoda								
Tatsuro Toyoda								
Hiroshi Okuda								
Fujio Cho								

TMS: Toyota Motor Sales
TMC: Toyota Motor Corporation
N.B. dashed lines show active periods, solid lines show presidential tenures

Sakichi Toyoda

Sakichi Toyoda was born in 1867 in the city of Kosai in Shizuoka Prefecture. The spiritual legacy of Nichiren[2] and the moral and economic teachings of Sontoku Ninomiya[3] are deeply rooted in the region, and both exerted a strong influence over Sakichi as he grew up. Although Sakichi devoted his career to inventing looms, his beliefs as an inventor (resolute follow-through, contribution to society and country, hard work as a human duty) were a natural outgrowth of the teachings of Nichiren and Ninomiya.

In his last years, Sakichi came to believe that automobiles were more vital and useful to humans than looms were, and he entrusted the family's foray into the automobile business to his eldest son, Kiichiro. Indeed, the fortune amassed by Sakichi through his loom inventions later provided the capital for Kiichiro Toyoda's entry into the automotive business. "Build cars!" Sakichi is said to have told Kiichiro. "Build cars and serve your country."

Sakichi Toyoda died in 1930 at the age of sixty-three, but the principles he espoused were passed down to future generations. Figure 1.2 summarizes Sakichi's words and deeds in the form of the Toyoda Precepts.

Figure 1.2 The Toyoda Precepts

1. Regardless of position, work together to fulfill your duties faithfully and contribute to the development and welfare of the country.

2. Always stay ahead of the times through research and creativity.

3. Avoid frivolity. Be sincere and strong.

4. Be kind and generous. Strive to create a home-like atmosphere.

5. Be reverent and conduct your life in thankfulness and gratitude.

The Toyoda Precepts

The Toyoda Precepts were articulated five years after Sakichi's death by his son-in-law, Risaburo, and his eldest son, Kiichiro. Sakichi's beliefs combined the lessons he had acquired as a lifelong inventor with the teachings of Sontoku Ninomiya and the doctrines of Nichiren Buddhism.

As company policies or management principles, the Toyoda Precepts continue to be used—either in their original form or modified according to the times, the environment, or particular company characteristics—in eleven companies of the Toyota Group, including Toyota Industries Corporation, Denso, and Toyota Auto Body. Common to all these companies is an emphasis on the key words: "research and creativity" and "cooperation and consistency." Sakichi's philosophy has become the traditional spirit of Toyota and the Toyota Group companies. It lives on as the ideology that binds the Toyota Group together.

Quotations from Sakichi

"You have no allies but yourself."

Sakichi had to rely on other people's capital when he first began to put an invention to practical use. The words cited here came from his experience of jumping through hoops to get what he needed. Kiichiro inherited his father's sense of independence and self-reliance. Under his management, Toyota was not content simply to import technology from Europe, the United States, and other countries with advanced automotive industries. Indeed, this conviction became the motive behind the awakening in Japan of an automotive industry based on distinctive Japanese technologies.

"Open the window over there and take a look. It's a big world out there."

Sakichi is reported to have said this to doubters around him when Toyoda Boshoku was expanding into China. He recognized that although new behaviors always provoke opposition, those who are complacent will be left behind and ultimately defeated. Sakichi's words remind us that active engagement with the new is the principal business of managers.

"The ultimate goal of invention is total practical application."

"Don't talk about true value without conducting exhaustive market trials."

Hard work is needed to bring an invention to completion, but practical application requires comparable effort. Japan is often criticized in the world for simply applying things that have been invented in other countries. But invention without practical application is no more than a hobby. Invention becomes innovation only when stable duplication is achieved on a meaningful scale and at a realistic cost. Sakichi was an innovator who believed that invention only achieved its goal through practical application, and it was in practical innovation that Japan's strength exceeded that of all other countries.

Kiichiro Toyoda

Kiichiro Toyoda, the eldest son of Sakichi, was born in Kosai City in 1894. He entered his father's company, Toyoda Spinning and Weaving, in 1920, after graduating from Tokyo Imperial University.

In 1921, Kiichiro embarked on a tour of European and American industry in the company of his sister and his younger brother-in-law, Risaburo Toyoda. It was in America that he became convinced that the age of the automobile had arrived. This was the genesis of Kiichiro's dream of building automobiles. He established an automotive division within Toyoda Spinning and Weaving in 1933, and set about the serious study of how to build cars. Nineteen thirty-five saw the landmark unveiling of Toyoda's GI Truck.

Outlined below are Kiichiro's basic concepts regarding automotive manufacturing as formulated in *Toyota Motor Sales—A History of the First 30 Years* (1967, Toyota Motor Sales Company).[4]

1. The key to automotive manufacturing must be passenger vehicles, more specifically, passenger cars priced for the general public.
2. The production of passenger cars priced for the general public must rely on mass production supported by substantial research laboratories and all necessary equipment.
3. Selling passenger vehicles priced for the general public is far more difficult than producing them.
4. Research and development are important. One must always stay ahead of the times.
5. The automotive industry is an integrated industry that relies critically on basic manufacturing prowess.
6. Actively adopt whatever technologies and knowledge of advanced nations that can be beneficial in establishing the Japanese automotive industry. This is not an argument for simple copying, however. Ingeniousness should modify imported techniques and ideas to adapt them to Japanese realities.

After World War II, Japan's economy entered a period of extreme deflation. Even Toyota had trouble raising capital. Throughout this period, Kiichiro repeatedly insisted that "managers are duty-bound to avoid layoffs." His guiding moral principle was "to avoid layoffs whenever possible." He sent memos to labor unions flatly stating that he would not "engage in layoffs."

But things got worse. By the end of 1949, with the company on the brink of bankruptcy, Kiichiro barely succeeded in obtaining a loan from a consortium of banks. The terms of the loan stipulated that "sales operations were to become independent" and that "excess manpower would be let go." Labor unions responded by launching a strike, and a major battle ensued. With troubles coming to a head, Kiichiro reasoned that he could not stay in his job if the only way to do so was to fire employees. In 1950, he stepped down as president.

Kiichiro was succeeded by Taizo Ishida, who got the company back on a firm footing by relying on the procurement boom prompted by the Korean War. In 1952, with the firm's fortunes on the rise, Ishida asked Kiichiro to return as president. But two months later, at the age of fifty-seven, Kiichiro suffered a cerebral hemorrhage, which ended his career.

Just-In-Time

Productivity in the United States in 1935 was estimated to be nine times that of productivity in Japan. For Kiichiro, being able to compete on an equal footing with automotive manufacturers in the advanced countries of the West meant having to work out uniquely Japanese methods for high productivity and low cost. One of the elements of this approach was the "just-in-time" method (i.e., making what is needed, when it is needed, and in the quantity needed). Just-in-time was born from the realization that each process in the automobile industry required massive storage capabilities and from Kiichiro's desire to find some breakthrough that would allow him to take on companies in Europe and the United States.

The just-in-time concept can be traced back to Henry Ford's belt conveyor system. But because of Ford's view that the market was production-driven—that everyone would buy black cars as long as they were cheap enough—the original purpose of the belt conveyor system was lost. Ford's philosophy was transformed into a philosophy embracing mass production: Whatever could be produced, should be produced in large quantities.

Ford's *My Life and Work* was Kiichiro's favorite book. Indeed, it was Kiichiro's study of Ford's management and production system that led him to discover the belt conveyor system's original purpose and eventually to the idea of just-in-time.

The phrase "just-in-time" was already in use when construction began on the Toyota plant in Koromo in 1935. Just-in-time thinking permeated the 10-centimeter-thick manuals that Kiichiro himself compiled for each process and distributed to key players. He drove the point home to Toyota employees in energetic lectures on the subject. Kiichiro's thick manuals are the roots of Toyota's production system. They lead directly to the subsequent establishment by Taiichi Ohno of the *kanban*-system-based Toyota Production System that we know today.

Kiichiro never challenged the advanced nations of the West with any particular hope of success. Instead, he acted upon an unshakable desire to "always stay ahead of the times through research and creativity." Later, Eiji Toyoda would write admiringly of the extraordinary courage Kiichiro showed in founding an automotive company and establishing the Koromo plant. Kiichiro, armed only with his own convictions, had plunged into the automotive business when even the great industrial conglomerates had deemed such a move too risky. Kiichiro's resolve was shaped by the pioneering spirit he had inherited from his father, Sakichi, and the moral support he received from his stepmother, Asa, who once had declared that if her son was reduced to begging, she would willingly join him.

Quality Improvement

Even sixty years later, Toyota employees recite the wise words of Sakichi Toyoda and Kiichiro Toyoda.
Sakichi Toyoda:

"Always stay ahead of the times through research and creativity."

"Don't talk about true value without conducting exhaustive market trials."

Kiichiro Toyoda:

"Study what customers want and reflect that in your products."

"Improve the product by auditing the production system, as well as the product itself."

Sakichi's clear and simple words call straight to the heart; they are really a psychological doctrine. Kiichiro's phrasing may have a less direct appeal but is the concrete expression of a considered methodology. It is fair to say that modern Toyota quality represents a fusion of Sakichi's psychology and Kiichiro's practicality.

In November 1935, during the era of Toyoda Automatic Loom, Kiichiro announced the completion—and the sales of several score—of the company's first vehicle, the GI Truck. Unfortunately, the GI was prone to mechanical failures and the newspapers had a field day: "*Toyoda Breaks Down Again*," the headlines read.[5] Shotaro Kamiya, who was then responsible for sales, insisted that the vehicles had to be repaired for free, no matter how much the repairs cost the company. This policy gradually reduced failures, but the episode persuaded Kiichiro that it was extremely difficult to resolve problems entirely by means of market trials within the company. It was at this point that he began to emphasize "studying what customers want and reflecting that in the product." Vehicles were turned over to customers for evaluation, and the results were collected and analyzed. Subsequent improvements to the cars reflected what customers wanted. In organizational terms, the company set up exclusive Inspection and Improvement Offices and Inspection and Improvement Committees.

Kiichiro's advice to "improve the product by auditing the production system, as well as the product itself" was an even more progressive idea. Tracing the causes of quality problems upstream revealed a variety of contributing factors. These factors included immature design and production technologies, ignorance about how a product was used, and careless design errors. The ability of production inspections to discover such problems is extremely limited. Inspections are simply incapable of capturing the kinds of quality problems that arise during product use. Kiichiro realized that manufacturing quality is determined by work done across a range of processes, including design, development, manufacturing, inspection, distribution, and service. Quality, he concluded, would not get better without improvement of the work in all processes. Audits could objectively assess work methods and suggest ways of improving them.

Kiichiro's view of quality was precisely the one codified in 1987 by the International Standards Organization as the ISO Quality Standards 9000 Series. The basic philosophy behind ISO 9000 is that all processes that generate products contain numerous quality problems and that the auditing and improvement of those processes is necessary for quality assurance. Seventy years after the formulation of Kiichiro's view concerning process management, his insights became international norms in the form of ISO standards.

Cost Reduction

Kiichiro also had firm ideas about pricing: "How many vehicles does Japan have to make for its domestic cars to reach an appropriate price level? Everybody wants to know this, but nobody can answer the question with certainty. What we do know is that we have to offer cars at a price at which customers will buy them."

At the time, the prevalent view of an appropriate selling price was that PRICE = COST + PROFIT (i.e., that one determined price by adding required profit to cost). Kiichiro, however, believed that a more appropriate formula—which later came to permeate Toyota—was that PROFIT = PRICE – COST. In other words, profit was determined by subtracting cost from a price set by the market. This concept was one that Kiichiro learned from Henry Ford, who posited:

> It may in some narrow sense be scientific to determine price by adding up costs, but in a broader sense this method is not scientific at all. A price determined in this manner is utterly useless if the product does not sell. The price should be set low, first of all, so that everyone will have to work efficiently for the business to be viable. Setting low prices forces everyone to make an effort to squeeze out a profit. A company discovers methods for manufacturing and selling when it has to make do in straitened circumstances.

Kiichiro, who had studied Ford's management and production methods, is thought to have applied Ford's idea regarding the determination of prices, profits, and costs to his own company philosophy.

Taking the Broad View

> "When technology is in the hands of individuals, you can make superior parts but you can't make superior vehicles."

Consider the strange wooden bucket depicted in Figure 1.3. Its staves are different lengths, and if you put water in it, it is the shortest stave—or the hole situated even lower—that will determine the water level. An automobile comprised of tens of thousands of parts is built through tasks performed by thousands of people. If the technical or skill level of even one of those people is not up to par, it is that person's skill that will end up determining the quality and reliability of the car.

Rather than focusing on individuals with extraordinary technical skills, Kiichiro emphasized creating teams whose average skill level was high. His primary tool for accomplishing this was the formulation of standard operations.

Figure 1.3 A Strange Bucket

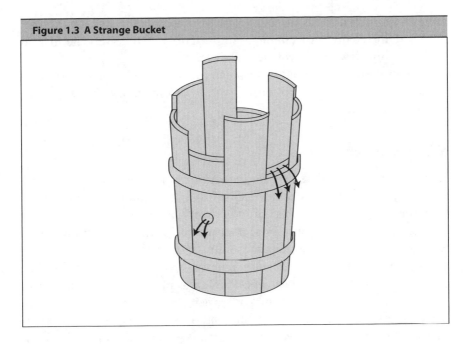

"Cars are not built by automotive companies alone. First-tier suppliers, in particular, must be partners in research. We don't just buy things from them. We have them make things for us."

Kiichiro saw the automobile as being a product of great breadth and believed that stabilizing its quality could be assured only by going into every nook and cranny of supplier plants and stabilizing quality there. As the volume of Toyota business increased, Kiichiro rejected both uncontrolled increases in the number of suppliers and the rush to the suppliers with the lowest prices. On the contrary, he emphasized the need to establish and maintain stable business relationships with first-tier suppliers and to foster and guide the specialization of partner plants.

This policy stabilized relationships with suppliers, deepened personal relationships, and laid a foundation for mutual prosperity with partner plants. Like the strange bucket in Figure 1.3, the policy illustrates the wisdom of taking the broad view.

The Legacy of Kiichiro's Management Innovations

After founding the Toyota Motor Company, Kiichiro instituted an extraordinary number of management innovations.[6] Broadly speaking, one sees Kiichiro's legacy as the fundamental strategies to overcome the important management challenges of each stage of the company's development. Rather than relying on technology imported from the West, he instead took the long view that Toyota would never be able to compete with Ford and General Motors without securing an independent automotive manufacturing base. Kiichiro's extraordinary gift was that he saw through to the essence of things.

Kiichiro's Documentary Record

Kiichiro was a man of neither eloquence nor narrative skill, but he left a great volume of writings behind, allowing us to gain a clear idea of his thinking. Table 1.1 provides a chronology of his major writings.

It is astonishing to consider that nearly all of these documents were written by Kiichiro himself, either as founder or as chief executive. Nearly all of them are in the form of rules, memos, or manuals—procedures or standards for running the business. This is exceptional as most executives the world over, East or West, pick up a pen only when they have something to sign. They conduct their business orally and express their priorities by the spoken word. Few chief executives write their own business standards! As a manager who wielded his own pen and wrote out his own business standards, Kiichiro was indeed extraordinary.

Shotaro Kamiya

In 1935, in order to strengthen Toyota's sales department, Kiichiro recruited Shotaro Kamiya, who at the time was the assistant manager of GM Japan. Kiichiro had gone headhunting on his own, telling Kamiya, "We can muddle through manufacturing because we have a good group of technical people, but we don't have anybody who knows anything about sales. If you come over to Toyota," he added, "you can have complete control of sales."

Kiichiro expected Kamiya to bring to Toyota a knowledge of market strategies, covering franchise systems, store management, installment sales, advertising, and service. He wanted Kamiya to do what he believed was right and to bring on board the people he needed.

So Kamiya joined Toyota, bringing with him a number of his subordinates from GM Japan. As Kiichiro had expected, Kamiya proceeded to build a Toyota tradition of emphasis on sales.

We can identify three elements of Kamiya's thinking that live on in Toyota today: emphasis on the customer, a long-term perspective, and an orientation toward information.

Table 1.1 Kiichiro Toyoda—A History of His Documentation

Year	Document name	Contents
1937	Job Functions & Job Descriptions	Drafted to clarify and simplify lines of authority in the context of building an organization for the new company founded in 1937. These assigned and distributed authority so that decision-making could respond immediately to situations on the shop floor.
	Guides (job procedures) Work Rules (job performance standards)	Kiichiro compiled many Guides and Job Rules so that jobs in all departments would be performed efficiently. The Guide for purchasing clerks pointed out "Fourteen Things to Remember About Purchasing." Among them, he writes, "Consider Toyota's subcontractor plants to be divisions of Toyota and make it a principle not to inflict change on them without good cause. Strive as much as possible to raise their performance." These laid down basic purchasing policies that are still alive in Toyota today.
	Process Manuals	When the Koromo Plant was under construction, Kiichiro personally compiled these 10 cm-thick manuals in order to spread the idea of Just-In-Time in the company. He devoted himself to making sure JIT penetrated the organization, distributing the manuals to the appropriate people and gathering employees for his energetic lectures. These manuals constitute the roots of today's Toyota Production System.
	Memo on Cost-Cutting	This memorandum records Kiichiro's view of cost reduction. You begin with a set selling price and then generate profits by lowering production costs. The Memo is displayed in the Toyota Museum.
1938	Inspection Regulations	These set up an organized inspection system to guard against difficulties with incoming inspections of outsourced parts.
	Regulations for Inspecting Outsourced Parts	These Regulations clearly state that, in order to cut down on defects in outsourced parts, "we must provide guidance to subcontractors and strive to bring their level of defects down to nothing." They assign to inspections the important function of improving supplier materials and processes. This grew into the Toyota attitude toward supplier management, i.e., that of guiding and nurturing suppliers.
June 1939	The Company Organization and a Survey of its Rules	Kiichiro reorganized many of the Guides and Work Rules he had compiled at the time of the founding of Toyota. "You can do any job as long as you work according to rules," he wrote. This idea of "job standardization" became the basis for a summary of the company and the some 83 job rules that make up "The Company Organization and a Survey of Its Rules." He compiled this with a view to efficient management and smooth flows of information, with the president and vice presidents looking after business policies and other executives in charge of their alloted areas of responsibility. For the Toyota organization, this sort of organizational reform clarified management levels, departments and the relationships between authority and responsibilities. It resulted in a functional division of work.
September 1939	Rules for Improving Audits	Kiichiro believed that "the most shameful thing one can do is send a defective car out into society." To prevent this, he established an Audit Improvement Section under his own direct jurisdiction and created Rules for Improving Audits. He brought Eiji Toyoda and others into the Section and they studied information on all defects collected by the people in charge of service in the sales departments. When they determined what needed improvement, they transmitted this information back to the service people by return notice.
November 1939	Purchasing Regulations	These "Purchasing Rules" were a rewrite of Guides for purchasing clerks. "Consider Toyota's subcontractor plants to be divisions of Toyota and make it a principle not to inflict change on them without good cause. Strive as much as possible to raise their performance." This has been consistent policy up to the present day.
1940	Internal Regulations for Control of Automotive Parts	Increased production accompanying the outbreak of World War II in Europe led to a change in policies for dealing with supplier parts—parts that accounted for 70% of costs. In addition to making a distinction between domestic and foreign products, this document defines internal and external sources and specifies such matters as inspection frequency (i.e., when they can be omitted) and inspection methods.
February 1941	Essentials of Establishing a Planning Department and Deliberative Council	Kiichiro instituted the Essentials of Establishing a Planning Department and Deliberative Council on the occassion of his accession to the presidency of Toyota. This document enlarged the Planning Department, a central organ for strengthening overall managerial competence, and clarified details of its organization, authority and management. Kiichiro himself served as chairman. To assist him, he set up a Deliberative Council composed of six members, and the two entities covered all aspects of planning work. Taizo Ishida, who at the time was a director of Toyoda Automatic Loom, was named as a member handling machine tools, steel and automatic looms. The formation of these organizational entities both professionalized the running of the business and made responsibilities and authority clear.
February 1943	Toyota Motor Corporation, Inc., Corporate Regulations	As the company grew in size, Kiichiro and others instituted the Toyota Motor Corporation's Corporate Regulations with a view to raising management efficiency. They then set about organizing internal systems. Together with previous regulations concerning the organization, work, and other matters, this document clarifies both the Board of Directors system and the status of executives and employees.
October 1943	Audit Improvement Committee Regulations	Under continuing harsh wartime regulations, Kiichiro re-established an Audit Improvement Committee in order to raise quality and productivity. He assumed the chairmanship himself and issued Audit Improvement Committee Regulations. The purpose of the committee was described as follows: "The purpose of the present committee is to investigate and improve aspects of Toyota automobiles that usage reveals to be inconvenient or deficient...we will investigate and improve areas that should be improved as a result of use in actual society." Based on information from outside Toyota, this committee conducted comprehensive examinations and research on market quality problems and functioned as the supreme voting body on all technical matters. Kiichiro's management practices became a primary factor in Toyota's priority on service and on the company's marketing power.

Source: From information in Sato, Yoshinobu. 1994. Sources of Toyota Management.

Emphasis on the Customer

"The user comes first, the dealer second, and the manufacturer third."

Even before World War II, a corporate customer came to the sales division and pressed Kamiya, who was then in charge of the division, for Toyota's position on selling cars. Kamiya didn't hesitate: "The first person we think of is the customer. The last person we think of is the manufacturer."

It was a desperate and evasive answer. But the customer is said to have gone away satisfied. The substance of this declaration later became a Toyota slogan: "The user comes first, the dealer second, and the manufacturer third." This insight was ahead of its time, anticipating the modern rule of marketing that dictates "Customer-oriented marketing first, then sales-oriented marketing, then production-oriented marketing."

The Long View

"Sales needs start-up capital every bit as much as production does."

From the beginning of Toyota Sales, no problem proved as perplexing as the question of how to exploit latent demand. Kamiya inaugurated many businesses in order to make this occur.

In 1954, he established the Toyopet Maintenance Company. He then invested in a series of ventures, which included the purchase of the Japan Driving School in Tachikawa, the establishment of Toyota Used Car Sales, and the opening of Chubu Japan Driving School, said to be the largest such school in East Asia. Additional capital went into Chiyoda Fire and Marine, the Japan Design Center, the Japan Research Center, International Highways, Nagoya Broadcasting, The Japan Industrial Film Center and the Chubu Japan School of Automotive Maintenance.

Kamiya's reasoning was difficult for people outside Toyota to understand. He was sharply criticized for imprudent use of capital at a time when funds to support monthly installment sales were in short supply.

Kamiya's response to his critics was that "sales needs start-up capital every bit as much as production does."

The company's business," he argued, "would come to a halt if we concentrated exclusively on latent demand for today and tomorrow. We have to think five and ten years out and work to expand latent demand on that scale. We must do it, even at the expense of immediate profit." And he moved resolutely ahead with this plan.

Later, Kamiya observed, "A lot of people misunderstood me, but now they seem to acknowledge that my judgment was correct."

"A peck of trout can only hold a peck."

In 1956, Kamiya overhauled the existing arrangement of one dealership per prefecture and introduced a system of multiple nationwide dealerships. Kamiya's celebrated response to the objections of existing dealers was to say "A peck of trout can only hold a peck." But increasing the number of dealerships amounts to fitting in two pecks. Kamiya's argument was that doing so would generate huge cost reductions that would benefit even the existing dealers. Surprisingly, the existing dealerships were won over by this reasoning and Kamiya's concept became reality. Kamiya articulated his commitment to the broad view and to balance when he pointed out that "even if production takes the lead in strengthening the system, things won't balance out if sales is going its own way. Real management begins when you enhance production and sales simultaneously."

Information Orientation

When Iwao Imazu left the Nagoya Bureau of Industry and Trade to join Toyota, Kamiya greeted him with a request. "We have no place for collecting and analyzing information for the organization as a whole," Kamiya said. "I'd like you to set up a department that can help us understand the whole picture." Imazu responded by setting three conditions: that no expense be spared, that he have access to first-rate people, and that consideration be accorded the notion of work as play. Kamiya agreed, and in December 1956, an Information Office was inaugurated as the prime strategic entity within Toyota Motor Sales. The successor to the Information Office, the Planning and Survey Department, is currently staffed by some 60 people and brings together specialists in mechanical engineering, mathematics, statistical analysis, and other fields to conduct wide-ranging and ongoing studies and surveys.

As Imazu had requested, this internal organization draws on extraordinary funds. In addition to semiannual Demand Trend Surveys, it conducts a variety of sample surveys. Each year, the office carries out more than five or six surveys at a cost of roughly 60 million yen; it requires some six or seven hundred million yen annually, a sum that very few companies would spend on market surveys.

Kamiya was known as the "god of marketing," but he did not attain that status by experience or razzle-dazzle. He earned it with his relentless focus on information.

Taizo Ishida

When Taizo Ishida was 38 years old, Sakichi Toyoda invited him to join Toyoda Automatic Loom, saying, "You've been a businessman. So make me some money!" Ishida, who had a natural gift for business, was later appointed president of Toyoda Automatic Loom. When Kiichiro withdrew from the presidency during the labor troubles in 1950, Ishida, while still chief executive of Toyoda Automatic Loom, was named president of Toyota as well. Accepting the promotion, he said, "In the event that I am able to conform to each of your expectations, I would like to ask for your approval in advance for Kiichiro Toyoda to return to the presidency."

In essence, Ishida saw himself as Toyota's caretaker. He had been trained directly by Sakichi and sometimes called himself a "medium for Sakichi's spirit." Ishida expressed himself with more than the usual self-confidence and was endowed with verbal gifts rich in wit and polished humor. Indeed, the record he left of many of his sayings remains the best guide to the genes he bequeathed to Toyota.

Independence

"Guard your own castle."

"Whatever you do, you need to accumulate capital resources that you can use as you like."

"Traditional self-reliance is a strong element in Toyota culture."

The agonizing experience of moving from invention to business without money had led Sakichi Toyoda to adopt the philosophy that one had no allies but one's own self. "Don't rely on others," he had said, "but move ahead by your own efforts."

Ishida was deeply marked by Sakichi's determination, and the painful experience of dealing with banks during Toyota's fiscal crisis in 1949 only confirmed this attitude. Facing bankruptcy with a year-end balance shortfall of ¥200 million, Ishida had been faced with the humiliating experience of going to banks and having low-level clerks ask him what he wanted. The experience had nearly brought him to tears. For him, the first principle of business was to take precautions that would preclude chasing around after money.

Stinginess

"I'm a very greedy guy. That's what makes me work so hard. Always wanting money drives me to work harder. And even when I'm making money, I wonder what sort of manager I'd be if I didn't make any."

"I don't recognize the utility of financial dealings. And I particularly dislike the current fashion for financial activities involving companies that exist only on paper. I believe the owner should always be around to mind the castle. It's fine to be a loner and it's fine to be stingy."

"Don't begrudge money that's being used."

Ishida's stinginess and his spirit of independence were two sides of the same coin. He believed that he had to be tightfisted because independence required some sort of capital guarantee to avoid relying on others. He was convinced, in other words, that a manager's primary mission was to make the company profitable. Ishida's managerial style was inherited by those who promoted Toyota's financial independence through the 1980s.

The Primacy of Equipment

"Plow the money you make back into equipment. You're not going to raise efficiency with people. Do it with machines."

"Investing profits in equipment rather than people is the way to avoid layoffs."

"Beat the other guys in the competition for equipment."

Ishida's notion that money has value when it is being used fed his view of the pivotal role of equipment for continued production. He focused on investing in equipment rather than people because he was determined never to repeat the humiliation of being forced to lay off 2,000 workers during the company's great labor crisis. One example of Ishida's adherence to this ideal was the Motomachi Plant. Built in 1959, it gave Toyota a decisive lead over Nissan at the dawning of the age of motorization.

Improve, Improve and Improve Again

"We inherit an insistence on 'better products and better ideas' from old man Sakichi. Creativity and ingenuity are what I want everybody to pursue."

"Our final and highest goal is to make things better and cheaper. Quality improvement and cost reduction will probably always be important themes for us."

Eiji Toyoda and Shoichi Saito brought Ford's suggestion system to Japan as a souvenir of their visit to the United States in 1951. At first, they used it as a system for eliciting creativity and ingenuity from employees, simply translating it and substituting the word "Toyota" wherever the word "Ford" appeared. But within six months, the system was rewritten in the Toyota fashion, and the result is the system the company uses today.

A contest among employees was held to choose a slogan. The winner, "better products and better technologies," was later modified to "better products and better ideas." Ishida may have used this phrase only to promote creativity and ingenuity, but Toyota's intoxication with improvement, or *kaizen*, began in Ishida's day.

A Rural Spirit

"A rural spirit is Toyota's greatest virtue and the one of which she should be most proud."

"A farmer's strengths are that his temperament and habits lead him straight forward, that he doesn't mind hard work, and that he doesn't shirk hardship. A farmer studies twice as hard as anyone else."

"Do what's right and do it the right way."

Ishida's "rural spirit" was his own interpretation of the third of the Toyota Precepts: "Be sincere and strong." If Toyota's location in the heart of the Mikawa district gave it an inferiority complex vis-à-vis the center, Ishida's words transformed this sense of inferiority into a source of company pride.

The phrase "suffers from rural location" for Company A in Figure 0.2 contrasts sharply with "benefits from rural location" for Toyota in Figure 0.3. Clearly, depending on how you look at it, being in the countryside can be a source of pride or shame, a strength or a weakness.

Nothing can be simpler than to say, "Do what's right and do it the right way." Yet nothing can be more difficult to understand or put into practice, especially because most people have a hard time understanding just what "what's right" means in concrete terms.

"What's right" means what's good for the company and "doing it the right way" means rejecting clever schemes and, instead, working steadily and logically. When this way of thinking is commonly accepted in a company, conflicting views converge at "what's good for the company," and energies are multiplied by tireless application instead of being dissipated by internal discord.

In most companies, the notion of "what's right" is often confused with the idea of "what's convenient for me," or "what will bring easy money." When this occurs, internal wrangling saps energy, and absurd and illogical policies are formulated. The company's issues and problems are postponed or not resolved at all, and the organization grows exhausted. We need to reflect anew on the meaning of doing what's right and doing it the right way.

Eiji Toyoda

Eiji Toyoda was born in 1913, the second son of Sakichi's younger brother, Heikichi. After Eiji's graduation from the Department of Engineering of Tokyo Imperial University in 1936, Kiichiro invited him to join Toyoda Automatic Loom, where Eiji was charged with working on Toyota's automotive business.

In contrast to Taizo Ishida, Eiji was a man of few words. Reticent and seldom one to play to the crowd, he nevertheless ran the business single-handedly, and it was he who built the Toyota we know today. Taizo Ishida, with his first-rate merchant's instincts, provided management support for Eiji's suggestions. Rather then citing Eiji's words, we will take a look at the genes Eiji left behind by citing a few examples of his thinking.

Eiji's Dream

Eiji never forgot what Kiichiro had said to him when he invited him to join the automotive division of Toyoda Automatic Loom: "Nobody has any business deciding whether we can make cars or not. The fact is that it's too late to back out. If you're a true engineer, then let us dream."

This one sentence was the start of Eiji's involvement with automobiles. Eiji didn't show his feelings much, but he was imbued with the romance of what engineering could achieve.

Seeing Through to the Essence

Shigemitu Miyake, the former chairman of Tokai Bank, had this to say about Eiji: "He has an astonishing genius for being able to discern point-lessness and waste."

Eiji's ability to see waste and to see through to the essence of things is said to have been developed soon after he joined Toyoda's Automotive Division, when he was working in the company's Auditing and Improvement Center to resolve quality problems. Toyota had so many quality problems at the time that it seemed almost as though the company was using the market-place as a testing ground. Eiji remembered that period well:

> "When we'd build a car that turned out to have a defect, we'd ask why the affected part was bad and look for the process that caused the prob-lem. My role was to improve the process, since we figured that if we fixed the process, then there wouldn't be any more defects. Basically we were doing what would now be called QC."

> "Many companies have accounting departments and general affairs departments, but both the name and the function of our Auditing and Improvement Department were unique. It's the same now as it was then. We search out problems that need to be taken care of, and we focus knowledge and wisdom on them until they're solved."

Continuing this sort of work for years results in the ability merely to look at a problem to reveal its origins and true causes. The work formed the background of Eiji's belief in the primary importance of the shopfloor and physical phenomena—a way of thinking that, through Eiji, went on to permeate Toyota.

Linking Departments

The 1960s in Japan were the Age of Motorization, and the Toyota organization swelled rapidly during this period. As the company grew, links between departments deteriorated and quality problems became more common. Eiji was executive vice president of Toyota Motor Cor-poration at the time and had jurisdiction over engineering, production technology, and production. Several times a year, the president would gather top managers—section chief, and higher, for meetings, and Eiji would invariably appeal for cooperation among departments. "I have three things to ask of you," he would say, and one of the three was always better interdepartmental cooperation. This went on for about ten years.

Eiji's ideas about linking departments very likely originated in his ability to see through to the core of things. He had the insight to recognize that product quality problems arose from insufficient cooperation among departments.

Interdepartmental cooperation constituted one of the reasons for Toyota's subsequent development of TQC. It became a cornerstone of Toyota's growth, giving rise to such distinctive practices as Management by Policies and Management by Functions.

A Philosophy of Manufacturing

In a talk at the Hall of Industry and Technology in July of 1994, Eiji cited three points to explain his philosophy of manufacturing[7] or the significance of manufacturing:

"Fabrication is the foundation on which civilization is created."

"Fabrication is the motive force of technological progress."

"Fabrication moves people's hearts and enriches their minds in the same way that art does."

These are profound words, spoken by a man who spent more than half a century striving to build things.

Reading the Times

Eiji set great store in "reading the times." In November 1989, he revealed his secret for doing this in a speech presented at Nanzan University, which had awarded him an honorary professorship.

"Experience has taught me two things. The first is, 'Don't oppose the course of Nature.' In other words, you have to understand the great currents of history and determine to follow them. The second is, 'The future you build will conform to what you want it to be.' It's fair to say that the history of Toyota is the constant practice of these two seemingly contradictory principles. The judgments we've made, I think, have been consistently based on the notions of putting the customer first and on contributing to society.

"Think seriously and think hard. You won't often go wrong if you do. The most important thing of all is to do your own thinking and to act on it."

Eiji's Distinctiveness

What made Eiji unique was his limitless humility and diligence in the face of facts and truth. The manager at the top is a mirror of the company. With a man such as Eiji leading them, all employees and all managers could not help but be humble and diligent.

Taiichi Ohno

Taiichi Ohno went to work at Toyoda Boshoku in 1932. Sakichi had passed away two years earlier, but for Ohno, the great genius of the inventor remained in the company, and this "presence" would teach him what it meant to work in a world-class company.

Ohno transferred to Toyota Motor in 1943 and set about reforming its manufacturing division. After the war, Kiichiro instructed Ohno to "catch up to America" in three years. As Ohno came to grips with the task of revolutionizing production, he began crafting the unique Toyota Production System that some have referred to as the "Ohno Production System."

Ohno's own words reveal his thoughts and allow us to survey the genes that he passed on to the Toyota Production System and to Toyota.

Going Beyond Common Knowledge

"Break free of conventional thinking. Think of each downstream process as pulling from the one upstream."

Conventional wisdom had always been that upstream processes send parts to downstream processes in a "push" arrangement. Ohno turned this idea on its head and devised a "pull" system, in which each process goes to the previous one to draw only what it needs. This was the genesis of the *kanban* system.

"Look at the production floor as a blank sheet of paper. Focus on the issue at hand and ask 'Why?' five times."

Kiichiro Toyoda had often told inexperienced managers to stand on the shopfloor. His expectation was that direct observation of the shopfloor would reveal essential truths about manufacturing. Ohno's "Go watch the production shopfloor!" harks back directly to Kiichiro's admonishment. However, standing absentmindedly on the production floor serves no purpose and Ohno's insistence on asking "Why?" five times precisely expresses the method of observation he had in mind. This technique revealed the essential causes of problems by forcing the observer to look beyond what was visible.

"What matters for equipment isn't the operating rate. It's the potential run rate."

Equipment operating rates are used as indexes of manufacturing productivity. This index has value as an indicator of resulting productivity. But the minute you use operating rates as targets, you inevitably generate quantities of unneeded products and components, and you waste materials, electrical power, and other resources. Ohno stressed that equipment had to be available to run when needed. He took aim at the heart of the issue by creating the term "potential run rate"[8]—a Japanese homonym for the word meaning "operating rate."

Inventory Awareness

"As soon as processes are stable, reduce inventories between process steps. This will bring new problems to the surface."

"The purpose of reducing stocks between processes is to make latent problems visible."

Kiichiro had been interested in more than just inventories between process steps. He had directed that all stocks be reduced because he saw inventories as idle money. Ohno went one step further, declaring that revealing latent problems was the real purpose of inventory reduction. He believed that once processes were stable, reducing inventories between process steps was a matter of constant repetition. It is likely that Ohno was aware that this idea would not be universally popular; on one occasion, he was nearly struck by a hammer wielded by a violent operator. Ohno dared the man, "If you're going to hit me, then hit me." From that day forward he refused to wear a helmet.

At the same time, Ohno was aware that "you won't solve anything by burdening operators. Always use equipment to solve problems," he said. "And don't frustrate people who are basically willing. Even when things don't turn out well, you have to give them a reason to do their best because you appreciate their efforts. You don't cut down on inventory between process steps to torment operators. Your sole purpose should be to reveal latent problems."

A Human Element in Automation

"Overproduction is the worst waste of all. Equip all your high-speed machines with automatic shutoff functions."

"Automation should always include the human element."

Ohno's "automation with a human element" was a reference to mechanisms that prevent high-speed machines from making defects because they have the sense to automatically stop when defects occur. Later, this notion was linked to the idea of a "stop cord" for operators along the production line. Such devices make it obvious to everyone which process steps generate defects and thereby make it possible to carry out rapid investigation of root causes and take preventive action.

Visitors from Europe and the United States are often astonished at these stop cords. In their plants at home, only a plant manager or higher manager has the authority to stop the production line; any operator who stops the line would be fired on the spot. Even in Japan, many managers think it is more advantageous to keep a line running when defects occur and to rework bad parts later. Certainly, in the short term, it often seems less problematic to rework parts. But reworking parts makes it more difficult to investigate the root causes of problems and to prevent their recurrence. And, in a vicious circle, latent problems will again rear their heads and cause new defects.

Reaching Out

"The handoff from one process step to the next shouldn't be like a swimming relay; it should be like a track-and-field event."

In a swimming relay, one swimmer dives in when the previous swimmer touches the wall. In track-and-field, however, a baton passing zone is set up within which one runner hands the baton off to the next as they run side by side. Ohno's analogy suggests that the handoff of work from one process to the next should take place within a fixed zone of cooperation, just as it does in a track-and-field event. Production processes will always be unevenly balanced, but the product can flow smoothly overall when processes can absorb one another's variability.

This idea, encapsulated in the phrase "reaching out," later spread throughout Toyota. The underlying premise here is that no job is ever finished in one person's work zone. A baton passing zone should be established and each person's responsibility includes seeing to it that the next process has the job firmly in hand. A typical example of this can be seen in the "resident engineer" system in which a development engineer takes up residence in the manufacturing division for a given period of time during a new product launch.

Shoichiro Toyoda

The eldest son of Kiichiro Toyoda, Shoichiro was born in 1925. He joined Toyota Motor in 1952 and built Toyota management alongside Eiji Toyoda. In the 1960s, when the introduction of TQC and the drive to receive the Deming Prize became great opportunities for Toyota's growth, Shoichiro carried out substantial activities in his capacity as deputy general manager supporting Eiji, who was general manager for QC Promotion. An engineer and a man of a quiet temperament, Shoichiro stayed in Eiji's shadow during Eiji's tenure as president of the company. Although little of what Shoichiro said ranks as quotable, we can view the genes he created and passed on by studying a few historical episodes that illustrate his thinking.

Fusing Toyota Motor and Toyota Motor Sales

In 1981, Shoichiro Toyoda moved from his position as executive vice president of Toyota Motor to the presidency of Toyota Motor Sales. One year later, the hopes of Toyota Motor's president, Eiji Toyoda, came to fruition when the two organizations merged to form a reborn Toyota Motor Corporation with Shoichiro as president. This period saw the spread of vigorous TQC activities:

- 1981 QC activities at dealerships
- 1982 Executive QC seminars
- 1983 Inauguration of the TQC Promotion Office
- 1983 TQC education for all managers
- 1983 Establishment of the QC Promotion Prize for Toyota dealers

These activities suggest that Shoichiro, the TQC standard-bearer in the old Toyota Motor organization, used TQC to merge that company with Toyota Motor Sales. While the pre-merger Motor and Sales organizations shared common roots, cultural differences had emerged between them. Their respective management philosophies were like oil and water, Taizo Ishida's "squeezing a dry towel" approach at Toyota Motor contrasting sharply with Shotaro Kamiya's "first the user, then the dealer, then the manufacturer" at Sales.

Shoichiro led an energetic campaign to blend the two cultures around the time of the merger and succeeded in infusing the old Toyota Motor Sales organization with QC perspectives and methods. Beyond that, the merger had the unexpected effect of bringing about organizational reform within Toyota Motor Corporation as a whole.

Organizational Reform at Toyota Motor Corporation

Managers from the mainstream old Toyota Motor company seemed quite unhappy with the thinking prevalent at the former Toyota Motor Sales.

Masaya Hanai, who was chairman of Toyota Motor Corporation at the time of the merger (and formerly executive vice president of Toyota Motor), rejected the "sloppy management" at Toyota Motor Sales. "I'm making them think hard now," he said, "and get by with a third of the funds they used to expect."

At the same time, managers and employees of the old Toyota Motor organization were influenced greatly by the "free and open" culture of the former Sales company. A new Toyota culture began to emerge, the genesis of the organizational revolution that took place at Toyota in the latter half of the 1980s.

Management in the old Toyota Motor emphasized "efficiency." The most effective way to expand an organization that emphasizes efficiency is by division of labor and stratification, in other words, by building a bureaucracy. Bureaucracies, on the other hand, lead to rigidity and so-called "big company disease."

Simply put, big company disease means the loss of creativity. Efficiency and creativity exist in a reciprocal relationship to one another. The "free and open" ethos of Toyota Motor Sales penetrated Toyota Motor just as the latter organization began to appreciate the reciprocal relationship between efficiency and creativity. This sparked a debate inside the company over whether Toyota needed to change and whether it could survive in an age of creativity.

Nineteen eighty-four saw the launch of a group to consider organizational reforms within Toyota. A series of institutional reform proposals came out of this group: "organizational flattening," organizational "clustering," the introduction of a system of performance evaluations, and a campaign in which all employees were to be addressed by their names and the honorific suffix "-*san*" rather than by their formal titles.

Iwao Isomura, senior managing director in charge of personnel at the time, commented on these proposed changes:

"Toyota's president, Shoichiro Toyoda, emphasized the 'Three Cs:' Creativity, Challenge, and Courage. But at every level of the organization, from division head down to team leader, new ideas coming up from below are quashed or lose their freshness. Our young people are losing their enthusiasm because even when they take on a challenge, they can't change anything. They conclude that their only option is to do as they're told. [Toyota's Great Experiment.]"[9]

Efficiency had driven out creativity.

In meetings of board members and executives, Shoichiro responded by evoking Toyota's "big company disease" and calling vigorously for steps to overcome it. In 1988, nearly all the recommendations of the Organizational Reform Study Group were adopted without modification.

The 1980s were distinctly upbeat years, with Japan lionized as "Number One" and with Toyota vehicles flying out of dealerships despite trade frictions. But with Toyota still harboring a sense of crisis, it was Shoichiro Toyoda's clear vision and decisiveness that allowed the company to lead the way and take command.

The Great Transition to the 21st Century

In 1990, Shoichiro initiated a shift in company focus from responsibility to service. Under his direction, the duty of social responsibility was abandoned and the mission of contributing to society was adopted.

Two years later, the Toyoda Precepts were brought up to date in the form of Basic Principles and issued in conjunction with the *Toyota Action Plan for Global Environment*, better known as the *Toyota Global Earth Charter*. The publication of these two documents occasioned considerable debate and criticism within Toyota, with some arguing that the company was headed into new sea lanes without a rudder and others that Toyota had crossed a river of no return. Even Toyota employees understood how different the values reflected in the new *Principles* were from previous Toyota culture.

Shoichiro's last accomplishment as president was to deal with the issue of Development Centers, the only one of the series of late 1980s organizational reforms that had not yet been implemented. The so-called "clustering" of the business had been hotly contested when first proposed and arguments and debates had continued into the early 1990s.

The premise behind the Development Centers was the following: As the division of labor progresses, the efficiency of individual workers increases. However, overall efficiency falls with the increasing need for communication between workers. Most importantly, creativity suffers. Creativity does not take place in the absence of contextual knowledge. The insight behind the Toyota Development Center System was to cap the burden on individuals by limiting the range of responsibility for vehicle models in those technical departments—such as product planning and design—in which creativity was needed most. Exploration of this idea began in 1984, but the system was not implemented until 1992. Toyota's movement from the structural reforms of the late 1980s to the Development Center System of 1992 constituted a pioneering experiment among large organizations worldwide. It attracted the notice of organizational researchers and became a revolutionary paradigm for global companies suffering from "big company disease."

In Chapter 2, we will take a closer look at *Toyota's Basic Principles*, its *Global Earth Charter*, and its Development Center System. Each of these decisions was Shoichiro's contribution to the Toyota gene pool. Hiroshi Okuda's generation inherited and applied the genes that Shoichiro created. Indefatigable managers kept them in use even during the so-called "lost decade" of the 1990s and have passed them on to the 21st century as part of the company's rapidly progressing managerial patrimony (see Chapter Six).

Even in his final years, Eiji Toyoda was a champion of 'rationalization,' or efficiency. Shoichiro Toyoda, who had at first carried the banner of efficiency with Eiji, became at the end of his life a man whose primary concern was coexisting with "people, society, and the environment."

From his father, Kiichiro, Shoichiro had inherited a family treasure, a maxim written in Chinese calligraphy. Hanging in his room where all could see, it read: "Heaven, Earth, and Man. Knowledge, Benevolence, and Courage." The underlying message was a reflection of Shoichiro's philosophy: Be mindful always of the rhythms of heaven, the utility of the earth and harmony among men, and do not forget to use your knowledge and wisdom to bring benevolence to society and to face challenges with courage. In his final years, as Shoichiro reflected on his father's career, his own purpose in life, and the time remaining to him, one might say, Shoichiro became a citizen of the Earth.

DNA: HOW TOYOTA GENES ARE TRANSMITTED

A Genealogy of Gene Transmission

Up to this point, we have looked at succeeding generations of Toyota leaders, and we have examined words and deeds that still live today. Now we must look at an important question: Why is Toyota alone in its ability to transmit and propagate continuously the spirit, words, and actions of its historical leaders?

Unlike Matsushita, Sony, or Honda, Toyota has not turned its inheritance into founder-worship. Instead, its legacy manifests itself as the veneration of principles.

Certainly, it is true that the founding family imparted a kind of centripetal energy to the organization via a heritage of words and actions. But every company is created by someone, after all. Having a founder doesn't by itself account for Toyota's distinctiveness.

Sakichi and Kiichiro Toyoda were not vastly different from most other founders of companies. They all share certain characteristics: extraordinary drive, an uncommon pioneering spirit, and stubborn perseverance. Yet none of that explains why the spirit of Toyota's creators continues from one generation to the next.

Certainly Sakichi and Kiichiro Toyoda were not alone in leaving inspiring words to their successors. Kiichiro was a taciturn man, with no special verbal gifts. And yet his spirit, views, and attitudes have flourished to the present day.

By contrast, we must look at Yoshisuke Aikawa, the entrepreneurial genius who founded Nissan Motors. There is no doubt that Yoshisuke Aikawa attracted many talented people to the Nissan organization by the force of his clearly stated mission to "establish a first-rate Japanese automotive industry." But those talented people did not inherit and build on Aikawa's spirit, words and actions.

The Toyota organization brings out the best even in ordinary people. As it does so, it steers extraordinary people clear of the "charismatic leadership" trap to which they are so prone and, instead, leads them to add their own wisdom to those of their predecessors and to pass on the results to their successors. This cannot be explained merely by referring to individual people. There is something else. Clearly, there is something beyond the company's particular founders and successors and employees that distinguishes Toyota from other organizations.

Professor Takahiro Fujimoto of the University of Tokyo is well known as an automotive industry analyst and student of the Toyota Motor studies. In his book, *The Evolution of a Production System* (1997),[10] he makes the following observation about unresolved issues in Toyota studies:

> *A clear picture or analysis has yet to emerge of internal organizational patterns that bear on the question of whether Toyota Motor, as an industrial organization, has drawn on unique evolutionary capabilities. What sets Toyota apart, for example, in terms of its decision-making patterns, its organizational culture, its managers' values, its system of formal procedures or its managerial style? And when and how did it get that way?*

Fujimoto goes on to cite what may be some of the distinctive elements constituting Toyota's evolutionary capability:

1. A pattern of thinking that links every trial to competitive strength
2. The tenacity to bring ideas to fruition even in spite of initial setbacks
3. A gritty willingness to use whatever means necessary to win
4. The successful maintenance of systems of formal rules
5. Succession practices that ensure policy continuity
6. Mechanisms for emphasizing the continuity of Toyota management thinking among employees

Yoshinobu Sato, a researcher celebrated for his historical studies of the Toyota Motor Corporation, lists prominent themes of Kiichiro's career in his book, *Sources of Toyota Management* (1994)[11]:

1. An inventor's philosophy influenced by his father, Sakichi
2. The confidence to build popular passenger vehicles gained through enterprising and careful planning
3. Ingenious sales arrangements that stress the importance of users
4. The creation of manufacturing technologies for mass production
5. Broad ideas on what an organization should be and how to manage it
6. An emphasis on basic research
7. A commitment to passenger vehicle development
8. The will to take up the challenge of diversified technical innovation and commercialization

Together, Fujimoto and Sato summarize some of the elements of Toyota's distinctiveness. By combining these elements with K's "Company Growth Model" in Figure 0.3, we can arrange them according to historical cause-and-effect relationships to form a "Genealogy of Gene Transmission at Toyota," shown in Figure 1.4.

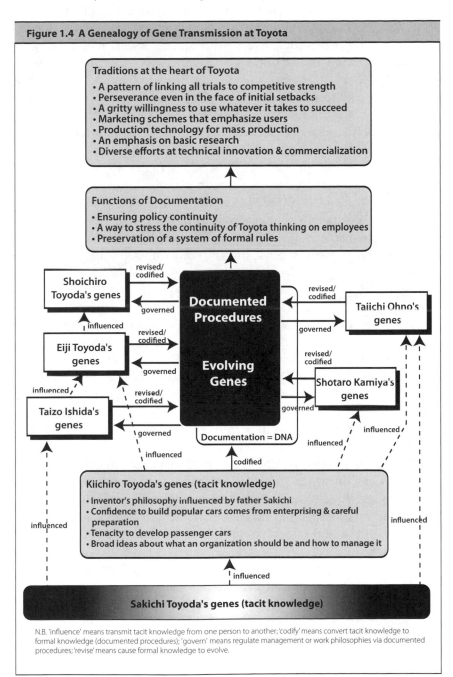

Figure 1.4 A Genealogy of Gene Transmission at Toyota

Traditions at the heart of Toyota

- A pattern of linking all trials to competitive strength
- Perseverance even in the face of initial setbacks
- A gritty willingness to use whatever it takes to succeed
- Marketing schemes that emphasize users
- Production technology for mass production
- An emphasis on basic research
- Diverse efforts at technical innovation & commercialization

Functions of Documentation

- Ensuring policy continuity
- A way to stress the continuity of Toyota thinking on employees
- Preservation of a system of formal rules

Shoichiro Toyoda's genes

Documented Procedures

Evolving Genes

Taiichi Ohno's genes

Eiji Toyoda's genes

Shotaro Kamiya's genes

Taizo Ishida's genes

Documentation = DNA

Kiichiro Toyoda's genes (tacit knowledge)

- Inventor's philosophy influenced by father Sakichi
- Confidence to build popular cars comes from enterprising & careful preparation
- Tenacity to develop passenger cars
- Broad ideas about what an organization should be and how to manage it

Sakichi Toyoda's genes (tacit knowledge)

N.B. 'influence' means transmit tacit knowledge from one person to another; 'codify' means convert tacit knowledge to formal knowledge (documented procedures); 'govern' means regulate management or work philosophies via documented procedures; 'revise' means cause formal knowledge to evolve.

As the figure shows, Kiichiro was influenced by the genes (tacit knowledge) of his father. Combining them with his own distinctive contributions, he created more evolved genes (tacit knowledge), which he then wrote down and codified in the form of "documented procedures" (formal knowledge). These procedures, representing the knowledge of the organization, governed the thinking and values of capable men who sustained Toyota in later years, men such as Shotaro Kamiya, Taizo Ishida, Taiichi Ohno, Eiji Toyoda, and Shoichiro Toyoda. Each of these subsequent leaders added his own unique wisdom and values to produce even more evolved wisdom. Everyone, in other words, introduced his own philosophy and values that then interacted freely and in multiple dimensions with those of every one else to produce new wisdom. In this way, organizational knowledge evolves and increases through a formal process in which the new knowledge is used to revise existing documented procedures or to establish new documents. One generation's tacit knowledge becomes genes passed on to succeeding generations. The equation of documents and DNA thus reveals "written procedures" to be "evolving genes."

Documented Procedures

DNA is deoxyribonucleic acid, the medium for genes. Taking an analogy from music CDs, the music is the gene and the CD is the DNA. To express this relationship in terms of the documented procedures of a company's organizational knowledge, we can say that recorded procedures are the genes and documents themselves are the DNA. The existence of the genetic medium DNA is what permits genes to be transmitted from one generation to the next and what permits evolution to occur in response to changes in the environment.

Without documents (DNA), words would fly about in a chaotic game of "telephone" in which information from one person would end up meaning something completely different ten people later. The transmission would be broken. In a culture of only spoken words, not even the finest managers and the finest people in the world can build a world-class organization.

Managerial perspectives shift as times change, and documented procedures are needed to keep those perspectives from disappearing altogether. If procedures no longer suit the times, they need to be revised. The process of revision is what we call "evolution," and it is in this sense that documented procedures are the same as evolving genes.

A passage from *Toyota: A History of the First 30 Years*, published in 1967, further explains this concept:

[With Toyota's launch in 1937,] a management organization was created and job boundaries became clear. As various business functions began to operate smoothly, notebooks of written procedures were established, as were rules defining standards for how work was to be performed. These rulebooks covered such areas as purchasing, ordering and warehousing, materials, regulations for supplier loans and investments, collections and sales, and rules for subcontractor orders. Rulebooks were gradually codified and at the time of the organizational shift in 1939, they were brought together as a set of nearly 83 Business Rules.

Let us take another look at Table 1.1, Kiichiro Toyoda: A History of his Documentation. Here, one sees that Kiichiro was influenced by Sakichi's values and applied them as he understood them in concrete form to the automotive business. These values acquired authority in the form of documents, and those documents eventually became the means for managing the organization.

A culture of documentation took root within Toyota because ways of working were written down under Kiichiro's leadership. After World War II, in 1948, formal rules for documentation were written down and Toyota's documentation culture came into full flower.

It is possible that Kiichiro, who reportedly expressed himself poorly and was not a very good speaker, needed written communication to run his company effectively. In any event, documents became a means for the transmission and propagation of Toyota genes. Without Kiichiro's documentation, the Toyota organization would have lost its genes and the company we know today probably could not have existed.

Toyota's Documentation Principle

Table 1.2 is a summary listing of internal rules as expressed in various Toyota-related materials.

The items we cite here (including some obsolete ones) are only a sample of Toyota rules, which are far more extensive. In addition, the table shows only those rules above a certain level of applicability. If we were to include low-level task instructions and the like, we would be listing tens or even hundreds of thousands of rules. Year after year, the 83 rules that Kiichiro formulated in 1939 are revised and amended as they are passed down. They are also expanded and can be viewed as a massive system of knowledge existing within Toyota.

Today, it is said that no Toyota manager can do his job without reading a 600-page document of standards. The management of standards occupies a central place in a manager's work, and not even the company president has the authority to change established standards at will.

Table 1.2 Internal Toyota Regulations

Level 1	Level 2	Level 3	Name	
1. Basic Business Regulations	1. Company Statutes		Board of Directors' Rules	☆
	2. Other		Board of Executive Officers' Rules	★
2. Employ. Regs.			Employment Rules	☆
3. Organizational Regulations	1. Org. Mgt. Regs.		Organizational Management Rules	★
	2. Job Allocation Regs.		Job Authority Rules	★
			Division of Duty Rules	★
	3. Council Functions	1. General Councils	Planning Council Rules	★
			New Product Council Rules	★
			Research Council Rules	★
			Equipment Council Rules	★
			Internal/External Mfg. Determination Council	★
			Investment Council Rules	☆
			TMC/TMS Joint Council Rules	★
		2. Committees	Safety Committee Rules	☆
			Audit Improvement Committee Rules	☆
			Rules for Handling Invention Ideas	☆
			Rules for Handling Innovations	☆
4. Work Regulations	1. Business Functions	1. Business Planning	Company Policy Management Rules	★
			Rules for Establishing Long-Term Plans	★
			Outsourcing Plant Financing & Invest. Rules	☆
		2. Quality	Quality Assurance Rules	★
			Guidelines for Audits of Quality or Assr. Acts.	☆
			Initial Management Rules	☆
			Rules for Registered Problems	☆
			Guidelines for Promoting Recall Countermeasures	☆
			Rules for Warranty Repair Work	☆
		3. Cost	Cost Management Rules	★
			Rules for Implementing Cost Planning	★
			Rules for Managing Departmental Budgets	★
			Cost Improvement Prescriptions	★
			Rules for Allocating Cost Mgmt. Work, annexed table	★
			Regulations for Controling Indirect Expenses	☆
		4. Office Work	Document Handling Regulations	☆
			Prescriptions for Circulating Drafts for Approval	☆
			Rules for Managing Forms	☆
			Detailed Rules for Implementing Forms Mgmt.	☆
			Rules for Technical Reports	★
			Rules for Classifying Technical Reports	☆
		5. Measure-ment	Rules for the Purchase & Storage of Meas. Equip.	☆
			Rules for Managing the Precision of Meas. Equip.	☆
	2. Production Functions	1. Prior Research	Product Research Rules	—
			Rules for Procedures Used at Toyota Laboratories	—
			Rules for Procedures Used by External Researchers	—
			Prescriptions for Experimentation Research	—
		2. Design & Development	New Product Development Rules	★
			Design Research Prescriptions	★
			Approved Drawing Prescriptions,	☆
			Dealing with Appr'd Drawings Presecriptions	★
			Guidelines for ~~~~~ Demand	
			Patent Gazette Survey Rules	☆
		3. Production Preparation	Production Engineering Development Rules	☆
			Guidelines for Constructing QA Tables	★
			Guidelines for Constructing Process Plans	☆
			Guidelines for Conducting Process FMEA	☆
			Guidelines for Process Surveys for Purchased Items	☆
		4. Purchasing	Guidelines for Constr. Comp. Insp. Methods	☆
		5. Inspection	Inspection Rules	☆
			Rules for Dealing with Defects	☆
		6. Manufac-turing	Rules for Op. Procedures and Compilation Guidelines	☆
			Guidelines for Constructing Operating Procedures	★
			Guidelines for Constructing Operating Guidelines	★
5. Preparatory Regulations	1. Technical Norms (TES)	1. Design	Automobile Design Criteria	—
		2. Experimentation		—
	2. Production Engineering Norms(TMS)			—
	3. Quality Management Norms (TQS)			—

Symbols

☆ : established before the introduction of TQC in 1961
★ : established after the introduction of TQC in 1961
— : date of establishment unclear

Terms

Regulation: a generic term for work standards
Rule: an obligatory regulation involving management fundamentals
Prescription: an obligatory regulation involving management fundamentals for a specific department or departments
Guideline: a fixed-form procedural regulation straddling organizational units
Norm: a regulation specifying a technical concept, thing or procedure

Remarks

- "Level 1" is a Toyota classification but levels 2 and 3 are the author's
- Regulations for running function councils are thought to be prescribed within the regulations for individual management functions.

When Eiji Toyoda was executive vice president of the company, subordinates could secure his reluctant agreement by showing him the procedural documentation to back up decisions they had made. "The documentation doesn't make sense," he would reportedly say. "Fix it next time." Most bosses would probably tell their people to ignore the documented standards and do what they were told. Of course, such companies probably have no standard work methods in the first place.

Japanese culture is traditionally hostile to documentation. A variety of reasons have been proposed to explain this: impatience with reading, a reluctance to do anything that might constrain future action, a desire not to waste paper, and so forth. Whatever the cause, the result is an unconscious habit that manifests itself as a reflexive rejection of documents. But Toyota is different. All the basics of Toyota business exist as documents, and written documents are the starting point for both action and thought. In the context of Japanese culture, this documentation principle marks a decisive difference between Toyota and other companies. (See the section on Toyota's Business Management System in Chapter 3).

It does not necessarily follow that documentation and standardization alone will automatically permeate a company and shape its organizational culture. Mitsubishi Motors, for example, adopted ethical guidelines in response to a 1997 scandal in which it was revealed that the company had paid off an extortionist who threatened to disrupt its annual stockholder meeting. These guidelines included an explicit ban on concealing recalls and stipulated the establishment of an office overseeing ethics. But, on a company level, rationality and conscience pretty much failed to function, and the scandals have multiplied. Snow Brand Milk Products, whose tainted products were at the center of an outbreak of mass food poisoning in 2000, was committed to HACCP (Hazard Analysis Critical Control Point) procedures and had implemented thorough document control. But HACCP never became pivotal for managers and people on the shopfloor because top executives did not take it upon themselves to build an organization in which fairness was either guaranteed or truly operational.

DNA and Organizational Capability

Figure 1.5 shows how organizational capability changes from one generation of managers to the next in a company with a documented corporate DNA (Company X) and in one without such DNA (Company Y).

When a company possesses DNA in the form of documents, the organizational capabilities cultivated by each generation of managers are transmitted undiluted to the next generation. The assumption here is

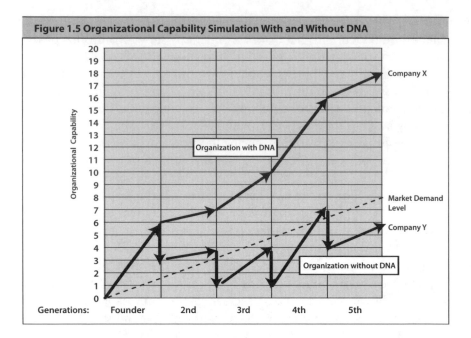

Figure 1.5 Organizational Capability Simulation With and Without DNA

that, without such documentation, the organizational capabilities of each generation of managers vanish at about level 3 when the baton is passed on to the next generation.

Suppose that corresponding generations in the two companies make the same contributions to enhancing organizational capability. In this example, the contributions made by the founder and the fourth generation of leaders are the greatest. We can think of the fourth-generation managers here as the "revitalizers." Other generations are ordinary managers.

This hypothetical example makes clear that in Company X, each generation stands on the shoulders of the preceding one and that by the fifth generation, managers have attained a high level of organizational capability. In Company Y, on the other hand, each generation of managers "ratchets back" to the level of the previous generation. After five generations, the organization has barely reached a capability level that is one-third of Company Y's. If we imagine that the level of market demand rises as shown by the dashed line in the figure, Company Y ends up constantly in the red in and after the third generation.

All companies tend to have founders and "revitalizers" who substantially raise their organizational capabilities. Over the long run, however, they also have many managers who fall into the "ordinary" category. What is important here is that the handoff from one generation to the next not lower the organization's capabilities. Some mechanism needs to be in place so that those capabilities accumulate constantly, even under "ordinary" managers. Even if a defective gene shows up, in other words, the fact that documentation makes it visual means that succeeding generations will evaluate it and weed it out, either by discarding or revising it. In this sense, the genetic medium—DNA—is vastly more important than the genes themselves. A company with DNA in the form of written documents is one that can evolve in the manner described by Darwin.

The Utility of Documented Procedures

Documented procedures means "standard ways of working" or what is commonly known as "work standards." A standard is the documented expression of the best method known at a given point in time; it enforces that method until a better one comes along. An organization as a whole keeps improving its methods via a process of formal revision in which improvements on past methods are incorporated into new standards. Standards are therefore a form of human wisdom hammered out with the aim of continually improving work methods.

The following quote from Shoichiro Toyoda eloquently describes the role and effect of documentation. (It is excerpted from a keynote address to the 67th Quality Control Symposium, sponsored by the Japan Union of Scientists and Engineers, December 1998.):

> An "innovative culture" is one we find in organizations that don't hesitate to change the current state of affairs, in organizations that strive continually to change and that accept that changing the status quo is good. What supports such organizations at the most fundamental level is the steady everyday business of continuous improvement (kaizen). Kaizen requires, first of all, that standards be in place for whatever business needs to be conducted in the workplace. And this doesn't mean simply pursuing results. The first step in kaizen is standardizing the processes that produce results. When this principle is weakened, team members lose a sense of where they belong and what their roles are. The cycle of management comes to a halt and standardization becomes inconceivable. Empty formalism takes over and no one does anything unless there is a precedent.

Hitoshi Kume, professor at Chuo University, professor emeritus of the University of Tokyo, and recipient of the Deming Prize, explains work standards in this excerpt (from an address to the 55th Quality Control

Symposium, sponsored by the Japan Union of Scientists and Engineers, December 1992):

> *Work standards give objective clarity to the question of what it is we do and where we do it. They illuminate the relationships between individual tasks and the system as a whole and allow us to understand the purpose of each activity in the context of the whole. They are at once cornerstones of management, analyses of the current situation and points of departure for* kaizen. *While records or data concerning the results of, say, sales and design are generally available in the form of statistics or drawings, many companies end up with management by outcomes and stalled* kaizen *because there is no information about the processes that produced those results. The role of documentation goes beyond simply specifying rules or capturing the current situation. Documents illuminate the current situation and should be used as the point of departure for improving it.*

Most standards are documents drawn up by staff members seeking only to ensure that shopfloor workers follow procedures. At Toyota, however, standards are both "points of departure for *kaizen*" and "evolving genes."

Many people tend to emphasize the negative regulatory or coercive aspect of standardization. But for an organization, it only makes sense to stipulate that one should not follow inferior methods when better standard methods are available. Standards are more than mere rules, however. Just like a high jumper's bar, standards mark the maximum height cleared by predecessors. A standard indicates the goal that everyone needs to attain and thereby induces everyone to rise to challenges and to be creative. Humans simply cannot display creativity or the will to meet challenges when they cannot see the goal. We need to keep this central aspect of standards firmly in view.

Standardization applies to four objects: concepts, protocols, procedures, and things. Even when they don't receive special attention, the standardization of procedures and things proceeds without much difficulty in manufacturing industries. This is because manufacturing could not take place without them. As Table 1.1 indicates, Kiichiro Toyoda placed particular emphasis on what we call "protocols."

Protocols, as used here, mean commitments concerning the execution of the business made by the organization or among various job functions. Typical protocols include regulations delineating jobs and regulations specifying the assignment of business duties. There are other organizational commitments, too, both great and small, and the effectiveness of the organization is determined by how well those commitments are coordinated and codified.

One form in which we encounter such protocols is in personal statements concerning what one's own organization does. The important thing here is to show the interactions among protocols that indicate what one does based on interrelationships specifying who (or which organization) has responsibility or authority with respect to whom (or which other organization). Clearly defining both protocol interactions and interrelationships of responsibility and authority spells out tasks and responsibilities for the future. Such clear statements may seem harsh, but if we make organizational allowances for human feelings, we will either be unable to establish protocols in the first place or else our protocols will become collections of useless and hollow personal statements.

Protocols at Toyota are created in the context of the Management System Scheme shown in Figure 1.6.

A general flowchart is used for simple interactions, but in complex cases, Input Process Output (IPO) charts, showing the inputs, processes and outputs of individual departments, are appended to or cited by the general flowchart.

Using words alone to express such organizational interrelationships and work interfaces would place an extraordinary burden on readers and would lead to unusable processes. Toyota's Management System Scheme makes everything clear at a glance and makes living, usable processes possible.

When applied to concepts, standardization is typically expressed in words or in tree diagrams. Standardizing concepts constitutes the basis of enhancing organizational efficiency. Even though there are different "Toyota dialects," vocabulary seems to be uniform within Toyota. There is, in addition, a strong impression that words are used with rigorous precision. A typical example of a tree diagram used at Toyota is the Job Structure Chart introduced in Chapter 3. Because these concepts are advanced at Toyota, communication is effective and both work analyses and *kaizen* proceed easily.

At this point, it is appropriate to introduce some observations made by K, who first appeared in the preface of this work:

- Technology is a kind of culture, and its inheritors must not be mere storytellers. Things need to be written down.
- Although devising new techniques may be a manager's principal job, an organization must be managed by balancing this function with the work of standardizing the best experience of the past.
- Written documents are indispensable for enhancing the precision of communications. Human culture arose from the written word. In the same way, a company culture needs to be formed by means of documents.

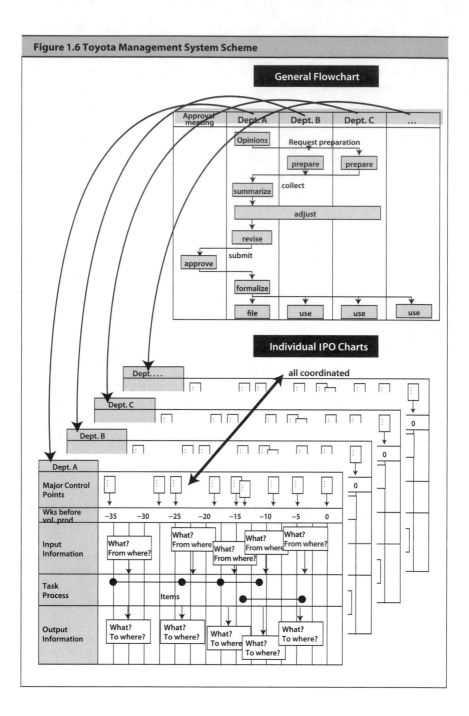

Figure 1.6 Toyota Management System Scheme

- Communication occurs when the other person understands. What a person may have said is secondary. True communication is difficult. This is where standards are required.
- Half of one's energy can accomplish 85 percent of a task; the other half is required to achieve the last 15 percent. Standards are what determine how effective that energy is.
- The cars that Toyota builds are not substantially different from those made by other automobile manufacturers. What is different is the efficiency of the Toyota organization.

Bureaucratic Principles and the Negative Effects of Bureaucracy

As central elements of bureaucracies, standardization and documentation are generally considered to be reactionary. For this reason, it is sometimes difficult to explain Toyota's evolutionary power in terms of standardization and documentation. In this context, it is important to remember that when sociologist Max Weber advocated bureaucracy a hundred years ago, it was not reactionary at all. In fact, it was the most effective methodology for managing organizations. The bureaucratic principles outlined by Weber are worth examining here:

- Standardization: Work is performed on the basis of universal and general rules.
- Specialization: Work is divided into specialties by function.
- Professionalization: The performance of work requires specialized training and education.
- Depersonalization: Inequities disappear because conduct is based on rules with the regularity of machines.
- Stratification: Hierarchies of authority are clear.
- Formalization: Jobs are in principle performed with documents as catalysts.

Such bureaucratic principles allow organizations to benefit from the effects of accuracy, stability, reliability, efficiency, and uniformity.

The word "depersonalization" seems to deny human individuality, but in its sense of "eliminating inequities," it does not at all contravene humanity. "Depersonalization" simply means eliminating the injustice of allowing people to live off an organization without obeying its rules. The term aims to express a situation in which all members of the organization conduct themselves in an orderly and harmonious way in pursuit of the organization's goals. Perhaps "regular conduct" would have been a more apt phrase.

Nevertheless, a carelessly run bureaucracy is prone to fall prey to negative effects:

- Trained impotence: Patterns of conduct appropriate to a previous state of affairs are carried over and randomly passed on when circumstances change.
- Occupational psychoses: Constant repetition of the same task leads to the development of particular likes, perceptions, and emphases.
- Goal shift: The observance of rules becomes an end in itself rather than a means.

The word "bureaucratization" arose precisely because such negative effects were observed in organizations of functionaries and civil servants. In time, bureaucracies came to be seen as having reactionary attributes. As a result, the word eventually became a synonym for "rigidity."

Task forces that cut horizontally across an organization can complement a vertically aligned bureaucracy as a method for suppressing bureaucracy's negative effects, energizing the organization and sustaining evolution. Indeed the adoption of such task-force-type management is one method that has allowed the Toyota organization to evolve, even as it rests on a bureaucratic foundation.

We will see in more detail in Chapter 3 how Toyota, since it was founded, has made liberal use of a "committee system" to complement its vertical management structure. When TQC was introduced into the company in the 1960s, it was woven into a uniquely Toyota system of "management by function" that cut across the organization. Even so, Toyota had to flatten and cluster its organization to overcome the first signs of "big company disease" that emerged in the 1980s. In the final analysis, Toyota has enjoyed the benefits of Weber's bureaucratic principles because it has proactively managed to cordon off the negative effects of bureaucracy.

Bureaucracy remains the fundamental principle of organizational management even today. A powerful organization can be constructed on a bureaucratic foundation as long as it institutes reliable measures to avoid falling prey to bureaucracy's shortcomings. It can be argued that Toyota has not entirely succeeded in constructing an organization that reconciles the advantages and negative tendencies of bureaucracies, but foresight and the search for optimal methods have made it the strongest bureaucracy-based organization in history.

A Learning Bureaucracy

Within its bureaucratic system, Toyota has made active use of the crucial principles of documentation and standardization to transmit the "genes" of previous generations. At the same time, these principles provide succeeding generations with controls and also with goals to be surpassed, so that new genes are added in a cycle of studying and revising improved ways of working. This is the epitome of a "learning organization."

The characteristics of a learning organization are worth examining here. Such an organization can be defined as one:

- in which people are ceaselessly stretching their capacities and are able to bring about results they sincerely desire
- that gives rise to innovative and expansive patterns of thinking
- that soars in pursuit of shared goals
- that constantly studies how people can learn together

Within this framework, Toyota is a prime example of a learning organization. Although Toyota has been referred to as a group with an "improvement addiction," it is more accurate to call it a group with a "learning habit." Toyota is an organization that makes use of bureaucracy to learn. It is, in other words, a "learning bureaucracy."

Becoming an Industry Leader

The developments we have described have brought Toyota to the role of industry leader (see Figure 0.1). Figure 1.7 summarizes the process by which Toyota achieved this status.

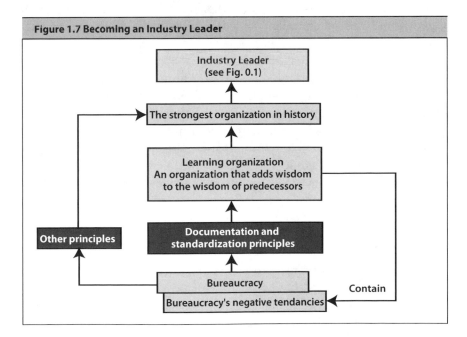

Figure 1.7 Becoming an Industry Leader

Bureaucracy lies solidly at the root of Toyota's organizational management. In particular, it was Kiichiro Toyoda's insistence on the most important basic bureaucratic principles of documentation and standardization that eventuated in a "learning organization" in which succeeding generations add wisdom to the wisdom of their predecessors. The development of a variety of measures to increase organizational effectiveness has allowed this learning organization to contain negative bureaucratic tendencies and bring out bureaucracy's positive principles. The result is the strongest organization in history, the industry leader depicted in Figure 0.1.

The principles of documentation and standardization constitute Toyota's DNA, the medium through which new wisdom is added to the wisdom (or genes) of preceding generations. It is the presence of this DNA—used to more effect than in any other company—that has been the key to Toyota's success.

We have now clearly seen Toyota's system for transmitting its growth genes. What makes it possible for an organization to transmit its growth genes is the creation within that organization of a transmission medium's DNA: a "culture of documentation."

THE MANAGERIAL TEMPERAMENT THAT CREATES ENDURING GROWTH

Creating a culture of documentation (i.e., a system for enduring growth that does not depend on individuals), is a fundamental condition for sustaining stable growth.

Yet it was one individual, Kiichiro Toyoda, who created this culture of documentation. In all likelihood, Shotaro Kamiya or Taizo Ishida could not have accomplished it. Without Kiichiro, Toyota would not be the organization it is today.

At this juncture, it is important to identify universal principles for selecting managers suited for permanent growth. What sort of managers, for example, have the temperament to be able to create the conditions for permanent growth? How does one find such potential managers, and how does one nurture them?

Level 5 Leadership

Managers with the potential to create the conditions for permanent growth need more than charisma. Charismatic leaders tend to see themselves as heroes and assume that a leader needs to compensate for the fact that ordinary people are powerless, lacking in vision, and incapable of change. One cannot expect permanent growth from leaders who have this view of employees—the people who carry the organization.

Leaders from whom one can expect permanent growth seem to be people, like Kiichiro Toyoda or Jack Welch, who are single-minded and focused. Some features of Kiichiro's character are presented below:

- Taciturnity rather than eloquence
- A monomaniacal approach rooted in a sense of mission
- An absence of sociability
- Meditative thought in pursuit of essentials
- An emphasis on knowledge and theory as well as realistic practicality
- A long-range, comprehensive vision
- Careful consideration followed by bold and fearless action
- Deep compassion for others through his work

Jack Welch more or less shares the same characteristics as Kiichiro. A figure celebrated in media headlines, Welch is a charismatic leader with a strong personality who gives the impression of great volubility.

But the real Jack Welch is quite different. He is a man of few words and speaks with a slight stammer. He is, in some ways, naïve and even shy. Because his massive restructuring and personnel reductions have emptied buildings of people, he has been compared to a neutron bomb. Few are aware of the pain he felt when hearing himself called "Neutron Jack." For Welch, public relations was an indispensable element of corporate strategy; his charisma was no more than an intentionally created role.

As we consider various theories of leadership, the examples of Kiichiro and Jack Welch draw our attention to "Level 5 Leadership," an article written by Jim Collins (the author of *Built to Last: Successful Habits of Visionary Companies*) and published in the April 2001 issue of *Diamond Harvard Business Review*.[12]

From among 1,435 Fortune 500 firms, Collins selected a group of eleven corporations that suddenly transformed themselves into "great" companies and then sustained extraordinary results for 15 years or more. He then compared them to companies that had achieved great results but had been unable to sustain them and attempted to discover the common variables that distinguished the two. Figure 1.8 shows the divergence of these two groups from the point at which the corporate transformation occurred.

Collins's study divides leadership into the five types shown as hierarchical levels in Figure 1.9 and discovers a statistical relationship of cause and effect. He posits that the corporate revolution cannot take place in the absence of "Type 5" leaders.

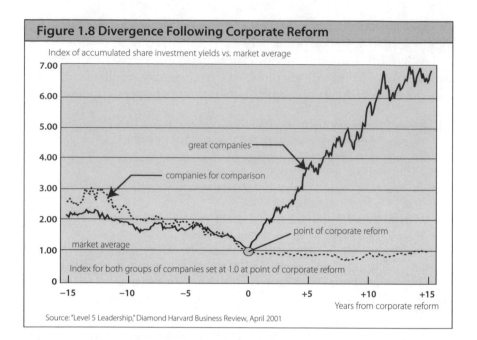

Figure 1.8 Divergence Following Corporate Reform

Index of accumulated share investment yields vs. market average

great companies

companies for comparison

point of corporate reform

market average

Index for both groups of companies set at 1.0 at point of corporate reform

Years from corporate reform

Source: "Level 5 Leadership," Diamond Harvard Business Review, April 2001

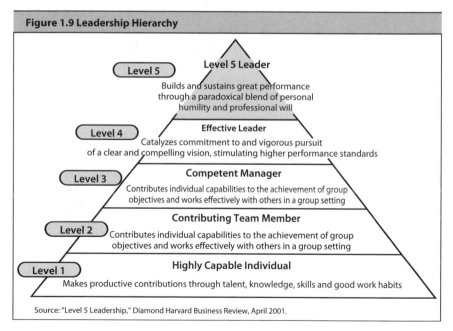

Figure 1.9 Leadership Hierarchy

Level 5 — **Level 5 Leader**
Builds and sustains great performance through a paradoxical blend of personal humility and professional will

Level 4 — **Effective Leader**
Catalyzes commitment to and vigorous pursuit of a clear and compelling vision, stimulating higher performance standards

Level 3 — **Competent Manager**
Contributes individual capabilities to the achievement of group objectives and works effectively with others in a group setting

Level 2 — **Contributing Team Member**
Contributes individual capabilities to the achievement of group objectives and works effectively with others in a group setting

Level 1 — **Highly Capable Individual**
Makes productive contributions through talent, knowledge, skills and good work habits

Source: "Level 5 Leadership," Diamond Harvard Business Review, April 2001.

Executives at the eleven companies Collins describes are, in all important respects, the same kind of people. Common characteristics are as follows:

- They appear to be shy, modest and even cowardly.
- They avoid the limelight.
- They are utterly without pretension, but draw on a powerful and even ascetic decisiveness in the face of reality.
- Their natures are divided between humility and strength of will, shyness and audacity.
- They don't talk much about themselves.
- They strive for betterment.
- They have wills of iron.
- They look outside themselves for the factors in strong performance and if they don't find them, they attribute success to "luck."
- They are stoic in their decisiveness.

When Collins conducted his analysis, he gave clear instructions to his survey team to avoid emphasizing the role of top managers in order to avoid the pitfall of simply ascribing success to leaders' achievements or leadership. The facts shown by his data, however, are unequivocal.

Level 5 leaders are, in summary, those who possess the following elements:

- In the face of reality, they are vigorously and stoically decisive.
- They have a passion for aiming high in whatever they undertake.
- They combine, on the one hand, a modesty that leads them to praise their staffs and not talk about themselves and, on the other, an almost pitiless steely determination.
- They put the company before themselves and expect succeeding generations to achieve greater success.
- They seek responsibility within themselves and the reasons for success outside themselves (i.e., in colleagues or employees, external factors or good fortune).

Collins cites the factors below to explain the behavioral characteristics of Level 5 leaders:

- People are more important than anything else. People are the starting point for these leaders. Strategy comes later.
- The Stockdale Paradox

This paradox is named for General James Stockdale, who was awarded a Medal of Honor after surviving seven years of brutal detainment in a Vietcong prison. Stockdale embraced two simultaneous and contradictory disciplines: He recognized that the extraordinarily harsh realities he confronted were real, but he held on to an absolute conviction that his side would prevail in the end.

- The flywheel powers the breakthrough.

The process that carries a good company to greatness is not achieved overnight. It resembles the task of tirelessly pushing a giant flywheel around.

- Hedgehog thinking

Think like a hedgehog and adopt a systematic and coherent approach. A hedgehog would ask simple questions: "Why do some companies perform better than any other in the world?" "How could the business models of such companies best function?" "What factors best ignite the passions of their employees?"

- Promote technological innovation

Resist the urge to pursue temporary technological fads. Be a pioneer in carefully chosen technologies.

- A culture of discipline

One observes three coherent kinds of discipline: disciplined employees, disciplined thought and disciplined behavior.

The qualities that distinguish Level 5 leaders from others can be recognized in the distinctive character of Kiichiro Toyoda. Kiichiro is said to have told his son, Shoichiro, "[In the automobile business,] all I did was wave the baton. It was the people around me who did everything else. Later on, people will probably make it sound as though I did it all by myself." This anecdote illustrates the temperament of a Level 5 leader.

Collins does not claim that the presence of a Level 5 leader is the sole factor required to shift a company from good to great. He argues only that it is an indispensable one. We can relate the results of Collins's research to the argument of this book as follows:

The indispensable requirements for moving from a good company to a continuously great one are a culture of documentation and the nurturing and development of Level 5 leaders.

Developing Level 5 Leaders

A group of newly appointed women CEOs put the following question to Collins:

"We believe that what you say about Level 5 leadership is real. But we're confused. One of the reasons we got the jobs we have now is that we have strong egos. Is the way to Level 5 leadership something we can learn?"

Collins's research had not taken him to the problem of how it was that Level 5 leaders got to be the way they were, so he admitted that he did not yet know the answer to that question. He hypothesized, however, that there were two kinds of people in the world: those who do not have the seed of Level 5 leadership within them and those who do. Then, he went on to say:

People in the former category are incapable of becoming Level 5 leaders no matter how many tens of thousands of years they try. For these people, work is a matter of 'What can I personally get out of it?' and has nothing to do with what they may build or create or how they can contribute. A cynical view is that the drive for supremacy or ambition of Level 4 leaders stands in direct opposition to the humility you need to be a Level 5 leader. What's more, there is a myth among boards of directors to the effect that becoming a great company requires an unusually self-centered leader. As a result, one just doesn't see companies with the persistence and soundness to transform themselves from good to great and then remain great.

Collins has also argued that, even among people who possess the seed of Level 5 leadership, the seed does not always germinate. In his view, no methodology has yet emerged to make it sprout.

No doubt it is not easy to discover effective methods for substantially increasing the proportion of seeds that will sprout. But a low germination rate does not matter because we are only looking for a limited number of top managers. What is important for a company is continually finding managers who possess the Level 5 leadership seed and then building programs that nurture their potential in such a way that their desire to contribute germinates and grows. These are not difficult tasks. Close observation will reveal people who carry the right seeds. Their seeds will sprout readily if one puts together education programs that touch off their sense of mission based on common destiny.

Jim Collins's book, *Built to Last: Successful Habits of Visionary Companies*, appeared in Japanese translation just before the manuscript of the current volume was completed. A summary of the arguments in Collins's new book appears under the title, *Reberu 5 Riidaashippu-ron*,[13] in the Japanese edition of the *Harvard Business Review*. I recommend taking a look at it.

Endnotes

1. In what follows, I draw heavily on the following sources: Yoshinobu Sato, *Toyota Keiei no Genryu* [*Sources of Toyota Management*] (1994), for material on (1) Sakichi Toyoda and (2) Kiichiro Toyoda; Fujio Wakamatsu and

Tadaaki Sugiyama's *Toyota no Himitsu* [*The Toyota Secret*] (1977), for my discussion of (3) Shotaro Kamiya; and Yoshinobu Sato's *Toyota Gurupu no Senryaku to Jissho Bunseki* [*Strategy and Substantive Analysis of the Toyota Group*] (1988) for information on (4) Taizo Ishida.

2. Nichiren Daishonin was a Buddhist monk in 13th-century Japan. He founded the Lotus (Hokke) sect, popularly known as Nichiren Buddhism.

3. Sontoku Ninomiya was a 19th-century Japanese agricultural leader, generally regarded, even to this day, as a symbol of hard work and perseverance.

4. *Toyota Jidosha Hanbai Sanjûnenshi.*

5. N.B. The company at the time was called Toyoda.

6. Details of these may be found in Yoshinobu Sato's 1994 *Sources of Toyota Management* (*Toyota Keiei no Genryû*).

7. *monozukuri no tetsugaku.*

8. *kadoritsu.*

9. Norioki Kobayashi. 1990. *Toyota no Daijikken.*

10. *Seisan Shisutemu no Shinkaron* (Yuikaku Press, 1997). This title, published in Japan, covers similar content to the re-edited English version, *The Evolution of a Manufacturing System at Toyota* (Oxford University Press, 1999).

11. *Toyota Keiei no Genryu.*

12. *Daiyamondo Habado Bijinesu* Rebyu.

13. *Level 5 Leadership.*

———— **2** ————

The Toyota Paradigm

The word "paradigm" is generally translated into Japanese as *kihan*, meaning standard or norm. We will use the term more broadly to encompass such concepts as corporate culture and organizational ethos. The Toyota paradigm has been formed by genes that are carried and transmitted by the DNA of documentation. This chapter weaves historical events into a look at just what sort of paradigm this is.

The development of the human race is the history of each generation's contribution to the wisdom or knowledge of its predecessors. The same is true for companies: The key to permanent growth lies in having a robust system for accumulating knowledge from one generation to the next. Toyota accomplishes this by the effective use of what is arguably the greatest of human inventions—documentation. From a layman's perspective, Toyota's knowledge encyclopedia constitutes a unique paradigm.

The Design Management Institute, a leader among Japanese consulting organizations, worked with Toyota after World War II. One of the senior people who worked with the Institute recalls that era:

> As an assistant to Shigeo Shingo[1] in 1955, I conducted training to introduce IE (industrial engineering) to Toyota. That was the point at which we discussed the introduction of the *kanban* system.
>
> The term "design management" emerged around 1957, when about twenty companies, including Toyota, Fuji Heavy Industries, Prince, Mitsubishi, and NEC, engaged in activities hosted by the Design Management Institute. Toyota was the most active of these, and we had more to learn from Toyota than to teach it.
>
> Around 1957, Toyota introduced twin reforms consisting of the *shusa* system (i.e., matrix organization) and a Technology Management Department (systematization). I was impressed to hear that Toyota had created a Technology Management Department at the same time that it introduced the *shusa* (heavyweight product

manager) system because it knew that merely fiddling around with the organization would distort relationships among people.

I was called to Toyota on several occasions to conduct improvement studies. After the oil crisis hit, Toyota also invited me to carry out a study of parts carryover, where there was much to learn from the company's thoroughness.

In 1980, I was asked to provide management training for Toyota employees one rank lower than the managerial level, but I refused, saying that I no longer had anything to do at such a company. I ended up going anyway because some of the members of the Design Management Institute at the time entreated me to. Toyota, they said, was in over its head. We used work sampling to carry out improvements in office work that led to "A Study in Raising White-collar Productivity."

As a result of these experiences, drawings management, data management, and design standardization all became crucial methods for improving the efficiency of the design department. Toyota spends about five times what other companies do on data management.

In this narrative, we glimpse a characteristic pattern of Toyota behavior that impressed even a senior figure in a professional management consulting organization. Toyota's unique paradigm was already well established.

VALUES

Management Philosophy

The most important determinant of the Toyota paradigm is clearly the company's management philosophy, including its management doctrines and basic policies. In most companies, management doctrines or basic policies take the form of empty incantations or ornamentation and tend not to penetrate the thinking of employees. Toyota, however, makes sure these are recorded as formal documents, that they reach all employees, and that their penetration throughout the organization is monitored. This allows Toyota to shape the values, thinking, and behavior of all employees.

Paradigms change with the times. The evolution of Toyota's management doctrines and basic policies reveals which parts of the Toyota paradigm have altered over time, thus giving us an overview of what at the company has changed and what has not.

The Toyoda Precepts

The Toyoda Precepts were drawn up by Kiichiro Toyoda and Risaburo Toyoda in 1935 as a summary of Sakichi Toyoda's teachings. Even after World War II, the Toyoda Precepts long remained enshrined as the principles of Toyota and the Toyota group. Because the precepts had been formulated before the war, certain aspects of their language became unsuitable for the modern era, but there was nothing dated about their spirit. As Table 2.1 shows, the Toyoda Precepts can be interpreted in a way that is quite modern. In their spirit, all of the Toyoda Precepts are perfectly comprehensible today. As a progressive doctrine expressing management as a mission, the precepts have lost none of their luster through the years.

Table 2.1 The Toyoda Precepts and a Modern Interpretation

Toyoda Precepts	Modern Interpretation
1. Regardless of position, work together to fulfill your duties faithfully and contribute to the development and welfare of the country	In their work, all company employees, without respect to rank, should join together to strive in concrete form for the development of the broader world
2. Always stay ahead of the times through research and creativity	You should dedicate yourself to studying the wisdom of your predecessors and to staying always on the cutting edge by creating ideas that surpass theirs.
3. Avoid frivolity. Be sincere and strong.	You should eliminate waste, concentrate energy on what is truly effective and build a lean and fit company
4. Be kind and generous. Strive to create a home-like atmosphere.	With a sense of shared destiny, you should help one another within the company and build family-like friendships.
5. Be reverent and conduct your life in thankfulness and gratitude.	As you conduct business with an awareness of belonging to the earth and a mindfulness of the blessings of your region and society, you should act with the intention to preserve the earth and to give back to society.

Postwar Basic Principles of Management

Toyota's team lineup and organization grew rapidly as the company rode the wave of motorization that began in the latter half of the 1950s. It soon became evident, however, that this growth was accompanied by a deterioration in quality and a souring of relationships among the company's various departments. Toyota decided to improve things at this point by taking on TQC, a movement that was evolving into company-wide QC. In the context of promoting TQC, in January 1963, Toyota announced a threefold corporate policy comprising a basic policy, a long-term policy, and an annual policy. The basic policy expressed the company's fundamental management philosophy:

1. We will strive to develop Toyota throughout the world by harnessing all energies inside and outside the company.
2. We will improve Toyota's results as a quality leader by our relentless pursuit of good products and good ideas.
3. We will contribute to the development of the Japanese economy through high-volume production and low prices.

The policy was not intended as a substitute for the Toyoda Precepts but as a business vision based on the precepts. It bears little relation to the precepts, however, and creates the strong impression that the precepts had been put on the back burner in the race toward high growth. The basic policy has historical significance as the motive force responsible for the Toyota we know today, but with its exclusive focus on company growth, it gave too prominent an expression to what Taizo Ishida at the time called vainglory.[2] During this period, Toyota was hardly progressive in its socio-economic activities and was ridiculed for its selfish isolationism. The basic policy certainly leaves an impression of self-righteousness and selfishness.

The first and second oil shocks constituted a turning point that led Toyota to grow into a world-class company. Heeding criticism of its isolationism, Toyota began to turn outward. In 1983, one year after the merging of Toyota Motor and Toyota Motor Sales, the company's basic policy was revised as follows:

1. While deeply cognizant of our mission in the automotive industry, we will actively contribute to economic and social development in Japan and worldwide.
2. We will strive for the sound development of Toyota throughout the world by harnessing all energies inside and outside the company.
3. Through ingenuity and effort, we will work to improve corporate efficiency as we sustain a youthful management culture.
4. We will improve Toyota's results as a quality leader by our constant and relentless pursuit of good products and good ideas.
5. On a basis of mutual trust between labor and management, we will develop people capable of meeting the challenges of the times.

On surface, this may appear to echo the principles of the Toyoda Precepts, but at closer examination, this revised policy does not appear to be grounded in the loftiest concepts of the Toyoda Precepts. One still gets the feeling that it has been extrapolated from a preoccupation with high growth.

By the latter half of the 1980s, European and North American companies were growing increasingly bitter over the flood of Japanese exports, and the backlash from overseas had become intense. Domestically, Toyota had become a mammoth corporation and there was mounting criticism of its persistence in maintaining a "Toyota first" attitude and of its inward-looking orientation.

Figure 2.1 shows public perceptions of the time. The consensus was that Toyota might have been a firm from which others wanted to learn, but that it could not be called a good company.

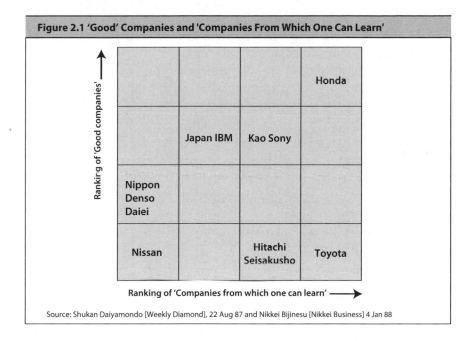

Figure 2.1 'Good' Companies and 'Companies From Which One Can Learn'

Ranking of 'Good companies'

Honda

Japan IBM   Kao Sony

Nippon Denso Daiei

Nissan   Hitachi Seisakusho   Toyota

Ranking of 'Companies from which one can learn' ⟶

Source: Shukan Daiyamondo [Weekly Diamond], 22 Aug 87 and Nikkei Bijinesu [Nikkei Business] 4 Jan 88

Even within Toyota, there was a sense of great crisis among those who saw the company and its employees losing public support. In study groups and other forums within Toyota, debates arose over how the company needed to change. From this point in time, Toyota finally began shifting from its defensive "What's wrong with good, cheap products?" to a sincere consideration of how it could become a "grown-up company capable of understanding other people's woes."

Toyota began to get serious about improving its corporate image. The man at the tiller for this important shift was the company president, Shoichiro Toyoda.

Basic Principles for the 21st Century

Shoichiro Toyoda presented his Basic Toyota Principles in January 1992. Table 2.2 shows these Basic Principles and how they reflect the Toyoda Precepts. A slightly revised edition of the Basic Toyota Principles was issued in 1997.

Table 2.2 Toyota Basic Principles and How They Reflect the Toyoda Precepts

Toyota Basic Principles (published 1992 and, with slight revisions, 1997)	Reflections from The Toyoda Precepts
1. Honor the language and spirit of the law and undertake open and fair corporate activities to be a trusted corporate citizen of the world.	(New)
2. Respect the culture and customs of every nation and contribute to economic and social development through corporate activities in the communities.	Industry and patriotism
3. Dedicate ourselves to providing clean and safe products and to strive for a liveable earth and the building of abundant societies through all our activities.	Industry and patriotism, gratitude and thanks
4. Create and develop advanced technologies in various fields, and provide outstanding products and services that fulfill the needs of customers worldwide.	Research and creativity being ahead of the times
5. Foster a corporate culture that enhances individual creativity and teamwork value and that is based on mutual trust and responsibility between labor and management.	Warmth and friendship, a home-like atmosphere
6. Pursue growth in harmony with the global community through innovative management.	(New)
7. Work in open dealings with business partners in research and creation to achieve stable, long-term growth and mutual benefits.	Research and creativity

With the Basic Principles of 1992, Toyota for the first time absorbed the spirit of the Toyoda Precepts, clarifying its relationship to customers, employees, business associates and other stakeholders, and expressing a clear awareness of the company as a corporate citizen of the world. The Basic Principles subsequently led to the formulation of a long-term vision, a medium- and long-term business plan, and long- and short-term corporate policies.

January 1992, the same month the Basic Principles were published, also saw the publication of a Toyota Action Plan for Global Environment, commonly known as the Toyota Global Earth Charter. Toyota began concrete action in February 1993, when it published The Toyota Environmental Action Plan, specifying more concretely how environmental policy would be reflected in company activities. The Toyota Global Earth Charter was revised in April 2000 and a third Environmental Action Plan was published for the years between 2001 and 2005. Toyota's homepage on the Internet records the plan in detail over five pages, giving specifics and agendas for such items as safety measures, a system of interventions, and internal structures and roles. Although one may question whether such openness is a good idea, the information provides a glimpse of the extent of Toyota's seriousness and confidence.

In fact, the rapid movement from the publication of the Basic Principles in 1992 to Toyota's safety and environmental initiatives has been impressive. The unveiling (in December 1997) of the *Prius*, the world's first hybrid passenger car (combining a gasoline engine and an electric motor) was the culmination of a project launched in 1992. Selling at the unprofitable price of ¥2.5 million per vehicle, the *Prius* symbolized Toyota's engagement with environmental issues and marked a break with the company's insistence on producing only cars that make money. To consumers, it imparted the strong message that Toyota was ahead of the curve in the environmental field. Toyota added a hybrid version of the *Estima* minivan in June 2001; in August of that year, a hybrid version of the *Crown* was also introduced. Fujio Cho, the president of Toyota, announced a plan to increase production of hybrid vehicles tenfold to 300,000 units in 2005.

Programs to recycle scrapped vehicles also advanced. In 1999, Toyota achieved a vehicle recycling rate of 88 percent, the highest level in the world. In Europe, with its progressive recycling regulations, the recycling rate for scrapped vehicles is expected to rise to 95 percent by 2015. Toyota announced its plans to attain that goal ten years earlier, in 2005.

Environmental policies are moving forward rapidly as well. In April 1998, Toyota's Design and Development Division became the first among domestic manufacturers to achieve ISO 14000 status for environmental management. In 1999, Toyota became the first carmaker to receive ISO 14000 certification for all its plants. At the same time, the company demanded ISO 14000 certification of all its suppliers.

In the *Year 2000 Environmental Management Survey* published in the *Nikkei Sangyo Shimbun* on December 5, 2000, Toyota had jumped from twenty-first place the previous year to fourth place. Ricoh was in first place, Japan IBM was second, and Canon was third, but when one considers that the industrial waste produced by such office equipment manufacturers is both miniscule and simpler in composition compared with the waste produced by automobile makers, Toyota's fourth-place ranking is extraordinary. Beginning with Nippon Denso, which jumped from eighty-ninth place to fifth place, there were seven major Toyota suppliers within the top 50 companies. Environmental protection had clearly become a paradigm for Toyota and its affiliates.

The year 1996 saw the formulation of Toyota's Principles for Social Contribution Activities:

1. In accordance with the basic themes of promoting research and creativity and building an affluent society, we will actively develop activities that contribute to society.
2. We will endeavor to foster an organizational ethos that allows each and every employee to carry out independent activities as an individual citizen.

The company launched these activities in 1998 by establishing a dedicated department and a Committee on Social Contribution Activities headed by the president and chief executive officer. These late 20th-century developments in company policies announced Toyota's intention to live as a citizen of the earth in the 21st century.

Perspectives on Work

Toyota's management philosophy includes views of work that are expressed neither in the company's management principles nor in its policies. Several of these merit a closer look.

Business Goals and Business Sense

The majority of people who look for jobs at automobile companies choose to do so for the simple reason that they like cars. Even if they rise in the organization and become managers, they may remain in the category of car buffs. As Figure 0.2 shows, groups of skilled craftsmen throughout the organization are composed of people enticed by the product but who never grow as company employees.

In Toyota's case, the organization was founded with the intent to, as the Toyoda Precepts put it, "contribute to Japanese society through manufacturing." Historically, the automobile was selected as the most appropriate means to accomplish this. Consequently, new employees who enter the company for the simple reason that they like cars will eventually be influenced by Toyota's founding principles and will become aware that automobiles are a means to achieving the real purpose of contributing to Japanese society. It is not difficult to imagine that a vast difference separates the business results of a group of people who come together merely because they like cars and a group of people with an ideological commitment to contributing to society.

Shuichiro Honda was an automobile enthusiast all his life. But Honda's business was entrusted entirely to Takeo Fujisawa, and it was Fujisawa's instructions that were followed in all matters relating to business. For Fujisawa, not surprisingly, automobiles were a means to achieve business ends.

In 1955, the Japanese Ministry of International Trade and Industry (MITI) came up with the idea of building a national car that would sell for $1,000. At the time, Toyota was selling its *Crown* for $3,300 to $3,600, and a price of $1,000 seemed out of the question. Eiji Toyoda, however, recognized that there was merit in MITI's idea. He justified immediate development plans by explaining, "Kiichiro built this company to make cars that ordinary people would use. We can't ignore an idea that had been with the company since its founding." After six years of unswerving commitment to the project, Toyota offered the first *Publica* for sale for $1,055 in 1961. Six years later, in May 1967, the price was lowered to $997 and the goal was finally achieved.

Nissan Motor considered the idea of a popular car to be premature and so hesitated before implementing MITI's concept. Its version of the $1,000 vehicle, the *Sunny*, was introduced in April of 1966, five years after the Toyota *Publica* went on the market at $1,055.

The *Publica* was judged to be too plain and didn't sell very well, but its five-year lead over Nissan gave Toyota a decisive edge in improving its sales network. Forthrightly facing the challenge of a popular, inexpensive vehicle, moreover, became the driving force that gave birth to cost planning, Toyota's revolutionary cost-management method (see Chapter 3). Toyota also learned that, at least when it came to high-ticket goods such as automobiles, Japanese consumers preferred deluxe models to standard models. All these lessons were applied with the unveiling (in October 1966) of the first-generation *Corolla*, a model that marked the definitive divergence of the fortunes of Toyota and Nissan.

The *Publica* could not have been developed without a clear business sense. Eiji recalled that the most valuable benefit of all was the satisfaction of having done a job worth doing.

Either at the time of a company's founding or during the early stages of its growth, a point arrives at which its employees have to see products as instruments of the business. From early on, managers have to imbue the organization with the sense that the business goal is to contribute to society and that products are a means to that end.

Perceptions of Competitors and Allies

Both leaders and ordinary employees in the Toyota camp will tell you that the target is GM. And they were saying this even back in the days when GM considered Toyota to be little more than "trash."

In his book, *Building People and Products the Toyota Way*,[3] Yoshihito Wakamatsu of Toyota OB recalls being asked by a Toyota director in 1963 to prepare a balance sheet comparing GM and Toyota costs. "In terms of sales at the time," he writes, "GM was 60 times larger than Toyota. Even if we knew the cost gap between two such dissimilar companies, I wondered, what was the point?"

Kiichiro Toyoda had the advanced automobile-producing nations of Europe and North America in his competitive sights from the very founding of Toyota, and he availed himself of every occasion to make the entire company understand that the big American and European carmakers were the competition. Hearing top executives tell of their grandiose dreams and their romantic ambitions is what led all employees to say that GM was the target. This premise of having a grand competitor was behind Kiichiro's hitting on the idea of just-in-time, Taiichi Ohno's work on the Toyota Production System, and Eiji Toyoda's commitment to building Toyota's solid business foundation by introducing TQC. It also induced all Toyota employees to rush excitedly toward the goal. Today, GM is within reach.

After the war, when feudal squabbling dominated the Japanese market for two-wheeled vehicles, Honda proclaimed itself the best in the world. It set its sights on winning the Isle of Man Race and finally became number one. Many readers no doubt still remember the front-page photographs and articles celebrating Honda's victory in the Isle of Man Race. One Honda manager at the time considered Honda's Shizuoka city plant's claim to world championship to be perilously close to bragging, but the world champion mentality later led Honda to achieve the best fuel efficiency in the world. This news, too, leapt to the front pages of newspapers. These brilliant achievements excited all of Japan and sent Honda surging ahead.

In Japan's period of rapid economic growth, the country's number two automaker, Nissan, settled on Toyota as its competition. For a while, Mazda, one of the automotive companies in the running for third place, set the goal of becoming a "clear number three." The result? Honda swallowed Nissan, and Mazda was overtaken by Honda and Mitsubishi. Nissan and Mazda had set goals they thought they could just reach with a little bit more effort. This mindset was an illusion, and they were taken over by stronger competitors.

There is a hardheaded rule of business to be learned from all of this. No matter how close a firm is to being "trash," it should set its sights on competing with the biggest and best companies in the world. Defeatism spreads through an organization the minute it assumes that underdog challengers will be swept away by the champion—and with defeatism, one way or another, comes an eventual need to withdraw from the market.

Firms that aspire to become world champions have a unique perception of their allies as well. At first glance, the Toyota group appears to consist of client/supplier relationships that are extremely cold and almost excessively stern. But suppliers sense that they are built on a well-intentioned motivation for mutual success, so that even the harshest demands rarely cause resentment or hostility. Shogo Tsuru, the former chairman of Nippon Oil Seal, has commented that "Toyota has two faces. It is a stern father and a compassionate mother."

Toyota's vendors and customers invariably recall having been trained by Toyota. Init, a company charged with creating the homepage for Gazoo, Toyota's e-retailing venture, underwent roughly three months of special training on multi-skilling, leveling, standardization, and techniques for building quality into processes. As a result, Init reduced its fees from ¥1.6 million for a 160-hour job to a half-million yen for a 50-hour job. A company already possessing a high level of technical expertise, Init absorbed the efficiencies of the Toyota Production System and now continues to enjoy rapid growth in both sales and profits. Yasuhiro Hayami, Init's president, recalls that "it didn't matter whether the product was automotive or digital. We had the *muda*-elimination (waste) mindset beaten into us."

While Toyota continues to set exacting goals, it sends people out to provide guidance on improving quality, cost and productivity, and to share its knowledge. The result is that streamlining continues and profits rise for Toyota suppliers. Customers are pleased, and gratitude toward Toyota produces a kind of centripetal force. This arrangement has enormous advantages for Toyota. Being able to grasp the true state of the workplaces of parts makers and sales and logistics companies allows Toyota to accumulate valuable knowledge needed to reduce manufacturing costs.

With buyers eager to buy parts at the lowest prices possible and sellers always wanting to sell for the highest prices possible, suppliers and their customers often try to outfox one another. On the other hand, when companies and their vendors work together to lower costs and improve profits, the entire car becomes a more competitive product, and sales allow both sides to prosper. Companies with the desire to succeed need to work out positive and concrete policies that foster diligence and trust between them and their suppliers.

Attitudes Toward Work

For many decades now, Toyota has continued to organize independent study groups[4] to conduct *kaizen,* or improvement, activities. Certainly, these activities do receive a certain amount of human and financial assistance from the company, but an examination of the activities suggests that the Toyota employee's attitude toward work is one of "group research into work."

The Toyota Technology Group and the Toyota Management Study Group are representative examples of independent study entities. Because of the tremendous influence it has had over Toyota management for many decades, the historical activities of the Toyota Management Study Group, in particular, should not be overlooked.

Toyota Motor—A History of the First Twenty Years[5] (1958) describes the Toyota Management Study Group as follows:

> *Doing a job well calls for unremitting study and effort. Persuaded of this fact, like-minded managers and workers independently organized a Toyota Management Reading Group (later called a study group) on February 7, 1955. At the beginning, participants read management-related journals and hosted lectures and studies and discussions in order to learn about various issues relating to modern management. Currently there are 200 members. The group subscribes to such journals as* Manejimento *[Management],* Jimu to Keiei *[Business and Management],* Kojo Kanri *[Factory Management],* Manajimento Gaido *[Management Guide] and* Kigyo Kaikei *[Corporate Finance], and the company helps out with part of the expenses. Early in 1957, group members formed a reading circle to study* Office Management and Control *by Professor George R. Terry, an American authority on office management. Later, in March 1958, the group began publishing the quarterly journal* Toyota Management. *In this way, members worked to improve their management skills by studying together and by learning from one another.*

The Toyota company history may point to the importance of the Toyota Management Study Group, but outsiders are unaware of the group's existence. *Toyota Management* became a monthly journal soon after its inception and is still published today.

Toyota Management is not generally circulated, but it is widely distributed among Toyota's customers, suppliers, and dealers. The author of this work had an opportunity to see the journal some ten years ago and was amazed at the scope and extent of the study group's activities.

It is surprising enough to realize that independent study group activities have been maintained for nearly half a century. What is even more astonishing is the comprehensiveness of the journal, *Toyota Management.* Its 50 to 60 pages brim with management studies, survey results, articles, descriptions of new management techniques, roundtable discussions, lecture reports, occasional essays, literature from abroad, reports of translations of foreign documents, summaries of speeches from inside and outside the company, sales and production data for a variety of companies, reader's pages, and even space for thumbnail book notices. Naturally enough, the principal content consists of management studies, articles, and descriptions of new management techniques, all very comprehensive and of high quality.

To cite an example, new management technique descriptions and lecture reports from the 1960s include the following titles:

- Industrial dynamism
- Investment and production
- How to assess and evaluate educational needs
- Recent design theories and their applications
- New planning and management techniques
- Cost management
- The Monte Carlo Method applied to capital investment planning

Even the brief book notices, which include insights by the likes of Peter Drucker, are written in a style that allows readers to absorb the essence of the books without reading them. No space is wasted.

Thus, at a time when the expressions "business management" and "management technologies" were not even current in Japan and when companies were concentrating on improving proprietary technologies, Toyota, through its independent study group activities, was surveying and researching progressive business management techniques and disseminating them throughout its organization.

Masao Yamamoto, a company director (later executive vice president) and the originator of Toyota's management study groups, makes the following observation in the preface to the March 1958 inaugural issue of *Toyota Management*:

Recognizing that significant recent issues in industry involve technological innovation and modern management, the Toyota Technology Group addressed the subject of technological innovation and the Toyota Management Study Group squarely took on the problem of modern management methods. In doing so, they advanced the modernization of Toyota management and both became influential internal study organs. In the three years since the founding of the Toyota Management Study Group, the board of directors has been run following the recommendations of the group, and the efforts of the group have, in both tangible and intangible ways, spilled into the boardroom like a breath of fresh air. There is no denying that the group has served to steer us in new directions.

The observations of members of the Toyota Management Study Group are also worth including here (the quotes are excerpted from *Toyota Management*'s special 40th Anniversary Issue, December 1995, Vol. 38):

"I still clearly recall Taizo Ishida, the president at the time, telling us jokingly that if we young people knew so much about management, we could take over his job for him."

"Three issues preoccupied me as we moved ahead with the activities of the Toyota Management Study Group: first, that we root ourselves in macroeconomic views, second, that we relate our work to regional, national and world society, and third, that we take steps to be ahead of the times."

"In those days, the Toyota Management Study Group would actively give advice directly relating to the business. On many occasions, suggestions from special editions of the Toyota Management Study Group's journal were actually implemented in the business."

The orientation of *Toyota Management* shifted over the years. In the TQC era of the 1960s, the journal reported many studies, surveys, developments, improvements, and implementations on such topics as quality control, cost management, office and information management, personnel and labor management, plant management, and computer systems management. The vitality of solid management research activities seen in submissions from that period is almost overwhelming.

In the 1980s, perhaps influenced by the free and easy culture of the old sales organization after the merger of Toyota Motor and Toyota Motor Sales, research papers submitted to the journal centered around new questions, for example, "Is it all right for Toyota to be greedy forever?" or "What stance should the new Toyota adopt in order to break free of the old Toyota?"

In the 1990s, studies and debates in the journal were preoccupied with addressing 21st-century issues, including how to be a global company, rebuilding relationships with suppliers, ecology studies, studies on the information society, the role of women in the company, and Hiroshi Okuda's theory of corporate morality. These writings hastened Toyota's reinvention of itself as a "beloved" company.

In the May 1988 issue of *Toyota Management*, a corporate organization study group, composed of six members drawn primarily from the Development and Technical departments, published a major thirty-page essay under the title "Creating a New Corporate Organization."[6] The authors argued that the Toyota organization, having matured and become a large corporation, was falling prey to a Gresham's Law of managerial behavior, in other words, that urgency was taking precedence over importance. They pointed out that big company disease, which stifles the flowering of individual ability, was creeping through Toyota. They went on to analyze the lessons to be learnt from the past—i.e., Henry Ford's system, Alfred Sloan's system of business divisions at GM, and Japanese management of the 1980s—and proposed a new paradigm for Toyota. Achieving it, they determined, would require an organizational revolution in development (the weak spot of Japanese management and historically the slowest area to reform), and they proposed the creation of an organizational entity they called an Ultimate Development Department (*Kyukyoku no Kaihatsu Bumon*). Structurally, this entity was basically the same as the Development Centers that Toyota implemented in September 1992 in what was billed as the greatest organizational reform since the company was founded.

In his book, *On Organizational Reform at Toyota*[7] (1990), Kozo Nishida tells the story of these proceedings:

> *Nineteen eighty-four saw the launching within Toyota of a 100-member "Personnel Systems Study Group." And between May and June of 1985, I lectured on the theme of solutions to current organizational and personnel issues. As an organization grows in size, it loses its institutional vitality and develops what has been called big company disease: bureaucratization, symptoms of institutional Gresham's Law and declining morale. I argued that the solution requires a steady transformation into a creative organization, and that organizational clustering [okukurika] and flattening were important steps in that process. One can't tell how much influence this argument had on Toyota's later institutional reforms, but the changes I advocated seem to have taken place.*

Kozo Nishida's lectures were most likely sponsored by a branch of the Toyota Management Study Group. From the late 80s to the beginning of the 1990s, this sort of independent study group activity seems to have prompted a string of reforms in organizational culture. Among these were the *sanzuki* campaign to address people using the neutral suffix –*san* rather than their official company titles, the three stamp campaign to reduce the number of stamps needed for the approval of decisions, and organizational flattening. The study group activity also seems to be connected to the historic Development Center reform implemented in 1992 (i.e., the limiting of responsibilities and the clustering of work for particular vehicle types). We will discuss the Development Center system later, but as we see from these examples, there can be little doubt that the activities of the Toyota Management Study Group brought fresh air into the executive suite for nearly half a century.

The Toyota Management Study Group consisted of 70 people at its inception in 1955, but by the mid-1990s that number had grown to 16,000. As an interesting contrast, an annual subscription for *Toyota Management* cost ¥600 (or ¥50 per issue) in 1958, but the price has not changed since then.

Eiji Toyoda, then senior managing director, was the chairman of the Toyota Management Study Group at the time the journal *Toyota Management* was founded. Even as Eiji moved up through the ranks to become executive vice president, president, and chairman, he remained chairman of the study group for nearly 30 years. In every January issue, he contributed a New Year's message in which he outlined his expectations for the study group commensurate with the management environment of the time.

All the same, the Toyota Management Study Group's activities have come catastrophically near collapse on several occasions in the course of the entity's long history, and the group has faced the possibility of suspension or disbanding. However, it has survived until the present day, probably because of Toyota executive management's unequivocal support.

Another independent study group, the Toyota Technology Group, was centered in the engineering division and focused on technological issues. Founded in 1948, it has since published the quarterly *Toyota Technology*.[8] In 1991, *Toyota Technology* was recast as the semiannual *Toyota Technical Review*. Formed so that members could learn from one another and polish their technical skills, the Technology Group's principal activities include research presentations, skills forums, technology festivals such as Idea Olympics, meeting proceedings, technology companions, and the publication of pamphlets on automobile technology. Pamphlets published by the group include *Automotive Facts, An Automobile Glossary, Production Facts, Car Electronics,* and *Automobiles and Data Processing*.

Large companies that have similar study groups are probably not very numerous. And firms that have been running such groups actively for a half-century are certainly rare. If one reflects on the research on work, the bold and frank initiatives transcending horizontal and vertical boundaries, and the free and open discussions that characterize them, it is easy to conclude that these study groups are an important source of vitality for Toyota Motor as a whole.

Perspectives on People

A View of Human Beings

Some people have the impression that Toyota management conceives of humans as cogs in a machine whose primary aim is always production. In fact, there are numerous books that have criticized Toyota for its inhumanity. In a typical example, Masaki Saruta offers this criticism in his book, *Labor Management in the Toyota System:*[9]

> *The superior suppleness and flexibility of Toyota's production system are due to the fact that all systems are built to give priority to production, that—from hiring, working hours and the wage system to human relations and even voting behavior—everything subordinates human beings who can be manipulated at will.*

Here, however, it is important to counter with Toyota's basic philosophy regarding people:

"Respect for human beings means not having people engage in wasteful work or jobs. That elevates the value of human beings and in turn constitutes respect for them."

Toyota's philosophy has been defended by Yoshito Wakamatsu and Tetsuo Kondo in their book, *Building People and Products the Toyota Way:*[10]

> *There seem to be people for whom the name Toyota Production System conjures up an image of inhumanity, but this is a mistake. The essence of the Toyota Production System is that each individual employee is given the opportunity to find problems in his own way of working, to solve them and to make improvements, and that employees work as one to build a better company. This organizational culture is the most important key to adopting the Toyota Production System and making it work.*

Jack Welch of General Electric attached great importance to people and through Work-out and Six Sigma activities tapped their creativity to raise their sense of participating in management. He tells this story in the company's 1989 Annual Report:

> *I want GE to be the kind of company whose employees hurry to work every morning because they want to try out things they've been thinking about the night before. And when employees go home, rather than*

forgetting what happened at work that day, I'd like them to tell their families about it. When the whistle blows at the end of the day, I hope workers will be surprised that they haven't noticed the time go by; I hope the plant becomes a place where people will question why the whistle is needed at the end of the workday in the first place. And I hope that employees will improve their jobs every day. I hope that by organizing their experiences they make their own lives richer and, by doing so, that they make their company into the best one on earth. This is a corporate culture with no boundaries: open, participative, and exciting. And you can see it in new companies that are reaping one success after another.

Welch has said that Japan (and by Japan, he means primarily Toyota) served as a business school for GE. He hints at this when he refers to "new companies that are reaping one success after another" and "a corporate culture with no [national or other] boundaries." From GE's perspective, Toyota is a new company.

Since most of us take it for granted that American and European workers do not take work home, it is surprising to see this idea openly expressed in a Western company's public relations magazine. At the same time, Welch's words suggest that we have entered an era in which such a notion has become essential to improving corporate performance.

Mochio Umeda, the president of Muse Associates, describes Japanese corporate culture as follows (excerpted from "The Magic C-Grade Nature of Japanese Companies," February 12, 2001. *Nikkei Business*):[11]

For many years, we have been raised in a work environment in which the company functions not simply as a place for work, but as a place for living and even playing. Playing through work is truly enjoyable. Nothing can replace the joy we feel when the work goes well and when work and play come together in the "simulated family" of people whose faces we see every day. This was the "salaryman" culture of Japan after the war. Companies in the United States are nothing more or less than places to work and there is a growing trend toward stockholder management and speed management. Companies like this may get good results, but they are lonely places. From the vantage point of anyone who has ever experienced the enjoyment of working at a Japanese company, the sense that something is missing in Western corporate culture is acute. At the same time, Japanese companies probably pay too high a price for sustaining this enjoyment.

Even if companies that view people the way Toyota or GE do are the only ones that can grow in the 21st century, that doesn't mean we should forever feel nostalgia for Japan's salaryman culture to the point where we sacrifice work and life. In trying to learn from Toyota and create new paradigms, perhaps the greatest challenge will be the ability to accept Toyota's view of people.

Toyota employees come in contact with Toyota's corporate view of people from the time they enter the company, so they are naturally accustomed to it. By changing our values, we, too, should be able to accustom ourselves to it. But to do so, we truly need a paradigm shift.

Approaches to Developing People

Toyota managers often wrap up their talks with references to "building people."

> "Production is the starting point for creating value and creating civilization. Without production there is no technological progress. Production always takes place by virtue of people and their accumulated know-how. Unless you nurture people, therefore, you can't even begin working." (Eiji Toyoda)

> "IT is ultimately nothing more than a tool. We must not forget that its effectiveness rests on the foundation constituted by production. Developing engineers and technicians is crucial to expanding production. As we communicate the importance of production to the younger generation, we also need to take a new look at what forms education should take." (Hiroshi Okuda)

We may think that all of this is obvious and that we don't need to hear it. But the "people building" here seems to differ in nuance from what we usually have in mind. When we talk about "building people," we generally mean developing their technical knowledge and abilities. But Hiroshi Okuda and Eiji Toyoda were talking about building enthusiasm for the work. Where motivation exists, technical knowledge and skills will follow.

Abraham Maslow, the psychologist famous for his five-step hierarchy of needs, explains this another way: "People will rarely come to grips with programs imposed upon them in a situation where there is no sense of crisis. But they will enter the fray willingly if they themselves have contributed to creating the program."

This seems to be Toyota's approach to developing (or motivating) people.

We often hear the following view about developing people: "You can lead a horse to water, but you can't make him drink. It's the individual who decides whether he wants to develop his abilities or not."

This is a frequent excuse for not educating people. It amounts to saying, "We won't teach anyone who doesn't ask to be taught."

Toyota's approach is to make the horse want to drink by making it clear to him that he'll die of thirst if he doesn't. The idea is constantly to draw out the motivation in people.

The education provided to new employees, for example, can have an enormous impact in their lives at a company. In Toyota's case, general technical employees are given two months of factory training in the first year and three months of sales training in the second year after hiring. The reason for the sales training in the second year is that it gives employees a sense of the direct connection between their jobs and the sales floor. At Toyota, it is important to draw a lifetime of motivation from people by taking them away from their usual jobs at the high point of their second year of employment and having them experience the cutthroat environment of sales.

Another motivational technique may be found in Toyota leadership's constant talk of crisis. The prime motive force supporting Toyota's prosperity in the 20th century was a sense of crisis in the company and an insatiable drive to reduce costs.

Toyota uses such methods to build "creative tension" within the company. By minimizing the number of employees who merely rent their physical labor and who mentally draw a line around their work lives, Toyota has become a "*kaizen* organization," striving constantly for improvement.

An economist once observed that "managers use human psychology to raise morale," and Toyota takes a psychological approach to nurturing individuals and the organization.

Perspectives on Things

Perspectives on Information

In Chapter 1, we recounted how Shotaro Kamiya, the president of Toyota Motor Sales, told Iwao Imazu in December 1956 that Toyota had no central location for collecting and analyzing information for the company as a whole; he wanted to establish a department that could understand the big picture. We explained that this was the genesis of Toyota's Information Strategy Department and the basis for later Toyota excellence.

Toyota Motor chairman Hiroshi Okuda, who came out of the old Toyota Motor Sales organization and who was probably trained directly by Kamiya, elaborated:

> *Toyota's information network is informal but impressive. For example, Toyota people excel at gathering information about, say, who's visiting the U.S. from which company and what sorts of people they're meeting with. They just don't talk about it. Because they have this information, they know really fast what steps they have to take to avoid running into trouble.* ("How Far Does Toyota's Competence Go?" April 10, 2000, *Nikkei Business.*)

Okuda's observation that Toyota's network is informal means that, in addition to an organization of information-gathering experts within the company, all departments in the entire company collect information as part of their everyday activities.

In the spring of 2000, Toyota's own information network caused considerable agitation when it picked up the news that GM was considering investing capital in Honda. Quite apart from the question of whether the information was accurate, it is just one example of the power of Toyota's information network.

Toyota is a company that happily publishes internal information of the sort that most companies treat as secret. But as Okuda suggests, not many details leak out about Toyota's information-gathering or information-management methods or systems. Toyota is known as generous when it comes to gathering and transmitting information, but the range of information gathered and transmitted is strictly managed. This is hardly surprising, since Toyota leadership believes that "information determines a company's destiny."

In recent years, a typical method of using information has been popularized as "benchmarking," a procedure for designating another company or organization as a criterion for comparison and then studying its "best practices." Tadaaki Jagawa, the president of Hino Motors (and former executive vice president of Toyota Motor) has noted that "Toyota's motive power probably lies in its eternal benchmarking." Toyota's long history of establishing its own best methods after scrutinizing Ford and General Motors stretches back to the days of Kiichiro Toyoda. Since that time, Toyota has grown by devoting extraordinary energy to the collection and management of information and then, using benchmarking procedures, by setting specific goals and working out its own best practices.

Perspectives on Knowledge and Documentation

We have explained how Toyota systematically manages the genes representing the wisdom of earlier generations, how it enhances them, and how the mediating DNA of documentation is required to transmit them. It does not matter whether the documents are on paper or in computer media. Valuing documents makes it possible to operate a system of knowledge management in the organization.

In the context of knowledge management, there are three kinds of knowledge: (1) unprocessed data; (2) information and records that have been processed once and express significance and value; and (3) rules (standards) derived from multiple sources of information and records that answer the question "if this, then that." In Chapter 1, we discussed in some detail the philosophy and values behind Toyota's standards; here we will examine Toyota's information and records.

In the article entitled, "Another Look at Toyota's Integrated Product Development," published in the July–August 1998 issue of the *Harvard Business Review, Diamond Harvard Business,*[12] Durward K. Sobek, II et al. explain Toyota's effective use of documents as an efficient means of exchanging information:

> When a problem arises that requires coordination between departments, the standard procedure is to put together reports including a "problem-solving plan," "important information," and a "recommendation," and then distribute these documents to the departments concerned. The recipients are expected to read and study the documents and to provide feedback by telephone or individual meetings or sometimes by compiling reports based on other documents. One or two iterations of this will result in a considerable volume of information going back and forth and the participants will reach consensus on most points. Only when insurmountable disagreements occur will meetings be held to resolve the problem through direct dialogue.
>
> Problem-solving meetings of this sort are prepared for by making sure that all participants understand the important issues beforehand and that everyone has considered proposals and countermeasures that approach the problem based on the same data. Since such meetings focus on resolving a specific problem, time isn't wasted obtaining a consensus among the participants. This contrasts with many U.S. companies in which attendees show up at meetings without having done any preparation at all. The first half of the meeting

is wasted in defining the problem and then participants scramble to deal with a problem they've hardly had time to think about.

Toyota frequently relies on written communication as the first step in problem-solving, but the company avoids the massive paperwork that afflicts bureaucracies. In most cases, engineers will write clear, concise reports on one side of a sheet of A3 paper. These reports are all written in the same format so that everyone understands where to find the problem definition, the engineer and department handling it, the results of analysis and proposals for resolution. A standard format also allows engineers to check whether all important aspects are covered.

Toyota has built a culture, moreover, in which reading this type of report is seen to be valuable and indispensable for the smooth conduct of work.

The reference here to a standard format on A3 paper means a standardized form on which questions of "why?" and "because" need to be written in designated places by the engineer.

Toyota also excels at meticulous recordkeeping. In examining Toyota documents that trace the progress of the company in detail from the prewar period on, including the period in which Toyota Motor was separate from Toyota Motor Sales, one can find a number of appended records and minutes. A close look at such documents reveals past approaches toward the business and what steps need to be taken in the future. Toyota's records are not simply records. They can be viewed almost as chronicles because they provide a summary of the past and lessons for the future.

The most chronicle-like of all company records is the official company history. In most companies, such official histories are treated like PR magazines or commemorative works rather than as historical records. Their principal purpose seems to be to introduce the marvelous company products or the company's factories or equipment. Toyota's official company histories are clearly histories of the company's management. Obviously, they also include descriptions of the company's products and factories and equipment. For the most part, however, they are devoted to improvements and innovations in management, such as the streamlining of transport operations, the evolution of quality control, supplier assessments, and systems to promote creativity, the supervision improvement system, the mechanization of administrative work, and the promotion of TQC. The emphasis, in other words, is on recording how the company has revolutionized the *way it works*.

As one of the editors of Toyota's company history explains: "Former British Prime Minister Winston Churchill is said to have kept his own published World War II memoirs at his side as he contemplated the future of Britain and governed the country. As editors of the company history, we would be overjoyed if we were able to put together a history that will be used the way Churchill used his memoirs."

Many Toyota scholars, including this author, have sought the secrets of Toyota's growth by collecting and analyzing quantities of information contained in Toyota Motor's official 20-, 30-, 40- and 50-year histories and in the 30-year history of Toyota Motor Sales. It is likely that this is not the fate the editors of those histories had in mind for their works; nonetheless, there is much we can learn from these histories and from other records.

Toyota's system of Failure Reports, developed from an observation made by Eiji Toyoda, is perhaps an example of how such records can be systematically used as one element of knowledge:

In our company we tell people to take bold action because it's all right if they fail. If they do fail, we have them write a report on the failure. We have to do this because if they just remember it without writing it down, then the lesson doesn't get transmitted to the next generation. There used to be a time when somebody new would have some triumphant approach to something and then end up repeating a mistake that had been made ten years earlier.

Eiji said this in the early 1960s and Toyota staff subsequently took up the idea and created a system of Failure Reports. (See the section on cost planning in Chapter 3.) To prevent the repetition of even small errors, everyone is expected to write up the reasons for the failure and what steps can be taken to avoid it. Even if the players change, a recurrence of the same error can be prevented by checking these records. The accumulation of these improvements forms the basis for what are known as the world's most reliable cars, (see Chapter 5). With increasing interest in recent years directed at actively evaluating the "value of failure," we see that Toyota was 40 years ahead of the trend.

PATTERNS OF THINKING

Perspectives

Toyota people have the habit of looking at things from two perspectives: "*muda* elimination" and "foresight." In this section, we will examine how these perspectives are expressed and how they are acquired.

Muda *Elimination*

Toyota management is centered on the elimination of *muda*, or waste. But Toyota's perspective on waste is substantially different from the perspective adopted by the rest of us. By now it is common knowledge that inventory is *waste*, but when we actually see inventory on the shopfloor, we tend to see either something necessary for production to run smoothly or else evidence of healthy manufacturing. Even for production line problems, as long as we build systems to fix the problems after the fact, we consider it more efficient on the whole not to stop the line. We are willing to make things we don't want because it would be a waste to stop our machines.

Toyota does not view inventory in terms of productivity but in terms of cash flow. Nearsightedness is rejected even when it comes to productivity on the line, which is measured by the long-term losses incurred when problems recur. Even in the case of equipment, Toyota sees greater evil in cash flow impediments resulting from overproduction than it does in lower operating rates. In other words, Toyota looks at things from a company management perspective rather than a shopfloor productivity perspective. Although this explanation may make intellectual sense, developing the reflexes to respond to conditions in this way is extremely difficult. At Toyota, these reflexes are nothing new.

Taiichi Ohno said, "There is a secret to the shopfloor just as there is a secret to a magic trick. Let me tell you what it is. To get rid of *muda* you have to cultivate the ability to see *muda*. And you have to think about how to get rid of the *muda* you've seen. You just repeat this—always, everywhere, tirelessly and relentlessly."

Later, Eiji Toyoda commented, "Problems are rolling all around in front of your eyes. Whether you pick them up and treat them as problems is a matter of habit. If you have the habit, then you can do whatever you have a mind to. You don't have to look for them. You just pick them up."

These were not merely words. When Kiichiro Toyoda ordered Taiichi Ohno to catch up to Western automobile companies in three years, Ohno looked for ways to do just that—every hour of every day. When Kiichiro told Eiji to deal with product problems fast, day in and day out, Eiji analyzed and took action to eliminate the causes of problems. For both men, this experience honed an ability to "see through to the essence." It cultivated in them a *muda*-elimination perspective and the instinct for finding and dealing with latent problems.

Although formal knowledge—standards, procedures and documentation—may be important to improving business outcomes, in the end, it is tacit knowledge—human instincts—that is decisive. This is why organizations need systems and mechanisms to hone the instincts of individuals. At Toyota, a paradigm of "cultivating the ability to see *muda*" permeates the entire organization.

Foresight

Toyota is said to manage from a sense of crisis. But as Hiroshi Okuda said, "A sense of crisis comes ultimately from being able to see what's up ahead." And "seeing what's up ahead" means "trying to see what's up ahead," in other words, an anticipatory perspective or foresight.

Representative examples of this anticipatory perspective are Eiji Toyoda's "decision-making that grasps major historical trends" and Shoichiro Toyoda's "21st-century shift in the nature of Toyota."

Eiji's foresight is shown to perfection in the construction of the Motomachi plant on the eve of the motorization boom of the 1960s. At a time when Japan's total monthly production of passenger vehicles was around 7,000, the Motomachi plant, completed in September 1959, had a production capacity of 5,000 passenger vehicles per month. Furthermore, the plant had the potential for expansion, up to 10,000 cars per month. The Motomachi plant by itself was large enough to have satisfied the total demand for the country, and executives from other companies who were invited to the plant's opening ceremonies could not hide their astonishment. Dealers, on the other hand, feared they would be unable to handle cars produced at the plant that would be forced on them. Yet the plant was running at capacity by the end of 1959, and the Motomachi plant became a major factor in Toyota's gaining a decisive lead over Nissan. Everyone praised Eiji's foresight.

Early in 1990, Eiji gave voice to a sense of crisis when he questioned whether it was really a good idea to keep making cars the conventional way and whether Toyota could, in fact, survive in the 21st century without major developmental changes. His observations triggered the start of Toyota's "Project G" (for "global"), which led to the development of the *Prius* hybrid car. The *Prius* was originally scheduled to come out in 1998, but Hiroshi Okuda's remark that Toyota "risked being in second place again" spurred the company to be the first in the world to bring such a vehicle to market, and the *Prius* was introduced in December 1997.

Honda people were furious because they were convinced they should have been first with a hybrid vehicle. It wasn't until 1999 that Honda introduced the world's second hybrid car, the *Insight*. Being second does not create the same stir as being first, and the media barely noticed. *Prius* was an epoch-making event for Toyota. Ranked as number two at the end of the 20th century, the company jumped into first place. And this was the result of Eiji Toyoda's and Hiroshi Okuda's "sense of crisis"—in other words, their foresight.

Shoichiro Toyoda's foresight is revealed by the shift in the nature of Toyota that he implemented during the period between the second half of the 1980s and the arrival of a new company president in 1992. Examples of his relevant activities include the flattening of the organization in 1989, the *sanzuki* campaign to address everyone the same way regardless of rank, and the reform of the seniority wage system. Other examples are the NOW (New Office Way) 21 campaign to improve office work in 1991 and the unprecedented shift to an engineering Development Center system. The move to a Development Center system, in particular, is seen to be the greatest organizational reform since the founding of the company. It was decisive in determining how Toyota would build products in the 21st century.

The Development Center system is extremely interesting and holds many lessons from a management perspective. We can summarize its implementation as a series of steps:

- In 1989, with dissatisfaction intensifying among the young engineers who constitute the backbone of engineering functions, engineering began to take a hard new look at things.
- After a year of study in which outside consultants were brought in to provide objectivity, it was observed that the functions of both chief engineers and junior engineers had been falling.
- A draft of measures specifying what to do in order to move things in the desired direction began early in 1991. A year of study resulted in a proposal that, without increasing the burden on individual engineers, said engineering jurisdiction over models should be "clustered" and that the range of models for which engineers would be responsible should be limited. For example, the plan proposed that, within a limited group of models, an engineer who may have specialized for decades in designing wiper systems, would now be responsible for designing entire upper bodies—including wiper systems. The plan combined job enrichment and job enlargement, with outstanding results.
- In 1992, came the decision-making phase of the reorganization. A "Future Program for the Twenty-first Century" (FP 21) organizing committee was established, with the senior managing director and managing director at the time (Kinbara and Wada) appointed as chairman and vice chairman, respectively. After the decision had been made to introduce a Vehicle Development Center system, Chairman Kinbara made provisional appointments of the center's director and of the department heads

within each center. They formed several individual teams that started working on the specifics.

- General Motors, in order to promote the use of common components and to reduce costs, had carried out organizational reforms that concentrated design and engineering teams into three groups: luxury cars, mid-size cars, and compact cars. Toyota studied the history of these reforms and concluded that GM had not achieved the desired results because of an inadequate understanding (before the fact) of the needed changes. Based on this judgment, Toyota began to explain to the relevant departments the aims and nature of the reorganization—several months before implementing the changes.
- Having gone through this process, Toyota waited until the time was ripe and launched the Development Center system on September 25, 1992. Four centers were established: Development Center 1 for mid-size and large front-engine, rear-wheel-drive vehicles (FR); Development Center 2 for small front-engine, front-wheel-drive vehicles (FF); Development Center 3 for commercial vehicles and RVs; and Development Center 4, responsible for developing basic common technologies, such as drive trains and electronics.

"Mainstays of Technical Department, Young Engineers Vaguely Dissatisfied," published in the May 1988 issue of *Toyota Management*, is a clear example of the sort of study group reports that were noted above in the discussion of attitudes toward work. Taking this into account, we see that the impetus for the shift to the Center system goes back to 1984 independent study group activities focusing on institutional reforms (see the section on Shoichiro Toyoda in Chapter 1).

This is a summary of what we can learn, directly and indirectly, about the transition to the Development Center system. What we would like to focus on here is the New Development System Concept that Toyota's TQC Promotion Office presented at the Toyota Group's Quality Management Conference in November of 1991, about a year before the transition to the Development Center system. The New Development System Concept is shown in Figure 2.2.

What we might call the "traditional pattern" of development involved a 48-month process in which each model went through planning, design, trials and evaluation, and preproduction steps before arriving at volume production. In the "future pattern," a separate development and planning process prepares engines and major components (α, β, γ, etc.) that have the potential for common use among models. Then, considerable time is spared planning the development of new models, while the time required for design, trials, evaluation, and preproduction is minimized. The con-

Figure 2.2 New Development System Concept

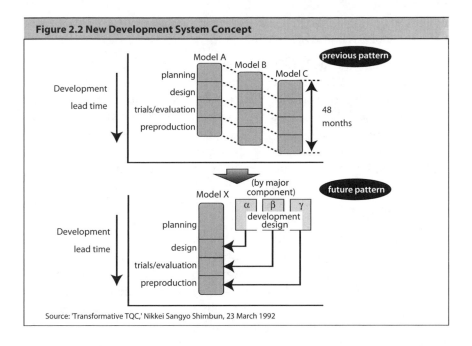

Source: 'Transformative TQC,' Nikkei Sangyo Shimbun, 23 March 1992

cept of the future pattern aims to simultaneously enhance product strength and shorten development lead time.

In the Development Centers as actually implemented, core technologies for common automobile components (α, β, γ, etc.) are assigned to particular centers, and a horizontal linking mechanism (called the "mother" system) is built into the network. This "mother system" covers Design Center 1, which handles body and chassis engineering; Design Center 4 (engine and electronics technologies); the Design Division (design policy), which doesn't belong to any of the centers; and the Engineering Management Division (development systems and development resource management). The "mother" division has authority over personnel in the other centers, and the role of other functions becomes that of spreading practices laterally.

The facts we have just examined suggest that the reasons for shifting to the center system can be summed up in terms of three farsighted aims developed with an eye to the 21st century:

1. Energize engineers who had developed tunnel vision because of extreme specialization.
2. Restore the proper role to chief engineers whose jobs had been reduced to negotiating with too many people and scraping together components to build cars.

3. Establish a new development system that enhances product strength and shortens lead-time.

Toyota made the move to a Development Center system in September 1992. In March 1993, August 1993, and January 1995, Nissan, Mazda, and Ford, respectively, reorganized their own development organizations on the Center model. Each of these companies adapted its organization to its own scale and none built a system exactly like Toyota's. Fundamentally, however, they were the same.

Toyota had begun concrete investigations of the Center idea in 1984, and it took a full eight years for the reorganization to come to fruition. The other companies spent about a year in their transitions, and it is no surprise that things did not go smoothly for all of them. Mazda, whose organization was too small for a Center system, went back to the traditional arrangement of departments by product function in June 1996. Ford launched a system with five centers, but the view within the company was that five was too many; in 1998, Ford pared back to three centers. At Toyota, the story was rather different. A system for electronics engineering development had been of some concern when the company shifted to a Center system in 1992; but after nine years, in January 2001, Toyota succeeded in launching a fifth development center.

Toyota's formal deliberations about a Center system began in 1989, at a time when the Japanese automobile industry was riding high and Toyota's own sales and business profits were soaring. Why consider a change involving fundamental revolution at such a time? As Kinbara, who was then senior managing director of engineering, said, "If we had waited until problems came to the surface, then it would have been too late. We had to solve them before that."

Switching to the Center system was a revolutionary shift in the history of the company. Reorganizing at a time when there seemed to be no problems was clearly a reform made with a view to the 21st century. The effect of the change was a reported 30 percent reduction in development costs and 10 percent savings in resources. The *RAV4*, the first vehicle born after the change to the Center system, was built with 40 percent of its components coming from other models.

But the aims of the Center system were not limited to this sort of effect on resources. They also showed up in the product itself. Toyota's introduction of the *Prius* and a series of other "un-Toyota-like" products in the late 1990s can also be traced to the Center system. Truly, these are examples of Shoichiro Toyoda's foresight.

Habits of Thinking

Systems Thinking

The just-in-time concept advocated by Kiichiro Toyoda is a good example of Toyota's systems thinking. Just-in-time does not treat each process step as independent, but, rather, sees an entire system of linked processes. Construing things in this way naturally leads to a broad view, to a view oriented toward the future, to a view that seeks optimization of the whole. Within the company, the *kanban* system was worked out as a result of such thinking. Outside the company, *keiretsu*, or group relationships, were established with suppliers.

From the end of the 1980s to the early 1990s, the *keiretsu* of Japanese industry were criticized in the United States and the West as being closed systems. Toyota faced such criticism head on, declared that it would become an "open" company, and inserted the words "open and fair" into the *Basic Principles* it promulgated in 1992. Not long afterwards, the United States worked out the concept of Supply Chain Management, its own version of *keiretsu*, and sang the praises of the economic prosperity of the 1990s. American and European countries, which are said to be strong at systems thinking, learned systems thinking from Toyota's *keiretsu*.

Meanwhile, the culture at Toyota, as we saw in Chapter 1, was one of "reaching out." An upstream process would establish a "baton passing zone" with the next process, without a rigid boundary, and work would flow from one process step to the next. This has allowed Toyota plants to achieve a high degree of line balance by absorbing unevenness between new and experienced workers and between the loads of different process steps.

Because work proceeds along overlapping processes in the development stage, upstream process work can be adjusted by anticipating the needs of the next process, and the next process can prepare itself for a changeover as it anticipates the impact a new product will have on its own operations. The chief engineer resolves differences of opinion between upstream and downstream processes. This is the system that *Product Development Performance* authors Takahiro Fujimoto and Kim Clark, along with other automobile industry researchers, later dubbed "concurrent engineering" or "synchronized simultaneous engineering."

By rejecting absolute delineations among departments, this system allowed people to share in work beyond their traditional jurisdictions and made that sharing one of the company's strengths. The idea of unclear boundaries may be incompatible with the concept of a system, but Toyota has always been ready to overturn traditional concepts when the need arises.

Getting at Essences

Toyota employees don't perform their work aimlessly. Their perspective on work drives them to ask why their own jobs and activities exist in the first place. Their goal is to get at the essence. A typical example of this is Taiichi Ohno's admonition not to confuse work and movement. (In Japanese, these two words are written with characters differing only in that the former includes a graphic element meaning "person"). Work, Ohno said, refers to production activities (such as actually processing or assembling things). Movement, on the other hand, is mere motion (such as transport or changeovers) that generates no added value. One of the focal points of the Toyota Production System is its insistence on removing motion from processes.

This culture of looking for essences also lives in administrative departments, which are prone to slip into bureaucratization. Titles of articles published in *Toyota Management* (e.g., "What is Administrative Work?" or "What is the Point of Compiling House Organs and Company Histories?" or "Why do we Manage Documents?") reveal administrative workers taking a hard look at the meaning (or essence) of their own jobs.

At its most fundamental, reengineering asks *why* we do something in the first place rather than asking *how* we can do it faster or better or at a lower cost. Reengineering, which was fashionable several years ago, is said not to be an idea imported from Japan, but it is a strategy that has been utilized at Toyota for many years. The habit that Toyota employees have of looking for the essence of everything consistently allows them to create things one or two steps ahead of other companies.

An Emphasis on Theory

Toyota management emphasizes theory. A clear example of this is Toyota's product strategy.

Toyota's leaders—whether Eiji Toyoda, Shoichiro Toyoda, Hiroshi Okuda or Fujio Cho—all advocated the theory of an annual production of 200,000 to 300,000 of their basic models, which constitutes the economic production unit, the minimum needed to reap the benefits of the mass production effect.

What we are calling a basic model here refers to cars of a single type or platform, a production line or car line.

In 1956, G. Maxcy and A. Silberston published their "automobile production cost curve," commonly known as the Maxcy-Silberston curve, shown in Figure 2.3.

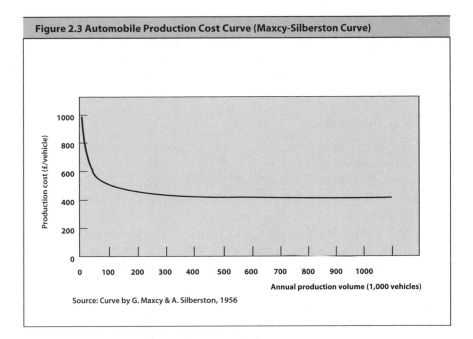

Figure 2.3 Automobile Production Cost Curve (Maxcy-Silberston Curve)

Source: Curve by G. Maxcy & A. Silberston, 1956

At Toyota, the Maxcy-Silberston curve (elsewhere a nearly forgotten theory) continues to hold sway. The fact that Toyota leaders all say the same thing means that this theory is at work throughout the company. A company so thoroughly permeated by a given theory avoids a good deal of guesswork.

In his 1997 book, *The Evolution of a Production System*,[13] Takahiro Fujimoto analyzes the Toyota experience of simultaneous model diversification and production growth during the period between the dawning of motorization in 1960 and the collapse of the economic bubble in 1992. According to Fujimoto, the number of passenger vehicles Toyota produced (*a*) and the number of basic Toyota models (estimated platforms: *b*) both increased steadily from 1960 to 1992, while the number of passenger vehicles per model ($c = a \div b$) reached a ceiling of just over 200,000 after 1970. Toyota's progress can be summarized as follows:

1960s

In order to achieve recognition in the market, Toyota concentrated its energies on a limited number of models based on the ability of Taiichi Ohno's Toyota Production System to deliver high productivity even under high-diversity, low-volume conditions.

1970s

Without increasing the number of basic models, Toyota strove (through marketing and other means) to reach a production volume of 200,000 vehicles per model. We can assume that, at least peripherally, the first and second oil crises had some influence in shaping this policy.

1980s and Afterward

Toyota gave birth to a new model each time production of a basic model reached 200,000 vehicles.

The introduction of belt-conveyor flow operations and relentless standardization allowed Henry Ford to produce two million Model T cars per year and to lower the price of automobiles through the mass production effect. GM's Alfred Sloan established a strategy of "wide variation," but at its peak around 1955, GM was producing 1.5 million Chevrolets per year. If we view these events in terms of the Maxcy-Silberston curve, however, the mass production effect is reduced once the level of 200,000 to 300,000 vehicles for each basic model is reached.

Working within the parameters of the Maxcy-Silberston curve, Toyota did not seek a mass production effect once the production of a basic model reached 200,000 to 300,000 vehicles per year. Toyota judged that it would be more profitable to increase overall sales by bringing out new models and developing and absorbing new customers. Toyota, in other words, combined the Maxcy-Silberston curve and Alfred Sloan's "wide variation" strategy to create a new strategy and introduced a new model whenever an existing model's production reached 200,000 to 300,000 vehicles per year. By combining Ford's strategy of mass production using conveyor systems and Sloan's strategy of "wide variation" to match every customer's pocketbook, the company developed a third strategy, one which "generated new models the Toyota way."

It is not only to automobiles that Toyota has applied the Maxcy-Silberston curve. Soon after the Maxcy-Silberston curve was published, Toyota began using the theory for components as well, investigating what the curve would look like for each component and how many parts would constitute an economic production unit. It then established component production plans and common component plans aimed at achieving those economic production units (see the section on Cost Planning in Chapter 3).

FORMS OF BEHAVIOR

Decision Making

Initiative from Above

Decision making in Japanese companies is generally a bottom-up affair, in which employees on the shopfloor make suggestions that are then scrutinized and decided on by senior executives. With enough effort, that approach may have been sufficient for an era of economic growth, but the 21st century has brought with it the need to shift the role of planning functions upward. The reality is, however, that many companies are still operating by "team management." This may be because they cannot find a suitable new management style, but one suspects that there is also a fundamental unwillingness to replace a style that managers find comfortable. At Toyota, from the executive staff on up, the higher your position, the more you lead in making decisions and taking action.

In addition to regular board meetings and meetings of executive vice presidents, Toyota's decision-making organization includes individual departmental conferences to promote management functions, general meetings to promote line operations, and a project organization encompassing regular committee meetings for the purpose of problem solving (see Chapter 3, Figure 3.3). A company executive presides over each of these groups and, depending on the matter under consideration, the president or executive vice presidents may take personal charge of activities. This is not management in which senior managers comment on suggestions coming from below; instead, they take personal responsibility for thinking, deciding, and acting. Strong managerial leadership is exerted in all forums for resolving issues and solving problems. Whenever a serious issue arises, executives are at the center of investigating the matter.

All companies have executive training programs, but these can be sporadic and diffuse. Toyota conducts regular and intensive training based on real management issues. Normally, an executive training session is held at the end of August each year.

In a keynote address given in 1998 at the 67th Quality Control Symposium sponsored by the Union of Japanese Scientists and Engineers, Shoichiro Toyoda presented some interesting insights on management:

I'd like to point out three fundamental principles of TQM that need to permeate an organization—that need to breathe—in order to build a culture, which dares to change or to draw out the creativity in people. The first is an emphasis on the customer, the second is constant improvement [kaizen], and the third is the participation of all employees. A lot of managers preach total participation, but don't participate themselves. Total participation is fundamental for breaking through sectionalism and the tendency to sub-optimize.

At Toyota, total participation means that executives participate by leading. Toyota executives have a good grasp of what is going on. They share an understanding even of fairly technical matters. This is true of the Maxcy-Silberston curve we introduced above and also of the following technical remarks by company leaders:

"Presses and the bodies that come out of the presses give us a prime example of the mass production effect. In the automobile industry, consequently, press plants will always have a difficult time matching the competition unless they attain a standard size." (Eiji Toyoda, senior advisor, 1996)

"We need to limit variety of unit parts we make (with dies), but it doesn't matter how many of those are in sets, or assembled components, as long as the customer demands them. Currently we are avoiding costs by using a (computerized automation) system for sets." (Akihiro Wada, then senior managing director, 1993)

The fact that Toyota executives share this sort of theoretical knowledge suggests that they are all exposed to lectures given by experts both inside and outside the company. Within Toyota, in fact, study sessions aimed at executives are held so that leaders thoroughly understand planning proposals based on new concepts. While the phrase, "study sessions aimed at executives" makes for odd grammar, it means, essentially, that providing a forum for executives to acquire specialized and theoretical knowledge is the rule whenever planning proposals are made.

Busy executives in most companies steer clear of new concepts or theoretical knowledge that would take much time to understand. Some feel that learning things from subordinates is beneath their dignity in the first place and would find the idea of "study sessions aimed at executives" unpalatable.

Debate among Toyota executives is lively, so much so that Toyota board meeting discussions sometimes resemble brawls. Through heated debate, everyone tries to figure out what is best for the company. Taizo Ishida has commented on this phenomenon:

They call Shotaro Kamiya the "god of sales" and often I would be completely dominated by him. But making and selling are jobs with their own distinct premises and legitimate characteristics. When it came to work, I would say what I wanted to say and sometimes we even got into fierce fights. But fights involve an intensely close relationship and in that sense we were a perfect combination.

Eiji Toyoda entrusted production management to Taiichi Ohno, production engineering to Masaaki Noguchi, and accounting to Masaya Hanai. There were fierce arguments among the three, and it was Eiji who settled them.

A description of Toyota board meetings appears in *The Toyota Secret* by Fujio Wakayama and Tadaaki Sugiyama (1977):[14]

Kyube Tanaka, a Mitsui Bank advisor and Toyota Motor auditor, was utterly impressed. According to Tanaka, Toyota Motor board meetings would run for a minimum of two hours without any chitchat. One would hardly have thought this was the most profitable company in Japan. Everybody focused on how costs could be lowered further and whether there was any waste (muda) in systems or materials. From around a square table, opinions flew from all directions.

Tanaka himself has made similar observations about these meetings:

Toyota board meetings are more animated than any I've ever known. . . . Toyota is one of Japan's top companies, but it feels like one that's in the prime of its youth. . . . Toyota is utterly without pride. It's always talking about trying harder and harder. Even now, when exports are booming, they're working out actions based on the importance of domestic demand. They change their minds fast, too. We meet once a month, and I feel rejuvenated every time. . . . On the other hand, it completely exhausts me.

In 1977, Toshihiko Yamashita became the new president of Matsushita Electric Industrial Company, one of Japan's premier corporations, at the age of 57. On that occasion, there was much talk of this exceptional promotion, such as company founder Konosuke Matsushita's decisiveness, and how, from a position as a director with no title, Yamashita leaped twenty-five senior board members to the presidency to deal with details. One newspaper carried the following remark by Matsushita: "Yamashita's an interesting guy. He keeps speaking up from the back of the room in executive meetings."

A young Toyota executive reacted to this story by saying that it made him think that Matsushita must be behind the times. "If the new president speaking out from the back of the room is so noteworthy," he said, "then does that mean that other executives aren't talking very much? In Toyota meetings, we've long thought it normal for people to speak up even from the back of the room."

Osamu Katayama, in *The Toyota Method* (1998),[15] cites Kingo Saito, the director of the Toyota Commemorative Museum of Industry and Technology:

> *(Hiroshi) Okuda doesn't just make decisions fast; he makes them almost instantaneously. His in box is nearly always empty. He comes to decisions while the documents are being prepared, so when he gets them, all he has to do is sign. On the other hand, fierce debates and incredibly intense communications go on during the process leading up to a decision. For us, telephone calls at home or in the car are a daily occurrence. We grab people at lunch to talk. There are no assigned seats at the tables, so we sit next to the person we need to and sometimes argue while we're eating our special of the day or our curry. This image is the true face of Toyota, although maybe it's not well understood.*

Historical events have influenced the activism and leadership of Toyota managers. When the company was founded in 1937, Kiichiro wrote the following description into the job duties he defined. (Excerpted from *Toyota Motor—A History of the First 30 Years*, 1967. Emphasis mine):

Department manager

The department manager supervises the entirety of the department and does so to the utmost of his ability and without omission. Consequently, *the department manager deals with important issues directly* and *takes personal charge* of matters not attended to by subsection managers and subsection chiefs. He strives to ensure that all work assigned to his department is performed without omission.

Subsection manager

The subsection manager is in charge of the subsection as a whole and, in addition to striving to ensure that subsection work is performed without omission, *handles important subsection matters personally*. He performs the work of subsection chiefs and subsection staff when they are not present and *accepts as his personal responsibility* any matters that may arise that do not fall within the jurisdiction of either subsection chiefs or subsection staff.

It is rare to find formal job descriptions that lay out so explicitly what leadership by example really means. The requirement that one lead by example has been formalized at Toyota ever since the company's founding, and those who have not complied have not been promoted.

Eiji Toyoda is said to have accorded special emphasis to the responsibilities of executives. When Eiji was president, he gave a speech to all his section heads in which he made the following point (excerpted from the January 1996 *Special 40th Anniversary Issue of Toyota Management*, vol. 39):

> *I want you to use your own heads. And I want you actively to train your people on how to think for themselves. You may all be in charge of departments and sections in this company, but it won't do for you merely to leave to your subordinates everything that needs thinking. I'm not saying that you should think about all problems by yourselves. But, at the least, I do want you to be trained to think about and resolve major issues on your own.*

A quote from the director named to the chairmanship of the 1977 Parts Commonization Committee (Sachio Fukushima, 1978. *Toyota Parts Commonization from the Parts Planning Stage*, supplemental edition of the journal *IE*) further illustrates this commitment to Toyota's management style:

> *The purpose of this committee is not limited to minimizing, through standardization and commonization, the number of parts existing at this particular point in time. It is to establish a system for managing the work of design so that true standardization and commonization can be accomplished on a permanent basis.*
>
> *We need to satisfy the demands of performance and durability on the basis of fundamental design principles of lightness, compactness, low cost and commonization.*
>
> *Commonization should proceed from current designs. Our basic approach should be to select from what we currently have. But we should also be willing to use new designs if they result in parts that are lighter or more compact.*

Words such as these can come only from one accustomed to developing solutions and policies.

The administrator of the Commonization Committee responded:

These [i.e., the Chairman's] words were harsh ones, but they gave us a point of reference for making decisions in situations where we were grappling with conflicting demands. This was enormously helpful in giving designers a positive understanding of parts commonization activities.

It is obvious that Toyota's monolithic management has taken shape on a foundation resting on this paradigm of leadership initiative.

Plodding Along

Toyota leadership takes a long time to make up its mind, but when it does, its ability to execute is amazing. We have already seen how it took eight years of deliberations before the Development Center system was implemented. Another typical example is the 1997 launch of the *Prius* hybrid car that had its roots in the G21 Project of 1991.

Before implementing a new project, Toyota works its way through deliberations of purpose, means, risk equivalence, and consensus building, and all this inevitably takes time. Toyota's "anticipatory perspective" brings the company to such deliberations much sooner than is ordinarily the case, and the time spent in exhaustive discussions up front allows a quick response to unforeseen issues that may emerge later. The result is that Toyota achieves its goals much faster than most companies do. In his *Inventor's Journal*, Sakichi Toyoda uses the expression "plodding" (*chin'utsu chidon*) to describe the preliminary deliberations required to anticipate what will come next. Toyota has taken Sakichi's teaching to heart.

Smaller companies often like to talk about taking "quick, small steps," or the value of "quick and dirty" actions. Such a view calls for caution, though. Even when a manager emphasizes the need for quick action as a warning against endless deliberation, skimping on preliminary investigations or skipping preparatory discussions results in treating the symptoms rather than the disease. Managers are cheered by a flurry of activity on the shopfloor because it is easy to see and it can raise equipment-operating rates. Hope eventually fades when positive business results fail to appear over the long run.

In *The Fifth Discipline: The Art and Practice of the Learning Organization*, Peter M. Senge urges us to "beware of treating the symptoms. A solution that deals with only symptoms, rather than root causes, is often profitable only for a short period of time. "Over the long run," he warns, "the same problem crops up again and there will be more calls to treat the symptoms. At the same time, there is the danger that one's ability to eliminate the root causes of problems will deteriorate. . . ."

"Plodding" has the same meaning as "careful and slow," the opposite of "quick and dirty." Cultivating institutional foresight means that "plodding" actually gets you to deliberations more quickly, and preparatory discussions mean that the overall time is shorter. The result is a "careful and quick" approach that speeds the attainment of goals.

"Quick and dirty" and "quick, small steps" never result in "careful and fast."

Follow-up, Yokoten

Follow-up and *yokoten* (lateral propagation) are distinctive features of Toyota's organizational culture.

To meet someone from Toyota is to be astonished by his habit of following up. You may expect that he has been kind enough to forget about some troublesome matter that once came up, but he is sure to ask about it. When you tell him that, for some reason or other, you want to pretend that it never happened, he will have the good grace to drop the subject. We are not talking about absolute rules of behavior. As long as the reason is clear, then the Toyota employee has the flexibility not to make an issue of your having stopped in midstream. The purpose is to monitor what is happening and to reject vagueness. The idea that Toyota is "monitoring" must make a lot of industrial ears burn.

Activities that followed after Toyota won the TQC and Deming Prize introduced in the 1960s are typical examples of Toyota follow-up. Toyota not only spread improved practices to its suppliers and its dealerships, it conducted rigorous training every few years for staff and for department and section heads, a practice that continues to this day (see Chapter 3). This example takes follow-up beyond the level of monitoring and raises it to the level of active building on what has been learned.

Koichiro Tokuoka, a vice president of Fleishman-Hillard Japan who used to work at Nissan Motor, had this to say (Nikkei Information Strategy, June 2001: Lectures on Nurturing Change Leaders): "The difference between Toyota, which built solid production and sales systems, and Nissan, which failed to do so and never manifested its strengths, resides in whether or not the company put the principle of *hansei*, or reflection, into practice. [This is why] Nissan never developed the organizational ability to create change leaders."

When Tokuoka talks about reflection, he is not referring simply to retrospection. He means follow-up.

Another word frequently heard at Toyota is *yokoten* (lateral propagation). Around 1985, an executive at Daihatsu grumbled:

At Toyota, when a problem shows up in one type of engine, they consider every way to deal with it and then make improvements (follow-up). Up to that point, Daihatsu does the same thing. At Toyota, though, the rule is that they take the improvement and try it out with other engine types to see whether it is better or worse than the current practice. If it's not worse, then they change the design and apply the improvement to all engine types (yokoten). Toyota points to three benefits of this approach: (1) It enhances their image or appeal vis-à-vis the customer; (2) they can lower costs by producing common parts in volume; and (3) it makes things easier for service plants. We think the idea would be good for Daihatsu, too, but we can't manage to keep up.

To find the origins of Toyota's *yokoten* culture, we have to go back to the 1960s, when Eiji Toyoda was introducing TQC into the company. Toyota was expanding rapidly in the midst of the motorization movement at the time, and the company was awash in problems concerning quality, manpower, and internal communications. Eiji brought in TQC to resolve these problems. In the course of TQC activities, Eiji would constantly call for laterally linked improvements. Then executive vice president of the company, Eiji made this appeal in June of 1963 in an address to all division and section heads at a ceremony announcing salary raises and new appointments:

There weren't too many managers when the company was small. We'd see one another from time to time and we could talk to each other. I think contacts among us were very smooth and close. The size of the staff has ballooned recently, though, and I think our contacts with each other have worsened considerably. This is why I want those of you in managerial positions to work hard at staying in touch with people at your same level and at exchanging accurate information. Now that we have multiple production plants, there are several groups of people scattered throughout the company who do the same kind of work that you do. When each plant learns something—this includes, for example, knowledge about accidents and knowledge about performance—I'd like you to transmit this knowledge to the other plants immediately. Our main plant has done a terrific job of increasing efficiency while the Motomachi Plant, unaware of this, has looked at other companies' plants and come away impressed. We don't make an issue of this. (January 1996. Toyota Management, Special 40th Anniversary Issue, vol. 39).

Just as Eiji's admonition to record failures prompted the staff to set up a system of "failure reports," it is not difficult to imagine that his call for improvements in lateral solidarity was transmitted to staff departments, who then devised *yokoten* mechanisms.

Dynamism

Experimentation

The Tokai Research and Consulting Company, a private economic think tank, issued a pamphlet entitled, "Companies that Win and Companies that Lose." The excerpt reproduced here is particularly relevant:

Here are the characteristics of winners: They are driven by the urge to make interesting plans. They determine what tactics to adopt by looking at projected business results a few months out. They find original and ingenious ways to ensure that management policies permeate the organization. Losers are different: They only look at the current month's figures and criticize people because of them. People who don't know the shopfloor determine new plans on the basis of past actions. Their instructions consist entirely of invoking manuals, rules and conformity. They delude themselves into thinking that management policies can permeate an organization by being distributed in printed form. They only write daily business logs when it is convenient. In other words, the difference between winners and losers boils down to the people who are doing the managing.

"Don't be afraid to fail," is a phrase heard in almost all companies. But companies in which that attitude is truly embedded in the culture are few and far between. The reason is simple. Most companies have loser-type managers, as described above, whose daily behavior contradicts the meaning of "don't be afraid to fail."

Kaneyoshi Kusunoki, former executive vice president of Toyota Motor, notes: "Toyota's top managers berate people who don't try to come up with new ideas or who don't take up new challenges, but not people who try something and fail. The role of senior managers is said—and is perceived—to be to help subordinates with new ideas or challenges and not to criticize them. That's what makes trial and error possible."

According to Eiji Toyoda, "It's fine if you fail in this company. Just don't shy away from taking action."

Iwao Isomura, vice chairman of Toyota Motor, has gone so far as to declare that "success is the mother of failure and failure is the father of success."

Toyota suffered for a long time from its image as conservative or second-rate when it came to doing business. In terms of technology, though, Toyota has always been progressive. The launch of the *Prius* finally brought a more accurate image of the company to the world's attention.

Honda and Toyota share very little in the way of common culture, but they are alike in their drive to confront challenges without fear of failure. One might even say that Honda surpasses Toyota in this respect. Where Toyota uses a negative expression (Don't be afraid to fail), Honda puts it in the affirmative: "Fail!" Senior workers and bosses at Honda tell new employees over and over again to fail. An affirmative phrase has a much greater impact on people than a negative one. Honda even awards an annual Failure Prize of one million yen to the employee who has achieved the biggest, i.e., most significant, failure. Failure will not be feared in such an environment. Indeed, at Honda, there have been numerous employees who have taken on what can only be considered crazy challenges. Honda was the last entrant to the automobile business, but this aspect of its culture is said to have enabled it to achieve a rate of operating profits in excess of Toyota's and allow it to tread an independent path without getting caught up in the global rat race.

It is easy to talk about not fearing failure or confronting challenges, but good results can hardly be expected if efforts are haphazard. Independent hypotheses and an experimental approach to verification are indispensable. This experimental spirit is very much encouraged at both Toyota and Honda. It is important that managers, senior employees, and bosses urge their subordinates to experiment once a hypothesis has been established.

Risk Taking

The willingness to take risks has features in common with a spirit of experimentation, but there are slight differences. By risk taking, we mean the willingness to leap into the unknown once you have thought a problem through and still don't know what the correct answer is. You select one alternative from among those that are possible, and then try it.

This willingness to take risks is exactly what Sakichi Toyoda was referring to when he talked about research and creativity and getting a jump on the times. "Open the windows," he said. "It's a big world out there."

From his engineer's perspective, Kiichiro Toyoda also wrote about the willingness to take risks: "Japan has a lot of engineers who work at desks. When it comes to implementation, though, they lose confidence and haven't got the courage of their convictions when other people criticize them. Engineers like that can't build cars. Success in this industry demands engineers who have the courage and the decisiveness to implement ideas."

In an interview with Eiji Toyoda, which appears in the 2001 book *Origins of the Toyota System*[16] by Takahiro Fujimoto and Koichi Shimokawa, we see further evidence of this mindset:

Question: You've been directly managing Toyota since it was formed. What's the most difficult decision you've had to make?

Mr. Toyoda: No decision was particularly difficult. Or maybe they were all difficult [laughter].

Question: I once heard from an Honorary Chairman that the decision to build the Takaoka Plant was quite a difficult one. Production of the *Publica* had just begun and it was only selling about 7,000 vehicles per month at the time. The entirely new Corolla was still in the design stage and you built the new plant to make 30,000 Corollas. It was said that was an amazing leap.

Mr. Toyoda: It was certainly a big decision. I can look relaxed about it because things turned out well, but if they hadn't, then we would have gone under.

Question: That turned out to be a good decision. And that's what opened the gap with Nissan. . . .

Mr. Toyoda: It was a tremendous risk.

Question: For Motomachi it was a big decision and then for Takaoka it was a big success.

Mr. Toyoda: It was a risk. I must have thought about it long and hard when I made the decision, but when it went well, I forgot all that [laughter]. That's why I say there were no difficult decisions. If I had messed up, then I'd remember.

Eiji Toyoda's modest tone somewhat masks his true meaning: When faced with an issue, you think about it as hard as you can and if things work out, then you forget about it. What is clear, however, is that he was naturally willing to take risks.

A willingness to take risks is not the same as recklessness. Ultimately, it is a choice of one of several carefully considered alternatives that is illuminated by one's own personal convictions. Basically, none of the alternatives is going to result in a big mistake because all of them have been thought through.

Eiji often spoke about a mathematics teacher he'd had in high school who told him, "When you think you're right, when you think your answer's good, then following through can make you lord of heaven and earth. Keep forging ahead. Stay the course. Keep going."

This mindset, which naturally expresses itself as a willingness to take risks, also protects against the failure that comes of being a prisoner of success.

Endnotes

1. Shigeo Shingo was a pioneer who analyzed the Toyota Production System from the standpoint of industrial engineering and popularized it through numerous books, including, *A Study of the Toyota Production System from an Industrial Engineering Viewpoint* (English translation published by Productivity Press, 1989).
2. *yuiga dokuson.*
3. *Toyota-shiki hitozukuri monozukuri.*
4. *jishu kenkyukai.*
5. *Toyota Jidosha Nijunen-shi.*
6. *Atarashii Kigyo Sosiki no Sozo.*
7. *Toyota no Soshiki Kaikaku o Kangaeru.*
8. *Toyota Gijutsu.*
9. *Toyota Shisutemu no Romu Kanri.*
10. *Toyota-shiki Hitozukuri Monozukuri.*
11. *Nihon kigyo ga motsu 'C-kyu-sei' no maryoku, Nikkei Bijinesu.*
12. Sobek, II, D.K., Liker, J.K., and Ward, A.C., "Another Look at Toyota's Integrated Product Development," *Harvard Business Review*, Vol. 76, No. 4, July-August, 1998; pp. 36–49. *Toyota Seihin Kaihatsu o Sasaeru Soshiki Noryoku. Daiyamondo Habado Bijinesu.*
13. *Seisan Shisutemu no Shinkaron.*
14. *Toyota no Himitsu.*
15. *Toyota no Hoshiki.*
16. *Toyota Shisutemu no Genten.*

3

Toyota's System of Management Functions

TQC AT TOYOTA

The systematic establishment and consolidation of Toyota's management function system began with the introduction of Total Quality Control (TQC) in 1961. TQC activities at Toyota went beyond quality to target all important management functions, including cost, personnel, administrative work, and information. As a result, TQC at Toyota involved activities to consolidate and facilitate all management functions at the company. Toyota's distinctive management system came into being while the company was competing for the Deming Application Prize, which it won in 1965. The management-system setup at this time form the foundation of the current Toyota system. To discuss and learn from Toyota's management system requires that we unravel the history of TQC at Toyota. It is no exaggeration to say that the secret of Toyota management lies in Toyota's TQC. Reading the official thirty-, forty- and sixty-year Toyota Motor's company histories makes this clear.

Masao Nemoto, a former senior managing director of Toyota Motor who played an important role during the 1960s when TQC was introduced and developed within the company, claims that Toyota methods consisted of seven elements: "(1) TQC, (2) concurrent engineering (CE), (3) the Toyota Production System (TPS), (4) human resource development, (5) labor-management trust, (6) long-term relationships with parts manufacturers, and (7) long-term relationships with dealerships." (Fujimoto, Takahiro and Koichi Shimokawa. 2001. *Origins of the Toyota System*).[1] Figure 3.1 takes this fundamental assertion and gives it a structure.

A management or business system is composed of two subsystems: a management function system, which runs the organization, and a production function system, which generates products. At Toyota, (1) TQC was brought in and positioned to encompass both the management function system and the production function system.

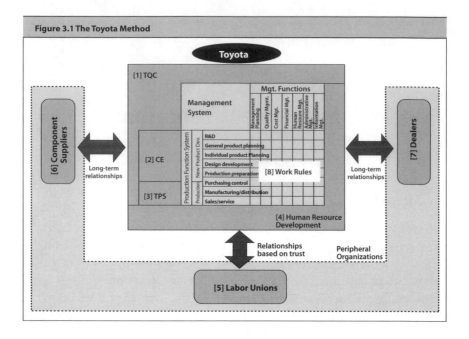

Figure 3.1 The Toyota Method

The production function system can be further divided into a new product development process for bringing new products to the marketplace and a more narrowly defined production process, which steadily manufactures, ships, sells, and services products. At Toyota, the former is carried out by (2) concurrent engineering (CE), and the latter is the focus of the (3) Toyota Production System (TPS).

Since TQC deals with managing the quality of people, (4) human resource development can be situated in the same region as (1) TQC. (5) Labor unions, (6) parts manufacturers, (7) dealerships, and other organizations are located in appropriate positions around the periphery of Toyota.

Nemoto does not touch on the subject, but one element of the Toyota management system that we cannot ignore comprises the administrative regulations (rules, prescriptions, and guidelines) discussed in Chapter 1. Administrative regulations work as a management system connecting the management function system with the production function system, so I have inserted (8) work rules at the intersection of the matrix formed by these two elements. Toyota's administrative regulations document and systematically formalize the tacit knowledge generated by TQC, CE, TPS, and human resource development activities. In doing so, they form a solid framework for the Toyota management system as a whole.

We discuss the Toyota management function system in Chapter 3 and the production function system in Chapter 4.

Please note that, in what follows, we have quoted liberally from the Toyota Motor Corporation's twenty-, thirty-, forty- and fifty-year histories and have not indicated the precise sources of citations from those works. Sources for other citations have been noted.

What Is TQC?

We should begin by defining the essence of TQC. The Deming Prize guidelines issued by the Union of Japanese Scientists and Engineers (JUSE) give the following ten evaluation categories:

1. Top management leadership, vision, and strategy
2. TQM management system (daily management, policy deployment, etc.)
3. Quality assurance system
4. Management systems by management element (cost, delivery, safety, etc.)
5. Human resource development
6. Information use
7. TQM philosophy, values
8. Scientific methods
9. Organizational strength (core technologies, speed, vitality)
10. Contribution to the achievement of company goals
    a. Continuous attainment of company goals
    b. Good relationships with customers, society, business connections, and stockholders, etc.
    c. Results and future plans

Because of its name, TQC tends to be construed either as a quality system that targets only the quality function of management or else as a management system with a quality bias. As the Deming Prize evaluation categories show, however, TQC encompasses nearly all management functions, from the attitudes of top management and management systems to costs, human resources, and information. These categories may not have been defined this way when Toyota introduced TQC and when it applied for and won the Deming Prize in the 1960s, but, considering the subsequent course of events, we think it fair to say that Toyota embraced TQC from a similar perspective.

How Toyota Came to Introduce TQC

In remarks he made on the occasion of a Deming Prize on-site assessment on September 20, 1965, Eiji Toyoda explained what led Toyota to introduce TQC into the company:

We launched sales of the Crown, Japan's first real passenger car, at the beginning of 1955 and were fortunate that the market's reaction was very positive. The company grew rapidly after that. Various problems showed up, too. Personnel doubled and production increased nearly sevenfold, but quality improvements didn't keep pace with efficiency gains. With the increase in new employees, inadequate education, inexperienced and insufficiently skilled managers and poor lateral communications all became conspicuous problems. At the same time, competition on the basis of quality was intensifying among companies in the same line of business. For our part, we realized, first, that top management had to make quality targets clearer and to ensure that all employees understood them. Next, we had to build systems to enhance functional cooperation among the various departments. On the basis of these two realizations, we decided to expand our QC activities to the entire company.

Toyota's rationale for introducing TQC involved facing up to how badly the company was doing (i.e., to its organizational and personnel weaknesses) and then stating its problems honestly. This was the first factor in the company's success with TQC, and it allowed Toyota to avoid Packard's Law, which asserts that no company can succeed when sales growth consistently outpaces personnel growth.

Introducing TQC and Winning the Deming Prize

The following have been cited as goals or were clearly key issues in Toyota's introduction and promotion of TQC:

Purposes of Promoting TQC
1. To withstand trade liberalization and other challenging conditions by developing a world-class Toyota, both in name and substance
2. Conduct an epoch-making reform of management
3. Enable the development and production of high-quality, low-priced products

Critical Promotion Issues
1. Raise awareness of quality and cost through total employee participation and establish a management system by function
2. Conduct new product planning appropriate to demand trends and smooth new product startups
3. Strengthen systems of cooperation with Toyota Motor Sales and major vendors

Basic Principles for Activities

1. Thoroughly apply the principle of Quality First
2. Thoroughly apply the principles of building quality into the process and of assuring subsequent processes
3. Raise problem awareness and promote continual *kaizen*
4. Be relentless in seeking problem causes and in preventing recurrences
5. Promote management based on facts and data
6. Clarify job responsibilities, improve and standardize the conduct of work
7. Promote management by total employee participation (policy deployment, QC circles)

Figure 3.2 shows the history from the time Toyota introduced TQC to its winning of the Deming Prize.

Stage One (Introduction, 1961–1962)

The Quality Control Committee and its administrative office, the Quality Control Department, played central roles in the first stage of the introduction of TQC, carrying out an educational campaign to raise cost and quality awareness and spreading QC training. At the same time, a move was launched to reduce defects by half.

As these efforts deepened awareness of the benefits and effects of QC, the traditional and long-rooted manufacturing shopfloor view that qual-

Figure 3.2 Before Winning the Deming Application Prize

Stage	Stage 1 (Introduction)		Stage 2 (promotion)		Stage 3 (stabilization)
Year	1961	1962	1963	1964	1965
General Audits		Round 1 July	Round 2 Jan.	Round 3 Oct. / Round 4 Feb.	Round 5 June / Round 6 March
Emphasis/ Policy		1. Introduce TQC throughout the company. Attain international quality and cost standards. 2. Conduct campaign to cut defects in half.	1. Promote TQC. Prepare system for winning the Deming Prize. 2. Prepare system for management by function.	1. Clarify management philosophy for each function and complete management system. 2. Raise level of statistical techniques.	1. Establish management system with particular emphasis on quality assurance and cost management. 2. Thoroughly roll out, apply and manage company-wide policies in every department.
Main Promotion Theme		Reduction by half of defects involving claims, mat'l shortages and rework, etc.	Smooth RT40 (Corolla) launch		Preparation and completion of management system, promotion of overall system, including Toyota Motor Sales and suppliers
Dept.		Quality Control Dept.	Planning Office-->Planning Research Office		QC Promotion Office

ity will improve if you tighten inspections began gradually to shift in the direction of what in QC is called "building quality into the process." These efforts bore fruit and, for customer complaints, materials and processing defects and rework, Toyota succeeded in reaching its initial goal of cutting defects in half.

Over the course of three days, from July 19 through July 21, 1962, Toyota conducted its first company-wide audit. This audit revealed several problems, including insufficient understanding of the true purpose of company policies and resulting inconsistencies among the divisional policies designed to implement them.

Almost immediately, management policies that had already been announced were codified, and plans were made to ensure that every employee was thoroughly cognizant of them. In early 1963, a company policy composed of three parts—a basic policy, a long-range policy, and an annual policy—were given to department and deputy department heads and section chiefs. These specified guidelines for how Toyota should proceed and what goals it should achieve; it also clarified various measures for the purpose of meeting those goals. At the same time, the gist of company policy was communicated and distributed to managers of group-leader class and above, so that everyone might become thoroughly familiar with it. The results of the audit were connected to the establishment of Toyota's Policy Deployment System, which we will discuss later.

Settling on a company policy—consisting of a basic policy, a long-range policy and an annual policy—and then making sure that all managers are thoroughly familiar with it is fundamental to managing a company, but a surprising number of companies fail to implement such policies systematically. Studying Toyota's policy deployment would benefit any firm in which basic policies, long-range policies, and annual policies are unconnected with one another, in which the president's annual policy speech does not match previous company policies, whose policies for one year are developed without taking stock of the previous year's policies, or in which policies written by each division are simply stapled together.

Stage Two (Promotion, 1963–1964)

Toyota's first company-wide TQC audit had highlighted another problem: that of insufficient coordination among different departments of the company. In the second, promotion, stage, the company took a fresh look at the work of each department in terms of its functions and consolidated and secured a new system of management by function. A system map of management by function was drawn up (see Figure 1.6), and work flow and relational rules both within functions and among functions were examined and consolidated. At the departmental and section levels, documents and other materials were prepared in order to distribute and coordinate work among various sectors according to the work flow shown on the system map and to clarify management issues and control points for managers.

In March 1963, the old assignment of staff members to divisions was abolished in favor of a system in which multiple staff members were given cross-functional responsibilities (see discussion below). This was done because, at the time of the second company-wide audit, some staff members had become profit representatives for their functions and this was understood to be one element that damaged divisional cooperation. At first, this new system was taken to refer to staff meetings by function; it later evolved into function councils.

Stage Three (Stabilization, 1964–1965)

Fukio Nakagawa, Toyota's president and CEO, asserted that the company was to win the Deming Prize within one year. This was the starting point for Stage 3 activities. Relations among the various functions were consolidated along the two themes of quality and cost control. On the quality control side, painstaking work was invested into achieving the goals of building quality into each process and of assuring quality at the next process. This effort was underscored by the substitution of the term "quality assurance" for "quality control." To make sure this philosophy penetrated the organization, Toyota standardized the items that needed to be implemented at each post and used those standards to establish a basis of quality assurance activities throughout the company.

On the cost-control side, Toyota focused on three areas: cost planning, cost maintenance, and cost improvement. At the same time, it renewed links with quality-assurance activities and took a new look at the details of cost-control activities at each step of the process, from product planning to sales. The results of this were summarized in formal Quality Control Rules.

In this way, a system of management by function was finally established by the systematic interweaving of quality assurance and cost control.

Staff members involved with individual functions and administrative offices were to play central roles in promoting quality assurance, cost control, human resource management, administrative management, and other functions that cut across the entire company. The development of each sector connected to these functions, furthermore, was to be coordinated and promoted through company-wide audits and other means.

Toyota also put together staff training programs, QC teams, QC circles, and other promotion units at each level, and vigorously and relentlessly carried out what was literally QC by total participation.

In May 1965, Toyota formally announced its candidacy for the Deming Application Prize to be awarded that same year. It submitted a quality control status report to the Deming Prize committee on June 20 and underwent a documentary review. A total of 74 outside evaluators subsequently conducted thorough on-site inspections, beginning with the Tokyo branch office on August 25, the Motomachi plant on August 30-31, and company headquarters on September 20-21. As a result of these inspections, the Deming Prize committee decided at its October 11 meeting to award the 1965 Deming Application Prize to Toyota.

The competion for the Deming Prize was a major operation for everyone in the company. One observer recalled that "employees couldn't help but be motivated to try their hardest when they saw that staff members were cutting down on their own sleep time in order to compete for the prize"—evidence that the example of staff leadership energized and invigorated everyone to reach the goal.

Effects of Introducing TQC and Winning the Deming Prize

Then Managing Director Shoichiro Toyoda, who, as vice director of Toyota's QC Promotion Office personally led the TQC effort. He summarized the effects of introducing TQC across the entire company in a speech delivered on July 30, 1966, to a special executive course at the 10th Quality Control Seminar:

Effect Number 1

Product quality improved. The costs of material and processing defects and per-vehicle claims declined, and in March 1963, based on estimates proceeding from this, we confidently led other companies in extending our warranty period.

Effect Number 2

Our share of the domestic passenger car market grew and exports increased overall. This was a result of applying TQC thinking and methods to the goals of new product planning and to new product startups. In addition, the system of cooperation among related sectors advanced, and the time it took to achieve target production figures improved markedly. This allowed us to satisfy the demands of the marketplace.

Effect Number 3

Costs decreased as we had planned. Quality awareness and cost consciousness penetrated to every corner of the company and, as a result, the promotion of TQC along the themes of quality and cost brought about extremely favorable results. The company's balance sheet improved, and we were able to render significant service to consumers by lowering the prices.

Other Effects

We saw considerable improvement in Toyota's "constitution," or basic health. Managers learned management methods and human relations improved markedly throughout the company. A system took shape in which everybody, from vendors to vehicle sales, cooperated to achieve common goals. Responsibilities and authority became clearer and forums were created in which frank discussions could take place. Quality Assurance Rules and Cost Control Rules were standardized as a result, and management stabilized.

The following comment about the introduction of TQC, made by an employee of the company at the time, shows how TQC was perceived by the rank and file:

At meetings in which team members reported on the results of QC activities, the consultant would let fly with questions about why a particular problem had been chosen or what the point was. Each time he did that—even when somebody else was doing the presentation—I felt that I was gradually learning what management was all about and that I was growing day by day. I'm sure, when they heard that the Deming Application Prize winner had been chosen, that everybody in the company was secretly thinking that now we'd start doing real QC. It's true that preparing to win the Deming Prize involved a lot of formal stuff and that we spent a lot of energy doing it. Now I'm ready to start working on a new QC, though. In addition to taking another look at the business, I'm looking forward to a second campaign to develop a kind of QC that's down-to-earth, that involves everybody and that's integrated with our jobs.

Activities After Winning the Deming Prize

The Toyota we know today would not exist if TQC had been a one-time affair. Introducing TQC and winning the Deming Prize was only a starting point. Toyota has been diligently continuing and expanding TQC-related activities right up to the present. Nissan Motor won the Deming Prize in 1960, five years before Toyota did, but a backlash after winning turned the Deming Prize into a "graveyard for QC." Toyota, on the other hand, made the Deming Prize into a "cradle for QC," and has sustained its QC efforts to the present day. Below, we look back at Toyota's TQC activities from the award of the Deming Prize to the present.

Follow-up Activities After Winning the Prize

At the 10th Quality Control Seminar previously mentioned, Shoichiro Toyoda described what happened after Toyota won the Deming Prize:

> From the moment we put ourselves forward as candidates for the Deming Prize, my greatest concern was how we would sustain QC after the evaluation process was over. The objectives provided by the Deming Prize allowed us to make rapid progress in QC, but I was looking around to see what form the backlash would take. Things are different now. Everybody in the company realizes that QC is a useful and convenient tool and everyone is eager and happy to continue doing QC.

Toyota paid close attention to the route by which QC ended up being a QC graveyard at Nissan and took great care not to fall into the same trap. When it was awarded the Deming Prize, it took the opportunity not only to review TQC progress to date but also to lay out policies for promoting TQC in the future:

1. We will promote a comprehensive QC, centered on Toyota but also encompassing our partner companies such as vendors and dealerships.
2. We will not be bound by form, but will establish simple and effective management systems. We will turn the management cycle rapidly, with rigorous emphasis on check and action steps.[2]
3. We will conduct full and comprehensive planning and, in harmony with the various management systems and with a long-term perspective, we will implement swift and correct decisions.

In December 1965, with the memory of having won the Deming Prize still very much alive, Toyota conducted its seventh company-wide audit, checking, among other things, which company policies of the year had been achieved and what action plans had been set up in response to the recommendations of the Deming Prize committee. The results of this audit were reflected in a 1966 company policy statement and slogans ("Assure Quality in All of Toyota," "Eliminate Wasted Materials and Time"). At the same time, the company began enhancing its cooperation with vendors on QC matters.

"Assure Quality in All of Toyota" Activities (1965–)

When Toyota won the Deming Prize, the prize committee indicated that one pending issue was the improvement of relationships with vendors. Toyota had known that this was one of its weak points and so, beginning in 1966, the company began extending TQC into its supply base. It encouraged vendors to educate themselves about TQC and to promote TQC independently. Toyota offered assistance from the sidelines and kept an eye on outcomes in terms of quality and costs.

Toyota also introduced an All Toyota Quality Control Conference as part of the Seventh Annual Quality Month in November of that same year. The first conference was held on November 25 at the Toyota Education Center and Toyota Hall. On that day, 250 people from seventy vendors, fifteen people from Toyota Motor Sales and the dealerships, and 250 people from Toyota Motor Corporation enthusiastically participated in presentation sessions and panel discussions.

Efforts such as these bore fruit. Kanto Jidosha Kogyo applied for the 1966 Deming Application Prize and carried away the award. In 1967, Kojima Press Industry Co., Ltd., won the Deming Application Prize in the small- and medium-sized enterprise category.

Toyota, in other words, did not relax after winning the Deming Prize. Both internally and outside the company, it continued to expand and apply TQC.

Second Deming Prize Evaluation (1970)

The motorization of Japan proceeded at a swift pace in the 1960s, and in the space of a few short years, Toyota grew rapidly in the number of vehicles produced, number of employees, and production equipment. The philosophy and methods of TQC aided greatly in this brisk expansion, but the number of people unfamiliar with TQC thinking grew as well. For this reason, Toyota decided to disseminate TQC philosophy and methods. The company adopted a policy of TQC promotion aimed at a second Deming Prize evaluation in 1970.

At about this time, the Union of Japanese Scientists and Engineers (JUSE) decided to award a Japan Quality Control Prize to companies that a second Deming Prize assessment identified as having achieved a high level of excellence. A group from the Deming Prize committee visited Toyota in September of 1970 and conducted a vigorous assessment over two days. As a result, Toyota achieved recognition for outstanding results in the maintenance and improvement of quality through company-wide activities, and JUSE decided to award the company the first Japan Quality Control Prize.

Establishment of the Toyota Quality Control Prize and Activities to Expand Practices to Suppliers (1969–)

Toyota had promoted TQC activities among its suppliers ever since winning the Deming Prize. To further increase the penetration of TQC practices among its vendors, the company instituted a Toyota Quality Control Prize in 1969 with a view to motivating suppliers by providing them with an attainable goal.

Shoichi Saito headed the evaluation committee that carried out the first prize assessment at Kojima Press Industry Co. in June 1970. Subsequent assessments were conducted at companies such as Futaba Industries, MTP Chemical, and Taiheiyo Kogyo, all of which were awarded the Excellence Prize that same year.

In the face of imminent capital liberalization, suppliers were highly motivated to rationalize their businesses. Recall problems also abounded, and quality-assurance concerns were growing more serious. This system proved to be a tremendous stimulus for many companies.

Deepening TQC with Programs to Enhance Management Skills (1979–1980)

In early 1978, Toyota began reviewing the way it was managing its board meetings and strengthening the management of function-specific councils for quality, cost and engineering, etc. One of the high-level issues to be dealt with was a perceived need to improve management skills. Company leaders felt that improvements in the efficiency of managerial and indirect functions were lagging behind rationalization of the manufacturing shopfloor and that there were more and more managers who had not experienced the assessments connected with the Deming Prize or the Japan Quality Control Prize. A pledge to "improve managerial capabilities and polish proprietary technologies" was added to the company policy for 1979, and a two-year management skills improvement program was developed over the course of two years.

The following year, Toyota's 1980 policy statement urged each division to make its work more efficient by establishing an entirely new system for conducting business. The engineering division had, in the past, been exempt from this sort of activity and some were of the opinion that managers and supervisory personnel in the professions should not have to participate. President and CEO Eiji Toyoda would have none of that, however, declaring that "the people who need management skills most are precisely those who have to operate by persuading people who are not their subordinates." He made this a truly company-wide activity; all staff members, from executive vice president Shoichiro Toyoda on down, were to spend two years hearing improvement examples from all the department and deputy department managers and grasping the essence of their problems.

Relentless TQC Education After the Merger of the Toyota Motor Company (TMC) and Toyota Motor Sales (TMS) (1983)

The new Toyota Motor Corporation was born from the merger of the Toyota Motor Company and Toyota Motor Sales in 1982, with Shoichiro Toyoda assuming the post of president and CEO of the new company. In February of the following year, Shoichiro launched a TQC Promotion Office to press ahead with the All Toyota program in the new company, to improve the health of the Toyota group, and to promote the development of new people internally through TQC.

In June, the company conducted general QC training for all executives below the chairman. After a lecture by University of Tokyo Professor Emeritus Tetsuichi Asaka, group discussions were held on management problems facing the company. More than 40 executives stayed and took meals together by Lake Hamana for three days, taking part in numerous successful discussions.

Penetration of TQC into Sales (1981–)

Nineteen eighty-one saw the introduction of QC activities for sales outlets. A top management study session was held in 1982 to identify knowledge and practices needed to strengthen management. In and after August of the same year, QC Circle activity presentation sessions were held to provide a forum for the exchange of information about the status of activities and of sample results, as well as for dealers to learn from one another. A Toyota Dealers' QC Promotion Prize was established in 1983 to provide recognition to model dealerships and to raise the level of sales outlets generally.

Expansion of TQM into Toyota Central R&D Labs (1995)

Toyota's Central Research and Development Labs had always been sacred territory, but in 1995 the company introduced TQM even there. (JUSE changed the TQC designation to TQM [Total Quality Management] in 1995.) The aim was to revolutionize management to raise the value of the labs in an increasingly perilous economic environment. Policy deployment had more or less taken root after a trial period of a year and then three years of expansion into the entire organization, and a number of new systems for the laboratories were developed and implemented in that period. Policy deployment proved as effective for the labs as it had for other departments, and the company reported that the TQM philosophy and methods provided a number of clues for streamlining research. (*Hinshitsu* [Quality], the journal of the Japan Quality Control Society, October 2000 and January 2001).

THE BUSINESS PLANNING SYSTEM

Decision-making Bodies

The managerial decision-making bodies at Toyota today are shown in Figure 3.3.

The basic form of these Toyota decision-making bodies was established in 1962 during the introduction of TQC and has not changed in the forty-odd years since that time.

The executive vice presidents' council is composed of managers at the rank of executive vice president or higher. The council, which is Toyota's highest practical decision-making body, deliberates on major policy questions concerning the business environment or internal conditions, and on business strategy, often involving matters requiring referral to the board of directors.

The management council was formerly positioned to bring the function councils and general councils under unified control; even now, it oversees function councils, general councils, and committees. Its role, at least nominally, is to deliberate on major matters of business execution. In fact, however, nearly all matters are considered and decided in function councils, general councils, and committees in which key executives serve as chairmen. The management council, in actuality, constitutes a forum for deliberating and deciding on overall executive strategies relating to these other bodies.

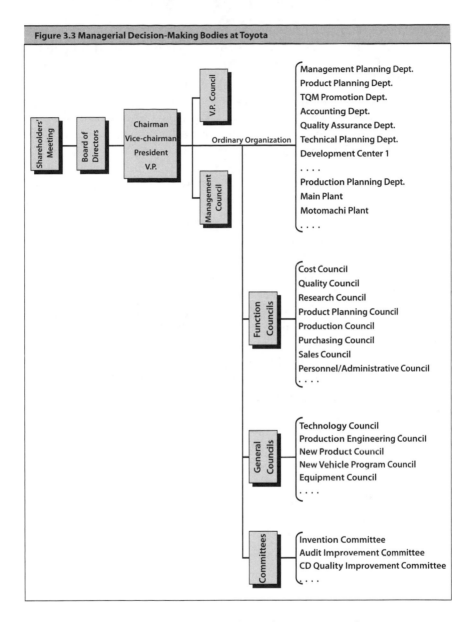

Figure 3.3 Managerial Decision-Making Bodies at Toyota

Shareholders' Meeting — Board of Directors — Chairman / Vice-chairman / President / V.P.

V.P. Council

Management Council

Ordinary Organization

Management Planning Dept.
Product Planning Dept.
TQM Promotion Dept.
Accounting Dept.
Quality Assurance Dept.
Technical Planning Dept.
Development Center 1
. . . .
Production Planning Dept.
Main Plant
Motomachi Plant
. . . .

Function Councils

Cost Council
Quality Council
Research Council
Product Planning Council
Production Council
Purchasing Council
Sales Council
Personnel/Administrative Council
. . . .

General Councils

Technology Council
Production Engineering Council
New Product Council
New Vehicle Program Council
Equipment Council
. . . .

Committees

Invention Committee
Audit Improvement Committee
CD Quality Improvement Committee
. . . .

Function councils, general councils, and committees do not appear on formal organizational charts because they change year by year and according to the issues at hand. Their existence is nonetheless clearly recognized by Toyota company regulations.

Stockholders' meetings, boards of directors, and vice presidents' councils are organizations that can be found in any company. The distinctive feature of Toyota's organizational form is that function councils, general councils, and committees exist as formal organizations and function at the center of the ranks of management.

Function councils are bodies that carry out Toyota's management by function. They are established by selecting a number of functions important to the entire company—e.g., quality, cost, personnel, administration, engineering, production, sales—from among the management and production function systems shown in Figure 3.1. Function councils choose yearly objectives, which they present to general councils. During the course of the year, they also conduct periodic reviews of progress. In a sense, function councils are organizational bodies concerned with individual business strategies. The chairman of a function council is a managing director or a senior managing director; closely concerned division managers or director-level division officers also participate.

General councils are organizational entities that deliberate and decide on major issues in specific sectors, such as development, preparation for volume production, or purchasing. Such issues may include, for example, the content of new products, new product development schedules, equipment investment planning, or responses to market difficulties. They receive yearly objectives from the function councils, incorporate them into annual business plans, and conduct periodic reviews. They are, in other words, bodies whose role it is to take individual business strategies coming down from the function councils, integrate them into plans at a practical level, and then execute them. In order to avoid any confusion about lines of authority, general councils are chaired by managers who are lower in rank than those who chair the function councils—ordinary directors responsible for specific departments or regular department heads. Other closely concerned divisions also participate.

Committees are bodies that handle ordinary matters not dealt with by business strategy. They may deal with important company-wide issues that are common to all periods of time or with issues that are specific to a certain period of time. In the former case, committees may be semi-permanent; in the latter, they may function within a limited time frame. Committees are chaired by the staff members who are most suitably positioned to deal with the issue in question. On occasion, the president or executive vice president may chair a committee.

TQM's *hoshin kanri*, or policy deployment, distinguishes between the management of strategic issues, which are the seeds of future meals, and issues of maintenance and control, which are grains for today's and tomorrow's meals. At Toyota, function councils and general councils deal with strategic issues, and committees deal with matters of maintenance and control.

Toyota makes decisions according to the complex system described above, but the system is not rigid. Depending on the subject, the councils can operate by changing shape like amoebae.

Policy Deployment

We have already cited Eiji Toyoda's explanation for the need to introduce TQC: "We realized, first, that top management had to make quality targets clearer and ensure that all employees understood them. Next, they had to build systems to enhance functional cooperation among the various departments." Policy deployment was adopted to address the first need.

Policy deployment refers to numerous systematic activities across an organization by which it sets an overall business policy, or objective, and then translates, or deploys, plans for achieving business targets into specific long-term plans, annual plans, sector plans, and personal plans, all the while monitoring them and driving them forward.

Management by objectives was introduced from the United States in the early 1960s and was widely used in Japan at the time in the context of TQC activities. The strong tendency of management by objectives to stress results, however, prevented it from achieving its original purpose of motivating employees, and it was usually applied as a kind of quota scheme in which management targets were simply distributed among individuals and organizational units. In response to this, a system was hammered out in which specific measures to attain business objectives were proposed by each organizational unit and then deployed downward. This system was dubbed *hoshin kanri*, or policy deployment. The prototype of policy deployment was the flag management system piloted by Komatsu Seisakusho Co., Ltd., a Deming Prize winner in 1964, one step ahead of Toyota.

Toyota adopted policy deployment in 1961, at the same time it introduced TQC. After several years of trial and error, the company created a system of company policy deployment rules shown in Figure 3.4.

In the world of TQM, what is known as general policy deployment centers on the "annual plan" portion of the lower half of Figure 3.4. In recent years, however, increasing consideration has been accorded strategic policy deployment, a conception of policy deployment that includes the long-range plan portion in the upper half of the figure. Toyota has been implementing strategic policy deployment for more than twenty years.

Toyota's General Planning Office (now the Business Planning Department) is the administrative unit responsible for formulating the long-term business plan. The primary mission of this general staff function is to analyze the demanding environment and to formulate strategy for the future.

The company policy (annual plan) published at the beginning of each year is a melding of individual plans made by the staff within each management function and of an overall company plan produced by the General Planning Office. The policy's formulation is predicated on the idea that individual staff groups are not free to proceed with whatever plan they want; for this reason, periodic adjustments are made so that work can proceed along lines fixed by the General Planning Office.

The annual plan, shown in the lower half of Figure 3.4, is implemented according to the following sequence of steps:

Step 1

Function councils determine specific company-wide actions needed to achieve annual policy (objectives) derived from the long-range plan. These objectives and actions form a matrix. The councils choose numerical indices and target values to measure implementation status and then assign the objectives to the various departments in the form of departmental objectives.

Step 2

General councils in each department determine actions to implement in order to achieve all departmental objectives received from each of the function councils. Departmental objectives and departmental actions form a matrix. The councils choose numerical indices and target values to measure implementation status and then assign the objectives to the various sections in the form of sectional objectives.

Step 3

Each section draws up actions according to the same pattern and then sets indices and assigns the actions to subsection heads, foremen, and group leaders in the form of personal objectives.

Step 4

Finally, each individual draws up individual actions.

After this process of deploying objectives, the values of action indices coming from individuals are aggregated and checked to see whether or not they are sufficient to meet the targets. By repeatedly deploying objectives and checking actions, the company settles on its overall objectives as

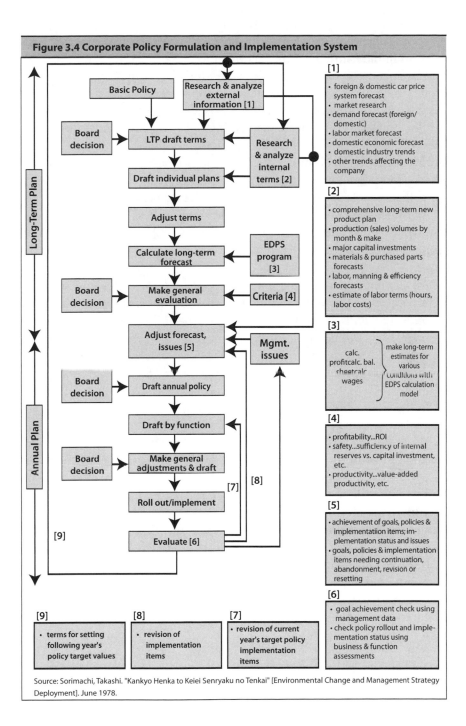

Figure 3.4 Corporate Policy Formulation and Implementation System

Long-Term Plan

Annual Plan

Basic Policy

Research & analyze external information [1]

Board decision → LTP draft terms

Research & analyze internal terms [2]

Draft individual plans

Adjust terms

Calculate long-term forecast

EDPS program [3]

Board decision → Make general evaluation

Criteria [4]

Adjust forecast, issues [5]

Mgmt. issues

Board decision → Draft annual policy

Draft by function

Board decision → Make general adjustments & draft

[7]   [8]

Roll out/implement

[9]

Evaluate [6]

[1]
- foreign & domestic car price system forecast
- market research
- demand forecast (foreign/domestic)
- labor market forecast
- domestic economic forecast
- domestic industry trends
- other trends affecting the company

[2]
- comprehensive long-term new product plan
- production (sales) volumes by month & make
- major capital investments
- materials & purchased parts forecasts
- labor, manning & efficiency forecasts
- estimate of labor terms (hours, labor costs)

[3]
calc. profit calc. bal. sheet calc. wages   make long-term estimates for various conditions with EDPS calculation model

[4]
- profitability...ROI
- safety...sufficiency of internal reserves vs. capital investment, etc.
- productivity...value-added productivity, etc.

[5]
- achievement of goals, policies & implementation items; implementation status and issues
- goals, policies & implementation items needing continuation, abandonment, revision or resetting

[6]
- goal achievement check using management data
- check policy rollout and implementation status using business & function assessments

[9]
- terms for setting following year's policy target values

[8]
- revision of implementation items

[7]
- revision of current year's target policy implementation items

Source: Sorimachi, Takashi. "Kankyo Henka to Keiei Senryaku no Tenkai" [Environmental Change and Management Strategy Deployment]. June 1978.

all sectors approach agreement on the suitability of targets and the possibility of implementing specific actions.

Managers at each level conduct quarterly or semiannual reviews at which they check for discrepancies between targets and results and, if need be, either speed up the plan or revise objectives and actions.

One important point in implementing policy deployment is that objectives and the specific actions needed to achieve them be determined and deployed downward simultaneously. If objectives are communicated downward before actions are proposed, then policy deployment becomes nothing more than a quota system. Management encouragement will bring no results.

As Shoichiro Toyoda explained in a keynote address at the 67th Quality Control Symposium sponsored by the Union of Japanese Scientists and Engineers in December 1998:

> *It's also important that the system proceed on the basis of shared views between the team determining objectives and actions above and the individual units or individuals below. That's why, at Toyota, we decide these things through exhaustive discussions in study sessions or off-site retreats. Merely communicating through documents will give you a kind of policy deployment in form only, long on work and short on results.*

In the Toyota policy deployment system described above, top management sets strategic policy, middle management makes tactical plans, and work improvements are carried out at the bottom. This clear structure makes it possible for everyone at every level in the company to cooperate in achieving company goals.

When we talk about the "bottom" at Toyota, we are referring to subsection heads, foremen, and team leaders; we do not include general employees and workers. The term also excludes QC Circles. The purpose of QC Circle activities is education and training.

Policy deployment is a powerful device if it is applied smoothly. It is currently enjoying a boom in popularity in the world of TQM.

Even ISO 9001, overhauled in December 2000 to yield practical results, refers to policy deployment as a systems approach and positions it at the root of quality management.

Policy deployment translates overall company goals down to the level of the individual and so naturally expands as the deployment proceeds. As long as suitable documentation and management procedures are established, the system can be applied without problems.

Toyota publishes its current policy and business objectives on its Internet homepage. Proposed and executed in the context of Toyota's policy deployment system, these policies and objectives are invariably aggressive and can easily be viewed as one reason Toyota is becoming the world's number one carmaker in the first half of the 21st century.

Management by Function / Cross-Functional Management

Under the guidance of various TQC experts and based on Eiji Toyoda's second reason for introducing TQC (the need to "build systems to enhance functional cooperation among the various departments"), Toyota focused on its key business functions and created a method of linking them horizontally.

In what follows, we have drawn principally on an article by former Toyota managing director Shigeru Aoki. "Cross-Functional Management for Executives" appeared in the February–April 1981 issue of *Hinshitsu Kanri*,[3] a journal published by the Union of Japanese Scientists and Engineers. Extracts from other documents will be cited where they appear.

Figure 3.5 shows a diagram of the general concept of management by function at Toyota. In this example, we select six key functions (from quality to personnel and administration) from among all the functions in the company that need to be managed and relate them to organizational entities within the company, from product planning to sales operations. Policy deployment is a method of managing horizontally according to the strength of these relationships.

Management by function is a technique created by Toyota. Because there was no precedent, the technique was conceptualized and re-conceptualized quite a bit before it took hold.

Management by function was first applied in April 1962. Thirteen functions (nine business functions and four production functions) were selected for this purpose, and management of these functions was assigned to a body called the Planning Council.

After a second company-wide audit in March 1963 found that executives tend to become profit representatives for their sectors, the company entrusted the management of most sectors to nonexecutive division heads and abolished the system of executive responsibility for the divisions. Function councils were created and a system was adopted in which management team members would concentrate on management of the functions. This increased the number of functions to twenty-four in a single stroke.

Too many functions became difficult to manage, so the number of functions was halved and functions were switched around. In the end, the system of executive responsibility for the divisions was revived in March

Figure 3.5 Toyota's Cross-Functional Management Scheme

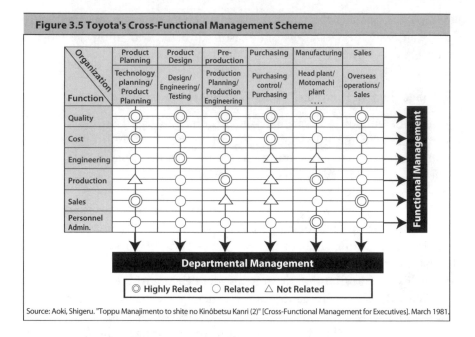

Source: Aoki, Shigeru. "Toppu Manajimento to shite no Kinôbetsu Kanri (2)" [Cross-Functional Management for Executives]. March 1981.

1965 and, with the number of functions squeezed down to eight, staff were assigned clear functional responsibilities.

This, finally, established the Toyota system of management by function. The number of functions has risen and fallen somewhat since then, but the basic contours of the system have remained in place.

The cause of these vicissitudes at Toyota boiled down to a lack of uniformity within the company as to the concept of a "function." With quality assurance and cost control being the most essential functions in the company, it was necessary to go to each department to determine what it had to do to fulfill those functions.

For each function, every department had to be clear about what it had to do, and function councils were run for the purpose of achieving the company's function objectives for each year. The agenda of these function councils is presented below:

1. Goal-setting
2. Planning and actions to achieve goals
3. Planning for new products, equipment, production, sales, etc.
4. Critical "bottom-up" issues
5. Policies to remove obstacles to DO actions
6. ACTION required by the results of CHECKing
7. CHECKs of yearly actions called for by company policies and the following year's policies and actions

8. Other matters necessary for fulfilling the functions

Function councils are also important bodies in terms of budget management and are centers for function budgets (one kind of departmental budget). Among fixed cost budgets, the production function council determines the equipment investment budget, the personnel function council determines the employee budget, the sales function council determines the marketing budget, the engineering function council determines the research budget, and the administrative function council determines the expenses budget. (*Toyota's Production System.*[4] The Japan Society for Production Control, ed.)

Shigeru Aoki cites three key points necessary to the success of management by function:

1. Select and define functions rigorously. Three issues are important here:
   a. Clarify which functions are important to achieving the aims of the company.
   b. Clarify the roles of each department with respect to those functions.
   c. Clarify the support functions required so that each of those departments can achieve its functions.
2. Don't think of management by function as an informal system.
3. Make it clear that function councils, as organizational entities, occupy a place next to the highest practical decision-making bodies within the top management organization. Give them the power and authority they need.

Vertical Departments Must Have Strong Implementation Capabilities.

The job of the function councils is to PLAN. Departments have to DO. Plans set by the function councils cannot be achieved if departments are unable to implement them. The power of vertical departments is not a self-interested strength that says, "I've done all I can do," but the strength to be able to implement plans set by the function councils.

Toyota's management by function has become an optimal system for the company for the simple reason that Toyota kept remaking it until it worked. Today's management by function system is the product of forty years of evolution.

In the West, management by function is referred to as "cross-functional management," and under that name, it has been re-imported back into Japan. This re-imported version, in reality, is often applied only to hybrid team activities or used for one-time projects. Few companies use management by function in the rigorous sense that Toyota does.

The Committee System

Table 3.1 gives an overview, by year, of the names of various Toyota committees culled from company documents and other materials. Be aware that the list is selective, not exhaustive, and committees formed to address issues specific to a particular era have fulfilled their functions and have been disbanded.

Committees that address themes of enduring importance—such as the Safety Committee, the Audit Improvement Committee, the Inventions Committee, the Ingenuity Evaluation Committee, the Quality Control Committee, and the Standardization Committee—are assumed to be still in operation. From this perspective, we may deduce that there are roughly ten to fifteen committees operating in all of Toyota at any given point in time.

There are three distinctive features of the committee system at Toyota:

1. A committee's place in the overall business organization is clear, and it is a formal business entity. (As Figure 3.3 shows, committees appear on organizational charts.)
2. Committees are run according to committee regulations and have specific briefs. The content of their activities is clearly specified.

   Regulations for running a committee are documented at the same time the committee is launched. These regulations clarify such matters as the committee's purposes, membership and roles, venue, issues for consideration, decision-making methods, conditions of formation, and budgeting procedures.
3. Managers personally take the lead in promoting the resolution of problems and issues.

   Committees are chaired by the most suitable executives for the issues addressed and, depending on the theme, even the president or an executive vice president of the company may serve as a chairman. The chairman takes the lead and conducts himself in such a way as to encourage the resolution of problems at hand.

The fact that Toyota accords explicit status to committees via organizational charts and committee regulations derives from the paradigm of documentation discussed in Chapter 2. The personal leadership of the committee chairman reflects the company's leadership-by-example paradigm.

In most companies, committees occupy an ill-defined place; it is far from clear by whom, where, and when a committee's plans and results should be reviewed. Somebody has an idea or gives instructions for forming a committee, people somehow show up, and everybody breathes in and out while doing whatever it is they're supposed to be doing. When the organization changes or people are shifted around, the committee dies a

Table 3.1 Toyota Committees at a Glance

are committees standing (S) or limited-time (L)

decade	year	Committee Name	S/L	Purpose	Chairman
1930	1938	Safety Committee	S	consider policies for creating a safe workplace	–
1940	1943	Audit Improvement Comm.	S	improve technology by auditing internal & external quality problems	President Kiichiro Toyoda
	1947	Mgmt Research Comm.	L	rationalize management methods; find better forms of management	
	1949	Invention Ideas Comm.	S	review & implement invention ideas	Sr. Mgr dir Eiji Toyoda
1950	1951	Trans. Ctrmeas. Comm.	L	establish & implement policies to improve transport efficiency	Mgr. Dir. Shoichi Saito
	1951	Innovaton Review Comm.	S	promote innnovation, review & reward suggestions	–
	1953	Quality Control Comm.		promote QC methods adopted starting 1949	–
1960	1960 aprox	Warranty Repair Comm.	S	negotiate claims compensation work between Toyota Motor (TMC) & Sales (TMS)	–
	1962	7-man Complaints comm.	L	set policy for vehicle complaints between TMC & TMS	–
	1963	TQC Promotion Comm. (TMS)	L	TQC promotion in TMS sales departments included in TMS Deming Prize drive	–
	1965 aprox	Expert Comm. on Simplification	L	promotion of parts norms, standards & references	–
	1966 aprox	Expert Comm. on Equipment Main.	L	establish company-wide production maintenance system	–
	1968	Toyota Traffic Environment Comm.	L	deal with changes in the environment around Toyota	Shoichi Saito
	1969	Comm. on Computer Use	L	consider the use of electronic computers throughout the company	–
	1969	Special Comm. on Recalls	L	deal swiftly & accurately with Transport Ministry's systemization of recalls	–
1970	1974	Cost Planning Comm.	L	consider cost planning from a company-wide perspective	Mgr. Dir Tatsuo Hasegawa
	1974	Corolla Cost Improvement Comm.	L	improve profitability hurt by 1st oil shock	–
	1975	Corona Cost Improvement Comm.	L	improve profitability hurt by 1st oil shock	–
	1975	Crown Cost Improvement Comm.	L	improve profitability hurt by 1st oil shock	–
	1977	Parts Commonization Comm.	L	improve profitability hurt by 1st oil chock	Dirs. Aoki & Moriya
1980	1980 aprox	Business Improvment Comm.	S	promote business improvement (hold sectional, departmental and company improvement meetings)	–
	1984	Info. & Coms. Network Comm.	L	overhaul Toyota-wide information and communication systems and examine future systems	Ex. VP Hiroyasu Ono
	1984	Distribution Comm.	L	promote streamlining of distribution expected from TMC/TMS merger	Dir. Shoji Bun
	1985 aprox	FQ (Flagship Quality) Comm	L	develop & promote highest quality for flagship car Celsior	–
	1985	Information Comm.	L	build information network extending from dealers to suppliers	Ex. VP Kaneyoshi Kusunoki
	1986	Officework Innov. Comm.	L	radical reform of work methods; 50% improvement in officework efficiency	Sr. Mgr. Dir Tsuyoshi Oshima
	1986 aprox	Appearance Enhancement Comm.	L	enhance aspects of exterior product appearance, including match, alignment & finish	–
	1986 aprox	Paint Quality Enhancement Comm.	L	enhance quality of exterior paint	–
	1988	Automation Comm.	L	improve & promote ergonomics as a means of lowering attrition in technical work areas	Sr. Mgr. Dir Tsuyoshi Oshima
	1989	CS Enhancement Comm	L	develop and implement CS (customer satisfaction) ideas introduced from the U.S.	Pres. Shoichiro Toyoda
	1989	Social Cont. Activities Comm.	L	promote shift from 'social responsibility' to 'social contribution'	–
	1989 aporx	Delivered Veh. Qual. Enhance. Comm.	L	improve & promote J.D. Power IQS/CSI product quality indices	Dir. Mamoru Kaita
1990	1990	Comm. to Enhance the Appeal of Skilled Wrkplc.	L	improve & promote issues relating to the decrease in skilled workplaces	–
	1990	Comm. to Reduce Supplied Parts	L	improve profits hit by the collapse of the bubble	–
	1990	Comm. to Adjust Nos. of Models and Comps.	L	improve profits hit by the collapse of the bubble	–
	1992 aprox	Design-In Promotion Comm.	L	expand purchases of high-price, high-function components from overseas suppliers	–
	1996 aprox	EQ Comm.	L	reform development of EQ (development code name for Corolla)	–
	1996	APEAL Comm.	L	improve & promote J. D. Power APEAL product satisfaction index	–
	1997	CD Quality Enhancement Comm.	L	improve CD (customer delight) quality, including APEAL	–
	1998 aprox	Long-Term Quality Improve. Comm.	L	improve & promote J. D. Power VDI long-term quality index	–
	1998 aprox	Platform Comm.	L	study platform integration strategies	–
–	–	Reliability Comm.	S	enhance product reliability	–
		Information System Comm.	S	review & decide on information systemization themes	–
		Standardization Comm.	S	promote internal standardization	–

N.B. Committees created for special events such as plant construction or the editing of company histories have been omitted, as have committees under function councils and lower organizational structures.

natural death. Even when an executive is named to chair the committee, he looks at proposals coming from below and then gives his own on-the-spot opinion or instructions; in many cases the proposals will have vanished from his mind before the next meeting. One cannot expect such committees to yield the kind of results that Toyota's committees do.

Line and Staff

Toyota is distinctive for the intricate interweaving of its line and staff organizations.

Among the various unusual names Toyota gives to its organizational entities, we find the designation *sokatsushitsu*, meaning general office or secretariat. This appellation originated in 1953 in an Inspection Department Secretariat established by then Inspection Department head Shoichiro Toyoda to handle such matters as inspection equipment design, precision measurement, and quality control. Later, organizations with the word "secretariat" attached were set up in departments throughout the company.

The role of the secretariat in modern-day Toyota departments is to take business strategies and managerial policies coming from the executive staff and spread them appropriately throughout the department. This system implements the management by function arrangement discussed above.

In most companies, organizational units corresponding to Toyota's secretariats are probably administrative departments or offices. But it is a rare administrative department that operates the way Toyota's secretariats do. In nearly all cases, the staff of administrative departments keeps a respectful distance from line departments. Unless management goes out of its way to make staff responsibility and authority crystal-clear, staff members inevitably stay in the background as "good wives and wise mothers." Only when problems arise do they rush like fire trucks to a fire.

The president of one company once referred to his staff department as his "nonline organization." He removed the words "management" or "control" from the names of organizational entities and replaced them with the term "administration." This would be like changing Toyota's "secretariats" to "administrative offices." In any event, the company president in question wasn't about to overhaul the organization of his staff departments. The staff were bound to the boss's decision, but their reason for being had been repudiated by the president and their departments withered. Far from being firefighters or even good wives and wise mothers, they ended up trapped. True management disappeared from the company in favor of routine. This might have been acceptable if the company was prospering, but, alas, that was not the case.

Even in cases that are not so extreme, executives with a "line first" mindset who want to set about restructuring activities by reflexively par-ing down their staffs, may want to consider the possibility that they may follow the same path the hapless company president described above. In the first place, the staff system is a modern one that came into being 100 years ago as a scientific management tool. Repudiating it pushes us back 100 years to an unscientific era of home handicraft industries and master-apprentice relationships.

We can cite the following as reasons to explain why staff functions do not drift away from line functions at Toyota:

1. Top management attaches just as much importance to staff functions as it does to line functions.
2. Line and staff are each given clear responsibilities and authority, and they must respect one another's authority.
3. Outstanding line people are periodically rotated into staff positions so that a bureaucratic and high-handed staff culture does not have a chance to develop.
4. More than anything else, staff people are educated to understand that their position is to support the work of the line.

THE QUALITY CONTROL SYSTEM

Quality Assurance

The idea of building quality into the process lies at the root of quality assurance at Toyota. In other words, whatever needs to be guaranteed is assured in every process, including product planning, design, production preparation, purchasing, *goguchi* production (Toyota's term for real production), inspection, sales, and service. The reason for this is that the majority of quality problems occur when a vehicle is in use; inspections at the point of shipment can never eliminate them. Nor can inspections at the point of shipment catch damage or dirt that occurs after vehicles have left the factory. Assuring quality during the period of a vehicle's use requires strict adherence to relevant standards during prior stages, such as product design and production preparation. Additionally, making sure that work procedures in the post-shipment process are strictly followed is an effective way to assure quality once a vehicle leaves the plant.

Toyota regularly conducts independent audits to evaluate and assess whether activities at quality assurance steps are performed appropriately and whether the quality of the resulting product is acceptable.

These two activities—building quality into the process and independently auditing the process—have been the basic elements of quality assurance at Toyota ever since Kiichiro set up an Audit Improvement Office.

These ideas inform Toyota's Quality Assurance Rules (standards specifying the details of quality assurance work) as well as a quality assurance system map, a flowchart showing how work proceeds through different departments.

Figure 3.6 shows a quality assurance system map presented in the October 1996 edition of the JUSE journal, *Hinshitsu* [*Quality*], by Katsuyoshi Yamada, a former head of Toyota's TQC Promotion Office.

Although Katsuyoshi Yamada presents this quality assurance system map as a typical current map from a "certain Deming Prize-winning company," the reader may be assured that it comes from Toyota. Careful verification is called for, however, because the chart contains a wealth of important information. It is important, therefore, to look critically at each of the rules, prescriptions, and guidelines that appear in the "major company regulations" column at the right of the chart. From these we see that this Deming Prize-winning company's overall system of development and production management is strikingly familiar. The review meetings mapped in the middle of the chart refer to design reviews, and the fact that the numbers on the chart skip around (DR1, DR3, DR6, etc.) indicates that the chart is an abridgement. In all likelihood, a complete quality assurance system map would occupy at least ten sheets of 11″ x 17″ paper. Such a map would reflect quality assurance for the whole company, but we would likely see quality assurance maps for individual departments as well, with the total running to nearly 100 pages. In an industry like automobile manufacturing, only a grand design can yield a functioning quality system.[5]

Since product quality is largely determined at the product development stage, cooperation between the quality assurance and product development departments is critical. At Toyota, a specially designated staff member coordinates the work of executives responsible for quality assurance and product development. The staff executive responsible for quality assurance, moreover, operates a "reverse Resident Engineer (RE)" system to check at the development stage that past problems do not surface in new products. The company also establishes product audit offices within product development departments as part of an umbrella quality system.

ISO 9000/QS 9000

The International Organization for Standardization (ISO) published its ISO 9000 International Quality Standards series in 1987. Using ISO 9000 as a foundation, the Big Three automakers in the United States drew up and published QS 9001 quality standards for their suppliers. Toyota

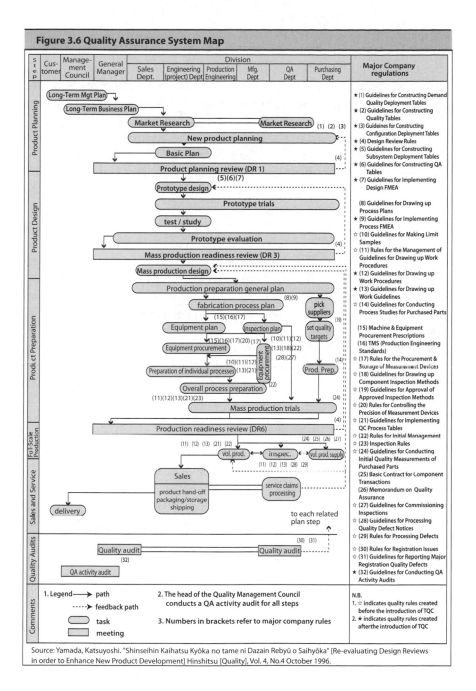

Figure 3.6 Quality Assurance System Map

Step	Customer	Management Council	General Manager	Division — Sales Dept.	Engineering (project) Dept	Production Engineering	Mfg. Dept	QA Dept	Purchasing Dept	Major Company regulations

Product Planning
- Long-Term Mgt Plan
- Long-Term Business Plan
- Market Research — Market Research (1) (2) (3)
- New product planning
- Basic Plan (4)
- Product planning review (DR 1) (5)(6)(7)

Product Design
- Prototype design
- Prototype trials
- test / study
- Prototype evaluation (4)
- Mass production readiness review (DR 3)

Product Preparation
- Mass production design
- Production preparation general plan
- fabrication process plan (8)(9)
- pick suppliers (19)
- Equipment plan — Inspection plan (15)(16)(17)
- set quality targets
- Equipment procurement (15)(16)(17)(20)(17) (10)(11)(12) (13)(18)(22) (28)(27)
- Preparation of individual processes (10)(11)(12)(13)(21) (14)
- Equipment procurement (22)
- Prod. Prep.
- Overall process preparation (11)(12)(13)(21)(23) (22)
- Mass production trials (24)

Full-Scale Production
- Production readiness review (DR6) (4)
- (11) (12) (13) (21) (22)
- vol. prod. — inspec. — vol. prod. supply (24) (25) (26) (27)
- (11) (12) (13) (28) (29)
- Sales
- product hand-off packaging/storage shipping
- service claims processing
- delivery
- to each related plan step

Sales and Service

Quality Audits
- Quality audit — Quality audit (30) (31)
- (32)
- QA activity audit

Major Company regulations:

★ (1) Guidelines for Constructing Demand Quality Deployment Tables
★ (2) Guidelines for Constructing Quality Tables
★ (3) Guideines for Constructing Configuration Deployment Tables
★ (4) Design Review Rules
★ (5) Guidelines for Constructing Subsystem Deployment Tables
★ (6) Guidelines for Constructing QA Tables
★ (7) Guidelines for Implementing Design FMEA
(8) Guidelines for Drawing up Process Plans
★ (9) Guidelines for Implementing Process FMEA
☆ (10) Guidelines for Making Limit Samples
☆ (11) Rules for the Management of Guidelines for Drawing up Work Procedures
★ (12) Guidelines for Drawing up Work Procedures
★ (13) Guidelines for Drawing up Work Guidelines
☆ (14) Guidelines for Conducting Process Studies for Purchased Parts
(15) Machine & Equipment Procurement Prescriptions
(16) TMS (Production Engineering Standards)
☆ (17) Rules for the Procurement & Storage of Measurement Devices
☆ (18) Guidelines for Drawing up Component Inspection Methods
☆ (19) Guidelines for Approval of Approved Inspection Methods
☆ (20) Rules for Controlling the Precision of Measurement Devices
☆ (21) Guidelines for Implementing QC Process Tables
☆ (22) Rules for Initial Management
☆ (23) Inspection Rules
☆ (24) Guidelines for Conducting Initial Quality Measurements of Purchased Parts
(25) Basic Contract for Component Transactions
(26) Memorandum on Quality Assurance
☆ (27) Guidelines for Commissioning Inspections
☆ (28) Guidelines for Processing Quality Defect Notices
☆ (29) Rules for Processing Defects
☆ (30) Rules for Registration Issues
☆ (31) Guidelines for Reporting Major Registration Quality Defects
★ (32) Guidelines for Conducting QA Activity Audits

N.B.
1. ☆ indicates quality rules created before the introduction of TQC
2. ★ indicates quality rules created after the introduction of TQC

Comments

1. Legend → path
   ----► feedback path
   ⬭ task
   ▭ meeting
2. The head of the Quality Management Council conducts a QA activity audit for all steps
3. Numbers in brackets refer to major company rules

Source: Yamada, Katsuyoshi. "Shinseihin Kaihatsu Kyôka no tame ni Dazain Rebyû o Saihyôka" [Re-evaluating Design Reviews in order to Enhance New Product Development] Hinshitsu [Quality], Vol. 4, No.4 October 1996.

already had TQC/TQM firmly in place and saw no need to obtain ISO 9000/QS 9000 certification, but its European plants needed ISO 9000 for business purposes, as did Toyota group suppliers doing business with companies in the United States and Europe. As the leader of the Toyota Group, Toyota applied for ISO 9000/QS 9000 certification, "for the purpose of learning." The engine division achieved ISO 9001 certification in 1996, and the Hirose Plant obtained QS 9000 certification in 1998. The certification was subsequently renewed after each mandated evaluation, and then was returned.

The requirements of ISO 9000/QS 9000 were more than satisfied by practices and systems that Toyota had established through its TQC/TQM activities, including policy deployment, management by function, top management diagnoses, process control, design reviews, document control, quality audits, and quality education and training. ISO 9000/QS 9000 was unnecessary for Toyota, moreover, because it was incomplete: It did not deal with cost, one of the twin pillars of management.

Its involvement with ISO led Toyota to translate a set of its quality documents into English and send them to its European plants to obtain ISO 9002 certification. For suppliers, Toyota set up an ISO consulting team in its quality assurance department and even began providing related assistance on its web pages.

Hitoshi Kume, a professor at Chuo University and professor emeritus at the University of Tokyo, has won the Deming Prize and is an authority on TQC. As the Japanese representative to ISO quality control and quality assurance councils, he has also been deeply involved in the formulation of the ISO 9000 series. Kume describes ISO 9001 and TQC in terms of a metaphor.

"ISO 9001," he says, "is like a university entrance examination and the Deming Prize is like a senior thesis." ISO 9001 can be compared to an entrance examination because it involves activities to prepare an organization to give specified, correct answers. TQC and the Deming Prize, on the other hand, can be compared to a senior thesis because those aspiring to succeed come up with their own issues and find their own path to resolving them.

The number of ISO 9001-certified companies continues to increase, but one rarely hears of companies that have transformed themselves using ISO. This is hardly surprising, considering that ISO 9001 specifies only minimum conditions. It goes without saying that a company becomes much stronger when it puts together a senior thesis for which it must find its own topic and solve its own problems through the independent application of TQC methods. This is precisely what Toyota did. It took up TQC to address its own issues and themes, and it hammered out its own solutions.

If the key thing is coming to grips with your own issues and themes, it does not matter whether the means you use are derived from ISO 9001 or TQC. It is probably fair to say that the reason for Toyota's success is that

Toyota would have gone after and solved its problems even if TQC hadn't called for it.

Gathering Market Quality Information and Handling Claims

W. Edwards Deming, who came to Japan in 1950 at the invitation of the Union of Japanese Scientists and Engineers, talked about new product development in terms of what he called "The New Way."

The New Way

1. Design products (on the basis of suitable tests).
2. Manufacture them and test and inspect them on the manufacturing line and in the laboratory.
3. Sell them.
4. In service, test the products and conduct market surveys to learn users' reactions to them and the reasons that some people don't use them.
5. Redesign products in response to consumers' reactions to cost and quality.

Deming advocated repeating the above cycle over and over again.

We see from the expression "in service, test the products" that Deming considered the market to be a forum for quality improvement in new product development. Toyota's founder, Kiichiro Toyoda, similarly saw vehicle quality as being difficult to verify and assure solely with tests performed at the company. He believed that the accumulation of responses to quality problems in the marketplace was one basic method of quality assurance. This belief was based on the premise that even if performance and function can be estimated by theoretical calculations, there are many aspects of quality that can be predicted only by rules of experience.

In order to make predictions from rules of experience, one needs a mechanism for collecting the experience of the marketplace, i.e., for gathering massive amounts of appropriate market quality information. Quality information from the marketplace is by nature extraordinarily difficult to organize, however, and its content is not easy to grasp. Such data depends, after all, on the voices of customers who are novices in terms of technology, and it arrives by telephone, fax, registration forms, sales slips, and a host of other means through a variety of organizations. Some customers send letters directly to the company, and some information comes from government agencies.

Toyota has adhered to Kiichiro's position on gathering quality information from the marketplace and has devised various means to increase the reliability of the information it gets. It has coded and entered as computer data the symptoms, circumstances, locations, conditions, and causes of product problems. Even specific locations on vehicle body panels that are susceptible to dings or scratches have their own codes, so it is now easier to gather, collate, and analyze reliable information. Having collected data in this way for decades, Toyota can use multivariate analysis (see the next section on Statistical Methods) and other statistical means to derive cause-and-effect formulas (rules of experience) to predict, for example, what factors result in what problems. Understanding these things helps clarify what needs to be done to eliminate problems.

It was in 1963, in the midst of the introduction of TQC, that Toyota began using the word "reliability" and collecting and analyzing information in earnest. One central type of quality information was data on claims during the warranty period. Other types of quality information that proved useful included the following:

1. Follow-up surveys of new vehicles on the market (these were called Initial Circulation Special Market Surveys)
2. Data gathered on commercial users and private users
3. Regular market surveys
4. Data collected from Japan and around the world on natural and social environmental conditions in which vehicles are used, national characteristics concerning how people treat vehicles, and other data on regional characteristics

Quality information gathered in this way is used in a problem registration system and followed up on until problems have been resolved. This system was established in 1962 in order to prioritize market quality information across the company clearly on the basis of urgency, not merely on the technical judgments of individual departments. The procedure for problem follow-up is outlined below:

1. Select problems from the marketplace on the basis of fixed criteria and then categorize and register them according to their urgency.
2. Determine the responsible departments and encourage resolution.
3. Measure the effect of actions taken, verify that steps have been taken to prevent recurrences, and remove problems from the register.

The key point here—verify that steps have been taken to prevent recurrences—lies in Step 3. All companies have groups assigned to work on preventing problem recurrences, but when recurrence prevention is perfunctory, it is virtually useless.

It is crucial to organize human resources and systems capable of checking—technically and theoretically—that recurrence prevention is really effective. Similarly, rather than setting a deadline at two months or three months, those involved in the process must be prepared to wait until measures are in place that will truly prevent a problem from recurring. What tests the competence of the organization is whether items on the register accumulate to the point where they clog the system. Managers who face problems squarely will be able to take truly effective actions to prevent problems from recurring. Companies that are casual about their system of problem recurrence prevention, on the other hand, will never see their quality improve.

Even by world standards, as we will see in Chapter 5, Toyota's quality stands out. This is the result of long years of steady engagement in quality control and quality assurance activities. Toyota's quality costs are low: Its ratio of customer claims to sales is half of what it is for other Japanese carmakers and one-third of what it is for American auto manufacturers. When quality improves, claims and costs decrease, and when claims decrease, products sell better. Quality sells.

Quality obeys laws of experience, so quality improvement requires planning for 100 years. If you look for results in three or five years, you will not get them. What you need is long-range policies and plans that will be in operation tens or scores of years after you are gone.

Using Statistical Methods

Experimental design, the Taguchi Method, and multivariate analysis are three typical statistical methods or quality control methods.

Where performance is determined by multiple and variable factors, experimental design or design of experiments is a method of drawing up experimental plans that make it possible to get to the top of the mountain by the shortest route. Toyota learned the efficacy of experimental design when its Inspection Department introduced the method from the West in 1951 and applied it to a cylinder block casting process suffering from a high rate of defects (*Toyota: the First 20 Years*). Use of the method subsequently spread throughout the company.

The Taguchi Method, also known as robust design, is a planning method that minimizes quality costs by seeking out those parameters that are the least sensitive to external disturbances. Its creator, Dr. Genichi Taguchi, has won many academic and industrial awards, including the Deming Prize in Japan in 1960 and induction into the American Automotive Hall of Fame in 1997. Taguchi used experimental design as a stepping-stone to develop and establish his unique Japanese statistical methodology in the 1970s. Japanese companies shied away from Taguchi's model because of its abstruse theories and idiosyncratic vocabulary; the method first gained currency in the United States in the 1980s. The

Taguchi Method is said to be one of the technologies responsible for the renaissance of United States industry in the 1990s. Still in the process of development, the method was re-imported into Japan in the 1990s under the name "quality engineering." A Quality Engineering Society was established in 1998, and systematization of the method continues.

Multivariate analysis is a method for analyzing multiple cause-and-effect relationships within a large mass of data. Wal-Mart's data warehouse became famous, for example, when the company deduced a cause-and-effect relationship between sales of diapers and beer, and subsequently moved beer next to the diaper aisle. The prime function of the data warehouse is to perform multivariate analysis.

As a statistical technique, the Taguchi Method came into the spotlight in Japan around the middle of the 1990s. Oddly enough, the words "Taguchi Method," "robust design" or "quality engineering" are rarely heard at Toyota. From the late 1980s into the 1990s, when Toyota was broadly promoting the teaching and diffusion of quality control and statistical methods under the banner of an "SQC Renaissance," the Taguchi Method was the one technique that failed to appear on stage. Denso and certain other companies in the Toyota group have vigorously supported Quality Engineering Society activities. Only Toyota has turned a cold shoulder.

What Toyota has done is to accumulate past examples and data from the entire Toyota group in a systematic, stratified, and electronic format and then use computer ("office automation") analysis of these to derive answers to most problems and issues. With two weeks provided for the resolution of problems, the time-consuming experimental design and Taguchi methods are hardly ever used. Multivariate analysis, on the other hand, is applied to past examples and data.

Ordinarily, since data from the past are not collected and managed systematically, problem-solving activities often call on experimental design or the Taguchi Method to find solutions to singular problems. When enormous quantities of past data are managed as systematically as they are at Toyota, however, multivariate analysis is certainly more effective than experimental design or the Taguchi Method.

We again recall the words of a prominent figure of a management consulting organization introduced at the beginning of Chapter 2: Toyota spends about five times what other companies do on data management. Toyota imported experimental design from the United States after the war and then painstakingly used it to solve problems. The company has been spending five times what other companies do to collect data, with the result that nearly all problems can now be solved by using past data.

Toyota does not scorn the Taguchi Method, however. To increase design speed and lower manufacturing costs in the future, Toyota recognizes the need for a technique that can identify robust design parameters, i.e., those whose impact on performance with respect to design tolerances is slight. For this reason, the Taguchi Method is beginning to find its own niche within Toyota and this niche is likely to expand in the future.

Toyota has 700 statistical specialists (at the Ph.D. and consultant engineer level) and a system that enables four of them to assist each department head. As a result, matters are proposed and considered on the basis of data even in departments, like design and sales, where decision-making relies on experience. When a new vehicle is launched, for example, estimates are made even of how many flyers distributed on which days of the week will draw how many people.

There are two underlying reasons responsible for these arrangements: (1) Staff departments control the key resources of people, material, and money. Actions that do not call on staff departments such as the TQM Promotion Office do not turn out to be Toyota's assets. (2) Improvement can neither take place nor be sustained unless the company as a whole comes to grips with quality problems.

Toyota has thirteen administrative centers, so that even if each one attains a 99 percent quality level, the total is only 0.99 to the power $13 = 0.88$ (88 percent). This serves to illustrate why statistical methods are needed.

Responses to Quality Issues in Recent Years

In the 1960s, a thriving consumer movement promoted by Ralph Nader and others in the United States transferred power over quality matters from the hands of producers to the hands of consumers. Organizations such as Consumers Union (publisher of *Consumer Reports*) and J. D. Power and Associates began publishing independent vehicle product evaluations. In recent years, quality surveys and reports have expanded beyond mere initial failures to address breakdowns over time, as well as appearance, feel, and other qualities, including sellers' attitudes toward customers and service.

As a result, manufacturers have had to shift away from production and sales-centered marketing policies—in which their sole energies went into selling—and toward customer-centered marketing, which entails making improvements in all quality areas important to customers. Toyota responded to data from Consumers Union and J. D. Power early on, and as a result, has grown to be the premier quality company in the world. In

Chapter 5, we look in more detail at recent quality issues, Toyota's responses, and the results.

THE COST MANAGEMENT SYSTEM

A History of Cost Management

Kiichiro Toyoda seems to have struggled more with cost than with quality at the time he founded Toyota Motor Company. If Toyota studied the technologies of the advanced nations of Europe and North America and gradually improved its products, then at some point it could be expected to produce vehicles consistently on a par with those nations. Cost, however, was hugely vulnerable to the mass production effect in Japan, a country far inferior to the United States in terms of geographical size, national resources, population, and purchasing power. Underground resources such as iron ore, coal, and petroleum, moreover, were as good as nonexistent. Given these limitations, Japan could not be expected to engage in mass production on the same scale as the United States. Even with Japan's low wages at the time, it was difficult to imagine building automobiles at a cost comparable to U.S. cost.

In the Toyota Museum, there is a treasured memo dating from the spring of 1937. Entitled "Cost calculations and future prospects," it is Kiichiro Toyoda's cost estimates for the founding Toyota Motor Company. In January 1987, addressing a joint meeting of the Kyohokai (an association of parts suppliers) and the Eihokai (an association of suppliers of molds, gauges, and jigs and of plant and equipment contractors), Eiji Toyoda spoke of Kiichiro's war on costs:

> *"Kiichiro worked out detailed cost reduction plans by component part and estimated the expected cost reductions. But he didn't start off having achieved 100 percent of his goals. He began under certain conditions and then devised other cost reduction measures on the basis of actual results. He was determined to forge ahead the way he had described in the memo. There's no doubt but that he was prepared to lose everything."*

It is likely that the question of cost was a constant concern for Kiichiro. This was the context in which he proposed just-in-time, a way for even small-lot production to be profitable. At Kiichiro's bidding (and to bring profits even with high diversity, small batch production), Taiichi Ohno hammered out the Toyota Production System, which kept costs down during the company's inception and expansion.

It goes without saying that a company cannot secure a sound financial footing merely through just-in-time or TPS cost-cutting on the shopfloor. Company-wide cost management methods must be established.

Toyota's introduction of scientific cost management methods begins after World War II, when it brought in standard costing and other management accounting methods from the United States in 1950. The details of this process are told in *Toyota: A History of the First Fifty Years* (1987), but certain pivotal events are discussed below:

> *The cost of a vehicle is largely determined at the planning and design stage. Moreover, not much in the way of cost improvement can be expected once full-scale production begins because manufacturing equipment in the age of mass production has become larger and more specialized. As one way through this problem, in late 1959, Toyota for the first time considered cutting costs at the planning and design stage by setting a target selling price of $1,000 for the* Publica, *then in the prototype stage. Results were good and the* Publica *managed to become a "people's car" at a mini-car price. This success in meeting price targets at the planning and design stage subsequently took root in the form of VE (Value Engineering), and the procedure came to be followed for the development of each new vehicle and for each model change. At the same time, a so-called cost planning system took shape in which the relevant departments at each stage of the process, including design, trials and production preparation, cooperated with one another to achieve target costs.*

Toyota introduced VA (Value Analysis) in 1962 and all the engineering departments worked together to hold parts reviews with each of their suppliers.

Toyota launched cost management first by putting together a system of cost maintenance that depended on managing departmental costs. Then the company established a system of cost improvement for further reducing estimated costs and added cost planning at the new product planning stage. The cost management system honed through this process eventually earned the acclaim of the Deming Prize evaluation committee when it conducted an audit in November 1965.

Toyota set up a cost planning committee in September 1969 to take a broad look at cost planning. This was followed by the establishment of a cost planning section in the Engineering Department and the realization and strengthening of cost planning systems in a number of departments, including the Production Technology

Planning Office, accounting and purchasing control. The forms of cost planning functions were able to evolve along with their goals.

The Cost Management System

Cost Management Rules, a document drawn up in the course of TQC activities in the 1960s, lays out Toyota's cost management activities. While prescribing a clear framework for various activities at each departmental level, *Cost Management Rules* emphasizes the tangible side of things as well: interdepartmental cooperation and raising cost awareness. Figure 3.7 shows the framework of Toyota's cost management system.

Cost Planning

- From new vehicle planning and design through production preparation, cost planning refers to early activities to ensure target profits by building in costs.
- Skillful planning at this stage is ten times more effective than cost improvements at the manufacturing stage.

Capital Investment Planning

- Cost planning looks at a vehicle vertically, whereas capital investment planning, which involves large sums of money and difficult issues of investment leveling, looks at a vehicle horizontally.
- Based on how total costs can be lowered, capital investment planning considers such choices as the innovative or the tried-and-true, dedicated or multipurpose equipment, and manual labor or machines.

Cost Maintenance and Cost Improvement

- Cost maintenance refers to activities for sustaining reference labor costs while adhering to standard operations and to maintaining raw material reference units. It is the foundation of cost management.[6]
- Labor, materials, energy, and other processing costs that vary according to operability are managed in accordance with variable budgets.
- Cost improvement [or cost *kaizen*] activities are those that lower reference labor costs and reference breakdown units[7] by changing standard operations, materials, or processing methods.

Although not shown in Figure 3.7, activities to create "opportunity profits" constitute one link of cost improvement. Unlike ordinary activities, these work toward significant cost reductions in major projects.[8]

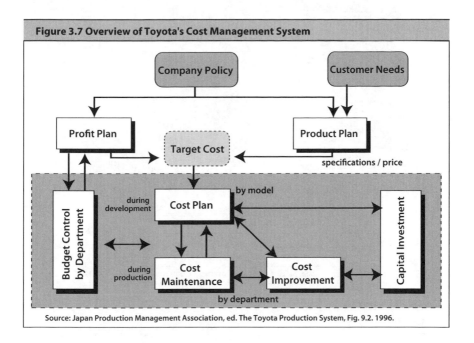

Figure 3.7 Overview of Toyota's Cost Management System

Source: Japan Production Management Association, ed. The Toyota Production System, Fig. 9.2. 1996.

Cost Planning

Cost planning occupies a particularly important place in Toyota's system of cost management. Figure 3.8 shows categories of cost by the point at which they arise.

The chart provides a qualitative illustration of Toyota's assertions that "the cost of a vehicle is largely determined at the planning and design stage. Not much in the way of cost improvement can be expected once full-scale production begins" and that "skillful improvements at the planning and design stage are ten times more effective than at the manufacturing stage."

It was Toyota's experiential grasp of what is shown in this chart that led the company to develop a new method of "cost planning that applies VE at the new car development stage" and to try using it in the development of the *Publica,* (see Chapter 2, Perspectives on Work).

VE is described as "organized research for the purpose of achieving needed functions at minimal cost." These needed functions are factors that assure quality, so that VE can be seen as a bridge or ferry running between quality assurance and cost management.

In February 1965, The Society of Automotive Engineers in Japan (JSAE), published an article in their Japanese-language journal, *Review of*

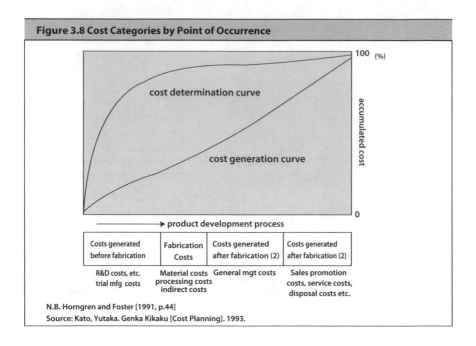

Figure 3.8 Cost Categories by Point of Occurrence

N.B. Horngren and Foster [1991, p.44]
Source: Kato, Yutaka. Genka Kikaku [Cost Planning]. 1993.

Automotive Engineering. Entitled "The role of VA in the Automobile Industry—with special reference to cost planning," it was written by Koichi Tanaka, the head of Toyota's Technical Administration Department. Tanaka's article is both crucial for understanding cost management—and, especially, cost planning—at Toyota and useful for grasping the way Toyota works and thinks. This article is considered to set the tone for cost management at Toyota even today and is summarized below section by section.

1. *Foreword*
   This paper is not a manual of specific VA/VE procedures, but, rather, an exposition of how an organization can draw maximal effect from VA/VE.
2. *VA Applications and Issues*
   At Toyota, VE is called cost planning, and VA is referred to as cost improvement. Toyota sets standards for accrual costs in the production department for each quarter and calls activities to maintain these standards cost maintenance. These three items—cost planning, cost improvement, and cost maintenance—are collectively dubbed the three functions of cost management. The following principally deals with cost planning activities, since these have the greatest effect.
3. *Managing the cost planning function*
   Cost planning at the new product development stage can be broken down into six steps, designated 0–5 in Figure 3.9.

Step 0 (cost planning target survey)

Collect and analyze information relating to demand forecasts and sales prices.

- Compare the sales price forecasts and quality targets of competing companies in Japan and in export destinations, conduct customer satisfaction surveys and other market research, and analyze information linking demand forecasts and sales prices.

Study sales profits by vehicle model.

- The sales price is not calculated by adding profit to costs. It is determined as a function of the competition's prices and the consumer's latent ability to pay.
- The total sales profit by model is also a function of the life cycle and the time required to implement model changes and minor changes. Other factors are price changes, development investment costs and capital expenditures.
- These considerations determine the time and substance of new product development, as well as which models have priority for the application of VE.

Analyze and quantify the relationship by model between production volumes and costs.

- Construct a Maxcy-Silberston curve (see Figure 2.3) for each process step—e.g., presswork, forging, casting, and machining—so that these steps can be aggregated into a picture of the model as a whole.[9]
- Make it possible to grasp the relationship of total life-cycle production volume to the choice between the depreciation of multipurpose equipment and the investment costs of dedicated equipment.

Understand the costs implied in technical trends.

- Understand the cost implications of trends in materials, production technologies, and factory management methods.

Step 1 (setting cost-planning targets)

- Clarify management's policies, strategies and intentions.
- Manufacturing costs and sales costs determined in this step are not immutable until the period of new product launch. Revise them as appropriate, depending on changes in market trends and the emergence of competing vehicles.
- Targets set at this stage are indicated by VE activities conducted in the course of the development process, during product planning, prototype studies, and production preparation.
- Use the basic production volume and projected vehicle life to check later estimates and conformance to goals.

Figure 3.9 Cost Planning Management System

	Stage 0 (planning, target research)	Stage 1 (planning, target setting)	Stage 2 (cost distribution)	Stage 3 (target costs & revised distribution)
Planning Council		decision		decision
New Product Council / Cost Council		target cost / target cost deliberations		target cost / target cost deliberations
Accounting Dept.	cost data	target sales profit ratio cost data		cost data
Eng. Mgt. Dept.	technical data; new product planning target	target price cost plan product target (basic plan policy production units)	plan for dist. of cost by function	plan cost est.; revised dist. of cost by function
Eng. Dept.1	functional component development		plan by function	trial drawing
Eng. Dept. 2	trials/ experiments; matls. development			trials/experiments
Business Export Dept.	Market information	demand forecast/model life sales price data (indicated requirements)		
Production Eng. Dept.				
Sales dept. 1 (maker)	cost data			
Prod Eng. Dept. Mech Eng. Dept Body Eng. Dept. Facilities Dept.	Production engineering Equipment information		Productivity equipment sales	Productivity equipment studies
QA Dept.	Market Information			
Casting Dept.				
Forging Dept.				
Motomachi Body Dept. Main/Motomachi Assy Depts. Motomachi No.2 Assy. Dept.				

Source: Tanaka, Kôichi. "Jidosha Sangy ni okeru VA no Yakuwari" [The Role of VA in the Automotive Industry], Jidôsha Gijutsu [Automotive Engineering]. February 1965.

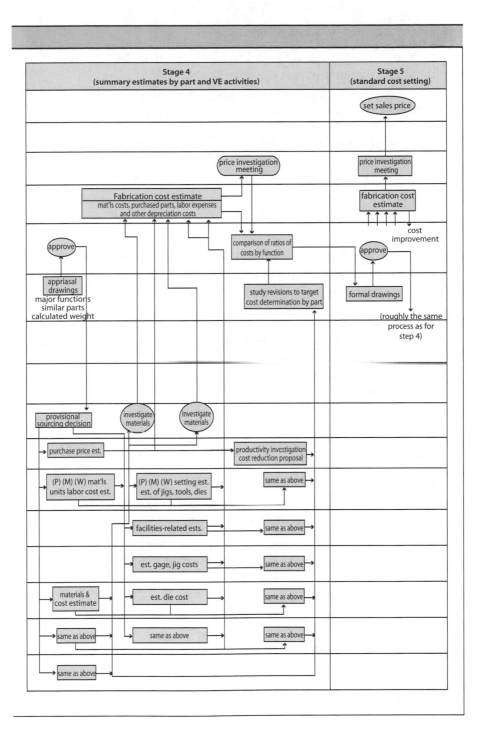

Step 2 (assignment of costs by function)

Survey and organize the costs and weight structures, by function, of each model currently in production.

- The Accounting Department generally puts together cost structures by departments, such as manufacturing and purchasing, where costs are generated. These need to be further subdivided by design function, e.g., engine, transmission, propeller shaft, white body, interior trim, and exterior trim.
- Again by function, create a table of cost per unit weight (¥/kg) for major components.
- These are useful because automobiles seldom undergo comprehensive or radical structural change.

Understand the cost structures by function of competing vehicles.

- Survey the retail prices of parts at competitors' dealerships. This method helps ensure fairly precise estimates of other companies' costs.

Determine the parts composition of the new product.

- Determine the parts composition for each model (type) before going into detailed parts designing.
- Study which components can be carried over from those currently in use and which need to be designed for the new model, along with how much commonality there is among new product types. The number of newly designed parts and the total number of parts will depend on the extent to which common (carried over and shared) components can be used. Capital expenditures will vary accordingly.

Combine basic plans and goals of the new product, break down costs by design function, and assign target costs according to basic specifications, weight, and principal materials.

- Assign costs in proportion to specific percentages by which elements such as seats, linings, and interior trim are to be upgraded with respect to previous models. These distributed costs, in other words, are a cost-based quality measure indicating the degree of quality that must be designed in.

Step 3 (target costs and their redistribution)

- Along with satisfying performance requirements, designers for each function put together detailed parts drawings within designated limits of weight and cost.

- Parts drawings are designed after detailed specifications are verified against the chief designer's intentions and then checked against the cost planning staff's macro-level estimates to make sure they fall within plan in terms of cost.
- If necessary, the allocation of costs to functions may be revised in response to problems during the prototype testing stage. When considering detailed parts drawings, the most important thing at this stage is to determine whether volume production will necessitate the rebuilding or redesign of the current equipment in use. Then compute the required capital expenditures.
- Technical standard costs are derived by multiplying the extent to which current parts will change by average cost variations. Production costs, on the other hand, are obtained by adding costs arising out of specific manufacturing elements.

Step 4 (VA in the prototype period)

Use standard parts.

- Shapes, dimensions, and monthly usage totals of basic parts such as nuts and bolts are arranged into tables that are distributed to all designers. Parts similar to existing parts cannot be redesigned without the permission of the responsible manager.

Commonize parts and processes.

- The first five digits of standard ten-digit part numbers at Toyota are standardized to the functional unit, so it is easy to compare drawings of similar parts. In designing new products, this makes it easy to use uniform parts and build uniform processes.[10]
- When problems or other reasons necessitate designing new parts that are different from parts already in use, the new parts are not designed in isolation. They are made so that parts previously used in other models can be changed as well.[11]

Conduct process capability feedback.

- Each part that is currently in production is classified according to the current processes. The capabilities of these processes are maintained according to the precisions as defined in design criteria. For processing methods such as casting, die-casting, forging, presswork, and machining in particular, data (technical standards) relating to dimensional differences, tolerances, surface precision, and difficulty (cost) can help prevent a drift toward excessive quality that does not show up in designs.
- Design criteria emphasize strength, function, and durability, but other items have recently been appended, such as cost-related selection of

materials and processing methods, cost calculation methods, and the capacities of related processes on an economic level. Failure histories and past problem recurrence prevention actions relating to similar parts have also been added.[12]

- Confirming producibility is not the only purpose of prototypes. Of greater relative importance is the verification of functions and performance. Occasionally, these two purposes contradict one another. When this is the case, prototype vehicles for functions and those for producibility are prepared separately, and comparative evaluations of the two groups of prototypes are conducted. Analysis then indicates how to secure both function and performance on the one hand and producibility on the other.

Use knowledge from supplier plants.

- Supplier plants must be treated with the attitude that they will generate good suggestions.
- Purchased parts deserve the greatest energy investment since they are responsible for over half the total cost of an automobile. At appropriate stages of prototypes, teams composed of designers, purchasing agents, people responsible for inspection, and production engineers should visit supplier plants to conduct VE investigations.

Make estimates with prototype drawings and prototype parts.

- Conduct cost estimates for key parts (the 20–25 percent of parts that account for 80–85 percent of the cost). Consider multiple key part designs, build comparative tables and compare these with technical requirement sheets before settling on a final version.[13]
- As data accumulate and the relationship between design specification variations and cost variations becomes clear, a comparative table of cost expenditures evolves into a [proper] cost table.
- Before prototype drawings assume their final form (i.e., when they are still in the study and planning phases), top managers attend and preside over parts study sessions with all concerned.
- These practices have the secondary effect of speeding up the decision-making process and saving time. They spotlight problems in the cost management system and facilitate its improvement.

Step 5 (Setting reference costs)

- Since none of the target costs in previous cost planning steps specify production conditions relating, for example, to what kind of production line will be used, a standard cost table is now used to arrive at target costs using the cost differentials among parts technologies. It should be noted that since the production line is determined at the production stage, costs will change depending on production conditions. They are called standard costs.

- Because the company's management strategy exerts enormous influence over profit plans at this stage, the following points are taken into consideration when effective capital expenditures are made and when serious study is invested in putting together economical manufacturing processes:
  - Reconfirmation of demand and production estimates
  - Operations estimates and plans for equipment and manning once volume production has begun
  - Comprehensive integration with all company long-term plans
  - Preparation of equipment, machines, tools, dies, and gauges for volume production
- Use the model life cycle to set profit and cost plans.
- Based on the model life cycle, the person charged with purchasing concludes parts purchase contracts with suppliers.

Cost improvement (Postproduction VA).

- Explain reduction targets for each model in terms that are easy to understand.
- Since costs are actually being generated, organize VA activities on a company-wide and systematic basis.
- Assign target reduction amounts according to responsibilities for cost generation.
- Speed up action to respond to VA suggestions coming from vendors. Whenever decisions are delayed, communicate the reason for the delay and specify the date a response may be expected.
- Clarify how VA-related cost reductions will be evaluated and make plans to reward the effort that goes into making suggestions.

Finally. . .

- I continue to pray that the Japanese automobile industry will understand the true essence of VA and that it will use creative VA in an organized way to develop into a global enterprise.

What we have seen above is the Toyota cost management system as developed over the course of the TQC activities the company introduced during the 1960s. The last sentence of Tanaka's paper is striking. In it, we glimpse both confidence in Toyota's cost management and Toyota's sense of responsibility as leader of the Japanese automobile industry.

Toyota has found it inefficient for the design department to implement VA by changing parts specifications after the start of production. The usual practice now is to concentrate VA on manufacturing method changes in the plant and for the design department to concentrate its principal efforts on VE during the new product development stage. The design department has practiced VA only twice: at the time of the oil crisis in the 1970s and during the collapse of the economic bubble in the early 1990s.

It is not at all unusual for companies to begin the production of new products without having met cost targets. In case targets are not met, companies want to conduct some sort of recovery operations (i.e., design changes for the purpose of VA) even after production on a completed design has begun, perhaps even as a punishment for designers who failed to meet the targets. If designers do not achieve targets, it is not for lack of effort. Assigning punitive recovery activities to them after the fact is demoralizing. It is wiser to use the same time to have them do VE for new products than to have them conduct inefficient postproduction VA. Toyota, like many other companies, begins production even when targets are missed. The difference is that Toyota does not burden designers with VA after production begins. As seen above, whether or not a company can take a total systems approach to the cost marks the difference between a vicious circle and a virtuous one.

We can cite an example of a president of a certain company who sighed with relief once his cost control system was up and running. "Now I'm free of the burden of cost," he said. The trouble was that his company never achieved its cost targets. "We always get off to a strong start," he lamented, "but we're always last coming around the final lap." In his company, recovery activities are the norm.

This company president is wrong on two counts. First, he assumes there will come a time when he can relax about costs. Secondly, he thinks he does not have to start managing until the final lap.

What built the Toyota we know today is that, even as the company set up a scientific system of cost management and developed cost management methods, it has always set aggressive cost targets and has endeavored to meet them.

FINANCIAL AND ACCOUNTING SYSTEMS

On its balance sheet for 2001, Toyota's consolidated profits neared one trillion yen, making it the most profitable company in the history of Japan. Its financial income was 553.1 billion yen, corresponding to ¥2.63 million per employee. In other words, Toyota would earn the equivalent of nearly half of the average of its employees' wages, even if it did not sell a single car.

Toyota: A History of the First 50 Years (1987) recalls the events that brought Toyota to this financial position:

Rationalization activities (following the first oil crisis in 1973), coupled with adjustments in the sales prices of exported vehicles, led to a rapid recovery in Toyota Motor Corporation business results after June 1975. Company policy had meant, too, that the massive capital investments of the late 1960s had in principle been covered by Toyota's own funds, so the company was able to exploit shorter equipment lives, accelerated depreciation, and a system of special depreciation. In addition, Toyota was well supplied with its own capital because it had made efforts to keep various reserves and contingency funds and had increased its capital by issuing stocks at market prices at just the right times. With its policy of limiting outside borrowing as much as possible, it was able to eliminate debts from the debit and credit categories of its accounts.

Even when reduced car production during the oil crisis rapidly cut into capital, suppressed capital investment and increased profitability led to a recovery, and capital exceeded 300 billion yen at the end of June 1977. Financial profits during the same period reached 45 billion yen. As a result, while the technical and production departments were working hard to cut costs through kaizen, *the accounting department was making efforts to put every bit of surplus capital to profitable use. Debt repayment and the redemption of company bonds led to a decreased interest burden, and this, coupled with increased profits, built a structure of profits outside of sales. The significance of this becomes increasingly evident in a period of low economic growth.*

Yasuhiro Monden, in his *Toyota Management System* (Productivity Press, 1993. tr. Bruce Talbot, pp. 26–27), analyzes Toyota's financial activities as follows:

1. To a very large extent, Toyota has tended to procure capital through so-called internal capital, which consists largely of retained profits and depreciation expenses. Even when Toyota turns to external sources to procure capital, such procurement is usually covered by owner's capital (stock) increases and convertible bonds. Consequently, we can recognize how Toyota has remained firmly committed to meeting its own capital needs in line with its policy of debt-free management.
2. To maintain and expand its capital from retained profits, Toyota has emphasized its positive support for plant investment, new car development funding, and investment in support of affiliated companies.

Nevertheless, Toyota has also recognized the need for an external security net for its main business, which is very sensitive to economic downturns. Therefore, it has also pursued capital operations outside its main business that can be counted upon to remain profitable regardless of conditions affecting the automobile industry. Such operations have concentrated on investing in negotiable deposits; temporary bonds, large-sum, variable-interest time deposits; and other investment vehicles that offer safe, reliable, and high-yield returns. Toyota has been conspicuous for its strong aversion to stock market investments. This conservative approach is seen as part of Toyota's staunch policy of putting its main business before all other considerations.

3. When increased investments toward tangible, fixed assets cannot be covered by Toyota's internal capital, Toyota has tended to liquidate some of its massive securities holdings.

4. Whenever Toyota has found itself with excess capital, it has tended to channel such capital toward further investments in support of affiliated companies or for acquiring more securities.

5. Whenever Toyota's main business has floundered amid depressed business conditions, Toyota has eased off on its tangible fixed assets investments and support for affiliated companies.

Another point bears mentioning here. A major contributor to capital creation at Toyota is the fact that the Toyota Production System cuts stocks of materials, parts, work-in-process, and finished goods to a strict minimum. There is, consequently, very little capital invested and stagnation in inventory assets.

In all probability, the foresight of Taizo Ishida is responsible for Toyota's financial health. In fact, the prototype of Toyota's financial system emerged from a combination of Sakichi Toyoda's formative experience of starting a company with other people's capital and from Taizo Ishida's post-World War II experience of being "penniless, pitiable and nearly reduced to tears."

Below, accompanied by quotes from Taizo Ishida, are Toyota's financial rules as summarized by Yoshimasa Kunisaki in his book, *Toyota's Rules of Management* (1979).

Financial Rule 1

Know that all loans are fearsome enemies.

> *"No enemy is more terrible than money, and no friend is more trustworthy. Other people's money—borrowed money—quickly turns into*

an enemy. Money is a trustworthy ally only when it is your own; only when you earn it yourself."

Financial Rule 2

If you have money left over, turn as much of it as possible back into equipment to raise the efficiency of your machines.

"Leftover money should be returned to capital. Increasing productivity through headcount is wrong. Production improvement always has to be achieved by raising the efficiency of machines."

Financial Rule 3

Always be prepared to welcome good fortune or luck.

"Good fortune or luck isn't simply a matter of chance. What makes for good fortune is always being prepared for it."[14]

Financial Rule 4

In using capital, always expect the worst.

"A manager should always manage under the presumption that the worst will happen; that the hard times will last all year."

Financial Rule 5

The bigger the company gets, the more you should cut expenses.

"This isn't a point one needs to drive home to salaried workers, but sales people need to have the discipline to maintain the same lifestyle with the same salary no matter how much sales go up."

During the period of the bubble economy, a prominent economics commentator observed that "any company that doesn't get into money management when it has 2 trillion yen of surplus capital is a fossil."

"Toyota is a manufacturing company," Eiji Toyoda retorted. "We don't need to make money in high-risk, high-return investments." After the collapse of the bubble it became clear which of them was right.

Hiroshi Okuda recalls that Eiji Toyoda "taught me that stocks are sometimes high and sometimes low."

Clearly, Taizo Ishida's lessons are still very much alive.

We see Ishida's words as being passed down, not by some oral tradition, but as documents within Toyota. Examples are the *Financial Man-*

agement Regulations, which codify the methods analyzed by Yasuhiro Monden, and the *Guide to Financial Management*, which records things Ishida actually said, words that would be impossible to transmit accurately by word of mouth.

MANAGING LABOR

Labor management encompasses such matters as hiring; employment, education and training, personnel, wages, welfare programs, and labor-management relations. Toyota's practices in many of these areas are distinctive, but in this section we will deal with career training and personnel management, two topics directly related to skills and motivation.

Career Training

Motivation

Table 3.2 compares levels of education of members of the board at Toyota, Nissan, and Honda.

Since it adopted a system of "corporate officers" in 1999, the Nissan Motor Company has very few board members, so a strict comparison is not possible. Still, the proportion of Nissan board members who graduated from the University of Tokyo is quite high. As a matter of interest, the proportion of University of Tokyo graduates among the 44 board members in 1998 was 45.5 percent. This is a historical tendency at Nissan. Before Carlos Ghosn, the current president, four generations of Nissan presidents had graduated from the University of Tokyo. Ironically, in 1999, when Nissan came under the umbrella of downgraded Renault capital, the front page of the *Asahi Shimbun* (March 28) mocked the weaknesses of "MITI, the Industrial Bank and Tokyo University."

For firms of their size, there are few University of Tokyo graduates sitting on the boards of directors at Toyota and Honda. Honda's nearly ten percent of high school graduates is noteworthy as well.

Toyota and Honda differ substantially from one another in terms of management policies and vehicle development aims, but they appear to have similar views on training. For each of these companies, human motivation, or "drawing out willingness," is central.

With the knowledge and grades one acquires at school of little use in the corporate world, it is *willing* people who carry a company forward. Table 3.2 probably looks the way it does because Toyota and Honda put their energies into developing and training willing people rather than into fussing over report cards.

Table 3.2 Educational Levels of Members of the Board (as of November 2002)				
	University of Tokyo Graduates	Other University Graduates	High School Graduates	Non-Japanese	Total
Toyota	10 (15.6%)	54 (84.4%)	0	0	64
Nissan	13 (48.1%)	14 (51.9%)	0	0	27
Honda	4 (9.8%)	33 (80.4%)	4 (9.8%)	0	41

Soichiro Honda created mechanisms for encouraging generations of willing people. His "Failure Prize," which awards one million yen annually to an employee who takes up a major challenge but fails is but one example. Eiji Toyoda declared in no uncertain terms that "the cardinal aim of personnel management is to motivate each person via the understanding that comes of education," and he worked to have that ethos permeate the entire organization.

The phrase, "cultivating people"[15] ordinarily means raising skill levels, but at Toyota, *hitozukuri* refers to the same thing that Eiji Toyoda talked about, i.e., motivating people. This is accomplished by a psychological approach, with education and training only one means among many. Managers and more experienced employees in Toyota are always asking themselves how to motivate people and are always looking for ways to maintain contact with junior colleagues.

Indeed, many aspects of Toyota's cultivation of people suggest a psychological approach. Whether consciously or unconsciously, Toyota freely uses a string of behaviorist theories such as Maslow's five-stage Hierarchy of Needs, McGregor's Theory X and Theory Y, Herzberg's Motivation-Hygiene Theory, Argyris' Immaturity-Maturity Theory, and various industrial psychology theories from the past few years as well as counseling and coaching theories that have recently been in the limelight. One of the points we would most like to emphasize in this book is the importance of using psychological approaches to increase the motivation of all employees.

Motivation lies at the root of Toyota's personnel management. With this in mind, we would like to turn to Toyota's education and training system.

The Education and Training System

Table 3.3 show Toyota's "Three forums for skill development."

"In the execution of work" means on-the-job training and (2) "group education" refers to systematic in-house education consisting primarily of off-the-job training (3) "Autonomous activities." refers to the informal education that was once the foundation of Toyota's personnel management.

On-the-Job Training (OJT)

OJT occupies the core of training activities at Toyota. It is supported by the personnel system and by group education, and these three elements function as one to promote effective training.

OJT may be defined as education and training in which a superior systematically and deliberately imparts to a subordinate knowledge, skills, problem-solving capabilities, and attitudes necessary for the job. OJT is conducted in four steps:

Step 1: Hold preliminary discussions with the person to be trained in order to inspire him to want to learn (motivation).

Step 2: Prepare learning materials, locations, and trainers. Rehearse the training session.

Step 3: In the actual training session, train by first demonstrating and then observing the trainee performing the task.

Step 4: Once the training is completed, assess what has been learned and repeat training if necessary.

Toyota and its affiliated companies post OJT Status Maps on their shopfloors that make it clear that OJT is being carried out in a planned and deliberate way.

The planned OJT described above is not carried out to the exclusion of everyday OJT. Toyota supervisors will toss out the following sorts of questions to employees while the latter are working:

1. How do you perform this job?
2. How do you know you're doing the job correctly?

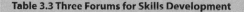

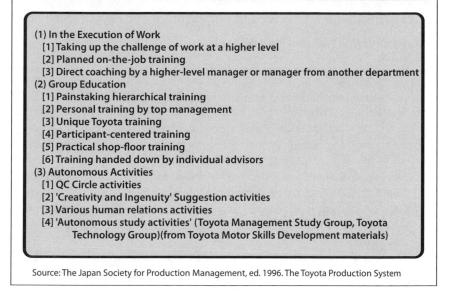

Table 3.3 Three Forums for Skills Development

(1) In the Execution of Work
  [1] Taking up the challenge of work at a higher level
  [2] Planned on-the-job training
  [3] Direct coaching by a higher-level manager or manager from another department
(2) Group Education
  [1] Painstaking hierarchical training
  [2] Personal training by top management
  [3] Unique Toyota training
  [4] Participant-centered training
  [5] Practical shop-floor training
  [6] Training handed down by individual advisors
(3) Autonomous Activities
  [1] QC Circle activities
  [2] 'Creativity and Ingenuity' Suggestion activities
  [3] Various human relations activities
  [4] 'Autonomous study activities' (Toyota Management Study Group, Toyota
        Technology Group)(from Toyota Motor Skills Development materials)

Source: The Japan Society for Production Management, ed. 1996. The Toyota Production System

3. How do you know that, when you're done, you haven't made any mistakes?
4. How do you handle problems when they come up?
   (Bowen, Kent et al. 1999. "Decoding the DNA of the Toyota Production System." *Harvard Business Review*, September–October).

Every businessperson—and not just shopfloor operators—ought to be able to answer these questions. Yet one wonders how many really can do so with accuracy. On the shopfloor, the answers will be provided in the form of (1) written procedures, (2) control points and inspection points, (3) control charts, and (4) procedures to follow in case of abnormalities. With these as a reference, one should be able to answer on one's own. And the quality of the work should rise markedly.

An examination of the data suggests that, even at Toyota, OJT does not always go smoothly in administrative and engineering areas. In most companies, in fact, OJT seems not to progress well in environments where work is not as routine as it is on the factory shopfloor. OJT in such cases has a tendency to turn into a sort of pre-modern "master and disciple" pair coaching.

Truly effective OJT (even in administrative or technical areas), requires constructing an OJT Promotion Map for everyone, preparing written procedures for the four OJT steps mentioned above, and insisting that they be used. Each department, moreover, needs to manage an OJT plan and track its OJT status, and the company as a whole needs to hold OJT reporting sessions and OJT assemblies.

Group Education (off-the-job training)

The following are distinctive characteristics of Toyota's system of group education:

- Education is fundamentally in-house. The human resource development department independently prepares a plan, arranges trainers to come from inside and outside the company, and implements the training. Even when educational programs developed outside the company are used, they are customized for Toyota. Toyota keeps its educational competence from deteriorating by implementing training plans on its own even when the content of the education is outsourced. The Toyota principle of self-reliance, evident in the manufacture of automobiles, also applies to education.
- That said, Toyota actively uses external education organizations. The company is careful to keep up with progressive educational methods.
- The company organizes courses (Critical Job Professional Seminars) that are expected to provide training for professional management as well as skills transmission in the workplace. These Critical Job Professional Seminars are classes in which managers transmit some of their own professional expertise to their subordinates at the chief clerk level and below.
- Training mechanisms are set up to take new employees in administrative and engineering areas and quickly make them into first-rate business-people and "Toyota people" who pledge allegiance to Toyota.
- In order to cultivate broad perspectives in its managers, Toyota organizes management lectures and exchanges, with a variety of industries and with the National Personnel Authority.
- The Toyota Production System is, of course, registered as a formal subject in the training curriculum. This training is given to managers in administrative and engineering posts as well as to technical managers.
- QC education, as one would expect, is extensive.
- Language education is popular, reflecting the current era of internationalization. In 1998, Toyota executives held discussions with professors from the Wharton School to construct a training program and launched a management school of short-term overseas seminars to train internationalists. This management school is another vehicle for spreading the Toyota way throughout the organization.
- Toyota provides training to assist customers and others outside the company.

Each person at Toyota undergoes approximately three days of group training annually. If we take into account the workplace training conducted in addition to this, the total comes to 6 days. Roughly 3 percent of labor hours, in other words, are invested in training.

Toyota also has a system of training for its executive staff, which can be loosely defined as a merit promotion encouragement system. Mechanisms are in place to help staff understand what they need to learn before they can qualify for merit promotions and to inculcate staff with the sense of responsibility they will need after such promotions. These mechanisms seem to constitute a thoughtfully elaborated system rooted in the psychology of cultivating a sense of mission that draws on both the desire for promotion and the satisfaction of having been promoted.

Autonomous Activities

We turn now to education through autonomous activities, the last category in Table 3.3. We find QC circles and the suggestion (*teian*) system here because at Toyota, the purpose of both of these systems is to develop personnel and skills rather than to make work more rational or more efficient.

Masao Nemoto, formerly in charge of Toyota Motor Corporation's TQC Promotion Office, puts it this way:

> *Improvements by shopfloor managers contribute far more to productivity and quality than do QC Circles or* kaizen *suggestion systems. The ratio between the former and the latter is about 80:20. Improvement (kaizen) activities were clearly worked out as the mission for foremen and team leaders from around 1955. Kaizen is their job and they are charged with making major improvements themselves. The basic idea is that you shouldn't be asking QC Circles to do the work of foremen and team leaders.*

When Toyota's suggestion (*teian*) system grew in the 1980s, many suggestions would be in progress simultaneously. Toyota consequently modified the system so that job improvement suggestions were linked to real skills development.

The designation, "Various human relations activities" in Table 3.3 refers to four things:

1. In-house group activities
2. PT (personal touch) activities
3. Activities to make company dormitories more cheerful
4. Toyota Club activities

Criticism has recently been leveled at the idea of exploiting informal organizations by formalizing them. This practice no longer suits the times and one sees fewer instances where it occurs. Nonetheless, it appears that informal organizations still play a quiet role in training at Toyota.

In Chapter 2, we discussed autonomous study activities, including the Toyota Management Study Group and the Toyota Technology Group, shown in Figure 3.3.

Personnel Management

Two effective means of imbuing all employees with company policies and goals are slow-acting motivation building and fast-acting personnel evaluations. Companies that suffer because their employees do not necessarily do things the way they are told or do not spring into action when the whistle blows should immediately link personnel ratings and company policies.

Toyota adopted the management by function system shown in Figure 3.5 when it introduced TQC in the 1960s. This was a "one man, multi-boss" arrangement, meaning that an employee's personnel evaluations would be made by more than one person. When the company brought in design reviews in the 1970s, it set up a system of conducting personnel evaluations that actively addressed design reviews (see Chapter 4). The introduction of the Development Center system in 1992 gave a "mother department" authority over personnel in other departments (see Chapter 2). The personnel evaluation system at Toyota, then, developed in step with major organizational innovations.

In his book entitled *The Toyota System*[16] (1998), Osamu Katayama offers the following analysis of recent movements in Toyota's personnel system:

- The "challenge program" launched by Toyota in July 1996 is a forum in which diverse people use their creativity in diverse activities to build a vital company. Against a background of structural change in the environment, the program places diversity and creativity at its core.
- Toyota has incorporated three pillars into its challenge program. The first is a revolution in the cultivation and use of people. As an example of this new orientation in personnel development, Toyota has worked out a progressive policy of enhancing labor flexibility to cultivate and support employee activities even outside the company. The second pillar is a revolution in the awareness and work methods of administrative and engineering personnel. This incorporates specific policies, for example, a system for self-study and training, casual days, the STRETCH individual development program, the U-TIME system, and flexible work hours. The third pillar is a revolution in organization and management. This

means better matching the framework of the organization to the content of the work, enhancing competitiveness in new businesses as well as old ones, and actively decentralizing with a view to improving service. Toyota assigns people full-time to limited-term project teams, moreover, to resolve issues that cut across the organization or to address topics of major importance or urgency.

- Personnel evaluation criteria are made explicit. For managers, for example, task creativity counts for 20 percent; task execution, 30 percent; organizational management, 20 percent; use of human resources, 20 percent; and popularity, 10 percent. Evaluation criteria for staff members assign 50 percent of the score to professional knowledge and ability and the remaining 50 percent to the same categories used to evaluate managers: creativity, execution, management, use of human resources, and popularity.

- Three features distinguish the promotion system introduced by Toyota. First, it abolishes chronological promotions in favor of a system in which employees always have the opportunity to move upward. Second, it evaluates each person in terms suitability, competence, and results. Promotions at the class-2 level of key posts and above are different. For managers, once need has been thoroughly investigated, placement is determined by fitting the right person to the right position. For staff positions, determinations are made by matching appropriate placement and remuneration to past performance.

- It is worth noting that multifaceted assessments form a subsystem of evaluations for promotion. These complement evaluations in areas that are difficult for superiors to judge and involve assessments from subordinates. One feature of this system is that assessments from other managers are called upon to sort out discrepancies among views coming from subordinates.

As we can see, Toyota is revising traditional Japanese employment practices such as lifetime employment, the seniority system, and corporate welfare at a rapid pace. But rather than trying to repudiate traditional Japanese management practices, it is refining them in order to activate its human resources for a new era.

In 1998, when a U.S. bond rating service threatened to downgrade Toyota on the pretext that it uses a lifetime employment system, then president of Toyota Hiroshi Okuda made headlines by protesting. "It doesn't make sense," Okuda said, "for Japanese companies and culture to be measured arbitrarily according to the culture of an American bond rating company. It especially doesn't make sense to reject lifetime employment."

Lifetime employment means just that—a guarantee that the company will not fire its employees. For managers, this is the highest moral imperative. The existence of this imperative is what makes managers strive desperately to be profitable. It is linked to their morale. Toyota may be revising its lifetime employment, seniority and corporate welfare systems, but it is inconceivable that it would abandon them completely.

Tokuichi Uranishi, the head of Toyota's Corporate Planning Division, puts it this way: "There is talk of the collapse of 'lifetime', but I prefer to keep thinking of this company as one where people would like to be for a long time."

THE OFFICE WORK MANAGEMENT SYSTEM

By "office work," I refer to work that mediates horizontal and vertical activities in an organization. Organizational activities would be impossible if there were no office work, and the organization itself could not exist. Toyota conceives of office work in this way and devotes extraordinary energy to its management. Figure 3.10 shows a schematic view of Toyota's office work management system.

In this section, I will look primarily at three aspects of Toyota's office work management system: the management of office work (office work efficiency), the management of documentation, and, within this second area, the management of standard instructions (job standards).

Managing Office Work (office work efficiency)

Toyota began coming to grips with the management of office work around 1950, at a time when the concepts of office work and office work management were as yet undeveloped. What follows is an overview of the history of office work management at Toyota taken from *Toyota: The First 20 Years* (1958).

With preparations for rebuilding the company complete in 1950, two managing directors with engineering backgrounds, Eiji Toyoda and Shoichi Saito, toured automobile industries in the United States and learned that mechanization was surprisingly advanced in America, even in office work. Astonishing statistical and accounting machines were in use everywhere, and office work proceeded with great speed and accuracy. As soon as the two executives returned to Japan, they directed the Management Research Office to begin looking into introducing IBM, Remington, Land, and other statistical and accounting machines into the company. As a result of their investigations, they realized that the organization of office work at Toyota was insufficiently rationalized and that no system suitable for mechanization

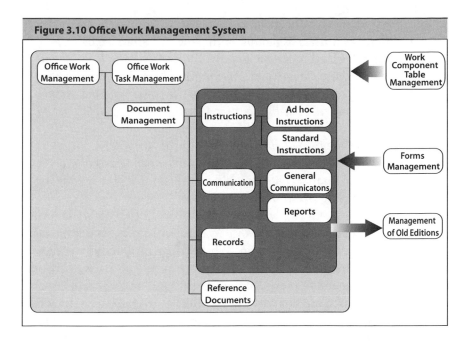

Figure 3.10 Office Work Management System

existed. *Mechanizing office work generally demands that office work organizations and procedures first be rationalized in such a way that they can be assigned to machines. The proper method is to wait until the work has been streamlined before you bring in machines. Rationalizing office work is not such a simple task, though. This is why Toyota, after various studies, decided to do things the other way around. It would be most effective, the thinking went, to introduce the machines first and use them to spur rationalization of the work. Fully expecting to have to pay a bit extra for the learning process, we signed a contract for two sets of IBM machines, including two brand-new accounting machines that had hardly been used in Japan at all.*

The mechanization of office work once more brought the problem of rationalizing work to the top of the agenda. The first issue we took on was the company-wide control and management of forms that, in a sense, constitute the tools and dies of office work. In early 1958, the Management Research Office collected forms from the entire company and inaugurated a system of form registration. The company laid a foundation for the use of the IBM machines by designating form managers for each department, plant, and section, laying out rules for forms and establishing criteria for form design.

Office work began to show its full potential once a balance was struck between technology and the work itself. While technologies advanced, office work always lagged far behind. In order to have office work improvements precede automatically, the Statistical Research Office (later the Management Research Office) took the lead in constructing a Business Component Table in May 1956. This table formed a basis for the rationalization of office work by specifying the components of the business itself in the same way that a parts table lays out the components of an automobile. Toyota put this table to regular use and completely revised it in May of each year. In order to promote rationalization, Toyota, in 1957, used the table as the basis of a Short Course on Flow Analysis that went a long way toward propagating the methods throughout the company.

All this took place soon after World War II, when office work management was still a new field in Japan. White-collar productivity is Japan's weak point even today, and in this context, the progressiveness of Toyota's office work management merits particular praise. The origins of Toyota's practices in this area are not well known, but, as we have seen, they take us back to Eiji Toyoda's visit to American automobile industries in 1950.

In the years since, Toyota has continued making improvements in office work, and has organized company-wide office work improvement events every ten years or so. In 1980, as we saw at the beginning of Chapter 2, for example, Toyota joined with one of Japan's top management consulting firms to improve office processes in its design department. The company implemented its C50 Campaign (to cut office work by 50 percent) in the second half of the 1980s and the NOW (New Office Working) 21 Campaign in the first half of the 1990s.

The Business Component Table described in *Toyota: The First Twenty Years* represents a critical concept in raising the efficiency of office work. A table of this sort, also known as an office work function system map, focuses on the work functions needed to achieve business goals and plots their cause-and-effect relationships on a tree diagram. In the sample table shown in Figure 3.11, for example, categories 1-3 give the structure of office work. At Toyota, this structure is uniform throughout the company up to category 3.

Below are five points highlighting the utility of standardizing the business component table:

1. *More efficient compilation of business component tables*
   A component table is drawn up whenever adjustments are made to the business. Standardizing the table saves work in constructing new ones.

2. *More effective organizational reform*

   One crucial point in constructing a business component table is to avoid being dragged down by current organizational structures. Functions always need to be developed according to what they should look like. At the same time, one needs to approach the current organization under the assumption that one is reorganizing it in accordance with the content of the business. Toyota's 1961 formulation of rules for apportioning office work on the basis of a component table (*Toyota: The First 30 Years*) raises the possibility of using such tables to change organizational systems.

3. *More efficient management of office work*

   A table of parts shows an automobile's manufacturing processes in a tree structure. Such tables make it possible to produce cars efficiently. As *Toyota: A History of the First 20 Years* points out, making administrative tasks more efficient demands a component table of business work analogous to a parts table. Standardizing the business task elements by the unit of business work component that appear in the right half of Figure 3.11—e.g., written procedure numbers, frequency, time required, input destination, input information, output destination, and output information —provides ready firepower to new and temporary workers and gives clues to improvements based on what is overall the most suitable thinking.

4. *Standardization of the management of data and research materials*

   Since common business components are used to manage items such as business standards, data, research materials, business plans, and minutes, the interrelationships among these materials can be accessed automatically.

5. *Linkages among different business functions*

   Different business functions are tied together by common business structures, so investigations can easily be made into compatibilities, balances, trade-offs, etc. As shown in Figure 3.12, for example, the component tables of business work on the leftmost of each of the quality assurance work and the cost management work tie together two different functions: quality function and cost function. This example shows only the first category of the business; ordinarily detail would extend to categories 2 or 3. Consequently, at each stage between product planning and sales and service, it is easy to investigate compatibilities, balances, and trade-offs between the distinct functions of quality and cost.

Figures 3.6 (the quality assurance system) and 3.9 (the cost planning management system) may appear to have no relation to one another, but in fact, as Figure 3.12 shows, they are tightly bound to one another by business structures.

If we take all management functions—cost, quality, engineering, personnel, information, etc.—and write them out in terms of their common

Figure 3.11 Sample Office Work Component Table

Work Component			Work Content					
Class 1	Class 2	Class 3	Procedure No.	Frequency	Time needed	Input @ Input info.	Output @ Output info	...
Sales and Marketing								
	Sales Planning							
		Basic Strategy						
		Market Research						
		Product Planning						
		Distribution Planning						
		Marketing Plan						
		Profit Plan						
		Advertising & Publicity						
		Results Management						
	Sales Promotion							
		Sales Promotion						
		Market Development						
		Negotiations						
		Product Establishment						
		Price Setting						
	Order Management							
		Order Processing						
		Production demand						
		Shipping Arrangements						
	Sales Recovery							
		Sales Processing						
		Invoice Processing						
		Recovery Processing						
		Conveyance						
	Direct Sales							
		Corporate Sales						
Service								
	Service Planing							

business components, the linkages among them automatically become accessible, and one sweep of the eye suffices to reveal their comprehensive relationships. The result will be improved management efficiency.

In his book, *The Evolution of a Production System*[17] (1997), Takahiro Fujimoto cites three distinctive characteristics of the competitive strength (or organizational routines) of Toyota-style development and production: (1) overcoming trade-offs, (2) flexibility, and (3) organizational learning and *kaizen*. Toyota did not create the first of these, overcoming trade-offs, out of thin air; it was a concept that evolved from the use of business component tables.

This, then, is what it means when *Toyota: The First 20 Years* tells us that Toyota created a foundation of business rationalization so that office work improvements would progress automatically. We can only marvel that this point of view emerged a mere ten years after the end of World War II. One clearly sees the fruits of work conducted at the time by the Toyota Management Study Group, whose activities centered on studying American office management (see the section on Views of Work in Chapter 2).

Managing Documents

In modern terms, we might refer to "document management" as "knowledge management." Knowledge first becomes useable by an organization when documentation turns the *tacit* knowledge of individuals into formal knowledge.

In this section, we will address the management of documents other than business standards. Since business standards play a critical role in Toyota's management system, we will deal with them in the following section.

All companies are aware that assistants manage documents. In the 21st century, however, when information and knowledge management can determine the fortunes of a company, that is simply not enough. Toyota invests enormous energy in the management of documents. Toyota tackled the rationalization of office work soon after the end of World War II, but it was not until the 1960s (with the introduction of TQC and the competition for the Deming Prize) that Toyota came to grips with reorganizing document management in a serious and systematic way.

An outline of Toyota's document management activities at the time is presented below:

Form Management (standardization of forms)

Documents converted to forms are sometimes called the tools and dies of office work. Standards should be imposed for office procedures that follow no standard, and documents that have no fixed format should be formalized. These measures will contribute to solving four problems simultaneously: expense, labor, time, and accuracy. In the same way that com-

Figure 3.12 The Tie-In of Different Functions by Job Composition

Job	Quality Assurance Work		Job	Cost Management Work
Product Planning	1. Forecast demand and project market share. 2. Meet market quality expectations. a. Set and allocate appropriate quality and cost targets. b. Prevent recurrence of major quality problems.		Product Planning	1. Set target costs and target investment costs based on new product planning and long-range profit plan. 2. Allocate target costs to departments responsible for design. 3. Allocate target investment costs to departments responsible for equipment.
Product Design	1. Design trials. a. Match with quality targets. b. Test and study performance, function and reliability, etc. 2. Design full-scale production. (verify necessary QA conditions)		Product Design	1. Estimate costs on the basis of prototype drawings. 2. Assess probability of achieving cost targets. 3. Conduct VE in order to minimize the gap between target costs and estimated costs.
Production Preparation	1. Arrange processes to fulfill design quality. 2. Create appropriate vehicle inspection protocols. 3. Assess full-scale production trials. 4. Ensure process capacities.		Production Preparation	1. Estimate costs based on process plan and equipment plan. 2. Assess probability of achieving cost targets. 3. Implement measures to minimize gap between the two. 4. Assess the economy of capital investment plans. 5. Assess the economy of production plan, production terms and sourcing.
Purchasing	1. Confirm qualitative and quantitative supplier capabilities. 2. Verify product quality through first-off inspections. 3. Support enhancement of suppliers' QA systems.		Purchasing	1. Assess economy of order plans and purchasing plans. 2. Control purchased part prices. 3. Improve purchased part prices.
Fabrication	1. Bring fabrication quality into conformity with quality standards. 2. Ensure suitable process management. 3. Maintain process and machine capacities.		Fabrication	1. Encourage cost maintenance and cost improvements. a. Manage fixed cost budget. b. Improve key project costs. c. Raise cost consciousness among employees.
Inspection	1. Check fabrication quality through first-off inspections. 2. Determine whether vehicles can be dispatched or not.		Inspection	1. (Same as above).
Sales & Service	1. Prevent quality deterioration during packing, storage and transport. 2. Train and conduct PR on correct use and maintenance. 3. Check new vehicles. 4. Analyze and feed back quality information.		Sales & Service	1. Measure and conduct overall assessment of actual new product costs. 2. Participate in analyses and deliberations of work checks, Cost Function Council, Cost Council and various committees.

Job Composition Ties in Quality Functions and Cost Functions

Source: Aoki, Shigeru. Amended and revised from "Cross-Functional Management for Executives (2)." Quality Management, March 1981.

puters are used to organize office data into databases, formalized documents are used to rationalize office work.

Document Circulation Rules

- Documents should flow in sequence only to people directly concerned and some work should be accomplished at each step in the flow process. (Do not transmit information that has no added value.)
- Have specialists transport documents.
- All documents should be handed over to the last management station in a timely manner.

Filing

Document classification numbers determine the success or failure of filing. At Toyota, such numbers derive from business component tables. Categories 1 to 3 are uniform across the entire company and individual departments draw up categories 4 and 5 as appropriate for filing or other managerial work. While the documents department from time to time conducts document audits, departments where the state of filing is poor are invariably those that have not made structures below category 4.

The System of In-house Technical Reports

Products have to be winners in the eyes of users if the company is to survive. To achieve this, technical product data needs to be collected, recorded, and fully reflected in the next generation of products. Engineering standards are a manufacturer's most valuable technical knowledge asset, but they are only effective when they are backed up by technical reports. Technical reports must be managed with the same care as engineering standards are. Toyota's tradition of technical development is built on this kind of thinking.

Toyota prescribed rules for technical reports in 1965 and at that time put together a company-wide system—still in use today—which includes such elements as a report structure for managing technical reports (hierarchically), data index criteria, and usage procedures. Nowadays all technical reports are kept in electronic form and from within Toyota and the Toyota group these can be freely accessed or subjected to analysis by data sampling or other statistical means. (See the section on using statistical methods in this chapter.)

Managing Business Standards

Knowledge management breaks down into four phases in accordance with Ikujiro Nonaka's Theory of Knowledge Creation:

1. Acquire tacit knowledge in reporting sessions or study groups (socialization)
2. Convert to explicit knowledge and common property (externalization)
3. Combine with prior knowledge in the organization to generate new explicit knowledge (combination)
4. Individually digest shared formal knowledge and make it one's own tacit knowledge (internalization)

Since results are generated by people, the most important step in this process seems to be (4) internalization, but since internalized knowledge moves with individuals, it cannot be used by an organization. This is why the highest form of organizational knowledge is the explicit knowledge created as a result of phase (3), combination, in other words, standards.

As the highest form of knowledge, standards include both goal-seeking processes and what-if mechanisms. Knowledge management, then, can be said to be a theoretical extension of procedures for highlighting and learning standards in an organized way.

Table 1.2 provided an outline of Toyota's business standards (or, in Toyota jargon, *kitei*, or regulations). From this outline, we can derive a comprehensive picture of the categories, systems, and content of the company's business standards. Table 1.2 assigns identifying marks to distinguish between standards that were developed before and after the introduction of TQC in 1961. Whereas most pre-TQC standards were established at the level of the shopfloor operations, we can see that many organizational and management standards were formulated after TQC.

When Toyota received the Deming Prize in 1965, there may have been some sense that the company had been engaging in the mass production of inferior business standards. When the Deming Prize Committee directed Toyota to overhaul its regulations, however, the company published this goal as part of its annual policy and inaugurated a system of regulation audits. Development ensued in both the quantity and the content of regulations.

Estimating Toyota's total number of regulations from sources such as Table 1.2 and the company's organizational charts, there are probably some 200 rules, an equal number of prescriptions, and perhaps 3,000 guidelines. If we include lower-level procedures, norms, and criteria, the total probably comes to tens or hundreds of thousands.

As a matter of principle, Toyota's business standards are not written out in long-winded prose, but expressed by management system maps such as the one shown in Figure 1.6. Explanations, attached to business standards, record such information as the standards' backgrounds, histories, bases, reference data, and issues for the future. The main text is a conclusion, in other words, and the explanation is process information. These explanations constitute important data that can be used as educational material, matter for discussion, or material for getting at the root of improvements.

Looking at these structures, systems and achievements of Toyota's systems for the management of documents and regulations, we can appreciate the astuteness of an assertion made by one of the elders of a top Japanese consulting firm previously cited in Chapter 2, i.e., that Toyota spends five times as much on data management as other companies do. Toyota operates on the premise that slashing resources that go to the production line while investing five times as much as other companies do to manage data and office work is the way to win.

COMPUTER SYSTEM MANAGEMENT

Toyota's massive computer system is described in detail in *Toyota: A History of the First 40 Years* (1978), *Toyota: A History of the First 50 Years* (1987), and *Automobiles and Information Processing*, published by the Toyota Engineering Society in 1989. Three aspects of this system promise to be of increasing importance: PDM (product development management), SCM (supply chain management), and the company-wide information system.

PDM (Product Data Management)

Designers ordinarily work according to the following process:

1. Receive product specification information—including product summary, destination, performance, and equipment specifications—from the product planning division.
2. Bring together the functional components (functional product components) needed to implement product specifications, and define for each component such characteristics as performance, function, and mass. This information is included in what is called product function information.
3. Construct a manufacturing sequence table (parts lineup) of prototype parts and production parts and use drawings and individual design documents to specify manufacturing methods, including materials, processing, and assembly techniques. Next, they release this information to parts suppliers, manufacturing, etc., via the prototype and purchasing

departments. This information, including the parts lineup, is referred to as parts specification information.

As shown in Figure 3.13, the relationships among product specification information, product function information, and parts specification information form a complex matrix. So, to support the designing, the manufacturing industry, as shown in Figure 3.14, puts together databases of these three types of information and develops application programs based on them. This total process is called Product Data Management, or PDM.

As Figure 3.14 indicates, Toyota has two computer programs in the area of PDM: TIS (for managing product specification information and prototype parts specification information) and SMS (for managing production parts specification information). Product function information cannot be managed in an integrated, company-wide system, and may be in designers' heads, handled by individual designers on personal computers, or managed separately as CAD/CAE data by the design department. Toyota's system, in other words, does not provide complete support to the design function.

Other companies have built systems similar to Toyota's TIS and SMS. There is nothing unique about these systems, so we will omit further discussion of them and turn, instead, to product function information.

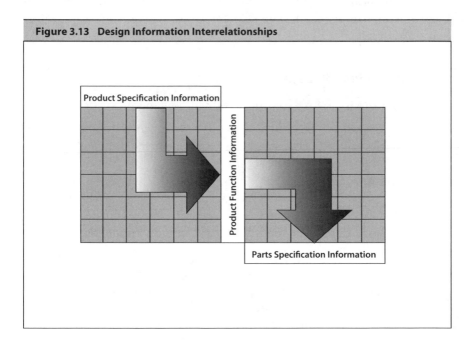

Figure 3.13   Design Information Interrelationships

Product Specification Information

Product Function Information

Parts Specification Information

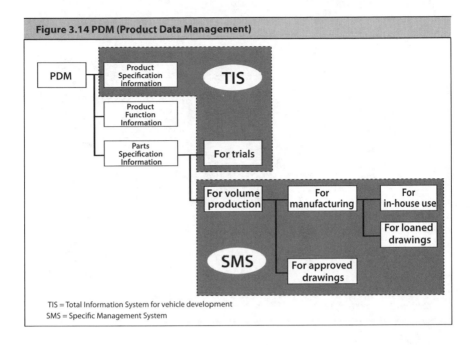

Figure 3.14 PDM (Product Data Management)

TIS = Total Information System for vehicle development
SMS = Specific Management System

In a paper entitled "Toward the Construction of an Information Basis for Automobile Manufacturing in the 21st Century," published in the January 1996 issue of the Japanese–language *Review of Automotive Technology*, the journal of the Society of Automotive Engineers of Japan, Satoshi Kuroiwa of Toyota Motor Corporation's IT Engineering Division describes a future PDM system for integrating data in the new vehicle development process. He sketches this out as a vision for all companies because the realization of such a system, shown in Figure 3.15, can be expected to have a revolutionary impact on quality, cost, and timing in new product development.

Kuroiwa looks to CALS (Commerce at Light Speed) as an enabler for PDM. CALS is an international computer data standard currently under development. Even before CALS is realized, though, establishing [robust] management of product models and of technical information for the development process holds the key to making a future PDM system like the one depicted a reality. Product models and technical information for the development process refer to the product function information (including functional product components) shown in Figure 3.14.

If development process information is managed in an organized fashion, it can be consulted rapidly and appropriately when needed for model

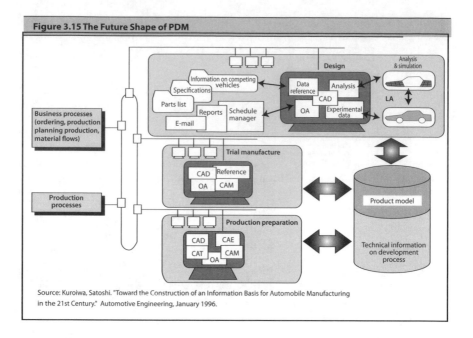

Figure 3.15 The Future Shape of PDM

Source: Kuroiwa, Satoshi. "Toward the Construction of an Information Basis for Automobile Manufacturing in the 21st Century." Automotive Engineering, January 1996.

changes and minor changes. One can expect marked improvements in product development speed, built-in quality and cost, and efficient parts carryover. In recent years, all carmakers have reportedly begun to focus on the challenge of cost management in the early stages of development, before parts specifications have been determined. Cost control becomes possible from an early stage if product function information, put together before parts specifications are determined, is managed in an organized way. Reforming and speeding up the development process has become central to competitive strategies in recent years and systematizing product function information is an important strategic theme.

In the automobile industry, one seldom, if ever, hears of companies that are managing product function information in an organized and effective way. Nissan and Ford began managing product function information in the mid-1980s, but functions and parts ended up jumbled together and true management seemed impossible. The sheer quantity of component parts in an automobile means that repeated design changes occur at the development stage, and this makes company-wide management of product function information difficult.

A decade has passed since Kuroiwa published his paper. There is still no unified management of engineering data in which CAD data, which is typical product function information, is not linked to parts specification information. Even now, it appears that Toyota has not developed a company-wide system to manage product function information.

How companies implement the sort of PDM shown in Figure 3.15 will be an important factor in their competitiveness.

SCM (Supply Chain Management)

There has been a great deal of talk in the past few years about supply chain management as a global standard for manufacturing industries in a new era. Dell Computer's supply chain management is often cited in such discussions. Dell's product inventory time—from receipt of an order until shipment—is only two days, which puts it far ahead of competitors like Hewlett Packard and Gateway (at both companies, product inventory time is a week). Dell has used its supply chain management as a weapon in a low-cost attack to drive the other two, formerly excellent companies, from the marketplace. The success or failure of supply chain management structures will soon determine the survival of companies throughout the manufacturing world.

SCM is a combination of Toyota's *keiretsu* strategy, M. E. Porter's value chain strategy, and Eliyahu Goldratt's Theory of Constraints. SCM arranges upstream and downstream organizations in a chain and globally optimizes quality, cost, timing, and quantities for all processes, from parts suppliers to sales outlets. To do this, it levels out the flow, both by feeding resources into the chain at the point where the most value is added and by solving problems at the bottleneck. Computer systems are indispensable tools.

Toyota began by moving toward SCM as a computer system in the 1980s, linking suppliers, Toyota itself, body makers, dealers, and the North American region with a Toyota Network System (TNS). Since the phrase, "supply chain management" did not exist at the time, Toyota referred to this process, which can be viewed as the prototype of SCM, as Production–Sale Integration. The overall structure of TNS in 1991 is shown in Figure 3.16.

Nineteen ninety-one was a time when networks were still in their infancy in Japan, so the satellite communications network seen in the figure indicates that the system was extraordinarily advanced for its time.

Toyota faced a number of challenges, including information systems issues (such as the standardization of communication systems) and concerns about how to deal with communication protocols. From a business point of view, there were additional challenges:

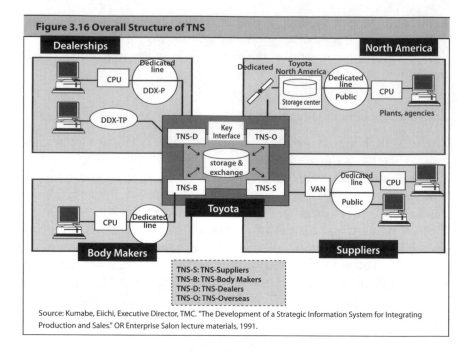

Figure 3.16 Overall Structure of TNS

TNS-S: TNS-Suppliers
TNS-B: TNS-Body Makers
TNS-D: TNS-Dealers
TNS-O: TNS-Overseas

Source: Kumabe, Eiichi, Executive Director, TMC. "The Development of a Strategic Information System for Integrating Production and Sales." OR Enterprise Salon lecture materials, 1991.

- The establishment of uniform and standard business protocols across the Toyota group
- Overall standardization of the Toyota group
- A revolutionary shift of criteria for evaluating the systematization of information, from costs and earnings to the concept of investment

The standardization of business protocols refers to standardizing the transactions (interfaces) among organizations. The fact that this emerged as an issue shows that within the Toyota group, nonvalue-adding conversion and processing were being performed by the receivers of information who were adapting it to their own organizations.

Overall standardization within the Toyota group means further standardizing areas in the Toyota group as a whole where work was not standardized. This shows that computerization was not reaching its full potential in places where work was insufficiently standardized.

Moving from costs and earnings to the concept of investment means evaluating information systems by opportunity creation rather than by efficiency. This hints at the degree to which Toyota sees opportunity creation in the field of SCM as its trump card.

A Company-wide Information System

In *Nikkei Information Strategies*[18] (October 2001), Susumu Miyoshi, a Toyota Motor Corporation executive vice president who is the company's Chief Information Officer noted:

> *The biggest problem with Toyota's information systems is that all the regions and companies have built different ones.*
>
> *We're in an age of furious change and it still takes a long time to close the monthly accounts.*
>
> *Unfortunately, other systems, like production management and materials sourcing and distribution, are in the same situation.*
>
> *When we developed systems in the past, we didn't look at how to link individual systems to the Toyota group's global information strategy.*
>
> *Frankly, a lot of people in Toyota management used to consider the information systems department to be no more than a team for processing business data. That was the past. Now we're in an age in which the activities of the information systems department can affect Toyota competitively.*
>
> *We repeat and explain that perspective, and in a variety of forums now, and the thinking of people in charge of shopfloor systems is changing fast. This gives us a foothold as we devote all our energies now to the current challenge of systems integration.*

Susumu Miyoshi describes Toyota's current system as a patchwork and indicates that improving the efficiency of its parts may not lead to a more efficient total system, but may even damage future prospects for systematization. In the area of PDM that we touched upon above, for example, the fact that SMS and TIS were set up without considering an overall PDM system now means not only that SMS and TIS do not work well with one another but that, together, they impede the systematization of product function information. Here, as in the case of SCM (integrating production and sales), the problem does not so much originate in the computer systems as it does from a lack of coordination and consolidation in the business. An information systems department regarded as no more than a business data processing team was in no position to take the initiative in revolutionizing or overhauling the business. Or the problem may have been that it intentionally avoided such issues. It shows, at any rate, that SCM still cannot operate at a satisfactory level in Toyota.

The fact that it takes more than a month to generate monthly balance sheets is a problem that exists everywhere, and Toyota has not managed to avoid this tendency. Improving such patchwork systems requires considerable effort, and because it is not considered a big problem, it is often put on the back burner. Toyota now realizes that the activities of the information systems department can affect it competitively, however, and it is looking to acquire new competitive strength by facing up to the difficult issue of rebuilding and integrating information systems throughout the company. Don't take your eyes off Toyota.

[N.B. The author is unable to locate the source of Takashi Sorimachi's paper, "*Environmental Change and the Development of Management Strategies*" (*Kankyo henka to keiei senryaku no tenkai*). Anyone with information on the matter is invited to contact the author.]

Endnotes

1. *Toyota Shisutemu no Genten.*
2. "Rigorous emphasis on check and action" later became part of Toyota's culture of follow-up and *yokoten*.
3. *Quality Control.*
4. *Seisan Shisutemu no Shinkaron.*
5. Toyota's quality assurance system is also described in an article by Ryosuke Ozaki, of the Toyota Motor Corporation's TQC Promotion Office, in the March 1993 issue of *Keiei Shisutemu* [*Management Systems*], a journal of the Japan Industrial Management Association. The reader is encouraged to refer to this as well as to Katsuyoshi Yamada's article. For an overall understanding of Toyota's quality assurance rules, these two articles, in conjunction with Shigeru Aoki's article, "Cross-Functional Management for Executives," published in *Hinshitsu Kanri* [*Quality Control*] (Feb–April, 1981), are highly recommended.
6. By "reference," I mean standards that should be challenged and improved.
7. In other words, the standard amount of raw material consumed per product per hour.
8. For details of Toyota's cost management system, it is worth consulting the Shigeru Aoki article, "Management by function for executives," that was cited in the section on management by function.
9. This is referred to in the "Emphasis on Theory" section of Chapter 2: The extension of the Maxcy-Silberston curve into parts.
10. The last five digits designate the specific part numbers.
11. This practice was the cause of the "Daihatsu lament" cited in the section on follow-up and *yokoten* in Chapter 2.
12. This may be seen as a system inspired by Toyoda's admonition to "write failure reports," cited in the section on perspectives on knowledge and documentation in Chapter 2.

13. Nowadays this procedure applies not just to key parts but to the management of all components.

14. Author's note: Ishida became president of Toyota in early 1950 when the company was near collapse as a result of its labor struggles. Toyota's fortunes recovered swiftly, when military procurement for the Korean War began immediately afterward, in June 1950. Ishida's assertion that "good fortune or luck isn't simply a matter of chance" was his response to the popular view that he had been lucky. The truth is that the military procurement boom was an opportunity that presented itself equally to all comers. What set Toyota apart from other companies was that Toyota knew what to do with the opportunity and that it took steps to prepare itself for the hard times that followed the boom.

15. *hitozukuri*, literally, "building people."

16. *Toyota no hoshiki.*

17. *Toyota Shisutemu Shinkaron.*

18. *Nikkei joho sutoratejii.*

—— 4 ——

Toyota's System of Production Functions

Production functions, as used here, are the series of process functions that, in a manufacturing industry, extend from research and development, through product planning, design and development, manufacture and sales, to handing over the product to the customer. This chapter looks at Toyota's production functions, with chapter sections following the numbering system shown on the production function system diagram in Figure 4.1.[1]

THE MARKETING SYSTEM

Product Policies

One important issue in the automotive marketplace concerns product mix strategy, i.e., how to structure products hierarchically and how to sustain derivative products. Establishing a product mix strategy makes it possible to draw in a broad range of customers with diverse values and to move customers to more luxurious vehicles as they advance in age and income. It makes it possible, in other words, to entice and embrace customers.

In strategic terms, Toyota pursued a fairly incoherent course of product development when it introduced the mid-size *Crown* in January 1955, the compact *Corona* in May 1957, and the low-priced *Publica* in January 1961. Afterwards, Toyota filled in the gaps in its vehicle lineup when it introduced a series of high-volume models starting with the launch of the *Corolla* in October 1966, followed by the *Carina*, the *Corolla Mark II*, and the *Vista/Camry*. Nowadays the product lineup is seamless and Toyota has put together a full line based on the idea of a product hierarchy.

This account suggests that something in Toyota's product strategy changed between the June 1961 launch of the *Publica* and the October 1966 introduction of the *Corolla*.

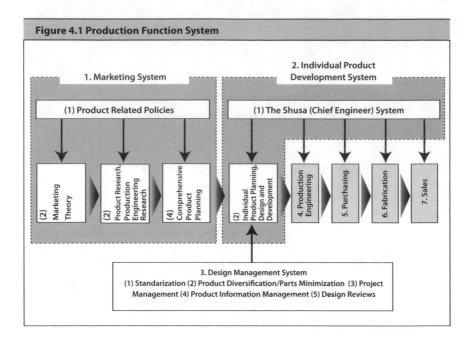

Figure 4.1 Production Function System

Akira Kawahara, former Toyota Motor Sales managing director and author of *The Essence of Competitivity*[2] (1995), tells a story that may explain the change:

I think it was the spring of 1964. I came across an article about former GM chairman Alfred Sloan's book, My Years with General Motors, *and immediately arranged with Toyota USA to get me a copy. The book taught us what we needed most to learn at precisely the moment we needed to learn it. It was published exactly at the time that Toyota's vehicle development had reached one set of goals and was groping around for where to go next.*

Sloan had to devote considerable effort to imposing coherent managerial control over an automobile company that had grown through a succession of mergers and consolidations. Since our aim was to grow bigger in the future, we thought we might perhaps be able to do better than GM by a careful reading of Sloan's struggles, experience and warnings. In developing new vehicles, for example, or in setting up a new sales network, we thought we could plan our expansion if we put a priority on not being bound by the legacy of the past. We felt we could refer to Sloan's extraordinary strategic thinking to develop and avoid wastefulness in ways that had been impossible for him. It was as though the book had been written especially for us.

We even thought that the longer it took our rival companies to become aware of Sloan's book, the better. Fortunately, the Japanese translation wasn't published until October 1967, long after the original (1963). Apparently, many automobile company managers and other Japanese didn't know of the existence of the book until the translation came out.

These nearly four years were a valuable period of strategy formulation that had an enormous impact on the subsequent development of the Japanese automobile industry. That in itself conferred an advantage on those who came in contact with the book and digested its contents earlier. The book was useful in many ways, one of them being in what it had to say about product policies.

The real story of the publication of Alfred Sloan's *My Years with General Motors* was that Part I of the book was first excerpted in *Fortune* magazine in 1963; the entire text was published in the United States in book form in January 1964. In Japan, a translation of the first *Fortune* Part I excerpt ran in installments in the journal, *President* (*Purejidento*) from November 1963 to April 1964. In October 1967, the entire text was translated and published by Diamond. Thus, only excerpts from Part I of Sloan's *My Years with GM* were available in Japan at roughly the same time the original version was published.

As a matter of interest, an abridged translation of Part II of *My Years with GM* appeared in installments in *Toyota Management* in the twenty months spanning February 1965 to September 1966. The original book obtained by Kawahara was subsequently acquired by the Toyota Management Research Association, which published installments of Part II in *Toyota Management*. I omitted Part I, of which an abridged translation had already appeared in *Purejidento*. Thus, prior to the publication in Japan of the entire text of *My Years with GM*, it is likely that many managers and others at Toyota had avidly read Part II of the book in installments and had read, as well, the abridged translation of Part I that had appeared in *Purejidento*.[3]

"This book demystifies the magician's tricks," recounts Yoshihiko Higashiura, the translator of Part II for *Toyota Management*. He further notes:

Sloan writes with true honesty of having been confused and of having made mistakes. This sort of thing is more useful to us than success stories are. It gives us the impression that even the great GM is within our grasp. We are given courage by the plain fact that GM is managed by entirely unremarkable people using entirely unremarkable ideas. This is why I felt I was looking at a magician's secrets.

The product policy that proved useful to Kawahara was the full-line policy of offering vehicles for every purse, every purpose, and every person. A brief outline of this policy follows:

1. Arrange products from lowest-price to luxury vehicles and manufacture a car in each price category. Build luxury cars in volume, however, and stay away from ultra-luxury cars that cannot be mass-produced.
2. Allow neither large gaps to open anywhere in the range between the lowest and highest price categories nor even occasional small gaps, to the extent that the greatest advantage of mass production might be lost.
3. No products should overlap in any price range or category.

This product policy formed the foundation for the competitive strategy that Sloan had implemented:

1. In the past, the market for automobiles was considered to be bipolar, with a mass market, represented by the *Model T* at one end and a luxury car market at the other. Sloan saw the car market as a homogeneous spectrum and arranged five models according to the policy described above, from the *Chevrolet*—considered to be a car for the masses—to the *Oakland* (*Pontiac*), *Buick*, *Olds* and the luxury *Cadillac*.
2. The troublesome market for used cars at the time was put to work as a means of dealing with the *Model T* Ford. In other words, GM's lowest priced vehicle, the *Chevrolet*, was planned as a more expensive and higher performance car than the *Model T* when new, but its second-hand value after a year would make it cost less than the *Model T*. Thus GM would be able to satisfy the demands of people looking for inexpensive second-hand cars.
3. GM adopted a method of competing with vehicles on both sides of its series. Sloan considered it dangerous to succeed without competition.

The product policy and competitive strategy described above constituted fundamental principles of GM product development. They allowed GM to push Ford aside in 1926 and to enter a golden age as the world's largest automobile maker and the world's largest manufacturer. An excerpt from Sloan's book provides an interesting insight on the history of GM's transformation:

From today's perspective, we may find it strange that GM in the 1920s not only lacked the concept of management, but even the concept of an automobile industry. That is the undeniable fact, however. Every business needs some notion of the industry to which it belongs. There is a logical way to run a business when you know the reality of the industry and the environment in which it is situated.

Sloan's policies were hammered out as the result of his keen perceptiveness. He had an astute understanding of the car market and, in turn, recognized what car manufacturers must do to respond to this market appropriately. *My Years with General Motors* is filled with pearls of wisdom about all aspects of modern business management, including finance-centered management, the division system, committee systems, and compensation systems—ideas that are almost taken for granted today.

But the book underscores a basic truth: If it was Ford who built the prototype of a 20th-century manufacturing industry, it was Sloan who built the prototype of 20th-century management.

As Kawahara notes, Toyota was ahead of its rivals in absorbing and integrating Sloan's product and business strategies into its own management system. In *Toyota Reborn—People and Strategy*[4] (E. Rheingold, 1999), Hiroshi Okuda extrapolates: "Sloan's and Ford's contributions continue to shape modern industry. Toyota employees will need to continue reading books about these two men."

Marketing Theory

It was from 1956 to 1957 that Toyota first came up with the idea of scientific sales promotion. Opinions were divided over a minor change to the *Crown*, and a suggestion was made that customers be consulted. Sales techniques that had relied on experience and "feel" were revised while the company developed demand forecast methods that polled consumer preferences and fashions.

Nowadays, scientific techniques of marketing and marketing research are widespread, and there are established theories in place for marketing methods and techniques. Examples are M. E. Porter's strategies of competition and competitive advantage and Philip Kotler's principles of marketing. All companies can be assumed to have built marketing systems according to Porter's and Kotler's strategies and principles.

During the period of the economic bubble, Mazda adopted a five-channel sales policy to compensate for its inability to offer full product lines. The senior managing director in charge of sales who suggested the five-channel policy boasted that he could "sell any vehicle with four wheels." Mazda came out with what one well-known industry critic denounced as a procession of "convenience cars," and sales collapsed along with the bubble. Mazda's abandonment of theory in favor of surprise moves and clever schemes invited the company's decline.

Toyota's advantage over other companies in this area stems both from its steadfast adherence to theory and from the fact that the ground-breaking research office created by Shotaro Kamiya in 1956 (see Chapter 2) is still vigorous and functioning. Apart from these, Toyota has no special secret plan.

Product Research and Production Technology Development

Figure 4.2 places Toyota's research and development system on a matrix formed of product system levels and research and development times.

Research based on a product R&D system of this sort proceeds as shown in Figure 4.3. Eventually, a practical proposal is compiled and referred to the New Product Council (see Figure 3.3) for approval.

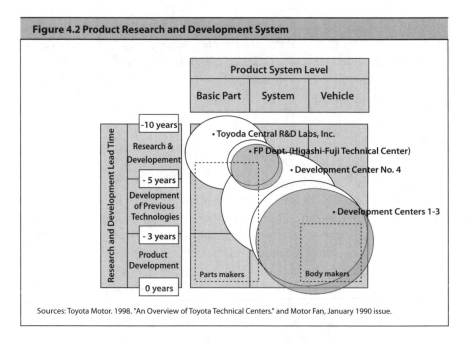

Figure 4.2 Product Research and Development System

Sources: Toyota Motor. 1998. "An Overview of Toyota Technical Centers." and Motor Fan, January 1990 issue.

What is distinctive about Toyota's new product research and development system is that Toyota devotes as much energy to the development of production technology as it does to product engineering research. The development of production technology proceeds as depicted in Figure 4.4.

It must be noted that, in the last step of Figures 4.3 and 4.4, both the accumulation of technology based on technical reporting rules and standardization based on technical standard registration guidelines are obligatory. All activities at Toyota conclude with a report and with standardization. This is the mechanism by which the company acquires and accumulates institutional knowledge.

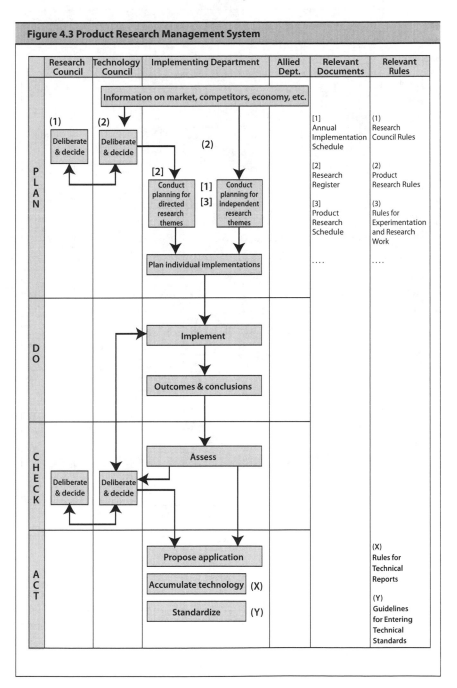

Figure 4.3 Product Research Management System

Figure 4.4 Product Engineering Development System

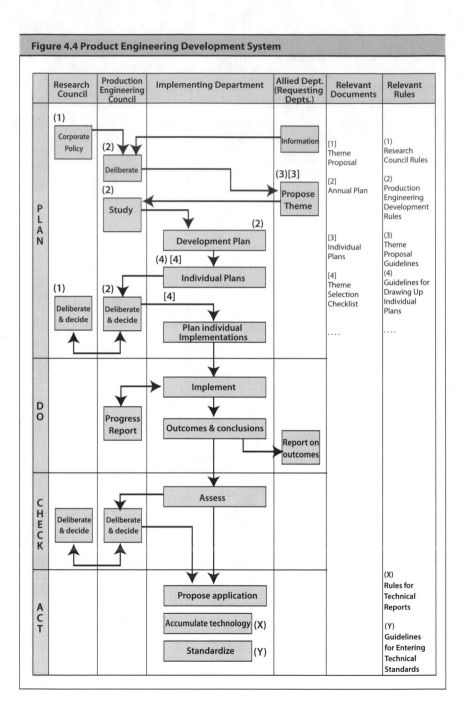

Comprehensive New Product Planning

Toyota's comprehensive new product planning process encompasses the following steps:

1. For the purpose of product diversification, a Product Planning Department reporting directly to the president conducts research and analysis, and solicits ideas and criticism. It then draws up a product plan that includes a product lineup and a schedule for introducing products to up to roughly ten years in the future.

2. The Technical Planning Department receives requests from the five development centers and domestic and overseas sales and, together with the Technical Management Department, studies the allocation of development resources and prepares a detailed comprehensive new product plan for the following five years. Each year in March, the comprehensive new product plan is presented to the Product Planning Council (see Figure 3.3) for the president's approval and decision.

3. Based on the comprehensive new product plan, all affected departments throughout the company settle on organizational staffing, equipment, long-term expense, long-term outsourcing, long-term production plans, and long-term sales plans.

4. For the development of new vehicle types or for model changes, a chief engineer (*shusa*) is appointed for each vehicle nameplate. Before the end of a concept submission deadline stipulated by the Design Research Prescriptions (see below), the designated chief engineer submits an engineering conception, detailing such items as the vehicle concept; its intended geographical markets; target customers; performance image; summary dimensions; cost, weight, and quality targets; and required resources. Activities during this period are a "black box," personally directed by the chief engineer.

The preparation of a thorough long-range sales plan in Step Three is a distinctive feature of Toyota's comprehensive new product planning. This recalls Chapter 3 (Automotive Planning Methods) of the *Handbook of Automotive Engineering*, mentioned above, where "Product Planning and Sales" is developed as an independent topic. This has been a Toyota strength ever since the days of Toyota Motor Sales.

INDIVIDUAL PRODUCT DEVELOPMENT SYSTEMS

The Shusa System

We have already discussed Toyota's *shusa*, or product manager, system at length. Below, with themes in parentheses, we list the chief documentary sources for information about the *shusa* system at Toyota. Toyota has abandoned the Japanese word *shusa* in favor of the term "chief engineer," but in order to appreciate the historical development of the position, the old term *shusa* (product manager) will be used here.

- Fujimoto, Takahiro, and Kim Clark. 1993. *Product Development Power.*[5] Tokyo: Diamond. (The heavyweight product manager).
- Fujimoto, Takahiro. 1997. *The Evolution of a Production System.*[6] Tokyo: Yuikaku Press. (The heavyweight product manager, origins of the *shusa* system, etc.)
- Japan Society for Production Management, ed. 1996. *The Toyota Production System.*[7] Tokyo: Nikkan Kogyo Shimbunsha. (Development of Toyota's *shusa* system).
- Nobeoka, Kentaro. 1996. *Multi-Project Strategy.*[8] Tokyo: Yuhikaku. (Development of Toyota's *shusa* system).
- Tamagawa, Shuji. 1988. *System Reconstruction as Seen in the Toyota System.*[9] Tokyo: Pal Shuppan. (shusa authority).
- Shiozawa, Shigeru. 1987. *Toyota Motors' Shusa System.*[10] Tokyo: Kodansha. (Ten *shusa* articles).
- Nakazawa, Takao, and Manabu Akaike. 2000. *Knowing Toyota.*[11] Tokyo: Kodansha. (The *shusa* system).
- Sobek, II, D.K., J.K. Liker, and A.C. Ward. July–August, 1998. "Another Look at Toyota's Integrated Product Development," *Harvard Business Review*, Vol. 76, No. 4, pp. 36–49.

Several topics related to Toyota's *shusa* system are discussed below.

Toyota's *shusa* system came into being in 1953 and from that time forward, the *shusa* were staff members with no authority to give orders to the line organization. One *shusa* who was struggling with this situation went to then senior managing director Eiji Toyoda and asked for clarification of the *shusa*'s authority. "On any matter you think will be good for the vehicle you're responsible for," Eiji told him, "you can give your opinion to anyone in the company. Know that you have the authority to give your opinion."

Tatsuo Hasegawa, a first-generation *shusa* in charge of the Corolla, compiled Ten Precepts for *Shusa* as a guide for staff members to succeed in the *shusa*'s role. Eiji's simple instructions, however, are probably a better and plainer way of defining what a *shusa* is and what he is expected to do. Nowadays, details relating to a *shusa*'s duties and the conduct of his job are spelled out in formal "product development rules" and elsewhere, but the basic spirit seems not to have changed since Eiji's time.

In the words of Akihiro Wada, a former senior managing director at Toyota:

The present system took root because the people who came before us worked in such a way that everyone around them treated their opinions the same way as they would do the president's. Officially, we were staff, but the system was built in such a way that we were called "emperors" because of the way we were able to work. Even if other companies try to install this system, they won't find it easy to make it stick.

From the 1970s through the 1980s, Japanese and Western automobile companies introduced the *shusa* system. Just as Wada warned, however, there were many companies in which the system never took root the way it had in Toyota.

Being a *shusa* is a dream job at Toyota, but in extreme cases in other companies, the *shusa*'s post can be a hated one. This happens because managers tend to make the *shusa* bear all the responsibility for a particular model and then blame him for any problem or issue that may arise concerning target performance, quality, cost, or delivery. Such targets are rarely met and processes always move on nonetheless. As a result, every time there is a development review, *shusa* in such companies are treated like criminals and mercilessly strung up by management. At the same time, line management is angry at the *shusa* as a management representative, and problems are neither treated seriously nor resolved. The *shusa*, drawn out and haggard, comes to work early and goes home late. One can hardly blame people in such companies for disliking the job.

Takahiro Fujimoto calls Toyota *shusa* "heavyweights," but *shusa* at other companies, although not exactly lightweights, are often treated like handymen.

A *shusa* ultimately occupies a staff position. He may have certain functional responsibilities, but it is the line organization that has to take final responsibility. The *shusa* will be blamed if his own dereliction is the cause of a poor outcome, but in most cases the cause is technical, and the line bears ultimate responsibility. Companies without an organizational management culture that clearly separates line and staff functions (see Chapter 3) will find it difficult, as Wada says, to implement the *shusa* system.

Toyota's *shusa* system is an important and indispensable part of the history of the company. Oddly enough, the *shusa* system is not once mentioned in any of the five official 500- to 800-page company histories (the 20-, 30-, 40- or 50-year histories of Toyota Motor, or the 30-year history of Toyota Motor Sales). One assumes that it was left out to avoid causing discord within the company with accounts that would inevitably be seen as lavishing praise on a particular position. Here again, we see vivid evidence of a "psychological Toyota."

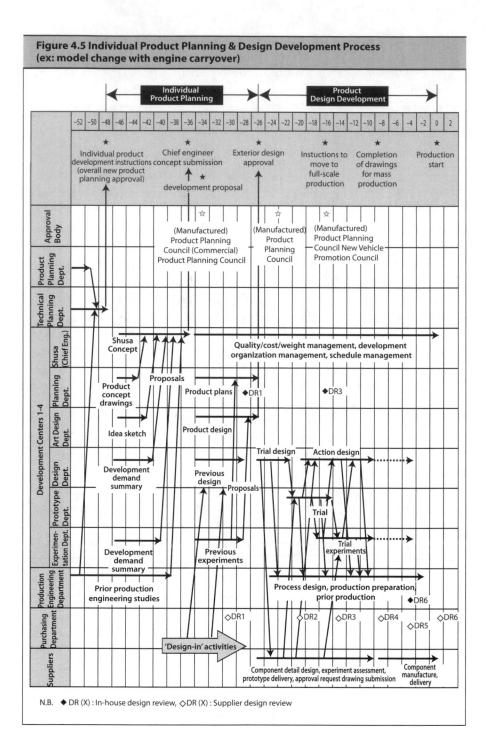

Figure 4.5 Individual Product Planning & Design Development Process (ex: model change with engine carryover)

N.B. ◆ DR (X) : In-house design review, ◇DR (X) : Supplier design review

Individual Product Planning and Design Development

Figure 4.5 outlines individual product planning and design development processes at Toyota at the beginning of the 1990s. We assembled this figure from a variety of sources. Toyota has dramatically shortened its product design and development cycle in recent years, and it is not likely that the basic shape of this development process has changed. New events and activities have no doubt been integrated into the individual product planning stage, and some types of events and their frequencies should probably have been deleted from the product design stage.

Individual Product Planning

The individual product planning period extends from individual product development instructions (minus 48 months) to exterior design approval (minus 26 months).

The first step of individual product planning involves the collection and analysis of market evaluation information for the current model (in the case of a model change) or a similar product (in the case of a new model). The sequence of flow is:

(1) Policy setting for individual new product, (2) setting of individual basic plan, and (3) design instructions to design department.

Broadly speaking, there are two kinds of market evaluation information: quality information and sales information. At Toyota, the *shusa* does not gather information regarding the market evaluation of current products each time a new product is planned. Instead, there is a system that channels this information to each department on a regular basis.

The *shusa* concept in Figure 4.5 encompasses mainly the formulation of the product positioning and product concept based on suggestions from each department. By product positioning, we mean clarifying the attributes of a given product and defining a user or market segment. Formulating a product concept means using the language of consumers to specify which attributes the product should have based on the lifestyle, values, tastes, behavior pattern, family structure, and income of the target user identified in the product positioning process.

The *shusa* next proceeds to draw up a product plan by elaborating the product concept in technical terms and clearly specifying the technical requirements of the product. "Product concept elaboration" is the name given to this translation from the language of consumers to technical language.

Product Planning

On the basis of the product concept development table, image sketches of external styling and interior design are begun, along with the design of a "product plan diagram." As the overall vehicle gradually takes shape, designs are begun for the engine, suspension, and other functional components. This process is called product planning.

Product planning is also called product packaging because it comprises planning activities that break the vehicle down into modules, such as the engine compartment, passenger compartment, underfloor, and trunk compartment.

It is a Toyota tradition that the job of product packaging falls to designers in charge of exterior styling and interior design. One rarely sees examples of this arrangement at other companies. Toyota's way may be more rational as the objects of styling, design, and packaging are nearly identical. In any case, better results are more likely if designers are permitted to work on designs with as few constraints as possible. This is why activities in Toyota's design department have recently been divided between design work, which takes place in a studio, and packaging, which takes place in a product room.

Design Quality Development

Figure 4.6 shows the flow of how, in the planning department of each development center, quality demanded by the customer is translated into manufacturing quality between the product plan and volume production.

Figure 4.7 extracts standards relating to activities for built-in quality from the Key Company Regulations column in the Quality Assurance System diagram in Figure 3.6 and assigns output categories for them. This is the flow:

1. Construct a "Demand Quality Deployment" table in accordance with the relevant guidelines for making such tables and replace the quality that customers seek in the product (consumer demand quality) with technical quality characteristics or with substitute characteristics (product demand quality).
2. Construct a "Quality Table" in accordance with the relevant guidelines and translate product demand quality downward in hierarchical order of product functions, defining demand quality (functional component demand quality) at each level down to low-end items.
3. Construct a "Mechanism Deployment Table" in accordance with the relevant guidelines and determine specific component mechanisms and component configurations (functional component mechanism characteristics) needed to achieve functional component demand quality at each level of the product function hierarchy.

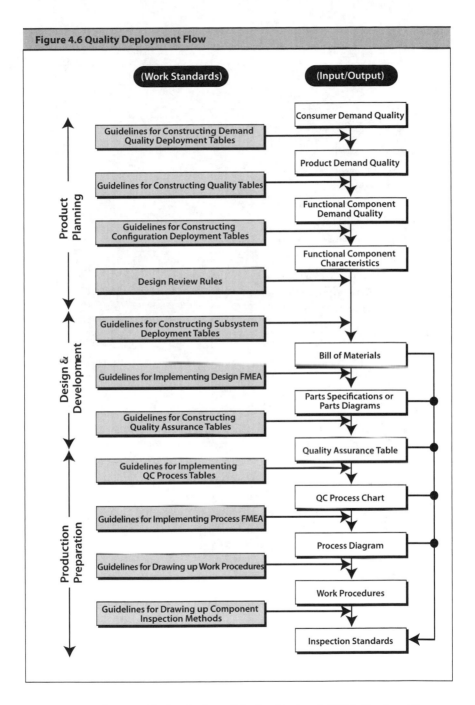

Figure 4.6 Quality Deployment Flow

4. In accordance with the timing of Design Review 1 (DR1, Product Planning Design Review), shown in Figure 4.5, and based on the Rules for

Figure 4.7 Planning Target Checksheet

Planning Target Checklist	Date:

Model Series	
(1) Examination of New Product Plans Overall (examination of management policies) • Balance of new plans in total model series (overal lineup) • New plan allocations by model (scale & time) • Model allocations by dealer group • Bonding among plans development, production preparation and sales department	
(2) Examination of Targets for Individual New Product Plans (by model) (examination of product policy) (A) Product quality targets • Series target markets (domestic/import) Product target focus (aims, basic shape, features • Quality level (class/competing products) • New scale (scope/investment) • Target life (model life/corrosion target) • Target price (proposed cost target/sales price)	
(B) Development Preconditions • Development target time ('line-off') • Target production volume (start-up/maximum) • Production development terms (plan conditions/ development conditions/production conditions) • Departments responsible for development (prototyping/production) Series model planning (by type/production department)	
(C) Responsibility (department)	

Design Reviews, carry out a design review using the Planning Target Checksheet, Demand Quality Deployment Table, Quality Table, Mechanism Deployment Table, and other tools.

5. When the first design review (DR1) is concluded, construct a Subsystem Deployment Table in accordance with the relevant guidelines, derive product structures needed to produce the product from functional component mechanism characteristics, and draw up a bill of materials (BOM).

6. In accordance with the guidelines for conducting design failure mode effect analyses, identify and eliminate latent breakdown factors and use the bill of materials to construct either parts specifications diagrams for suppliers or parts manufacturing diagrams for in-house or outsourced component manufacturing.

7. In order to assure a reliable transfer of this built-in planned design quality to manufacturing quality, collaborate with the production engineering department to construct a QA Chart, in accordance with the relevant guidelines, that clarifies manufacturing control points and control items.

8. Following this, the production engineering, manufacturing, and inspection departments, in accordance with the relevant guidelines, successively construct a QC Process Table, Process Diagram, Operating Procedures, and Inspection Criteria. Then volume production begins.[12]

Few companies define these procedures so elaborately or build in and transfer designed quality to manufacturing quality with such rigor.

Prototype Innovation

All companies that design products have some sort of prototyping or trial manufacturing process. At the same time, few can give a straight answer when asked the purpose of prototyping. For many, it is merely an experiment in manufacturing products within print tolerances using dedicated prototype jigs, tools, gauges, dies, processing machines, assembly equipment, and other tools.

Even when products or parts are built according to the blueprints, however, there will be subtle physical differences in the resulting parts depending on whether dedicated prototype tools or regular production tools are used. A prototype may be cut on a lathe, for example, when, in regular production, the part is made with dies. In a similar example, a sand-cast prototype may be produced with a metal die. Even though the drawings may be exactly the same, when prototype tools and production tools differ, problems often arise with production parts where there is no problem with prototypes. Some 50 percent of problems that occur before volume production are said to be this type. Narrowing the gap between prototypes and production parts, therefore, becomes a crucial issue affecting quality, cost, and timing.

Making prototypes with production tools would solve this problem, but, if design changes should be required because of specification-related problems found after fabrication of prototypes, they would necessitate modification or disposal of production tools, resulting in enormous losses.

On this subject, Toyota drives home the following philosophy in its own operations:

- Prototyping and regular production must be the same.
- Regular production methods are the foundation of both.
- Rather than seeing how close trial production tooling can come to regular tooling, the principle is to use regular tooling. If regular tools can be correlated to trial production tools, then trial production tools may be used.

Toyota has gradually increased the proportion of trial runs it makes with regular production tooling and set the goal of using all production tools in 2001. For some parts, this is not necessary, so it is likely that Toyota has not achieved this 100 percent. All the same, doing away with trial production tooling is necessary for the epoch-making reduction in development times that Toyota has set its sights on for the 21st century.

THE DESIGN MANAGEMENT SYSTEM

What is most distinctive about Toyota's product development system is the solidity of its design management.

Technical Criteria

A System to Promote Standardization

Standardization refers to methods and activities that make management more efficient by minimizing the variety of concepts, protocols, procedures, and things. Standards generated by standardization activities are the crystallization of an organization's highest knowledge, and the act of revising standards drives progress. Standardization is important for all organizations, whether they are in the manufacturing business or not.

Standardization may be the critical foundation supporting the Toyota management system, but there are few reports on Toyota's standardization system. It can be surmised, however, that Toyota maintains a hierarchical organization of regular and active entities charged with standardization: a Standardization Committee for the company as a whole, standardization working groups in each department, and standardization subcommittees at the office and group level. There are, for example, subcommittees for product engineering, production engineering, and service.

Toyota began organizing a company-wide system for managing standardization when it introduced TQC in 1961. In 1966, after having won the Deming Prize, Toyota's planning department norms, standards, and criteria were already several steps better organized than those of other companies, both inside and outside the automobile industry.

Standardization is among the most important aspects of a manager's job. For each component in teardown activities of a competitor's vehicle, for example, the designated working group leader (department or section manager) manages by identifying the optimum construction and then standardizing and commonizing it.

When new or revised standards are proposed, a subcommittee composed of section heads representing each of the departments prepares the work for consensus by a council at the department head level.

Rules that affect the entire company are deliberated and decided by the Standardization Committee. Once these rules are set, not even the president can change the standards. A change requires the committee's decision, even if this entails additional expense.

Below, are some examples of technical standards at Toyota that are organized by this kind of system.

Standardization of Product and Component Structures

The Nikkan Kogyo Shimbun published the following information in an article on December 23, 1992, after the economic bubble had collapsed:

> *Starting in January 1993, Toyota idled the No. 3 Assembly Line and carried out mixed production of the Celsior at Tahara Plant No. 4, where it builds the* Crown Majesta. *The aim is to raise the operating rate of the new line. Executive Vice President Toshimi Onishi emphasizes the flexibility of the Toyota Production System, saying, "We can always start Line 3 when demand goes back up again."*

The flexibility to put different vehicles on various production lines requires the standardization of vehicle structures (such as engine compartments, passenger compartments, and underfloors) as well as the standardization of the location of components within those structures. No matter how much apparent flexibility a production line may have, product designs and production line processes will have to be modified as long as vehicle structures and component locations are different for each model. Not only do such modifications incur extra, non-value-adding expense, they also entail opportunity losses when a company cannot respond quickly to fluctuations in sales or production.

As an example, three vehicle models (A, B, and C) would be nearly impossible to run down the same assembly line if the locations of batteries and air cleaners in the engine compartment, where components are densely clustered, were all different:

A: battery on the right, air cleaner on the right
B: battery on the left, air cleaner on the left
C: battery on the left, air cleaner on the right

What would forcing these three models down the same line do? For one thing, ergonomic considerations in an aging society would forbid requiring assembly operators to carry heavy batteries and mount and attach them on the left and then the right, depending on which models come down the line. A uniform location for batteries, on the other hand, would make it possible to use a mechanical mounting device.

When batteries and air cleaners are not always in the same place, the locations of numerous other components in the engine compartment will be different as well. For each car that came down the line, operators would have to go back and forth, left and right, carrying all sorts of things: parts, tools, assembly devices, equipment for adding water and oil, etc. This would result in substantially decreased efficiency and in operational errors.

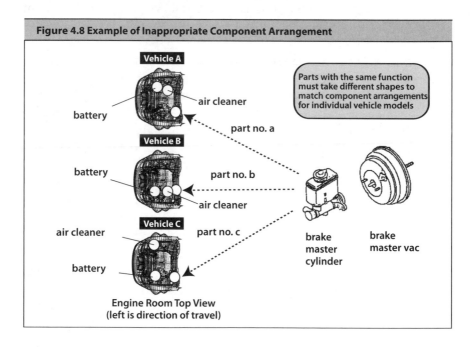

Figure 4.8 Example of Inappropriate Component Arrangement

Non-uniform component locations constitute a major cause of parts proliferation. Figure 4.8, for example, shows three vehicles (A, B, and C) for which the functions and performance of brake mastervacs and master cylinders are identical. These components connect to other parts, however, and because those other parts are in different locations, the vehicles require mastervacs and cylinders on which the orientations of such items as brake pipes and vacuum hoses are different. The result is a substantial increase in the number of parts.

Development is also burdened because when component locations vary, problems of interference, vibration, and heat damage have to be checked and revised for each vehicle type during the product development process. Cars these days are so rich in functions that tightly packed engine compartment components barely allow access. Even in an age of three-dimensional computer-aided design systems, avoiding interference among engine compartment components while limiting vibration from the engine and suspension remains the most time-consuming task in the product development process.

The engine compartment is also the source of vibration and heat emanating from the engine, and suppressing these requires considerable proprietary technology. If technology cannot be shared when the arrangement of parts in the engine compartment differs, then new technologies have to be developed every time a model changes.

Standardizing the arrangement of components greatly alleviates the sort of problems mentioned above. It brings the considerable advantages of shortening development times, reducing the number of part types and raising productivity at the manufacturing plant.

To return to the thread of our story, when we look at the locations of engine compartment components used in the *Crown Majesta*, *Celsior*, and *Aristo*, we find the air cleaners uniformly located on the right and the batteries on the left. Not all component locations are uniform because there are two engine types involved, in-line six-cylinder and V8. However, the locations that are not uniform are for a few components with low tooling costs, such as the power steering tank and the hydro-cooling fan tank. Most component parts and functional parts with high tooling costs are always in the same locations. Since this virtually eliminates the need for design modifications or process changes, adapting the production line, as Onishi says, to variations in sales or production becomes easy.

In historical terms, it was Nissan Motor that first tackled standardizing engine compartment component locations when it completed the standardization of its FR (front engine and rear-wheel drive type) passenger cars in the 1960s. Later, in the era of compact and popular FF (front engine and front-wheel drive type) vehicles, Nissan standardized its FF passenger cars separately, and this arrangement remains today. Component location standards for FR and FF vehicles have almost nothing in common, so each group has its own standards.

While Toyota was one step behind Nissan, it standardized engine compartment component locations for its FR and FF vehicles simultaneously from the 1970s on, with the result that nearly 70 percent of component locations are analogous.

What this means is that it is nearly impossible for Nissan to mix production of FF and FR vehicles on a single production line and that commonization of FF and FR parts shows no progress. Toyota, on the other hand, can mix FF and FR vehicles on its lines according to fluctuations in sales or production. Parts commonization has also improved.

In "Product Development and the Management of Standardization,"[13] [a 1971 article published in *Automotive Engineering* (vol. 25, no. 9), Akira Kaibara of Nissan Motor tells of the importance of—and gives methods for—standardizing part locations. He also reveals how advanced Nissan's technology was at the time. One might even say that, with respect to standardization of engine compartment components, advanced technology has backfired.

Honda, from the start, produced only FF vehicles and finished standardizing its engine compartment components in the 1970s. Perhaps in the pursuit of technological innovation or progress, however, Honda occasionally markets vehicles whose component locations do not conform to its own standards. In a legacy from its days as a motorcycle manufacturer, Honda's engines used to turn counterclockwise. In recent years, however, as it supplies engines to General Motors and uses engines and power train parts from other companies, Honda has gradually begun to switch over to the generally accepted clockwise standard. In conjunction with this change, Honda is revising its standards for engine and component locations, which apparently should have entailed a very huge investment.

In introducing its FF cars in the 1970s, Mitsubishi Motors conducted trial-and-error experiments with transverse-mounted engines facing left and right and then standardized by getting rid of all FR models, including the luxury *Debonair*, in favor of FF cars.

Mazda has not taken up standardization of engine compartment component locations, and components are configured differently even for similar models such as the *Demio*, *Familia*, and *Capella*.

Toyota has relentlessly standardized parts configurations for underfloors, cabins, and trunk compartments as well. Just as we saw in the case of the engine compartment, standardization in these other units does more than just increase the flexibility of responses to fluctuations in production. It also gives rise to many other advantages in such areas as development efficiency (including design, prototyping, and experimentation), productivity in manufacturing processes, product quality, and parts proliferation.

Toyota has also standardized unit construction and parts construction.

At Nissan Motor, for example, even for the same engine types, attachment locations for alternators, air conditioner compressors, power steering pumps and water pumps, and other auxiliary parts differ according to whether engines are mounted in FR cars or FF cars. At Toyota these are all the same. Even when the engine type is the same, Nissan changes the locations of engine accessories, depending on whether it is installed on two-wheel drive or four-wheel drive vehicles. At Toyota these are all the same.

Actually, in terms of function, space, mass, and variable costs, Nissan's separate standards are more advantageous than having a single set of standards to cover all cars.

Toyota, in contrast, follows the Maxcy-Silberston curve in Figure 2.3. The idea is to pursue the mass production effect with the application of uniform standards and not to optimize standards for individual models up to the level of 200,000 to 300,000 vehicles in a given model each year. Toyota adheres to this relentlessly.

Substantial results can be gained when this same principle of standardizing structures is applied in the context of value engineering (VE), i.e., to techniques for reducing costs and increasing value through VE. This is because standardized construction automatically extends the effects of VE. Efficiency is strikingly poor, on the other hand, when structures are optimized in isolation and VE has to be applied only to individual cases.

Toyota rules prescribe that the same assembly sequences and the same manufacturing equipment be used in all plants. There is no way that a profitable method originating in one plant is not extended to other plants. This is also based on the premise that a method that works at one plant but not at another cannot be a true solution to a problem. In other companies, each factory (or sometimes each production line) may have its own assembly sequences or its own manufacturing equipment. From the standpoint of local optimization, it is better for individual plants and lines to have their own assembly sequences and manufacturing equipment because they may have their own particular local conditions or environmental constraints. But the result is a proliferation of entities and higher management costs. Flexible responses to production fluctuations among lines become more difficult and knowledge cannot be shared.

Toyota's high degree of standardization and uniformity in both products and plants guarantees sufficient flexibility to, as Onishi says, combine production lines during economic downturns and return them to their original state when the economy recovers.

In the increasingly polarized, survival-of-the-fittest world of modern automobile manufacturing, the winners have product structures and production lines that do not require design or process changes when moving from one plant or line to another. At the same time, they produce at capacity in such a way that plant or line changes are unnecessary. The losers, by contrast, want to build and scrap plants and production lines in a hurry; consequently, they are bedeviled by rigid products and plants that require months to accommodate design or process changes. A full understanding of the disparity merits considerable attention.

When we consider Toyota's products and parts chronologically or when we line them up against those of other companies, what emerges is a method of working in which superior technological creations spread rapidly (across the entire company) to other vehicle families in the form of standard structures. One can only marvel at the thoroughness of this lateral propagation.[14]

Responding to a question about lateral propagation, one engineering division executive said it is "just a part of the company culture." He refuted the idea that any specialized organizational entity within Toyota takes the lead in this lateral propagation. Although he was right to say that no particular department takes the lead in lateral propagation, "company culture" is not a very specific answer. One gets the impression that the question was answered this way because he was hard put to explain things he did every day without thinking about them.

We may posit that the reason for this aspect of Toyota culture derives from a few relentless standardization rules for product and part structure:

- Superior technologies that people develop are obligatorily registered either in the form of new standard structures or as modifications of existing standard structures.
- When designing a new vehicle model, the person in charge of the design is obligated to consult the standard structures.
- It is recommended that individual models be simplified (subtracted) from standard structures.
- When the basis of a standard structure cannot be adopted, it is mandatory either to correct the cause of its unsuitability or to make a new standard structure and reregister it.

- Managers of design departments are obligated to administer and manage according to the above rules.

Anything less thorough than this would fail to achieve the level of culture.

Design Criteria

Design criteria refer to documents containing criteria for evaluating design procedures and design results. A table listing only the criteria for judging design results is an engineering checklist or a design review checklist.

In an article entitled "Another Look at Toyota's Integrated Product Development," (*Harvard Business Review*, Vol. 76, No. 4, July–August, 1998; pp. 36–49), Durward K. Sobek II et al. describe the quintessence of Toyota design criteria:

> Toyota, however, still maintains voluminous books of engineering checklists to guide design work. These checklists act as the first cut at designing manufacturable products that use common parts across platforms. Engineering checklists contain detailed information concerning any number of aspects, including functionality, manufacturability, government regulations, and reliability.
>
> Engineers use the checklists to guide the design throughout the development process. The checklists are particularly important for the intensive design reviews that every vehicle program undergoes. What keeps these extremely large meetings from becoming chaotic is that all engineers come with a list of all the items they need to verify from their perspectives. If the design conforms to the checklist, the part is highly likely to meet a certain level of functionality, manufacturability, quality, and reliability. If it does not, discrepancies between the checklists and the design become the focal points of discussion among the divisions.
>
> Once in place, design standards add predictability across vehicle subsystems and between product design engineers and manufacturing engineers.
>
> Engineering checklists also facilitate organizational learning across generations of vehicles. Toyota trains its engineers not only to record product histories but also to abstract from that experience in order to update existing capabilities. When an engineer learns something new, the knowledge can be incorporated into the checklist and

then applied across the company to every subsequent vehicle. Those lessons reside with the organization, not in one person's head. If an engineer leaves, the knowledge he or she has gained is captured in the checklists and remains with the company.

Just as standardization is the key to continuous improvement on the factory floor, standards are the basis for continuous improvement in engineering design.

Standards are revisited every couple of months (as opposed to being used once or put away for a couple of years); they never become outdated. The frequent changes to the checklists also give engineers continual opportunities to develop and hone their skills. [In other words, they] . . . build Toyota's base of knowledge.

Many of Toyota's current practices—such as an emphasis on written communication, design standards, and the chief engineer—seem to have been standard practice in the United States in the 1950s and earlier. But in the 1960s and 1970s, as U.S. automakers neglected their development processes, systems that were once sound and innovative gave way to bureaucracy, internal distrust, and other distractions that brought the companies close to the chimney extreme. In reaction, those companies seem to have swung toward the other end of the spectrum. Results in the short term have been encouraging, but the deficiencies of the committee extreme may well appear soon. Some companies are discovering them already.

This article provides an excellent description of where and how design criteria are used at Toyota. The last sentence of the paper refers to bureaucracy and the committee system that we noted in Chapter 1. U.S. automobile manufacturers, plagued by bureaucracy's dysfunction, fell into an extreme version of a "chimney" structure and then reacted by leaning too much toward a project-centered committee system. In the end, they ended up weakening the advantages of a bureaucracy, i.e., documentation and standardization. Toyota has struck a balance between bureaucracy and the committee system and manages to take the best from each.

The Production Engineering Structural Requirements Form

One distinctive feature of its product design is that Toyota excels in building new products from existing material. The Production Engineering Structural Requirements Form is a typical standard used to accomplish this. This standard summarizes the principal features of product construction to be adhered to during the product design stage from the point of view of production engineering difficulty and equipment compatibility.

With its own input already incorporated into the standard, the design department has used this standard to drive up Toyota's productivity and use of existing equipment dramatically. Clearly, the Toyota Production System is not the only factor responsible for Toyota's lean production.

Yoshio Komagine of production engineering comments on Toyota's TQC days in the 1960s:

> I'm absolutely convinced that all the work we did preparing for the Deming Prize has made a big contribution to the production preparation we do for body processing now. . . . One example of this is the feedback to design during the drawings stage. We made a master model that improved product quality reliability. The more we analyzed data, too, the more we were able to learn about how the quality of the plans determined overall quality, quantities, costs and timing. (*Toyota: A History of the First Forty Years. 1978.*)

The feedback to design during the drawings stage and the master model that Komagine mentions may be seen as precursors to the production engineering structural requirements form. This concept of taking knowledge from downstream processes and inputting it into the design department is one of the preconditions for Toyota's achievement of lean production. Most companies leave this step out and consequently fail in adopting the Toyota Production System.

Toyota's system of using production engineering structural requirements forms eventually spread to other automobile companies and then to other manufacturers. One suspects this was one of the reasons that Japanese carmakers and manufacturing industries outstripped international competition from the 1970s into the 1980s.

Product Diversification and Parts Reduction

Numbers of Vehicle Models and Engine Types

Figure 4.9 shows the number of passenger car and light truck models and engine types for major Japanese automobile manufacturers at the beginning of the 1990s.

Let's assume that the figures for Toyota are the optimum. It would be ideal, then, to plot the ratio of each company's vehicles sold compared to Toyota on a straight line connecting Toyota's figure with the origin. In

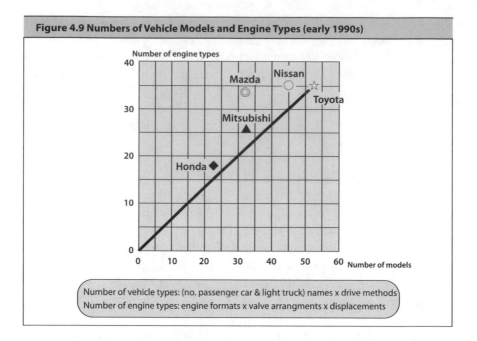

Figure 4.9 Numbers of Vehicle Models and Engine Types (early 1990s)

fact, however, we have to account for the fact that the lower ranking the manufacturer, the more models it has to carry.

Nissan, at forty-five models, carried six fewer models than Toyota at the time but had thirty-five engine types, the same as Toyota. Furthermore, as we have already seen, for a single engine type, Nissan changed the location of auxiliary equipment depending on whether the engine was destined for an FF, FR, two-wheel drive or four-wheel drive vehicle. Thus, the true number of engine types was even higher. Since Nissan's sales volume at the time was roughly half of Toyota's, it is clear that Nissan was overextended.

Mazda had thirty-two vehicle models—nineteen fewer than Toyota— but thirty-four engine types, nearly the same number as Nissan and Toyota and far in excess of the ideal line. This figure, moreover, includes rotary engines, which shared almost no common parts with gasoline or diesel engines, so it is fair to say that the number of engine types was actually greater. Since it sold roughly one-fifth as many vehicles as Toyota, Mazda had too many models and engine types far in excess of the company's capacity.

Although Mitsubishi is situated close to the ideal line, the fact that its sales volume was one-fifth of Toyota's means that it, too, was carrying too many car models and too many engine types.

Honda is also nearly on the ideal line. It, too, had a sales volume one-fifth of Toyota's, but when one considers that the lower-ranking manufacturers are obliged to overreach a bit, we can say that the number of models and engine types produced by Honda was more or less what it should have been.

We can see in this data one of the reasons that some companies grew during the 1990s and others dropped out. From time immemorial, the principle has been that the proper strategy for small and medium companies is to concentrate their resources.

It is not necessarily true to say that Mitsubishi Motors exceeded its capacity in terms of numbers of vehicle models and engine types. The company dropped out of the race in the wake of various problems, including the 1996 sexual harassment scandal in the United States, the diversion of profits to extortionists in 1997, and a series of recall cover-ups in 2000.

Numbers of Model Specifications

When the economic bubble collapsed in December 1990, Toyota inaugurated a Committee for Optimizing Numbers of Vehicle Types and Parts, which aimed for a 20 percent reduction in vehicle types and a 30 percent

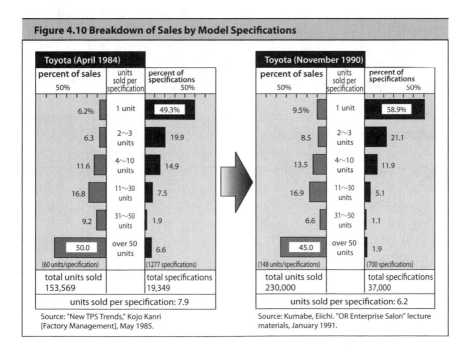

Figure 4.10 Breakdown of Sales by Model Specifications

reduction in part varieties. The *Weekly Oriental Economist*[15] (2 May 1992) explains how the targets were established:

> Toyota knew that for a given model, 80 percent of vehicle types currently being sold can satisfy 95 percent of the demand. The remaining 20 percent of vehicle types are inefficient, and this is the source of the target of a 20 percent reduction in vehicle types. It was concluded that 5 percent of the demand would shift to other vehicle types. Restricting the number of vehicle types would cut down on expenses for prototyping and experimentation. For parts, too, 70 percent were responsible for more than 90 percent of orders; therefore the target for parts reduction was set at 30 percent. For 187 critical items, the reduction goal was set at 45 percent.

Figure 4.10 shows the change in the sales structure of vehicle specifications for Toyota cars from 1984 to 1990.

The "model specifications" referred to in this figure are used to distinguish individual vehicles by defining, among other things, engine, body, options, and color.

In the mere six and a half years from April 1984 to November 1990, the total number of specifications rose by a factor of 1.9, from 19,000 to 37,000. At the same time, the number of vehicles sold per specification dropped from 7.9 to 6.2. In 1990, specifications for which only one vehicle per specification sold during the month accounted for nearly 60 percent of all specifications and almost 10 percent of all cars sold. At the same time, cars for which over 50 vehicles per specification sold during the month dropped from 50 percent to 45 percent of total sales over the period of six and a half years, while the number of vehicles per specification rose from sixty to 148.

In other words, a polarization separated those specifications that met the target from those that did not. Abandoning those specifications that did not meet the target was the basis of the vehicle type reduction policies and goals reported in the *Weekly Oriental Economist.*

Having absorbed Alfred Sloan's strategy of wide variations, coherent product diversification had been basic Toyota policy, and the company had continued to pursue expansion of its range of vehicle types. One might well question whether the company abandoned wide variation strategy at this point.

Quoted in *Nikkei Mechanical*[16] (5 April 1993), Akihiro Wada, the Toyota Motors senior managing director in charge of Development Centers 1-3, provides some insight on this.

[In 1993], I was made to take the chairmanship of an internal committee to reduce the number of vehicle types and component types. The trouble was that cutting the number of vehicle types wouldn't reduce costs very much. Even if we had cars that sold at the rate of only a score or two per month, it wasn't as though they required that many extra parts. It was just that there weren't that many of certain combinations. We could get rid of those cars, but it wouldn't improve operability very much because we take care of things like that with our system nowadays.

It isn't true, either, to say that we were strangling ourselves with model changes that were too frequent. Per-vehicle depreciation costs are minimal for vehicles that we produce at a given quantity. Just because we lengthen the model change cycle doesn't mean that profits will suddenly go up. Indeed, it's more profitable to come up with better ideas and create good, low-cost products.

A supplementary comment on Wada's notion of operability is in order. What Wada is saying is that any effect from reducing the number of vehicle types would be limited to factory operations. Since computer systems are used to manage combinations, eliminating car types that are really just different combinations of elements will not make operations any easier.

Wada also refers to per-vehicle depreciation costs. By this, he means that if any effect can be expected from lengthening the period of model change, it would only be per-vehicle depreciation costs from an increase in production volume during the model's life cycle. Since Toyota reaches the saturation point on the Maxcy-Silberston curve (see Figure 2.3), the easing of depreciation costs would be slight.

The greater part of the increase in the number of model specifications comes from combinations of options. There are many cases in which the number of optional components as such does not rise. An increase in combinatorial variety does not increase the number of expensive dies, and in this era, in which computers manage variety, the cost impact is insignificant.

Wada's words hint at some disagreement within Toyota over model specifications, but subsequent history makes it clear that Wada's ideas were understood within the company. The Committee for Optimizing Numbers of Vehicle Types and Parts afterwards focused its activities only on the "vehicle type" part of its mission, and the company continued its product policy of wide variation.

Returning to our discussion of Figure 4.10, Toyota in a mere six and a half years rapidly raised its total vehicle sales by a factor of 1.5. A 190 percent increase in total specifications was one factor in achieving this. Customers always lean toward diversification. In the final analysis, however, when satisfied with diversification, they select standard specifications. This is why the number of vehicles per specification sold above fifty grew two and a half times.

The Law of L-shaped Diversification (unless applied to purely single specification products like the black-only Model T Ford) holds that diversification will always lead to an L-shaped sales structure (i.e., one in which specifications that sell and those that do not will distribute themselves in the shape of the letter "L"). If, in 1990, Toyota had cut off specifications below the level of one vehicle per specification, the result would not have been zero. The remaining specifications would have formed another L shape, and gradually, sales would have assumed the same structure as in 1984.

In other words, if Toyota had abandoned product diversification, both total sales volume and the per-specification number of vehicles sold above the level of fifty would have slumped. Fortunately, Toyota did not "kill the bull in order to straighten out his horns."

Products that come of unplanned diversification as often seen in other general automakers are out of the question. Even for specifications that combine option components, the first step in marketing is as Alfred Sloan said, having, a concept of diversification from the customer's perspective.

Parts Commonization

As Figure 4.11 shows, parts commonization belongs in the domain of parts reduction.

Parts commonization can be divided into three methods: parts carryover, parts sharing, and parts substitution. Parts carryover refers to using existing parts in new products. Parts sharing means carrying newly designed parts across multiple new products. Both parts carryover and parts sharing call for specific intervention at the new product design stage. Parts substitution is a method for cutting down the number of new parts after they have been created by making them interchangeable and then eliminating some of them. Within the larger category of parts reduction, functional integration refers to the consolidation of functional components that have been divided into multiple parts. Functional substitution means modifying the construction of components to reduce the numbers of nuts and bolts by replacing fastening functions.

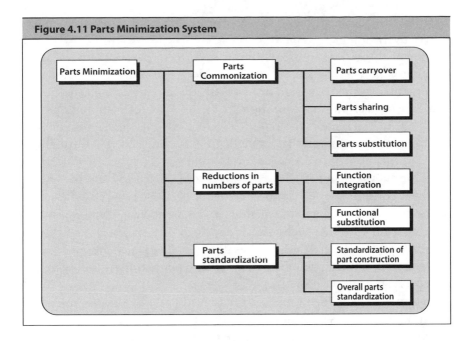

Figure 4.11 Parts Minimization System

Parts standardization means standardizing parts to be used in the future. Although parts commonization and parts standardization are sometimes confused, parts commonization involves activities that look at carryover and sharing of specific parts during the development of specific products; the concept of standardization does not enter into the picture.

In principle, parts commonization activities at Toyota involve the systematic carryover and sharing of parts at the new product development stage. Substituting already existing parts is inefficient and is rare. Parts standardization, on the other hand, is a daily routine because Toyota's policy is to avoid as much as possible dealing with such matters after the fact.

Yoshifumi Tsuji, former president of Nissan, once said "We're adept at many things when we're slimming down. We're not very good at all, though, when we're expanding." He added, "At Nissan, we don't do enough preparatory research before we start something new, so that what gets created ends up being like a wet towel. Our forte is squeezing the water out of the wet towel afterwards." Tsuji's description can be applied to many companies.

Even at Toyota, non-commonized parts tend to increase even where commonization is possible. In times of emergency (such as the oil crisis and the collapse of the economic bubble), Toyota sometimes works with suppliers in "cleanup" activities to commonize (or substitute) parts retroactively.

One of these cleanup events took the form of parts commonization activities following the first oil crisis. Sachio Fukushima of Toyota's engineering management division describes those activities in an article entitled "Toyota Parts Commonization from the Product Planning Stage."[17] (*IE*. 1978 Special Issue). His account is valuable for its description of Toyota's relentless organizational strength in spreading changes throughout the organization once a decision was made and of the revolutionary thinking among designers. These can easily be related to the senior management consultant's description of Toyota parts carryover studies cited in the beginning of Chapter 2. As the consultant noted, "There was much to learn from their thoroughness."

Also significant were the activities of the previously mentioned Committee for Optimizing Numbers of Vehicle Types and Parts following the collapse of the bubble economy.

Figure 4.12 plots the numbers of managed parts by various automakers and total Japanese automobile production in and after 1979.

The number of managed parts is the total of parts for current products and service parts covering older products. In the case of automobiles,

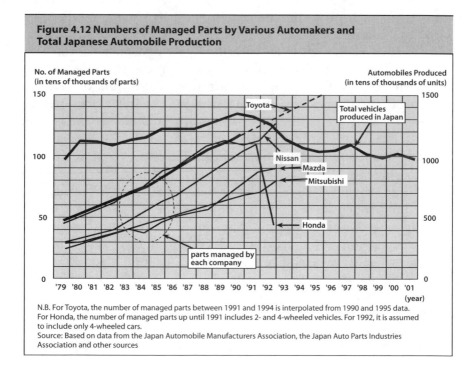

Figure 4.12 Numbers of Managed Parts by Various Automakers and Total Japanese Automobile Production

No. of Managed Parts (in tens of thousands of parts)

Automobiles Produced (in tens of thousands of units)

Toyota

Total vehicles produced in Japan

Nissan
Mazda
Mitsubishi

Honda

parts managed by each company

'79 '80 '81 '82 '83 '84 '85 '86 '87 '88 '89 '90 '91 '92 '93 '94 '95 '96 '97 '98 '99 '00 '01 (year)

N.B. For Toyota, the number of managed parts between 1991 and 1994 is interpolated from 1990 and 1995 data. For Honda, the number of managed parts up until 1991 includes 2- and 4-wheeled vehicles. For 1992, it is assumed to include only 4-wheeled cars.
Source: Based on data from the Japan Automobile Manufacturers Association, the Japan Auto Parts Industries Association and other sources

parts for previous products may be used in the marketplace for twenty to thirty years, so service parts need to be managed for at least twenty years after a product has been discontinued. In other words, the number of managed parts has a characteristic of going to be added up each time a new vehicle model is marketed.

This characteristic of the market accounts for a rapid increase in managed parts during the 1980s, when virtually all carmakers were increasing new model and derivative vehicle production. Although we have no continuous data for Toyota from 1991 onward (and for other companies from 1993), *Toward Maintaining the Automobile Base in the 21st Century*, published in *Automotive Engineering* in January 1996,[18] notes that total managed parts for Toyota reached 1.5 million in 1995, and it is likely that other companies followed suit. At the same time, with the collapse of the bubble economy in the 1990s, Japan's automobile sales volume as a whole declined and returned to the 1979 level.

The number of managed parts includes more than just parts stocks; it is also an index of quantities of jigs, dies, inspection fixtures, tools, machines, castings, and forgings. All of these must be managed for a minimum of twenty years, so administrative costs are enormous. In their book, *VRP (Variety Reduction Program)*,[19] published in 1988 by Japan Management Association, Toshio Suzue and Akio Takahashi of JMA Consulting state that parts management costs account for 45 percent of the total cost of parts in the automobile industry.

Easily performed parts management simulations led many to fear that, at this rate, none of the companies would be able to stay in business for long. All the manufacturers therefore focused on numbers of managed parts as a key improvement indicator and tackled the challenges of parts variety reduction and parts commonization.

Parts commonization became all the rage in Japan in the first half of the 1990s, and hardly a day went by when the topic was not mentioned in the newspapers. Companies competed by releasing parts commonization ratios each time they announced the launching of a new model car. Criticisms of designers were published as well; "designer ego," for example, was cited as the reason for Nissan's slow advance in commonizing parts.

Only the media were amused by such stories, however. The all-important customer viewed these news reports with a cold eye. Consumers in general want their cars to be gleaming and entirely new. They are not at all interested in new models with old parts. Car sales stayed soft and the trend prolonged sluggish consumption after the collapse of the bubble.

In this environment, Toyota was the only automaker that refused to publish parts commonization ratios even when asked to do so by the media, and this was the case despite the fact that Toyota had long carried over some 50 percent of its old parts. ("An integration-oriented system for registering and managing information on parts tables." *IE*, February 1975).[20] Nor did Toyota, always attentive to the impact its comments might have on consumers, ever say anything critical about anyone in the company. We described Toyota's "psychological approach" in our discussion in Chapter 3 of how the company cultivates people, and again in the current chapter, in the section on the *shusa* system. Here, we see that Toyota also excels in a "psychological approach" to dealing with its customers.

By combining Figures 4.10 and 4.12, we see that Toyota's number of managed parts per vehicle specification (known as the modular design [MD] index) fell from 39.8 in 1986 to 31.1 in 1990. A simultaneous drop in the MD index and rise in vehicle model specifications substantiates Toyota's ability to, as Akihiro Wada says, make vehicle types by combination:

> The MD index is illogical in the sense that it is the ratio of quantities in different dimensions. The denominator is the number of current product specifications and the numerator is the cumulative number of parts, including past parts. It is nevertheless valuable in revealing basic trends. Calculations of MD indices for other companies yield results that are several times greater than that for Toyota. In other words, Toyota has a greater ability than do other companies to commonize and to generate large numbers of specifications with small numbers of parts.

Even with this high degree of success, Toyota people would say that they have a long way to go and that commonization remains a major issue. To this day, one of Toyota's executive vice presidents is leading the effort to promote commonization.

Figure 4.12 tells us that the number of managed parts in all the companies in 2001 is about four times what it was in 1979. The number of vehicles produced, meanwhile, remains similar to what it was in 1979. This is one element that makes management difficult for car companies that have not reformed the way they run their businesses. Even auto companies that are currently doing well cannot relax, because the specter of the number of managed parts lurks in the shadows. Limiting part numbers remains the primary concern in the 21st century. In the final section of this chapter, we will show steps that Toyota is taking to hold down the number of managed parts.

Reducing Numbers of Parts

Methods of reducing the number of parts include functional integration (joining together functional components that were once separate) and functional substitution (or changing the construction of components so as to reduce numbers of nuts, bolts and other constituent parts).

In terms of manufacturing and service, functional integration is divided into several categories, such as body panels and intake and exhaust pipes. For each, the point is to consolidate nonfunctional parts. It should be noted that the consolidation of functional components such as radio cassette players belongs to a different genre whose purpose is not to reduce parts but to create multifunctional products.

Functional integration to reduce the number of parts involves production equipment improvements, which make it possible to press integrated body panels (see the section on Production Technology, below) and to switch from segmented intake lines to molded one-piece plastic units.

Functional substitution to reduce the number of parts includes reducing the numbers of fasteners such as bolts, nuts, washers, and the like. Parts reduction encompasses more than merely cutting down the numbers and types of parts. It brings many other advantages, such as increasing part hardness and strength, making parts lighter and quieter, and enhancing ease of assembly.

Toyota does a remarkable job of reducing the number of its parts. Relentless parts-reduction efforts target every product component, even often-ignored parts deep inside the engine. Toyota adopts a flexible approach in which exhaust pipes for manufacture are integrated and exhaust pipes for service are segmented for ease of handling. The total number of parts to be managed may rise, but there are few parts to be seen on the production line. Moreover, Toyota's special strength in *yokoten* (lateral propagation) comes into full play, so that a structure that proves itself for one model will be used in all models within a few years.

Parts Standardization

Because the standardization of product and component structures has been discussed in earlier sections of this chapter, there is no need to include the details of standardized parts construction within the broader context of parts standardization.

Overall parts standardization refers to standardizing the totality of components and focuses on bolts, nuts, and similar part elements. At Toyota, all part elements are standardized and registered, and no new design can be made for similar new parts without the permission of the Design Control manager. This system works because the Design Control department has the authority to determine part numbers.

Project Management

Managing the Development Schedule

The standard schedule for the development of a new product is prescribed by design research regulations stipulated in formal Rules for New Product Development. The design research regulations were formulated by the Technical Administration Department in 1974, originally as rough guidelines. Standard schedules were determined according to the scope of development involved, e.g., new product development, model changes, minor changes, or mini-changes. A standard schedule was printed on the top half of a calendar form, and detailed schedules for individual projects were filled in by hand on the bottom half.

Later, in 1984, a revised and more detailed version of the design research regulations was adopted. The Toyota Standard Development Schedule of the early 1990s took the shape shown in Figure 4.5. Detailed individual standard schedules were added in the form of the individual departmental IPO charts shown in Figure 1.6. This allowed huge information inputs and outputs to flow without contradiction among the departments during the development stage. Just like *kanban* on the production floor, moreover, this was a "pull" system in which each process would get information from the previous process at appropriate times. By exerting psychological pressure on the previous process, this pull system constitutes a mechanism that encourages product planning, design, and other upstream processes to adhere to the schedule set by the standard. Development-schedule delays would probably become the normal state of things in a "push" system in which upstream processes force information downstream.

Development lead times have now become so short that the standards in Figure 4.5 are already out of date. We can surmise, however, that Toyota continues to create and apply this sort of standard even in an age of short lead-times.

Different standards exist for long-term planning for engines. Toyota integrates design needs, layout needs, and comprehensive engine planning to construct long-term engine plans. At the point where the *shusa*'s concept is submitted (minus 36 months), a new engine can only be adopted for the new product once the Production Engineering Planning Office consents.

The benefit of standards such as these is that they raise the level of management. Managers do not always know what information is needed—and when—for their own and other organizations. These standards give managers a panoramic view of information needs and can be used both as checklists and as stepping-stones for improving the business. They make it possible for managers to actually manage. And, in the future, they will enable computerization of the management of development information schedules—something that has probably already been done at Toyota.

The development process depicted in Figure 4.5 was more or less the same one used at all Japanese automobile companies at the time. What differed was whether this process was standardized or not. The utility of standardizing the development process extends beyond eliminating the extra effort required to think about development schedules for each new product. Because the process does not change even when the product does, applying knowledge that arises from similar experiences promotes a learning effect. At the same time, the accumulation of similar knowledge gives rise to new ideas, all of which makes it possible to improve quality and cost performance and to shorten development times.

Some people hold that having standards does not change anything. After all, even companies without standards will set new product development processes by borrowing from previous models or other models. This view, though, emerges from a failure to understand the difference between standardization and carryover. Once standardization is in place, standards—even though they may be used with minor revisions—provide pivot points that do not wobble. They make similar experiences possible and they enable knowledge. Carryover does not have that firm pivot point of standards, so there is no telling where it will wander over the course of time. Similar experiences cannot be accumulated, and knowledge cannot be gained. This difference manifests itself over the long run in significant disparities in organizational capabilities.

Managing Development Resources

Toyota's Product Development Department employs about 12,000 people, with another 3,000 coming from outside companies. The Product Planning Department is a sales function that handles marketing and is not included in these numbers.

In the 1980s, there was a system for estimating labor costs according to the scale of development projects, and estimates often matched actual results. At the same time, numbers of prototype vehicles were set according to standards: testing was a given and there were no adjustments to development resources or development times. Nowadays, however, experiments with dramatic reductions in development times have made development resource estimates and (fixed) standards for numbers of prototype vehicles meaningless. These practices have been abandoned in favor of *hoshin kanri* (policy deployment methods).

In policy deployment, a time reduction target is set for the development of each new product, the developers bring together their brainpower to hammer out plans and policies to achieve it, and development resources are determined for such needs as manpower and numbers of prototype vehicles. In accordance with the Clark-Fujimoto Rule (Takahiro Fujimoto and Kim Clark. 1993. *Product Development Capability*),[21] which holds development resources to be proportional to development time, this approach generally yields a low estimate for needed resources. Excess development resources (such as manpower and prototype vehicles) get in the way and have to be eliminated.

If the pressure to shorten development lead-times ever slackens, Toyota will probably revive its system of labor and resource estimates.

Managing Product Information and Technical Information

In his book, *The Evolution of a Production System*,[22] Takahiro Fujimoto says that competitive product development and production planning systems in manufacturing industries must be superior to those of other companies in at least two respects:

1. Creating product concepts and translating them into product designs.
2. Embodying product designs in products.

We have discussed the first point in the section on Individual Product Planning. The second, an area of critical importance to a company's competitiveness, will be dealt with below.

Embodying product designs in products means conducting production activities to transcribe product design information accurately, effectively, and rapidly onto raw materials; the information is thereby embodied in physical products. Fujimoto says that the key here is the precision and effectiveness of the processing and communication of the product design information.

Product design information encompasses, among other things, blueprints, parts tables, design change notices, manufacturing instructions, adjustment guidelines, troubleshooting guidelines, and reports to governmental authorities. Blueprints, as used here, cover design-specific product plans, design review drawings, prototype drawings, manufacturing drawings for mass production, supplied drawings and approved drawings, etc. A product will not materialize if even one of these many forms of design information is missing. Imprecision in any of this information necessitates manual rework or supplementary operations and greatly increases the need for development resources and development time. Having a precise and effective system in place is the essential ingredient to becoming a robustly competitive manufacturer.

Work in this area is basically a thankless business. Because it centers mostly around maintenance, it is typically work that no one wants to do, and companies are reluctant to use their best people to do it. This fact alone creates the potential for such work to become a hidden bottleneck in efforts to shorten development times and other development reforms.

Toyota has not reported much information on this subject recently, but the reader is encouraged to refer to an earlier article published by Toyota in the journal *IE* in February and March issue of 1975: "An Integration-oriented System for Registering and Managing Information on Parts Tables."[23] The article explains Toyota's parts table management system and has many useful suggestions. It also provides a glimpse of the high level of competence of the people who manage Toyota's parts tables.

Managing technical information refers to the management of other companies' product information, legal regulations, patents, production engineering requirements, technical standards, design standards, technical reports, information on development costs and quality, examples of exemplary design, examples of design problems (i.e., failure records), and benchmarking data. It involves, in short, a knowledge management system for designing. At Toyota, management protocols for each type of information listed above are formalized. Because they are managed separately, however, they are a one-dimensional management system that does not reveal interrelationships, and this has been an issue of concern. The PDM concept depicted in Figure 3.15 emerged in 1996, but the actual system seems not yet to have materialized.

Of particular importance in the realm of technical knowledge is the development "white paper," which is compiled after development has ended and mass production has begun. At Toyota, the Product Planning Office (perhaps now the development center's planning department) draws up a development white paper within a month of the start of mass production. The white paper summarizes gaps with targets, explicit statements of responsibility, cost, weight, man-hours and expenses, etc. The findings are then submitted to top management and other concerned parties. This triggers the transformation of implicit knowledge to explicit knowledge (e.g., technical standards), passes on technology, and is linked to reviews of the product development system. Manufacturing industries generally have new product development programs jostling up against one another, and projects without development white paper are not unusual. As long as this state of affairs persists, the knowledge and wisdom needed to advance and reform technology and development will not appear no matter how often the development process is repeated. Any company that aspires to permanence needs to take stock of this and to implement this sort of "white paper" approach.

The Design Review System

The Significance of Design Review

Product development is a process that requires repeated exchange of information to find points of compromise between the demands of upstream processes whose role is to establish and modify products in order to create customers and downstream processes intended to maintain the status quo in order to constrain investment. The more frequently information is exchanged between upstream and downstream processes, the more likely it is that a company will reach optimum compromise points, i.e., good design prints.

If information flowing from upstream processes does not conform with the demands or conditions of downstream processes, reactions (often inconsistent reactions) will emerge from the downstream processes. Besides, reactions to downstream processes often contain contradictions. Since only upstream processes can coordinate the reactions of downstream processes, they have the complex and difficult job of coordinating these reactions while staying alert to conflicts that arise in downstream processes. Particularly demanding is the design work involved in the process of converting specifications information into physical information. Simply put, if imprecise information (prints) is sent downstream, parts cannot be made right away. So, the work of upstream processes has no escape called compromise, and their work is very rigorous.

In the automobile business, it takes five to ten years of experience with development work for a new employee to become a full-fledged developer. Even at that, there is a limit to the knowledge that any individual human can accumulate, and the number of design changes that take place during the product development stage of a single car model is on the order of ten thousand. This is the context in which Toyota introduced and implemented the Production Engineering Structural Requirements Form (see the section on Technical Standards, above). By using this form, later processes can systematically determine conditions and provide them to previous processes. This method has proved highly effective.

Reliability programs or design reviews (DR), developed by the U.S. National Aeronautics and Space Administration in the course of space flight planning in the 1960s, are another method that Toyota has introduced and developed for the purpose of mobilizing knowledge throughout the company and, particularly from downstream processes.

Design review is a system in which downstream processes (and sometimes earlier processes in product planning departments) review results from planning prints and other process information, blueprints, and prototypes from upstream processes. Design reviews are common practice in the space and aeronautics industries, where it is difficult to use repeated prototype fabrications and experiments for verification.

Design review systems have recently begun to receive serious attention in industries in general as mechanisms for preventing progress to subsequent stages until criteria for built-in quality set for each stage of development have been cleared. One typical example of a design review system is the "quality check gate" system that Mitsubishi Motors COO Rolf Eckrodt introduced from DaimlerChrysler in 2001 to support the corporate turnaround plan. The advent of design reviews marks an important event for product development, so much so that even the ISO 9001 International Quality Standards, which in principle avoid technical jargons, makes an exception for the term "design review" and stipulates its use.

Design Reviews at Toyota

In 1988, Katsuyoshi Yamada, former head of Toyota's TQC Promotion Department, gave a speech entitled "Design Review for Automobiles" at a seminar on reliability methods sponsored by the Union of Japanese Scientists and Engineers. In his talk, Yamada described design review (DR) techniques at Toyota. He traced the history of Toyota's interest in design review and explained how the company had cultivated and established it as an effective methodology.

Figure 3.6 (the Quality Assurance System) shows the positioning and implementation timing of design reviews at Toyota. Below, we will summarize Yamada's account of design reviews and supplement it with related information.

- There were two underlying reasons for Toyota's implementation of DR: [1] the start of exports to the United States (1957–) and [2] a response to emissions controls (1970–). Especially in the case of emissions controls, the company had few people with experience and needed to pass on that experience to later models. It was judged that conducting design reviews would be the most effective way for the organization to accomplish this. Design reviews were actually begun in the mid-1970s.

- There were four underlying reasons for pursuing DR implementation:
  1. While labor costs for testing in the development stage were on the rise in order to respond to more detailed and higher-level demands from the marketplace, the company had a strong desire to complete product development in a short period of time.
  2. The organization was growing with personnel increasing and getting younger.
  3. The massive scale of production led to huge losses if products failed.
  4. Consolidation of the information system meant that vast amounts of information were available from inside and outside the company, but the right information was not getting to the right people at the right time.

- NASA's design review system linked contractors with contractees and so could not be used as a model for Toyota. The company had to develop a design review methodology of its own.

- The term "design review" was itself a problem. Translated into Japanese as *sekkei shinsa* (design judging), it was misconstrued as a system for finding fault with designs. The concept thus created negative opinions (in some cases, flat-out rejection) before it could be explained.

- Encountering various bitter experiences along the way, DR finally took root and was implemented step by step through incremental stages of understanding (study, enlightenment, experimentation, acknowledgment, organizational promotion, establishment). The acknowledgment stage was reached between 1986 and 1987, when the Reliability Committee approved DR Implementation Guidelines in order to ensure the application of design reviews throughout the company. The committee also provided a supplementary manual of standards, added as an appendix to the standards.

- Design reviews were applied to intermediate entities of an appropriate scale, usually designated as units, assemblies, systems, and components.

Products and parts subject to design reviews were selected by the following criteria:

1. Entirely new mechanisms.
2. Materials for which there is no usage experience or newly introduced materials.
3. Newly designed parts susceptible to the influence either of the proximity of car attachments or of conditions of usage or environment (where problems have been likely to occur in the past).
4. Parts for which the management of process planning or manufacturing processes need to secure critical functions (e.g., safety-related items)

- Once products or parts subject to design reviews were selected, a design review planning form was filled out and then used by the Design Review Office to manage DR progress.

- Figure 4.13 shows a summary of design review implementation procedures.

- Design reviews are a type of gate management. The process stops when it goes outside some specified permissible zone. Development does not stagnate, however, because in actual practice, nearly all items remain in the permissible area.

- Different people are responsible for design reviews at each different stage of development. At DR1 in the product basic planning stage, the head of Planning is in charge of design reviews. At product design stages DR2 and DR3, this function is the responsibility of the head of design. For DR4, DR5, and DR6, when the design has moved into production, the head of the Production Engineering Department is responsible for the reviews. For designers, design reviews can be nerve-racking: The effects of DRs on personnel evaluations are significant.

- Too much data used in a design review adds to the designer's burden, so the following guidelines are set to prevent information overload:

    1. Blueprints
    2. Specifications forms (or simple written explanations)
    3. Design checksheets
    4. The actual product or part (where feasible)

Additional items are presented where needed, including quality tables, the results of design calculations, FMEA/FTA charts, and the results of experiments.

- A design checksheet (item [3] above), traditionally prepared as one link of design standardization, is a list of items (for each part) that are absolutely indispensable to proceeding with the design. The checksheet brings together in one place such items as the development schedule, required functions, product characteristics, print indications, pertinent laws, norms, standards, and past problems. Ostensibly it is to be used in tandem with design standards (standards that record pass/fail criteria for design procedures and design results). Bringing the checksheets into the

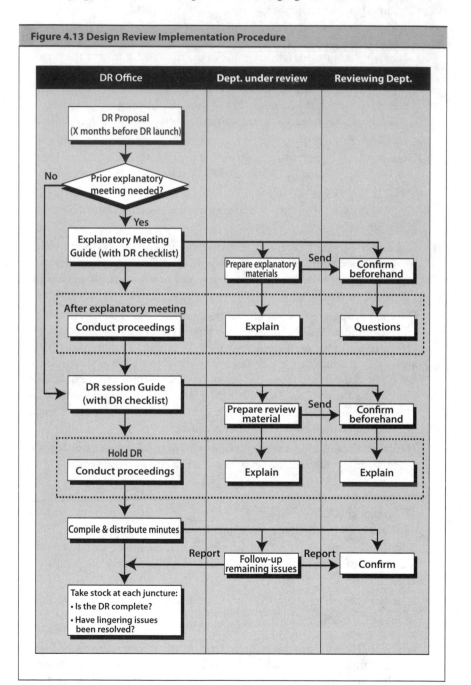

Figure 4.13 Design Review Implementation Procedure

   design review process is also useful since corrective action is indicated
when a design is deficient.

- When the reviewers receive design review data, they first verify them
  according to the design review checklist shown in Figure 4.14 and then
  conduct the review on the same day. Note that there are as many as 200
  detailed points to review.

- As we see from this DR checklist, evaluation in a design review is not
  confined to quality and reliability, but covers all aspects of development,
  including cost. The executive Function Council (see Figure 3.3) carries
  out independent quality, cost, production engineering, and other assessments, but it is within the practical course of a design review that a comprehensive assessment is performed.

- There are two styles of design reviews: one performed by Toyota in-
  house and the other used for suppliers (see Figure 4.5). Even for in-
  house design reviews, suppliers participate either by assisting the person
  responsible for the design or by presenting DR materials themselves.
  There is a strong desire in all this to have suppliers participate in the
  design review process as frequently as possible. The Kyohokai, an association of Toyota suppliers, has created and runs a system of supplier
  design reviews linked to the timing of the Toyota design reviews shown
  in Figure 3.6.

- The effects of design reviews are very difficult to assess, but the number
  of design changes at the start of production has dropped substantially.

- It has taken more than ten years since the introduction of design reviews
  for Toyota to confirm their effectiveness and to reach the point where
  they have become part of the daily work of the design department.

This summary of Toyota's design reviews is based on Katsuyoshi
Yamada's paper and other information. Toyota's design review system
becomes clearer still when the information presented here is read in conjunction with the Harvard Business Review article, "Another Look at how
Toyota Integrates Product Development," introduced earlier in our discussion of design criteria.

At the start of the 1980s, word that Toyota was putting energy into
design reviews spread, and DR became fashionable. Many companies
implemented DR, only to abandon it after a year or so. As Yamada noted,
design reviews either became forums for heaping blame on designers or
they did not last long because design departments resisted them, claiming
that design reviews were a wasteful duplication of discussions that designers had with concerned departments on a daily basis. Such problems
could have been avoided if DR implementation had been regulated by
guidelines. Guidelines might have dealt effectively with concerns about

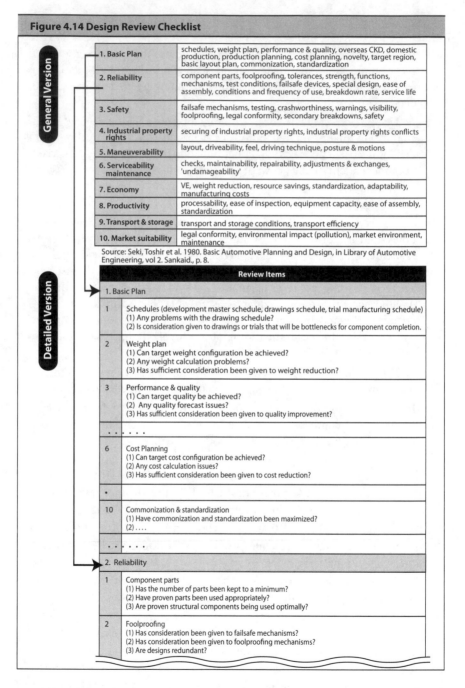

Figure 4.14 Design Review Checklist

General Version

1. Basic Plan	schedules, weight plan, performance & quality, overseas CKD, domestic production, production planning, cost planning, novelty, target region, basic layout plan, commonization, standardization
2. Reliability	component parts, foolproofing, tolerances, strength, functions, mechanisms, test conditions, failsafe devices, special design, ease of assembly, conditions and frequency of use, breakdown rate, service life
3. Safety	failsafe mechanisms, testing, crashworthiness, warnings, visibility, foolproofing, legal conformity, secondary breakdowns, safety
4. Industrial property rights	securing of industrial property rights, industrial property rights conflicts
5. Maneuverability	layout, driveability, feel, driving technique, posture & motions
6. Serviceability maintenance	checks, maintainability, repairability, adjustments & exchanges, 'undamageability'
7. Economy	VE, weight reduction, resource savings, standardization, adaptability, manufacturing costs
8. Productivity	processability, ease of inspection, equipment capacity, ease of assembly, standardization
9. Transport & storage	transport and storage conditions, transport efficiency
10. Market suitability	legal conformity, environmental impact (pollution), market environment, maintenance

Source: Seki, Toshir et al. 1980. Basic Automotive Planning and Design, in Library of Automotive Engineering, vol 2. Sankaid., p. 8.

Detailed Version

Review Items	
1. Basic Plan	
1	Schedules (development master schedule, drawings schedule, trial manufacturing schedule) (1) Any problems with the drawing schedule? (2) Is consideration given to drawings or trials that will be bottlenecks for component completion.
2	Weight plan (1) Can target weight configuration be achieved? (2) Any weight calculation problems? (3) Has sufficient consideration been given to weight reduction?
3	Performance & quality (1) Can target quality be achieved? (2) Any quality forecast issues? (3) Has sufficient consideration been given to quality improvement?
· · · · · ·	
6	Cost Planning (1) Can target cost configuration be achieved? (2) Any cost calculation issues? (3) Has sufficient consideration been given to cost reduction?
·	
10	Commonization & standardization (1) Have commonization and standardization been maximized? (2) . . . .
· · · · · ·	
2. Reliability	
1	Component parts (1) Has the number of parts been kept to a minimum? (2) Have proven parts been used appropriately? (3) Are proven structural components being used optimally?
2	Foolproofing (1) Has consideration been given to failsafe mechanisms? (2) Has consideration been given to foolproofing mechanisms? (3) Are designs redundant?

duplicated work or might have prevented excessive criticism of designers by promoting constructive criticism. As noted above, even Toyota struggled when it first introduced design reviews because it was unable to secure the understanding of designers and reviewers. Toyota, however, had the backing of its company-wide Reliability Committee, and within ten years, the company was able to institute design reviews. Toyota's strength lies in a willingness to spend ten years mastering something perceived to be worthwhile.

PRODUCTION TECHNOLOGY

Because it contains the word "production," the term production technology is often treated as an element of the Toyota Production System. Drawing from Taylorism, the Toyota Production System involves manufacturing operations improvements in the industrial engineering sphere. Production technology, on the other hand, is the field of engineering that exists independently between product development and manufacturing.

The Place of Production Technology within Toyota

Production technology [i.e., production engineering] has come to occupy a vital place at Toyota in its role of giving material form to the quality, appearance, reliability, and cost of Toyota products. The production technology development system shown in Figure 4.4 illustrates, for example, that production technology is on a par with the product research management system (Figure 4.3). Even in the setting of product specifications, the Production Engineering Office plays an important role:

1. Once mass production trials are completed, production technology evaluates and checks to ensure that the condition of new materials and new methods will cause no trouble on the line.
2. This applies across the board, whether to engines, airbags, or plastic parts.
3. Since production trials consume research costs, OK'd items need to be "sold" to the *shusa* (chief engineer). That is to say, when it comes to new products, the Production Engineering Department has the authority to accept or reject parts made using new materials or new methods.

Manufacturing Technology at Toyota

Manufacturing Technology and Its Position

Production technology can be divided into two types: technologies for plant layout and process design (making things flow) and technologies for assembling and processing (making things). There have been a fairly large number of studies and reports dealing with plant layout and process design at Toyota, so we will not deal with these topics here. We will concentrate, instead, on technologies for assembling and processing (hereafter referred to as manufacturing technologies).

The birth of new manufacturing technologies very often makes the birth of new products possible. In most companies, neither new manufacturing technologies nor new products come into being, because production engineering is treated as a downgraded form of product engineering.

Product engineering determines the functions and structures of products whereas manufacturing engineering determines the workmanship of products, including their quality, appearance, reliability, and cost. Getting at the truth behind the Toyota's reputation for high quality products requires research in the area of manufacturing technology.

Manufacturing Technology and Quality

The *LS430* and *RX300* (sold in Japan as the *Celsior* and *Harrier*, respectively) are models that Toyota markets in the United States under the Lexus brand. To understand why Lexus ranked first in the J.D. Power IQS (Initial Quality Study) survey of luxury cars in 2000 (see Chapter 5), *Business Week* interviewed Kousuke Shiramizu, Toyota's executive vice president in charge of production.

Question: How did Toyota go about setting a global benchmark for quality with its Lexus line?

In building the Lexus, our operating principle has been to cut the margin for error in half. Everything was fair game, such as reducing the small space between body panels. This helps reduce wind noise when the car is being driven. We also went to extremes to rethink the way we made cars—everything from the casting of the stamping dies used to form the car's metal parts to the exterior finish. Previously, our mainstay cars had gaps [between the front and rear doors] of about 7 millimeters. Our goal for the LS 400 was to cut that average in half, to 4 mm.

Question: How do you ensure that the quality will carry through the assembly process?

When we started, it was hard to systematize the way we put together parts. But we developed processes for everything, right down to the way the seat leather is cut. Now, thanks to advances in production technology over the past decade, it's all systematized to allow for mass production. All of that knowledge results in better stamping dies, which then makes it easy to produce on greater scale.

Question: Why are stamping dies, or molds, so important in the fit and performance of components?

Take the two exterior side panels on a car. Each of these is basically made up of four main components. When put together to form a panel, there's a lot of room for minor aberrations such as cracks and wrinkles. So we developed a mold press that stamps all four parts as a single component. That made it a lot easier to mass produce them with fewer quality problems. We've adopted these approaches in the manufacturing of all Toyota models. So that's a clear spin-off benefit from the development of the Lexus line.

(September, 2001. "From the Nexus of Lexus." *Business Week*, No. 3747, p. 28.)

An automobile body is a soft enclosure made of thin sheets of metal welded or bolted together. Distortion in the welding process or a part's own weight may deform a part section by 5 millimeters or so. There are as many as scores of other sources of distortion as well, including subtle factors such as differences in lots of sheet metal or inventory storage times. Controlling the causes of distortion in car bodies is an extremely difficult business. Given this situation, manufacturers establish fixed gaps to prevent doors and panels from interfering with one another even if distortion occurs. They also change from round to oblong bolt holes to make assembly and adjustment possible even in the presence of distortion.

The description above does not mention it, but bolt holes on Toyota vehicles are round. Success in controlling more than scores of subtle distortion factors made it possible for Toyota to narrow the gap between the front and rear doors from 7 millimeters to 4 millimeters. It is no ordinary technology that allows this level of gap reduction.

It is easy enough for Shiramizu to talk about building a press that could stamp out four parts as a single component, but, in fact, there is nothing easy about it. A car body functions as a single unit and by rights should be made as a single piece, but for ease of production it is broken up into several tens of parts with no individual, independent functions. Side panels should really be built as single units, but considerations of press capacity, space, transport difficulty, and other issues have always meant that automobile makers have divided them into four separate pieces. Being able to make four-part panels as single parts will strike anyone who knows the shopfloor as an amazing feat because it means that all impediments to this have been cleared.

Shiramizu also says that Toyota had systematized procedures for all processes, "right down to methods for cutting seat leather." Usually, seat leather is cut at first-tier or second-tier suppliers. Systematized procedures, therefore, encompass not only in-house plants and assembly lines but also the standardization and systematization of procedures at parts suppliers. Even the mighty Toyota must have found this difficult. Shiramizu's assertion that the completion of systematization of all processes has made large-scale production possible and that the knowledge they have accumulated along the way helps develop better dies merits attention. These are important words.

It is natural that making the gap between parts smaller or eliminating the gap itself by making them a one-piece part should contribute to radical reduction in wind noise and elimination of dents or scratches during the part assembly and transport.

J. D. Power began conducting IQS evaluations in 1986. Cutthroat competition to improve IQS performance has reduced major problems so much that IQS scores are now determined by factors such as wind noise at high speeds (when the gaps in parts are reduced or integration eliminates them entirely, wind noise automatically diminishes and damage to parts in assembly and transport naturally goes down) and slight scratches. It is easy to see why Lexus, when evaluated by IQS criteria, is rated number one.

If we compare cars with smaller panel gaps—or no gaps at all—to cars with wider gaps, the cars in the latter group are obviously perceived in a less favorable light. Differences like these are reflected in another J. D. Powers quality index: APEAL (see Chapter 5). Capable manufacturing technology is what accounts for the fact that Toyotas, in recent years, have been highly ranked in the United States for appeal.

Toyota builds the *Celsior* and *Harrier* at its Tahara Plant. When production of the *Celsior* began at the end of the 1980s, a Tahara Plant production engineer made the following observations:

We're confident we have the best fit-and-finish quality of any automobiles in the world. There is still no car anywhere that can compare with a Toyota.

Fit-and-finish quality is fundamentally a consequence of the way we manufacture vehicle bodies, of how much we can improve body precision.

All the "covers" on a car, including doors, hoods, trunk lids, and filler caps, etc., need to close correctly the first time, with no adjustments in assembly. This has been the rule for ten years (since the end of the 1970s). It's a product of merging production engineering and body construction technology.

In many ways, we are number one in the world in press technology.

Teardowns of other cars reveal a manufacturer's quality levels and technical capabilities. The assertion that "there is still no car anywhere that can compare with a Toyota" comes from tearing down other companies' cars. The reference to closing "correctly the first time, with no adjustments in assembly" can be linked to Toyota's round bolt holes. From this account, we also learn that "this has been the rule for ten years" (since the end of the 1970s). It is just this sort of long-term accumulation of manufacturing technology that has made it possible for Toyota to achieve its sensational shrinking of body gaps from 7mm to 4mm.

Toyota's reputation for a high quality fit in the interior and exterior trim is well established, too. Parts are built so that the quality of fit can be reproduced no matter who assembles or reassembles them. And this is not achieved by adding extra parts. On the contrary, it comes from ingenuity that works in the direction of reducing the number of parts and lowering costs.

A visit to the Tahara Plant reveals no special inspections going on to raise the *Celsior*'s IQS score. One gets the feeling, instead, that the principle of "building quality into the process" is an everyday practice. Full complements of manpower and equipment are at work on the finish of vehicles at companies that compete with the *Celsior* for high IQS rankings. Other companies, for example, will run high-speed chassis roller tests up to 160-240 km/hour whereas the test for the *Celsior* usually stays below the 120 km/hr range.

Process Capability

The Tahara Plant production engineer also commented on Toyota's process capability:

The Takaoka Plant has the best figures for defects, at 0.5 per vehicle, including body, painting, assembly, and components. The figure for assembly alone is 0.08 per vehicle, which corresponds to two rework operators per shift.

We have 55 people on kaizen *(improvement) teams for Takaoka's three lines. The company as a whole has been charged to reduce indirect labor, but we've been told at the same time to expand our* kaizen *teams.*

People in the industry will appreciate right away how extraordinary these figures are for defects per vehicle, assembly problems, and rework operators. Note, also, that the idea of expanding *kaizen* teams emerges in a context of decreasing numbers overall. Many companies that are still trying to increase the number of line employees at the expense of staff would benefit from studying the Toyota experience.

When compared to the numbers of other companies, Toyota's low numbers for both per-vehicle defects and rework operators, show that design tolerances (allowable manufacturing error) for Toyota products are broad enough to accommodate manufacturing variability—or, rather, that manufacturing variability is narrow enough with respect to design tolerances.

Generally speaking, fitting the variability in manufacturing processes into design tolerances requires either 100 percent inspections or Cp (process capability) index values of 1.33 or above, as shown in Figure 4.15.

A Cp value of 1.33 or higher means a rate of 3.4 defects out of 1 million (effectively 0), which makes it possible to get by with sampling

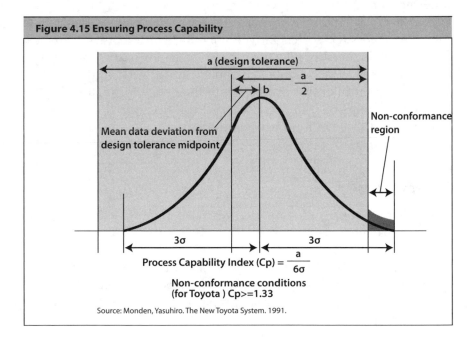

Figure 4.15 Ensuring Process Capability

a (design tolerance)

$\dfrac{a}{2}$

b

Mean data deviation from design tolerance midpoint

Non-conformance region

3σ 3σ

Process Capability Index (Cp) = $\dfrac{a}{6\sigma}$

Non-conformance conditions (for Toyota) Cp>=1.33

Source: Monden, Yasuhiro. The New Toyota System. 1991.

inspections or other simple inspection methods. Succeeding in making parts that "close correctly the first time" is the same as achieving Cp values of ≥1.33. Engineering capability at this level supports the claim that Toyota is the world leader in all aspects of production technology.

A Cp value of less than 1.00 requires 100 percent inspections. In our discussion of body assembly above, the justification for using oblong bolt holes and adjusting each part is that the Cp is below 1.00. One may imagine that the defect rate goes to zero when 100 percent of the parts are adjusted, but, in fact, human error enters into the adjustment, and the defect rate will inevitably rise above the 3.4 per million level achieved when the Cp is less than or equal to 1.33.

This is why Toyota works to bring the Cp for all processes to less than or equal to 1.33, either by enhancing the precision of manufacturing equipment or by broadening design tolerances. Blindly increasing the precision of manufacturing equipment would send capital costs soaring, so broadening design tolerances is desirable wherever possible. This is one incentive for using the Taguchi Method (for widening design tolerances) that was discussed in Chapter 3 in the section on statistical methods.

Toyota set out to achieve Cp≥1.33 for all processes in the midst of its continuous quality improvement activities after receiving the Deming Prize in 1965. This is why Toyota's reported achievement of Cp≥1.33 in car bodies at the end of the 1970s is reasonable and why we can assume that the company now possesses even more formidable manufacturing technologies.

In his book, *The Toyota Method*[24] (1998), Osamu Katayama publishes an interview with Kazuo Okamoto, a director at Toyota Motor in charge of the development of the Celsior.

First, we got together the production engineering people at the plant and formed a "flagship" quality committee to make dramatic improvements in manufacturing precision. Then we put together a system of design and experimentation support.

For example, we needed a device for balancing the propeller shaft as it turns that was capable of more precise measurements than the balancers used on previous Toyotas. Ordinarily, someone would say "You can't measure that precisely," and that would be the end of it. When Ichiro Suzuki (the Celsior's chief engineer) reported on the problem through the FQ Committee, though, he brought along some production engineers and had them ride in a vehicle with higher numbers and got them to admit the difference. The production engineers had no choice but to develop a higher precision inspection apparatus than had been used in the past. The same kind of thing happened for all the parts.

Here, we see a production engineering department recognizing its gatekeeper role and bringing about a revolution in attitude to open up a new era.

PURCHASING

Growing Together

The way Toyota sees its parts suppliers has not changed fundamentally since Kiichiro's day. The theme is "growing together." Kiichiro's view of suppliers is basically the same as the one we introduced in Figure 1.3 with the picture of the strange bucket. The notion of growing together grew out of the idea that the performance of the weakest supplier determines the performance of the entire group of companies.

Toyota's Purchasing Rules, formulated in 1939, contain the following statement:

> *"We consider subcontractor factories to be our branch factories and in principle do not change to other subcontractors for frivolous reasons. To every extent possible, we will endeavor to improve the performance of those factories."*

Takahiro Fujimoto cites a typical example of "growing together" in his book *The Evolution of a Production System*[25] (1997):

> *The B___ Company, when it was founded in the 1960s, would fabricate, test, and then manufacture parts according to complete manufacturing prints supplied by Toyota. It also undertook formalized work such as the compilation of parts tables and print control. During this period, the company kept sending "guest engineers" to Toyota and improved its percentage of print approval as it eventually went to the point where it could take charge of design nearly up to the vehicle level, i.e., from approved drawings (detailed prints based on parts specifications from Toyota) to assembly prints to structural design prints. As it entered the 1980s, the B___ Company added marketing planning to its capabilities and grew to establish itself as an independent parts supplier that could be entrusted with a comprehensive approved drawing design system.*

Thus, through a thirty-year association with Toyota, the B___Company expanded and grew to the point where it could participate with other manufacturer groups (*keiretsu*). Results of this sort were not achieved because Toyota grew, but rather, because both companies prospered through Toyota's philosophy of growing together.

As it had the previous year, Toyota came out on top in a 2000 ranking of corporate income. It had successfully joined with suppliers to lower manufacturing costs and reported a 40.6 percent increase in income. And lest one think that Toyota was bullying suppliers to get such results, consider this. Of the thirty top-ranking automobile parts suppliers on the list, twelve were from the Toyota group. (*Nikkei Business*. 27 August 2001).

Keiretsu

In Toyota's thirty-year company history (1967), we find an interesting observation about *keiretsu*:

> *"Growing together" had been at the center of Toyota's thinking about suppliers since Kiichiro's time, but concrete organizational improvements had to wait until after World War II. In September 1952, Toyota applied for the Diagnosis Guidelines for Machinery and Equipment Enterprise Groups (keiretsu) that had been formulated by the Japanese government's Small and Medium Enterprise Agency in July of the same year. Over the course of eleven long months, diagnoses were conducted at Toyota, as the parent company, along with approximately forty supplier plants. The results were edited in the form of diagnosis reports and these then became the basis for recommendations for improvement.*
>
> *Partly as a check on this process, Toyota conducted a second round of diagnoses in April 1954. From the results of this second round, it became clear that considerable improvements had been made to the management systems of companies where assessments had been carried out only two short years before. Sales-profit ratios, ratios of fixed assets to net worth, and production all rose one and a half times while defect rates had been cut in half.*

The formation of a Toyota enterprise group, or *keiretsu*, based on the philosophy of growing together proved to be extraordinarily productive. The *keiretsu* survived and grew stronger through the 1980s until, in the early 1990s, Toyota adopted the idea of an "open-door policy" in response to U.S. criticism of the *keiretsu*. The *keiretsu* were not summarily dismantled, but membership into the *keiretsu* was opened.

Nowadays the word *keiretsu* is taboo at Toyota; it has been replaced by the word "group." *Keiretsu* implies a system, a far stronger connotation, and the conclusion to be drawn here is that the taboo was adopted in order to avoid friction. Indeed, the issue of *keiretsu* was not solely of concern at Toyota. The following appeared in the August 20, 2001, edition of the *Nikkei Sangyo Shimbun*:

> *Koichiro Toda, president of Unisia JECS, lets his true feelings slip out when he says, "We never realized what a serious blow the disappearance of the* keiretsu *would be." As Nissan Motor starts to dismantle its* keiretsu *system, they're anxious to groom other suppliers outside of Nissan. "But you can't just go to a customer and start negotiating. It takes time to get to that point," he explains sternly. "Our customer had always been Nissan, so basically we don't have the sales know-how we need." Toda says that he needs engineers who can design and develop for other carmakers. "We may be adding people for a long time even though we haven't got the sales."*

Dismantling *keiretsu* put Unisia JECS into a new environment, and its cost structure can be expected to improve in the future. But even if it were to succeed in achieving a cost structure that, like the Toyota group, can "wring water out of a dry towel," it is not likely to prevail over Toyota group companies. It will continue to have the problem of the extra costs of sales and of carrying engineers for multiple carmakers.

In July 2000, Toyota launched CCC (Construction of Cost Competitiveness) 21, a campaign designed to bring about unprecedented cost reductions. The *Nikkei Sangyo Shimbun* reported on this development in on March 8, 2001:

> *CCC21 is not simply a campaign to lower the purchase prices of parts. It involves working with suppliers to lower their manufacturing costs. On January 1, 2001, in order to pursue comprehensive materials and other cost reductions, Toyota merged Procurement Departments 1 and 2, handling parts and materials, respectively, into a single integrated system. This was a major shift, transforming purchasing personnel from specialists in individual parts to generalists overseeing the stream from materials to production processes. The aim is to lower costs across the board, not by examining quality and cost in*

isolation, but by investigating their mutual relationships with methods and equipment.

The cooperation of suppliers responsible for 90 percent of the number of parts and 70 percent of the costs of parts is indispensable to fulfilling the promise of strategies such as CCC21. And the suppliers carry part of the strategy precisely because of their continuous relationship with Toyota. Dissolving the *keiretsu* means dealing with suppliers only on the basis of price. We see what is happening to automakers who ruin suppliers by pushing them to the point where purchase prices can go no lower or who engage in "scorched earth" purchasing by wandering about in search of suppliers with excess capacity. In the long run, they themselves will be ruined.

Faces of a Stern Father and a Compassionate Mother

Toyota does not cling stubbornly to *keiretsu.*

An executive in Toyota's Purchasing Department observes that, "The Toyota corporate culture of fostering parts suppliers is important, but you can't prevail in world competition without also adopting the Western culture of selecting suppliers." This was how a pilgrimage to Paris began among TMC parts supplier affiliates. The reason was that Toyota, in a joint-venture production of compact vehicles with the PSA Peugeot Citroen Group, had adopted a policy of entrusting parts procurement to PSA. Toyota is even forsaking parts suppliers from its own keiretsu, saying that it will "introduce them to PSA, but won't guarantee contracts." (December 13, 2001. Nikkei Sangyo Shimbun.)

When this Toyota executive refers to adopting the Western culture of selecting suppliers, he is not talking about shifting to a culture of selecting suppliers. He is referring, rather, to creating a new Toyota way that incorporates the European approach. The article uses the word "forsaking," but this should not be interpreted as dismantling the *keiretsu*. On the contrary, it means urging *keiretsu* suppliers to grow stronger by having them engage in another kind of competition, in much that same way that a lioness toughens her cubs by pushing them off a cliff.

Toyota is said to possess two faces: those of a stern father and a compassionate mother. Typical examples of this dual nature may be seen in the VA/VE suggestion system and in the claims compensation system for marketplace defects.

The VA/VE suggestion system, created with the introduction of TQC in the 1960s, is a system for getting parts makers to generate effective cost reduction suggestions. Toyota had already spent four years making cost tables and other preparations with a view to encouraging productive suggestions. In addition, the company decided to raise the motivation of parts suppliers by returning to them half of any cost reductions made. The arrangement gave parts manufacturers high cost reduction targets and a way to prosper if those targets were met. Even Toyota's most intense cost reduction efforts, then, would not impoverish its parts suppliers. Some automakers still run VA/VE suggestion systems in order to grab the profits for themselves, but with total vehicle sales volume not expected to increase in the future, such a practice threatens to ruin the group as a whole.

Here is how the system of claims for marketplace defects works. Ordinarily, when a design is outsourced, the outsourcing company fixes specifications and the supplier designs, manufactures, and delivers parts that conform to those specifications. If the part causes some problem in the marketplace, then responsibility for compensation is assigned depending on where the problem occurred. If the problem lies clearly in the supplier's design, manufacture, or delivery, then the outsourcing company seeks compensation from the supplier for any damages caused by the problem. Anything else is deemed to be a problem with the specifications, and responsibility falls to the outsourcing company. This way of thinking means that unless the outsourcing company's written specifications contain an unreasonable requirement that there be "no problems in the marketplace," the majority of marketplace problems become specifications problems, and the outsourcing company cannot seek compensation from the supplier.

Instead of adopting this "logical" approach, however, Toyota has a "unilateral" policy that market claims regarding components are basically the responsibility of the supplier. Not adhering to this, as Toyota tells it, would be "rude to the supplier" or would deny the supplier the "chance to grow." The real purpose behind this policy is to establish for suppliers a market problem analysis system and to promote market quality improvements by suppliers. Toyota's philosophy, in other words, is that there is no way an automobile manufacturer can, by itself, guarantee the quality of all of the twenty thousand to thirty thousand components in a vehicle. The quality of the automobile as a whole cannot be guaranteed unless each component maker sees itself as an independent manufacturer and puts in place all measures necessary to ensure the quality of its own components.

On the basis of this thinking, Toyota has put together a "supplier recovery system" (outlined below) in which claims cover the costs of defective components + costs of related components + labor charges for repair.

1. Toyota sets an initial ratio for sharing the costs of a claim (e.g., x percent for Toyota specification sheet and y percent for supplier approval request print).
2. When a claim occurs, Toyota seeks compensation from the supplier in accordance with the initial cost-sharing ratio.
3. The supplier investigates the claim and, if agreeing with Toyota's assessment, pays according to the initial cost-sharing ratio. If the supplier does not agree, it appends recovered problem parts themselves to its investigation data and applies to Toyota for a change in the cost-sharing ratio.
4. The supplier and Toyota make an adjustment and determine a new cost-sharing ratio.

Step 3 is particularly important. The supplier needs to have suitable market research and analysis capabilities in order to be able to carry out the third step.

When large enough sums are involved that this becomes a management issue, an assessment is made with Purchasing at the center, and Toyota sometimes assumes part of the burden. Here we see the "compassionate mother" side of the company.

Given that its sales-to-claim costs ratio is only half that of other firms, it is ironic that Toyota obliges component makers to shoulder nearly all of the burden of market claim costs when for many companies, the majority of such costs are borne by the finished goods manufacturer. Toyota's claim costs are low, however, precisely because Toyota has a clear ideology of toughening suppliers by "pushing them off the cliff," a philosophy that is directly connected to reducing the burden of claims costs on suppliers.

Design Outsourcing Methods

Historically, the enormous number of component parts in an automobile has compelled capital-poor Japanese car manufacturers to adopt design outsourcing methods for relying on outside companies to design and manufacture components. Design outsourcing takes place according to the following specific procedure, known as the "approved drawing method" (*shoninzu hoshiki*).

1. The carmaker draws up parts specification drawings that document required characteristics such as size, basic shape, design and performance, and reliability criteria, and asks parts manufacturers (often plural) to take charge of design, prototyping, and trials.
2. Based on the parts specification drawings, the parts manufacturers design part specifications including part shape, materials, components, internal construction, and various other elements, verify these through prototyping and trials, and submit approval request drawings and written trial results to the automaker.
3. The automaker checks these and, if no problems are found, makes them into approved drawings by stamping "approved" on the approval request drawings.[26] It then contracts with one or more parts manufacturers to produce the parts for mass production.
4. The parts makers produce the parts in volume based on the approved drawings.

Takahiro Fujimoto's book, *The Evolution of a Production System* (1997), details the historical development of the approved drawing method and the differences between Toyota's practices and those of other companies, especially Nissan Motor's approved drawing system. Among other things, Fujimoto points out that the approved drawing system has long been in common practice in automobile companies and that Toyota took the method, elevated it into a "system" through documentation, and polished it into a method that benefits both automobile manufacturers and suppliers. He also posits that Nissan Motor's documentation of its practice lagged behind Toyota's by about ten years and that Nissan's approved drawings were seen to involve multiple overlapping tasks between Nissan and its suppliers, with the result that Nissan was never able to draw as much benefit from the system as Toyota did.

The work of design evolves little by little from the "soft" images and ideas of designers into increasingly concrete and creative operations. Breaking off part of that evolution and assigning it outside the company inevitably creates a need for close communication. As a result, the practice has emerged of having engineers from parts suppliers take up residence at automobile manufacturers.

The conditions under which parts supplier engineers stay at Toyota vary depending on the part in question, but ordinarily between five and eight assistant design managers will be in residence for from one to two years, with experimentalists asked to put in shorter stays when necessary. The costs (salaries) of these residents are split, with Toyota's share paid in a lump sum.

Other companies use this system of resident parts suppliers as well. But in other companies, the resident suppliers work with car manufacturer engineers and are generally treated as employees on temporary assignments. In many cases, moreover, the residence of parts supplier engineers is considered to be a kind of "training" by the car company. Sometimes, too, the car manufacturer does not pay the expenses of the resident engineers on the pretext that supplier costs are included in the purchase price of the parts during mass production.

Toyota's view of this can be expressed as follows:

Any haggling or kickbacks between parts suppliers and the car manufacturer will eventually rebound and obscure the details of the problems. This will deprive the company of opportunities for improvement, so fees for work performed are paid strictly for the stated reasons and in a lump sum. The car manufacturer's role is development, and the parts supplier's role is parts designs. When supplier employees are treated on a par with Toyota employees, a kind of "complicity" arises that diminishes engineering performance. And this is why a strict line is drawn between the two.

Parts Outsourcing Policy

Shoichiro Toyoda said, "If we don't make a part, we lose our understanding of its cost unless we at least have a grip on the technologies involved. We should outsource after we've made sure that we could make the part ourselves at any time."

Toyota is said to have set its criteria for the switch to an approved drawing system in terms of its criteria for design outsourcing. These may be expressed as follows: Ensure that parts design outsourcing does not hollow out Toyota's technical strengths or drain away basic know-how. Consequently, design work should not be frivolously outsourced merely for the purpose of saving on in-house development resources.

Thus, at Toyota, the decision to outsource design work is made after prior assessments and confirmations to guarantee that outsourcing will not diminish the company's technical strengths. Toyota's fundamental outsourcing policy, in other words, can be expressed as, "build technology inside and build parts outside."

At the end of the 1980s, Toyota responded to Nippon Denso's[27] bid to take charge of electronics-related systems, by saying that parts technology was one thing, but that Toyota would handle the systems. And although Nippon Denso was a sworn Toyota ally, Toyota proceeded to build a dedicated semiconductor plant in Hirose to manufacture components as sophisticated as microcomputer circuit boards. This example shows Toyota's deep commitment to the principle of "build technology inside and build parts outside."

Thus, Toyota outsources nearly all parts once it is able to design and produce them at will itself. And through subsequent supervision and support of its parts manufacturers, Toyota arranges to prevent its parts design technology capabilities from deteriorating.

> Toyota has launched a revolution in production to a surprising degree. For the first time in the history of car manufacturing in the world, it produces tires inside an automobile plant and supplies them directly to the assembly line. . . . Above all, the system Toyota uses now makes it possible to reduce costs substantially. It is estimated that Toyota is able to hold the cost of supplying tires to less than 50 percent of what other automobile manufacturers pay. This is leading to a desperate realignment in the tire industry and there is a significant possibility that this will trigger a dramatic break in the price of tires. And that can only bring about a major restructuring of the tire industry worldwide. (May 8, 2000. Nikkei Business.)

Another characteristic feature of the relationship between Toyota and parts manufacturers is that, in principle, Toyota issues orders to multiple firms. Orders for a single part or similar parts are always sent out to two or more suppliers (including in-house Toyota manufacturers). Along with minimizing risk and guarding against unforeseen problems or defects, this is intended to raise the technical competencies of parts suppliers by having them compete with and against one another. This practice results in lower purchase prices, but that is not the sole purpose. Most companies will push hard for lower prices but will ease off once they get them. When prices fall for Toyota parts, Toyota pushes hard to find out why. This is because it is more valuable to understand why prices fall than to understand why prices do not fall.

The "continuing relationships" referred to in Toyota's 1939 Purchasing Rules apply nowadays to model changes and minor changes. For new models, orders are targeted on a competitive basis. Even then, however, such competition does not give undue weight to price. As illustrated in the Supplier Guide (described later), competitions to choose suppliers evaluate "overall managerial strength, including the attitudes of the company president."

Outside Toyota, there are many companies that have adopted policies of multiple supplier sourcing on the Toyota model. However, because they make too much of competitive costing and expanding business relationships, they often outsource items to three or four suppliers even for low-volume production models. This should lead to higher costs, but in fact, deals are made at low costs. Something is distorted somewhere, in other words, and the practice invariably leads to financial woes. Toyota sets extraordinarily demanding standards for its suppliers, but it also wants its suppliers to profit.

As we explain in detail in the final chapter, Toyota is moving toward earning more volume through its CCC21 campaign. In connection with this, Toyota is revising its policy of ordering from multiple suppliers and changing to a system of single supplier outsourcing.

Toyota Suppliers' Association Activities

No discussion of Toyota's purchasing management can omit mention of the activities of the Kyohokai and Hoeikai, which are associations composed of Toyota suppliers. Yoshinobu Sato's 1988 book, *The Toyota Group: An Analysis of Strategy and Substantiation*,[28] provides details on this subject; only one example will be cited in this work.

Toyota suppliers associations put together management organizational charts for parts manufacturers that are linked to Toyota's management structure chart, and they have made them the common property of the group. Around 1985, they created a Project Development System Chart for parts suppliers that corresponds to Toyota's Quality Assurance Regulations and Design Review Usage Guidelines. In 1988, they compiled and implemented a Cost Planning Activities Manual for parts suppliers that corresponds to Toyota's Cost Control Regulations.

Such activities have built up systems for partner plants that link to the Toyota system, with the result that the entire Toyota Group has a single system for quality assurance and cost management. The fact that Toyota has created this situation means that supply chain management (SCM) has long been implemented at Toyota. Other companies' groups cannot put together effective supply chain management because many have no quality control system chart or cost management system chart in the first place.

New Purchasing Policies

Toyota's new purchasing policies are summarized systematically in A Supplier's Guide (for dealing with Toyota), a bilingual (Japanese-English) booklet of sixty-eight pages, plus appendices, distributed to parts suppliers seeking to do business with Toyota. This booklet is, of course, updated yearly, with the latest edition summarized on Toyota's website homepage. Because this guide provides a very good understanding of Toyota's philosophy on purchasing and the purchasing system, an outline of its contents is presented below.

A. Introduction: Toyota <u>has always</u> made it a fundamental principle to develop open, fair, and equitable purchasing activities to contribute to society and to the economy (Emphasis added).
B. Toyota's Purchasing Philosophy and System
   1. Three Basic Principles of Purchasing
      a) Fair competition based on an open-door policy
      b) Mutual benefit based on mutual trust
      c) Contribution to local economies based on good corporate citizenship
   2. Three Pillars of an Optimal Global Purchasing System
      a) International cost comparison data base system—to help provide suppliers with improvement targets
      b) New supplier/new technology development programs—to engage new suppliers and discover new technologies
      c) Improvement support program for existing suppliers—Toyota supports supplier improvement activities
C. Toyota Purchasing Activities
   1. Global expansion of Toyota production activities
   2. Purchasing organization and cooperative system
   3. Purchase items list
   4. Characteristics of products sought by Toyota
   5. Toyota's active discovery activities (new supplier/new technology development programs)
   6. Profile of suppliers sought by Toyota (technology, delivery, production, quality, cost), what Toyota aims for with suppliers (basic philosophy)
D. Sales Promotion Method
   1. Contact address, what Toyota wants to know when making contact— summary of products promoted and company particulars
   2. Summary of initial contact
   3. Summary of presentation
E. Characteristics of Toyota Development and Production (approach)
F. Purchasing Process (original parts, materials)— System of supplier activities linked to Toyota development process
   1. Planning steps
   2. Prototype fabrication steps
   3. Mass production preparation/Mass production steps

(Ref: Toyota supplier selection criteria. In addition to general implementation capabilities in the areas of quality, cost, and delivery, management attitudes are included in the selection criteria).

   A. Purchasing Process (maintenance parts and accessories)
   B. Purchasing Process (equipment, machinery, office equipment)

Steps and procedures for prospective new suppliers are explained systematically in the handbook outlined above. Since it has made clear what companies need to do in order to do business with Toyota, criticisms of a closed *keiretsu* system are no longer applicable.

Moreover, the handbook and the appended contact form, which sets out the items that need to be filled out in order to contact Toyota (the form is also available on Toyota's website), — allows prospective suppliers to see for themselves whether they possess the capabilities necessary to do business with Toyota. This effectively eliminates wasted time on both sides.

In any event, as Toyota states in the beginning of this booklet, what the booklet contains has hardly changed over the years. Parts manufacturers have always been free to pitch their products to Toyota, and the capable companies have been able to join the ranks of Toyota suppliers. Companies that have suggested pricing their way into the ranks of suppliers have been told not to overtax themselves and have been turned away at the door.

MANUFACTURING (THE TOYOTA PRODUCTION SYSTEM)

Toyota's system of manufacturing refers to the Toyota Production System created by Taiichi Ohno. Many studies and explanatory books about the Toyota Production System already exist, so the present work will touch only on the main points concerning the introduction of the system into the company.

The following summarizes key factors in the success of the Toyota Production System (TPS).

1. The system reduces costs comprehensively through the relentless elimination of waste. The fundamental philosophy of the system is to ask how overall efficiency can be raised rather than seeking partial efficiencies.
2. The two pillars of the system are just-in-time and *jidoka* (autonomation).
3. TPS is a production system that works to (1) build only what is needed, when it is needed, and in the quantity needed, (2) have each downstream process pull what it needs from each upstream process, and (3) have a minimum of people.

4. **Leveled production:** Hourly production quantities and varieties are balanced for all processes.
   Synchronization: Every process is provided with a system to constrain it from producing too fast.
   Autonomation: Lines are set to stop whenever abnormal situations occur.
   Visual management: All of this, moreover, is arranged so that it can be understood immediately (e.g., using *kanban* and *andon*).
5. (A) Setup changeover times are made as short as possible in order to minimize batch sizes. (B) Jigs and tools are kept simple and low-cost.

Despite the celebrity of the Toyota Production System and despite the wealth of literature about TPS, very few companies have adopted the Toyota Production System in its entirety.

Robert Eaton, the former chairman and CEO of Chrysler, which used to be one of the Big Three automakers in the United States, declared in an interview in the beginning of 1994 that "we have achieved production efficiencies equal to those of the Japanese manufacturers. We have nothing left to learn from Toyota." Eaton's comment was prompted by changes in Chrysler that had come about when he hired consultants to introduce the Toyota Production System into his company. Chrysler had subsequently succeeded in achieving broad increases in productivity.

Some months later, however, a Chrysler executive visited Toyota's plant in Kentucky, saying that he wanted to "check that Chrysler had learned everything it could from the Toyota Production System." From early in the morning, he spent a full day earnestly touring the plant, and as he left, he made this assessment. "This has been a truly exhausting day. I have clearly confirmed that Chrysler hasn't learned anything from Toyota." (*Nikkei Business.* April 10, 2000).

Michikazu Tanaka, a former senior managing director of Daihatsu Kogyo who was personally trained by Taiichi Ohno, describes the main features of the Toyota Production System this way: "In terms of results, it involves reducing work-in-process, raising productivity and lowering costs. But the real aim is to bring out the capabilities of each individual. The ultimate aim is to draw out people's motivation." (Shimokawa, Koichi and Takahiro Fujimoto. 2001. *The Starting Point of the Toyota System*).[29]

Yoshihito Wakamatsu and Tetsuo Kondo in *Building People and Products the Toyota Way* (2001) and Masaharu Shibata and Hideharu Kaneda in *Toyota Shiki Saikyo no Keiei* (2001) make similar arguments.

All the same, these arguments do not seem to suffice to make it possible to adopt the Toyota Production System. For instance, the notion that inventory is evil or the idea of making stop cords to halt a production line when a problem occurs owe more to a way of seeing things—to a viewpoint or perspective—than they do to "building people." Conventional thinking would lead us to conclude that inventory is necessary for smooth production or that total efficiency is greater when we repair after the fact any problems that occur on the line.

So what is the fundamental "way of seeing" of the Toyota Production System, anyway? The question calls for a cogent and comprehensible explanation. Without a basic understanding of this point, we may adopt the Toyota Production System but we will be unable to apply it and therefore unable to build a version of the Toyota Production System that will surpass other companies. If we cannot apply it, then nothing will work.

Taiichi Ohno provides part of the answer: "There is a secret to shopfloor technology just as there is a secret to juggling or to a magic trick. And I'll let you in on the secret. To get rid of waste, train your eyes to find waste and then think about how to get rid of the waste you've found. Do this over and over again, always, everywhere, relentlessly and unremittingly."

Ohno, however, does not explain what he means by "eyes that can find waste," and therefore does not reveal the secret. The Toyota Production System remains as elusive as ever.

One book that gets to the heart of the problem is *Toyota's Profit System—a Thorough Study of Just-in-Time*[30] (1993), written by Noboru Ayuse, a former Toyota employee. Ayuse's perspective on TPS can be summarized as follows:

- There are two sources of profit in manufacturing. One is the generation of surplus value and the other one is capital turnover.
- What the Toyota Production System does, essentially, is to increase the capital turnover rate (i.e., invested resources versus sales). It's a question of how many times you go through the selling cycle or of increasing the capital utilization rate. Being flexible, responding quickly to shifting circumstances, and reducing inventories are means of achieving that.
- Taylorism and the Ford system seek to increase efficiency. Efficiency is the ratio of invested resources to production volume, or "productivity." There is no focus on whether what has been made sells or not, only on how much is being produced. Ford could efficiently produce uniformly black Model Ts, but lowering the manufacturing cost was meaningless unless the cars sold.
- The Toyota Production System, then, is a system that focuses on quickly building products that sell. This basic perspective is what resulted in ideas such as leveling, SMED, one-piece flow, stop cords, availability rate

(not operating rate, but the availability to run at any time). This is why the Toyota Production System emerging after Taylorism and the Ford System has been called revolutionary.

Even while Ayuse was at Toyota, he viewed Toyota from the perspective of an objective outsider. He began writing the precursor to the book, the internally published *The Toyota System—A Toyota-style Production System for the Purpose of Cost Reduction*[31] because he vaguely suspected that something was wrong. It is difficult for someone from Toyota to explain things in such a way that outsiders can understand, but Ayuse's book accomplishes this because of its author's objective stance.

SALES

Shotaro Kamiya is largely responsible for establishing Toyota's sales system. In 1935, when Kamiya was scouted by Kiichiro Toyoda and came over to Toyota from GM Japan, Kamiya had GM Japan's Chevrolet and Buick dealerships one by one change over to the Toyota group. When the Japan Automobile Supply Company (JASC) was dissolved after World War II, moreover, he had leaders from the old Nissan group throughout Japan switch one after another over to Toyota group dealerships. Both before and after the war, the gap between Toyota and Nissan sales capabilities was unmistakable. Later, when Toyota Sales split off from Toyota Motor, Kamiya became president of Toyota Motor Sales and, proclaiming his famous sales philosophy of "users first, then dealers, then the manufacturer," came to be known as the "god of sales."

In his book *Toyota Management Rules*,[32] Yoshimasa Kunisaki concisely sums up the sales rules that Kamiya formulated:

> **Sales Rule No. 1:** Sales is different from selling products. Sales is creating the conditions that make selling easy.
> **Sales Rule No. 2:** You don't make things and then sell them. You make things for people who buy them.
> **Sales Rule No. 3:** Trust in a product comes from trust in the sales.
> **Sales Rule No. 4:** The relationship between manufacturer and dealers is one of co-existence and mutual prosperity.
> **Sales Rule No. 5:** Sales should not skimp on investment.
> **Sales Rule No. 6:** "Unreasonable effort" is sometimes required to seize the right timing for a deal.
> **Sales Rule No. 7:** Always ask what you should be doing to win the competition for sales.
> **Sales Rule No. 8:** Not even orders from small countries are to be slighted.

Sales Rule No. 9: Make sure you can always cover your main line of work when you make forays into other businesses.

These rules were compiled during an era of production-driven marketing in which manufacturers could sell anything they could build. Kamiya's thinking, however, goes beyond sales-driven marketing to the concept of customer-driven marketing. It was an extraordinarily progressive idea.

Backed by this powerful sales network, Toyota garnered a 43.3 percent share of the domestic market in 2000. Yet this seemingly rock-solid sales network gives rise to a sense of crisis at Toyota, a situation noted by the editors of the *Weekly Diamond*[33] as quoted in *Toyota Management: The Law of Winner Takes All* (2001):[34]

> *A mid-level executive in the sales department says, "Seeing dealers as distributors puts them in the most backward category of all." Not enough action is being taken, he means, to respond to structural changes among consumers or to strengthen the value chain (i.e., to provide value and garner profit after new cars are sold). Such structural changes inevitably make heavy burdens of the large numbers of salespeople and sales outlets that support competitiveness. As the president of a Kanto Region dealership confesses, "I'm worried that, within five years, Honda and the others that have fewer dealerships and people could turn the situation to their advantage over Toyota."*

Certainly, the Japanese system of selling cars is said to lag far behind that of the United States. This is why serious Toyota-type streamlining was applied to the Kamiya-style sales system when Toyota Motor and Toyota Motor Sales merged in 1982.

Shoichiro Toyoda explained this at the 67th Quality Management Symposium sponsored by the Union of Japanese Scientists and Engineers in 1998:

> *Let me give you the example of one particular dealer. When we're talking about sales, the emphasis is always on market share and the number of vehicles sold, so there is a tendency to spend money in order to differentiate oneself. But this doesn't necessarily make for a healthier organization in the long run. This particular dealer hadn't had much success in his steady attempts to improve the process between selling a car and recovering payment and by lowering costs and returning profits to customers in a bid to improve CS in its true sense of the word.*

At this point, he put together a team including manufacturing kaizen *experts to improve material flows for new vehicles and service. This team succeeded in achieving results that until that time had seemed impossible: They shortened the time between order receipt and vehicle delivery, maintained 100 percent on-time delivery to customers, and recovered nearly 100 percent of payments. A culture of continuous improvement has taken root at this dealership and is beginning to penetrate throughout the organization. We are beginning to see many dealerships like this one.*

The team, including manufacturing experts that made improvements to the dealership's tasks, was the Business Improvement Support Office guided by Shoichiro Toyoda's eldest son, Akio Toyoda.

Within the sales division, the Business Improvement Support Office was launched in January 1996. Its purpose was to introduce the Toyota Production System into the sales division in order to increase the efficiency of distribution and sales and to shorten lead-times. Used car distribution became the first focus of the Business Improvement Support Office. At the time, it took as many as forty days to change a used car into cash when it was traded in. To speed up this cash conversion, a system was set up for dealers to post traded-in cars at other dealerships via information network terminals. As this developed, it was linked to the website Gazoo, which offers information about new and used cars on the Internet.

Gazoo is an information system whose purpose is to eliminate as much waste as possible in distribution and sales and to increase business efficiency. Its ultimate goal is to directly link to the production department's information system to achieve total make-to-order production. In this way, the Toyota Production System is on the verge of a major revolution in distribution and sales.

Endnotes

1. Chapter 3 (Automobile Planning Methods) of the first volume of the *Handbook of Automotive Engineering* (Jidosha kogaku benran), published by the Japan Society of Automotive Engineers in 1984, systematically describes the planning, design, development, and production preparation processes for an automobile and presents a brief discussion of marketing strategies. The chairman of the chapter's editorial committee and all eight of its authors are Toyota employees, so it is probably fair to assume that the chapter describes work methods at Toyota. In the somewhat incoherent

partial treatment of marketing strategy, we can see the lingering influence of Toyota Motor Sales. Although the technical details are somewhat dated, the chapter provides a good understanding of Toyota work methods. The *Handbook of Automotive Engineering* is recommended as further reading for anyone interested in more details.

2. *Kyosoryoku no honshitsu.*
3. The Japanese edition of Sloan's *My Years with GM* (Diamond, 1967) is out of print, but an abridged version was published in installments in the *Diamond Harvard Business Review* (*Daiyamondo Habado Bijinesu Rebyu*) in a series that began in January 2002.
4. *Shinsei Toyota—hito to senryaku.*
5. *Seihin Kaihatsuryoku.*
6. *Seisan Shisutemu no Shinkaron.*
7. *Toyota Seisan Hoshiki.*
8. *Maruchipurojecuto Senryaku.*
9. *Toyota Hoshiki ni miru Shisutemu Saikochiku.*
10. *Toyota Jidosha Shusa Seido.*
11. *Toyota o Shiru to iu Koto.*
12. For details on each of the tools used in the quality deployment process described above, please refer to the specialized quality documents.
13. *Seihin kaihatsu to hyojunka kanri (in Jidosha Gijutsu).*
14. *yoko tenkai.*
15. *Shukan Toyo Keizai.*
16. *Nikkei Mekanikaru.*
17. *Seihin kikaku dankai kara susumeru Toyota no buhin kyotsuka.*
18. Satoshi Kuroiwa. *Nijuisseiki ni muketa Jidosha Kiban no Seibi ni Mukete (Jidosha Gijutsu).*
19. *Giho ni yoru—Seihin Kosuto Daun Manyuaru [Manual of Cost Reduction using VRP Techniques].*
20. *Tôtaruka o siko suru buhinhyo joho no toroku—kanri shisutemu.*
21. *Seihin Kaihatsuryoku.*
22. *Seisan Shisutemu no Shinkaron.*
23. *Totaruka o siko suru buhinhyo joho no toroku—kanri shisutemu.*
24. *Toyota no hoshiki.*
25. *Seisan Shisutemu no Shinkaron.*
26. Author's note: The term "approved drawing" (*shoninzu*) is not currently in widespread use and individual companies use such equivalents as "received drawing" (*juryozu*). In this book, we refer to these collectively by means of the old appellation of "approved drawing."
27. An electronics supplier.
28. *Toyota Gurupu no Senryaku to Jissho Bunseki.*
29. *Toyota Shisutemu no Genten.*
30. *Toyota no shueki shisutemu—jasuto-in-taimu no tettei kenkyu.*

31. *Genka Teigen no tame no Toyota-shiki Seisan Shisutemu—Toyota shisutemu.*
32. *Toyota no keiei hosoku.*
33. *Shukan Daiyamondo.*
34. *Toyota Keiei Hitorigachi Hosoku.*

——— 5 ———

Product Power and Brand Power

In Chapters 1 through 4, we have taken a systematic bottom-to-top look at the infrastructure of the Toyota Management System. The suitability of a company's infrastructure can be judged in two ways: by the power of its products (that is, whether or not the products and services ultimately produced by its corporate activities appeal to customers) and by the power of its brand (whether or not the company is attractive to consumers). In Chapter 5, we will examine the power of Toyota products and the Toyota brand in order to judge the suitability of its infrastructure.

PRODUCT POWER

Indexes for Assessing the Power of Products

Citing assessments by third-party organizations is an appropriate means for making objective judgments. From the 1970s to the 1980s, the American consumer group Consumers Union and the market research firm J.D. Power and Associates began independent product ratings and published the results in their magazines and on the Internet.

Since 1986, J.D. Power has conducted independent automobile surveys by sending questionnaires to general American consumers and publishing the results of its evaluations by vehicle use and model category. In a broader survey of "customer satisfaction" data, the company rates not only the product quality, but also the attitudes of salespeople and post-sales service. With respect to quality, the J.D. Power evaluations are more technical—they also assemble peripheral data needed for problem solving. This helps explain why automobile companies have paid increasing attention to J.D. Power data in recent years and why the media has become interested in the Power ratings.

In this chapter, we will focus on five indices included in J.D. Power surveys and published reports for automobiles.[1]

IQS (Initial Quality Study)

Measured after ninety days of ownership, this index looks at the number of defects, malfunctions, and other quality issues experienced by consumers and rates them in terms of problems per 100 vehicles.

VDI (Vehicle Dependability Index)

This index surveys the number of defects, malfunctions, and other quality issues consumers experience after four to five years of vehicle ownership and scores problems per 100 vehicles.

APEAL (Automotive Performance, Execution and Layout)

Measured after ninety days of ownership, this index surveys the degree to which consumers are satisfied with the uniqueness of vehicle design and styling, ride and handling, engine and transmission performance, and comfort and convenience. The results are published as a score per 100 vehicles.

SSI (Sales Satisfaction Index)

Following vehicle purchase, consumers are surveyed on such matters as purchase processing, salesperson attitude, vehicle delivery and follow-up, price assessment and financing, and insurance processes. Responses are processed statistically to yield an index of customer satisfaction with sales.

CSI (Customer Satisfaction Index)

Measured after three years of ownership, the CSI calculates satisfaction with dealership service by statistically processing evaluations of dealership service department attitudes toward customers and experiences with repairs and warranties. This index focuses on matters of convenience, such as days and hours required to perform the job, the service area, and ease of scheduling appointments.

The Impact of Third-party Ratings

In 1976, Paul Bender published enormously influential research results showing a 1:6 ratio between the cost of servicing existing customers and the cost of acquiring new customers. The cost of turning an existing customer into a "repeater," in other words, is a mere one-sixth of the cost of winning a new customer.

In a 1975 to 1980 survey, the Office of Consumer Affairs of the U.S. Commerce Department first reported on the qualitative existence of a "word-of-mouth" effect by which repeat customers introduce others to products, brands, and dealers.

In 1986, TARP (Technical Assistance Research Program) conducted a study of the behavior of customers (in the United States) who have been disappointed by defects, malfunctions, and other basic functional quality problems. The survey results showed that 90 percent of customers go away without saying anything and do not return. In addition, 85 percent of those people tell at least 9 other people of their dissatisfaction, and 15 percent voice their dissatisfaction to 20 people.

This string of theories and survey data is corroborated in the car industry by J.D. Power research on the relationship between CSI scores and customer intentions to make a repeat purchase as well as on the relationship between CSI scores and the word-of-mouth effect. These are shown in Figures 5.1 and 5.2 respectively, each of which shows a clear positive correlation.

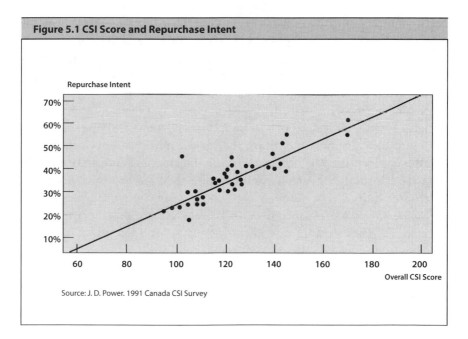

Figure 5.1 CSI Score and Repurchase Intent

Source: J. D. Power. 1991 Canada CSI Survey

Company awareness of customer service soared with the publication of a number of scientific survey results of this kind.

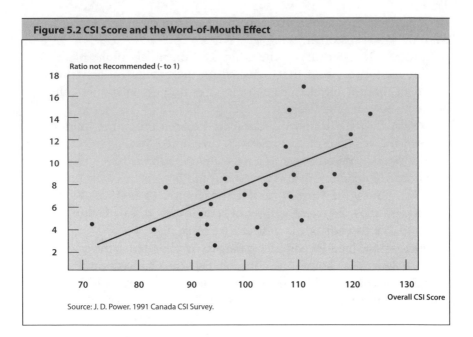

Figure 5.2 CSI Score and the Word-of-Mouth Effect

Ratio not Recommended (- to 1)

Overall CSI Score

Source: J. D. Power. 1991 Canada CSI Survey.

The publication of product ratings data by *Consumer Reports* (published by Consumers Union) and J.D. Power further raised interest in this area. New customers are not drawn to cars from companies with below-average scores and existing customers leave. New customers are naturally drawn to top-ranking companies' cars, and these are the cars that hold on to existing customers.

Because the publication of *Consumer Reports* and J.D. Power data was shown to have an impact both on the rate of new customer acquisition and on the retention rate of repeat customers, Japanese automakers began focusing efforts in the late 1980s on raising their *Consumer Reports* and J.D. Power ratings. The companies put particular energy into improving their J.D. Power scores since the J.D. Power data are based on technical evaluations. The effort to raise J.D. Power scores resulted in an improvement of *Consumer Reports* scores as well.

Toyota's Initiative

Of the five J.D. Power evaluation criteria, the oldest, inaugurated in 1986, is the IQS. Since IQS is the most basic assessment of early malfunctions, moreover, all the automobile companies began trying to improve their IQS scores. This approach was the most orthodox method of resolving problem items pointed out by the IQS. It, however, did not yield satisfactory results.

The quality of cars nowadays has increased so much that the IQS registers small, almost unnoticeable problems that customers point out as occurring "occasionally." It is human nature to try hard to come up with an answer, and when they are asked whether there are any problems, people will end up remembering even minor problems from the past. When there are many minor problems, addressing issues that come up "occasionally" is like playing "whack-a-mole": As soon as you fix one problem, consumers will point out other ones from different categories. In the end, there is little overall improvement. To improve IQS ratings, a broad range of issues must be voluntarily addressed, including problems not flagged by IQS surveys.

Toyota does not conduct any special activities in which the focus is limited to IQS. It has been quietly engaged in systematic activities to build quality based on various data since before J.D. Power IQS surveys began. Toyota can always come out on top of IQS ratings because IQS data are among the market quality data it already uses.

This issue of quality-related criteria is discussed in *Toyota—A History of the First Fifty Years*[2] (1987):

> *In the fall of 1978, a series of quality-related demands came out of the customary visits Toyota Motor executives made to dealerships. Quality had been built into each process step at the factories, but the emphasis had inevitably been placed on functional quality. As a result, the situation was that finishing touches on the products relied on new vehicle inspections and rework conducted by Toyota Motor Sales or by dealers.*
>
> *Toyota Motor Sales immediately adopted a company policy of ensuring quality at shipping. What it found was dirt inside vehicles, excess adhesive around vehicle bodies, out-of-position molding, and inadvertently omitted nuts and bolts. The company revised its process for checking intermediate processes in all the plants and took steps to eliminate these sorts of careless errors by introducing equipment and tools, securing labor for quality verification, and organizing a system of inspections.*
>
> *Improvement results were still unsatisfactory, though, and in 1980, critical items were divided into categories, with designated categories for improvement including, especially, the fit of doors, etc., wiring, wrong or missing parts, and paint work. These became the focal points for follow-up.*

Such activities had a tremendous impact on IQS improvements. As a result, Toyota ranks at the top of IQS assessments because, quite apart from the J.D. Power ratings, it engages in improvement activities that address all "customer-required quality" issues.

Toyota achieves high marks for VDI as well. Both IQS and VDI deal with "must-have quality," in other words, eliminating defects and problems that should not be there in the first place. Ever since the days of Kiichiro Toyoda, most improvement efforts have gone into must-have quality.

Toyota currently devotes the most effort to the category of APEAL (attractive quality), which J.D. Power has been surveying since 1995.

"Must-have quality" and "attractive quality," shown in Figure 5.3, are concepts defined by Professor Noriaki Kano of the Tokyo University of Science in 1984.

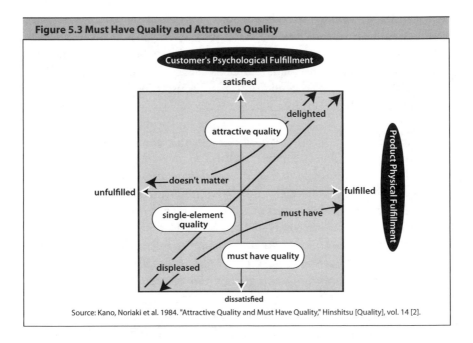

Figure 5.3 Must Have Quality and Attractive Quality

Source: Kano, Noriaki et al. 1984. "Attractive Quality and Must Have Quality," Hinshitsu [Quality], vol. 14 [2].

Must-have quality is quality that the customer expects as a matter of course even when a product is more perfect physically and has fewer problems than it used to. The customer will be displeased if a product is imperfect and problems occur. Attractive quality is quality whose absence customers will forgive. When attractive quality is enhanced, on the other hand, customers will be surprised, impressed, and pleased. There are other types of quality as well, including "single-element quality" that, like fuel consumption, fluctuates, and "indifferent quality," which the customer can take or leave.

Must-have quality is a negative quality involving breakdowns or dysfunction, whereas attractive quality is a positive quality exemplified by workmanship or craftsmanship. The Japanese word for quality (*hinshitsu*) principally denotes negative quality, whereas the English word has both positive and negative connotations.

Toyota devoted too much energy to raising CS (Customer Satisfaction) during the period of the economic bubble, and the market frowned on the "rich and fat" *Corona* and *Corolla* models it built. Around 1993, after the bubble collapsed, the pendulum swung too far in the other direction. Toyota introduced its excessively spare *Tercels, Camrys*, and *Vistas*, all of which were hammered in the marketplace. After this experience, the APEAL surveys begun by J.D. Power in 1995 were perfect for Toyota because they offered an objective index of product attractiveness.

Based on a Kano model with IQS on the horizontal axis and APEAL on the vertical axis, Toyota announced that it would henceforth put effort into the APEAL area. It formed an APEAL Improvement Committee in 1996 and tried to raise awareness through executive study sessions, presidential speeches, and information sessions for affiliate companies. Beginning in 1997, the company expanded these efforts by establishing a Customer Delight Quality Improvement Committee to evaluate representative models on a trial basis, and, in 1998, it extended this to model changes for all vehicle types. The result of these activities was a series of Toyota cars that scored high in the APEAL rankings.

Toyota's close relationship with J.D. Power can be traced to 1968, the year J.D. Power and Associates was founded. During the intervening years, Toyota has usually stayed one or two steps ahead of other companies in terms of collecting market evaluation data. It goes without saying that holding the lead in information-gathering means holding the lead in product quality.

In J.D. Power ratings conducted in the spring of 2001, GM aggressively advertised that it had improved its score by 11 percent compared to the previous year and had overtaken Ford and Chrysler. But GM's score put it only in fourth place, after Toyota, Honda, and Nissan. Guy Briggs, who led GM's North American Manufacturing Division, said that GM was tackling the lag in quality "as though it were a life-threatening disease." (*Nikkei Business*, September 3, 2001).

In an era in which anyone is free to read J.D. Power ratings on the Internet, Briggs's comment is not at all surprising.

But we have already noted that quality is not something that can be improved by individual countermeasures. Everything connected with quality must be improved. And to achieve overall quality improvement requires improvement in an entire infrastructure, as described in Chapters 1 through 4. This is why quality has been called a "comprehensive management index." The status a company accords to quality determines the quality of that company's management as well as the quality of its products and services. It also determines the life of its management.

IQS (Initial Quality)

IQS involves 135 questions in nine categories. It also surveys the conditions under which problems occur (which, for the automakers, are clues to the source of problems), and these bring the number of items studied to more than 300.

The 135 basic items studied include questions such as, "Does the steering wheel slip?" "Do the brakes pull to one side?" "Does the engine lose power?" Questions about the causes of problems might include such items as, "Does the steering wheel slip to the left or the right?" "Does the engine lose power when it is warm? When it is cold? If it is on city streets, does it happen when accelerating from a stop?"

2005 IQS Results

Table 5.1 gives the results (by top model in each category) of the J.D. Power 2005 IQS ratings.

Toyota products, including the *Lexus* (Toyota's luxury brand, sold in Japan under the *Celsior, Harrier,* and other names), comes out firmly on top of the IQS rankings, taking the number one position in ten segments, more than half of the total of eighteen.

Scoring next in best-of-segment rankings are the GM group with four segments, and Ford with two. They are putting up a good fight.

It bears noting here that Korea's Hyundai and Kia enter the segment rankings around second and third places. This shows the improved quality of the Korean carmakers, whose names began to show up in the top three spots in 2002. From the 1980s to the beginning of the 1990s, sales of cars from the Korean automakers stagnated as their position at the bottom of quality rankings led to a reputation for cheapness and shoddiness. Hyundai president Dongjin Kim expressed confidence in recent quality at the October 2001 Tokyo International Automotive Conference sponsored by Nikkei BP. In fact, U.S. sales for Korean automakers have shown strong growth since 2001.

Table 5.1 2005 IQS (Top Model by Segment)

Car Segment	Truck Segment
Compact Car	Midsize Pickup
Toyota Prius	Ford Explorer Sport Trac
Entry Midsize car	Light-Duty Full-Size Pickup
Chevrolet Malibu	Ford F-150 LD
Premium Midsize Car	Heavy Duty Full-Size Pickup
Buick Century	GM Sierra HD
Full-Size Car	Entry SUV
Buick LeSabre	Toyota RAV4
Entry Luxury Car	Midsize SUV
Lexus IS 300/IS 300 Sport Cross	Toyota 4Runner
Midsize Luxury Car	Full-Size SUV
Lexus GS 300/GS 430	Chevrolet Suburban
Premium Luxury Car	Entry Luxury SUV
Lexus SC 430	Lexus RX 300
Sporty Car	Premium Luxury SUV
Scion tC	Lexus GX 470
Premium Sports Car	Midsize Van
Nissan 350Z	Toyota Sienna

N.B. Shading indicates segment
Source: J. D. Power 2005 IQS

Past IQS Trends

Table 5.2 shows the movement of various top-ranked brands from 1996 to 2005. A review of these ten years shows that Toyota has continued to dominate with consistent first-place rankings.

Table 5.2 Past IQS Movement (Number of Segments in Which Manufacturer Captured Top Ranking)

			1996	1997	1998	1999	2000	2001	2002	2003	2004	2005
Number of Segments in which Manufacturer Captured Top Ranking		1st Place	Toyota (6)	Toyota (3)	Toyota (3)	Toyota (6)	Toyota (9)	Toyota (7)	Toyota (9)	Toyota (6)	Toyota (7)	Toyota (10)
		2nd Place	GM (2)	Nissan (3)	Honda (3)	Honda (2)	Honda (3)	Honda (2)	GM (4)	GM (4)	GM (3)	GM (4)
		3rd Place	Subaru (1) Nissan (1) Ford (1)	Ford (3)	Ford (3)	Nissan (2)	4 other companies (1)	GM (2) Nissan (2)	Ford (2)	Ford (2) Mazda (2)	Honda (3)	Ford (2)
No. of Segments			11	10	13	15	14	16	16	16	18	18

N.B. In parentheses are the numbers of segments in which the manufacturer achieved top ranking.
Results by brand name are given under the name of the manufacturer.

Source: J. D. Power 1996-2005 IQS.

In principle, the IQS sample size for each car is set at two hundred or more vehicles, which gives a statistical margin of error of +/– 15 percent. The fact that this 15 percent margin of error translates roughly into +/– three IQS ranks should give an indication of how extraordinarily stable Toyota's performance has been.

We see solid progress in quality from U.S. automakers. While Honda and Nissan used to occupy the second and third places in the rankings, in the past five years, these have been replaced by GM and Ford. Over the course of the last ten years, other Japanese and U.S. carmakers have never consistently shown up with the most first place segment rankings.

Assembly Plant Awards

Each year, J.D. Power gives Assembly Plant Awards to factories that build U.S.-market cars with high IQS rankings. Table 5.3 shows the assembly plant awards for 2005.

Table 5.3 2005 Assembly Plant Award Winners

	Award	Manufacturer	Location, Country	Score
Platinum Award	Platinum	Toyota	Tahara, Japan	59
Asia Pacific	Gold	———	———	—
	Silver	Toyota	Higashi-Fuji, Japan	67
	Bronze	Nissan	Tochigi, Japan	79
Europe	Gold	Ford	Halewood, UK	70
	Silver	BMW	Regensburg, Germany	79
	Bronze	BMW	Munich, Germany	85
	Bronze	Porsche	Stuttgart, Germany	85
North/South America	Gold	GM	Oshawa #2, Ontario, Canada	85
	Silver	GM	Oshawa #1, Ontario, Canada	89
	Bronze	Ford	Hamfranck, MI	90

N. B. Score indicates number of defects per 100 vehicles. The name of the winner of the Asia Pacific Gold Award is omitted because it is the same (Toyota's Tahara Plant) as the winner of the Worldwide Platinum Award.
Source: J. D. Power 2005 Initial Quality Study.

The Platinum Award is given to the best plant worldwide. Top-ranking regional assembly plants worldwide are given the Gold Award, and second- and third-place plants receive Silver and Bronze Awards, respectively.

In the past, North American plants of Toyota, Honda and other Japanese manufacturers had dominated the North American prizes, but 2002–2005 saw U.S. companies sweep this category. While this can be seen as a result of quality improvement efforts by the U.S. plants, Toyota still took the Platinum Award by a margin of more than 20 points.

VDI (Vehicle Dependability Index)

Based on the IQS study's nine categories and 135 problem areas, VDI points are derived from questions about repairs or additions to critical parts stemming from time-dependent characteristics such as deterioration, rust, corrosion, wear, looseness, rattling, and discoloration.

VDI is an index that infers the residual value of used vehicles, i.e., their trade-in price. Consumers have paid increasing attention to VDI in recent years, because this index determines the true value of a new car by subtracting the trade-in price from the new car price.

VDI Results for 2005

J.D. Power 2005 VDI rankings (with scores in parentheses) are as follows:

1st Place: *Lexus* (139)
2nd Place: *Porsche* (149)
3rd Place: *Lincoln* (141)
4th Place: *Buick* (163)
5th Place: *Cadillac* (175)
6th Place: *Infiniti* (178)
7th Place: *Toyota* (194)
8th Place: *Mercury* (195)
9th Place *Honda* (201)
10th Place: *Acura* (203)

Hyundai, which has recently made striking improvements in IQS (initial quality), ranked 21st in VSI and Kia came in last, at 38th place, lower than the industry average of 15th place. IQS and VDI survey questions are essentially the same and the two scores generally correlate directly to one another. IQS improvements for Hyundai and Kia have taken place within the past two to three years and so their effects may not yet have shown up in VDI (durable quality), which rates cars three years after purchase.

Past VDI Trends

Table 5.4 shows the movement of VDI rankings between 1997 and 2005.

Table 5.4 Past VDI Movement (VDI Rankings)

		1997	1998	1999	2000	2001	2002	2003	2004	2005
R A N K I N G	1	Lexus (217)	Lexus (167)	Lexus (208)	Lexus (216)	Lexus (173)	Lexus (159)	Lexus (163)	Lexus (162)	Lexus (139)
	2	Cadillac (240)	Cadillac (234)	Cadillac (241)	Porsche (220)	Infiniti (219)	Infiniti (194)	Infiniti (174)	Buick (187)	Porsche (149)
	3	Audi (242)	Infiniti (273)	Benz (254)	Infiniti (245)	Jaguar (250)	Acura (228)	Buick (179)	Infiniti (189)	Lincoln (151)
	4	Infiniti (261)	Benz (278)	Infiniti (269)	Toyota (299)	Lincoln (253)	Honda (251)	Porsche (193)	Lincoln (194)	Buick (163)
	5	Lincoln (2690	Acura (281)	Buick (288)	Acura (304)	Acura (255)	Toyota (276)	Acura (196)	Cadillac (196)	Cadillac (175)

N.B. VDI scores in parentheses
Source: J. D. Power 1997-2005 VDI Survey

Although this table does not show it, the Lexus brand boasts over-whelmingly superior durability, taking first place continuously in the eleven years following J.D. Power's inauguration of the VDI rankings in 1995.

The VDI shows solid improvement in quality from U.S. automakers after 2003, with GM and Ford vehicles appearing in the range of second to fifth places.

APEAL (Attractive Quality)

APEAL studies cover 114 items in eight categories.

These 114 items include questions such as passing performance on high-speed roads, overall braking performance, the suitability of cup holders for a variety of cups, and vehicle appearance and styling as seen from the side. Users rate each item on a ten-point scale ranging from highest (ten points) to lowest (one point).

APEAL Results for 2005

Table 5.5 gives J.D. Power APEAL rankings for 2005.

Out of a total of 18 segments, GM ranks first in the number of segments (five) in which it top-rated. Toyota and BMW are tied for second and Chrysler and Nissan are in third place.

Table 5.5 2005 APEAL Results (Top Model by Segment)	
Passenger Car Segments	**Truck Segments**
Compact Car[1]	Compact Pickup
MINI Cooper	Subaru Baja
Entry Midsize car	Light-Duty Full Size Pickup
Chevrolet Malibu	Cadillac Escalade EXT
Premium Midsize Car	Heavy-Duty Full-Size Pickup
Volvo S40	Dodge Ram Pickup HD
Full-Size Car	Entry SUV
Mercury Marauder	Chevrolet Equinox
Entry Luxury Car	Midsize SUV
Chrysler 300 series	Nissan Murano
Midsize Luxury Car	Full-Size SUV
BMW 5 Series Sedan	Nissan Armada
Premium Luxury Car [2]	Entry Luxury SUV
BMW 7 Series	Lexus RX 330
Sporty Car	Premium Luxury SUV
Pontiac GTO	Lexus LX 470
Premium Sports Car	Compact Van
Porsche Boxster	Toyota Sienna

1. Includes the Entry Compact Car and Premium Compact Car Segments.
2. Includes the Premium Luxury Car and Luxury Sport Car Segments.
N.B. Shading indicates segment
Source: J. D. Power 2005 APEAL Survey

Past APEAL Trends

Table 5.6 shows the movement of various brands that have achieved the top ranking between 1996 and 2004.

Table 5.6 Past APEAL Movement
(Number of Segments in which Manufacturer Captured Top Ranking)

			1996	1997	1998	1999	2000	2001	2002	2003	2004
Number of Segments in which Manufacturer Captured Top Ranking		1st Place	GM (4)	GM (6)	Toyota (4)	VW (4)	VW (3)	Toyota (7)	Ford (5)	Toyota (4)	GM(5)
		2nd Place	Chrysler (3)	Chrysler (3)	GM (3)	Toyota (3)	Toyota (3)	GM (2)	Toyota (3)	BMW(2) Nissan(2)	Toyota(3) BMW(3)
		3rd Place	Toyota (2)	Toyota (2)	VW (2) BMW (2) Chrysler (2)	GM (3)		VW (3)	GM (3) Honda (3)	GM(2) Honda (2)	Chrysler(2) Nissan(2)
No. of Segments			11	10	13	15	14	16	17	17	18

N.B. In parentheses are the numbers of segments in which the manufacturer achieved top ranking. Results by brand name are given under the name of the manufacturer.

Source: J. D. Power 1996-2004 APEAL Survey.

This table makes it clear that attractive quality has been a category in which European and American cars are relatively strong. As we have seen, Toyota experimented with activities to improve APEAL in 1997 and in 1998 extended these to all models. As we can see in Table 5.6, this has resulted in incremental improvements beginning in 1998 and coming into full flower in 2001, but not yet in a stable first-place ranking. Here we see evidence for the argument that, no matter how high the quality of Japanese cars, they are still bested in overall product strength by European and American cars, with their longer histories.

SSI (Sales Satisfaction Index)

Product quality exerts almost no influence on SSI, which is mainly an index showing the quality of treatment customers receive when purchasing a vehicle.

SSI Results for 2004

In the J.D. Power SSI ratings for 2004, *Jaguar* and *Lexus* are tied for first place, *Cadillac* is second, *Mercury* is fourth and *Mercedes* fifth, followed by *Lincoln*, *Buick* and *Hummer*. With the average manufacturer's ranking at twenty-two, the only other Japanese carmakers scoring above average were *Infiniti* at nineteenth place and *Acura* at twenty-first. American automakers are strong overall in this category.

Past SSI Trends

Table 5.7 gives trends in SSI rankings from 1998 to 2004.

From Table 5.7, we see that American cars such as *Saturn*, *Cadillac* and *Lincoln* occupy first place overall and that Lexus moves between second and fourth place.

The SSI measures customer satisfaction with the salesperson's attitude without regard to product quality. U.S. companies are probably strong here because they can offer comprehensive service rooted in locally-based sales personnel training, coaching and incentive bonuses.

CSI (Customer Satisfaction Index)

CSI Results for 2004

J.D. Power 2004 CSI rankings are as follows:

Table 5.7 Past SSI Movement (SSI Rankings)

		1998	1999	2000	2001	2002	2003	2004
R A N K I N G	1st	Saturn (144)	Cadillac (142)	Saturn (143)	Saturn (887)	Saturn (886)	Cadillac (889)	Jaguar (898)
	2nd	Cadillac (143)	Jaguar (142)	Cadillac (141)	Cadillac (885)	Cadillac (881)	Porsche (888)	Lexus (898)
	3rd	Lexus (142)	Volvo (142)	Lexus (141)	Lexus (884)	Lincoln (880)	Lincoln (885)	Cadillac (896)
	4th	Land Rover (140)	Land Rover (140)	Infiniti (139)	Infiniti (883)	Lexus (878)	Mercury (885)	Mercury (892)
	5th	Volvo (139)	Mercedes-Benz (139)	Buick & others (138)	Jaguar (882)	Jaguar (877)	Saturn (885)	Mercedes Benz (888)

SSI scores given in parentheses
SSI scoring method changed in 2001.
Source: J. D. Power 1998-2004 SSI Survey

1st Place: *Lincoln*
2nd Place: *Cadillac*
3rd Place: *Saturn*
4th Place: *Lexus*
5th Place: *Infiniti*

Other Japanese makes that ranked above the company average of 20th were *Acura*, at 8th Place, and *Honda*, at 13th Place. In CSI rankings, too, U.S. automakers are generally strong.

Past CSI Trends

Table 5.8 shows CSI ranking trends for the years 1999 through 2005.

The CSI involves the quality of service for breakdowns and other problems, so it is influenced by product quality as well as by the attitudes of service personnel. Lexus, which scores well in IQS and VDS, was top-ranked until 2001. The subsequent movement of U.S. companies to the top position is probably due to the improvement in the quality of American cars since 2002.

CSI is a valid measure for evaluating overall product and service quality, and CSI rankings are generally given more weight than SSI.

Table 5.8 Past CSI Movement (CSI Rankings)

		1999	2000	2001	2002	2003	2004	2005
R A N K I N G	1st	Lexus (815)	Lexus (811)	Lexus (903)	Saturn (900)	Infiniti (900)	Lincoln (512)	Lincoln (515)
	2nd	Cadillac (778)	Saturn (807)	Saturn (901)	Infiniti (897)	Saturn (896)	Buick (509)	Cadillac (511)
	3rd	BMW (775)	BMW (783)	Cadillac (893)	Lexus (894)	Acura (895)	Infinity (508)	Saturn (505)
	4th	Daewoo (774)	Volvo (778)	Infiniti (882)	Cadillac (890)	Lexus (895)	Cadillac (504)	Lexus (504)
	5th	Infiniti (771)	Volvo (769)	Acura (881)	Volvo (883)	Lincoln (895)	Lexus (502)	Infinity (501)

CSI scores given in parentheses.
Source: J. D. Power 1998-2005 CSI Survey

Consumer Reports Ratings

Table 5.9 shows the "Best 10 Cars" chosen by *Consumer Reports* on the basis of reliability and performance criteria.

Table 5.9 Consumer Reports—Examples of Best Cars in 2001 Edition

Luxury Sedans
BMW330i
Toyota Lexus ES300
Lexus IS300
Saab 9-52.3t
Small Sport-Utility Vehicles
Toyota RAV4
Subaru Forester-S
Ford Escape XLT
Minivans
Honda Odyssey EX
Toyota Sienna LE
Chrysler Town & Country LX

N.B. Overall ranking in test results
Source: "Consumer Report April 2001" Nikkei Business 2 April 2001

These ratings can be seen as comparable to J.D. Power IQS (Initial Quality Study) evaluations. Four Toyota models were chosen by *Consumer Reports* to be among the "Best 10 Cars," additional proof of Toyota's commitment to high quality.

Consumer Reports also publishes quality ratings of vehicles that have been used between one and three and four and eight years. These ratings are similar to J.D. Power VDI ratings. Here, Japanese cars are given nearly all the top ratings, with Toyotas leading the pack and cars manufactured by Honda, Nissan, Subaru, Mazda, Isuzu, Mitsubishi, and Suzuki following.

How Different Companies Have Responded

J.D. Power measures various data from the United Kingdom, Japan, Taiwan, Thailand, India, Indonesia, the Philippines, and elsewhere as well as U.S. data. CSI and SSI and other surveys have been conducted each year in Japan since 1993 but have not been made public. CSI and SSI studies have also been carried out for used cars, and partial results have been released to the public.

The leading five Japanese automobile manufacturers commission J.D. Power to conduct IQS surveys of the Japanese and European markets, providing funds for this purpose. Whether J.D. Power quality ratings and customer satisfaction indices are made public or not, all the companies recognize them to be a major factor influencing repeat sales. With the data they receive, all of these companies analyze problem areas, study causes, and take steps to make improvements. When problems and causes are difficult to understand, they may pay additional fees to J.D. Power for extended studies or follow-up telephone surveys of consumers.

All the data from Japan, the United States, and Europe (acquired at considerable expense) create great challenges. The work of analyzing the data, coming up with responses, and then implementing them is extremely difficult, especially for the design departments that come up with countermeasures. All of the companies have multiple models in Japan, the United States, and Europe, and it is a tremendous challenge to follow up on problems with existing models while simultaneously working on new model development projects. J.D. Power survey data do not, of course, provide all the information needed and various other means must be employed to gather related information or obtain new information. In the meantime, more pressing and immediate concerns must be dealt with. Therefore, even if executives give instructions to take immediate and comprehensive measures to address IQS, VDI, and APEAL issues for current models in Japan, the United States, and Europe, design departments have not got the time or manpower to deal with "trifling historical information" for which (unlike the J.D. Power data) there are no direct claims. Thus, information diligently collected at great expense often ends up gathering dust.

Toyota apparently limits its improvement activities to addressing data from American cars. Data from other regions is used only for assessing results. The reason for this is that, for Toyota, the results of improvements and corrective measures applied to its U. S. cars spreads to other areas automatically via lateral propagation.[3] (Recall the soundness of the "lateral propagation" phenomena we have seen in previous chapters.) It is basic Toyota policy, moreover, to avoid inefficient after-the-fact design changes in the absence of major problems and to address leftover problems thoroughly for the next model. As a result, Toyota is able to obtain maximum effect from minimal effort even when dealing with must-have quality and attractive quality. J.D. Power quality rating data from the United Kingdom, Taiwan, Thailand, and elsewhere shows that Toyota has a solid and comprehensive hold on quality throughout the world.

When quality is poor, managers cannot simply turn around and issue instructions to make everything perfect. They need to give instructions after drawing up realistic scenarios for making steady quality improvements with limited resources.

THE POWER OF THE TOYOTA BRAND

The "propensity to sell" can be defined as Product Power × Brand Power. In an age in which emphasis is laid on a company's social character, the weight of brands is increasing. No matter how great the power of a product, if its brand is weak, then the product will not sell.

As we saw in Figure 2.1, Toyota, in the latter half of the 1980s, was a company from which one could learn, but it was not a "good" company. In other words, its products had power but its brand did not. Shoichiro Toyoda saw this as a crisis, and from the end of the 1980s to the beginning of the 1990s, he turned the rudder of the Toyota ship sharply in an effort to steer the company in a better direction. (See the section on foresight in Chapter 2.)

Several indexes of how this shift in Toyota management manifested itself as changes in the power of the brand at the end of the 20th century are presented below.

Brand Power in the United States

The American public opinion polling firm Harris Interactive compiled a ranking of companies, Popular Brands in 2000, that placed Sony in first place for the second year in a row. Ford came in second (from fourth the previous year), GE third (the same as the previous year), Toyota fourth (from seventh the previous year), and GM fifth (from second in 1999). The survey asked 2,461 American adults for the brand names of three of their favorite products or services. Sony's ranking was to be expected, but Toyota pulled ahead of GM to an unapologetic fourth place. Ford's problems with Firestone Tire precluded speculation about where Ford might rank after 2001, and Honda was not ranked among the top ten. (May 5, 2001. Sankei Shimbun.)

Brand Power in Japan

Corporate Brand Score Ranking

Results from the Fourth (2000) Corporate Brand Score Ranking conducted by the Nihon Keizai Sangyo Shimbunsha put Sony in first place, Toyota in second, and Honda in third. (February 14, 2001. *Nikkei Sangyo Shimbun*).

Brand Japan 2001

In the Brand Japan 2001 survey carried out by Nikkei Business Publications, Toyota was in first place, NTT DoCoMo in second, and Sony in third. No other automobile company figured among the top thirty firms. These results came from questionnaires that went to some 3,000 business and technical Internet users, so the study can be seen as a survey of relatively intelligent "knowledge workers." With eight electronics or IT firms among the top ten, this survey favored IT-related companies; the fact that Toyota ranked first shows that Toyota was widely accepted within the target population of the survey. (May 21, 2001. *Nikkei Business*.)

Survey of Brand Recall

In a Brand Recall Survey conducted in September 2001 by Nikkei Business Publications, Sony came in first place, Toyota in second, and Honda in third, followed by Uniqlo, Louis Vuitton, and Matsushita Electric. Here again Toyota ranked very high.

It seems fair to say that the results above show that Toyota has already shaken off the vestiges of its earlier image and has moved from being a "company to learn from" to being a "good company."

Endnotes

1. The J.D. Power ratings data that appear in this chapter have been updated since the original Japanese publication of the book in 2002. This English-language edition incorporates the most recent data available.
2. *Toyota Jidosha Gojunen-shi.*
3. *yokoten.*

——— 6 ———

Toyota Management in the 21st Century

The aim of this book has been to analyze previous almost unchallenged information about Toyota and extrapolate from this analysis the principles of the company's enduring growth. In previous chapters, we have focused on the past, and we believe we have been able to achieve our aim.

In this last chapter, we will use recent Toyota data to view what sort of strategy the company is using as it sets about the task of management in the 21st century. Provided we gain the conviction that Toyota will continue to grow in the 21st century, we will substantiate the principles of enduring corporate growth.

THE OKUDA/CHO SYSTEM

In May 1999, Hiroshi Okuda, then president of Toyota, was named chairman of the Japan Federation of Employers' Associations. In June of that year, Okuda resigned as president of Toyota and assumed the chairmanship of the Toyota Motor Corporation. Shoichiro Toyoda, the direct descendant of the Toyoda family, withdrew from this position to become honorary chairman, and Fujio Cho was chosen as the company's new president.

At the time, Okuda stated: "I have turned over the day-to-day work of the presidency of the Toyota Motor Corporation. I will continue to make judgments and refine needed strategies from a broad perspective so that the Toyota Group as a whole will grow stronger and take its place among the major players in the world."

On his appointment to the presidency of the Toyota Motor Corporation, Fujio Cho made it clear that he would play his part in maintaining the Okuda system, declaring, "The company has had an easy time of it thanks to the decisive speed with which Mr. Okuda has set a clear direction for management. I will hold firmly to the same line." With this, these two men assumed control of the management of Toyota in the 21st century.

Okuda's Ambitions

On August 10, 1995, Toyota's president Tatsuro Toyoda succumbed to illness, and Hiroshi Okuda was abruptly named as his successor. He declared himself "truly shocked," adding, "I would have been happy to take on the job had I been ten years younger."

Such bluntness is typical of Okuda. When asked by the press about his aspirations as president of the company, he responded immediately, "I'm going to tackle three major management issues at Toyota. The first is our lag in product planning. The second is our declining market share in Japan. And the third is that we are behind in overseas expansion."

From that point on, Toyota moved at lightning speed in an automobile industry racked by upheaval. It went on the offensive in a series of managerial moves, including further consolidating management of the group by turning Daihatsu Motor Company into a subsidiary and by acquiring a controlling stake in Hino Motors Ltd. Under Okuda's direction, Toyota also speeded up overseas operations in North America, China, and Europe, rolling out a massive sales campaign and recovering a 40 percent market share while implementing measures for internal reform and new projects.

On September 9, 1996, one year after being named president, Hiroshi Okuda was interviewed by the Nikkan Kogyo Shimbun. In the interview, Okuda spoke candidly about what had been achieved and about his vision for the company's future:

> We've accomplished a lot, but I'd be embarrassed to take personal credit for it. I've just brought to fruition some projects that had been building up. This company has always been refining what it inherits, so even though you might talk about the "Okuda regime," that's not what's going on at all.
>
> I'd like to expand the company even more if I can. But it can't be about all take and no give. I want us to be a "moral" company to whose growth society will be glad to have contributed.
>
> Another ideal I have is that I don't want our management to spend all its time plugging leaks in the dike. I want us to build one or two new dikes.

Okuda was saying, in other words, that his celebrated speed management was equivalent to plugging leaks in the dike and that he did not want to be judged by such work. He wanted to be remembered for building one or two new dikes.

A Response to Hereditary Succession

Okuda has sometimes spoken bluntly to members of the Toyoda family, and because of this, there have been rumors of poor relations between the descendants of Sakichi Toyoda and the president. One typical example of the discord between Okuda and the Toyoda family concerned Toyota's participation in Formula One (F1) races and the purchase of the Fuji Speedway. The decisions to involve Toyota in these enterprises were Okuda's.

Shoichiro Toyoda, the honorary chairman of Toyota Motor, had other opinions: "I'm against participating (in the F1). Along with Eiji (Eiji Toyoda, supreme advisor), I say we shouldn't do it. . . . I never told anybody to buy (the Fuji Speedway). On the contrary, I'm the one who held the deal up. . . . I've always said that I wanted to use cars as a means of contributing to society. We're trying to be an industrial company."

Shoichiro went so far as to declare, "You don't elevate the fortunes of a car company by winning the Formula One." (May 18, 2001. Yomiuri Shimbun Chubu.)

Eiji and Shoichiro Toyoda had expanded Toyota while saving every last pencil stub, worn-out eraser, and scrap of wastepaper. That they should react negatively to Formula One, for which several billion yen might vanish in a single event, was perfectly natural.

In the end, though, Okuda announced Toyota's participation in Formula One in January 1999; in November 2000, he bought the Fuji Speedway. Fujio Cho, in referring to Formula One, said that "motor sports is a culture and young technical guys have grand dreams about it. This is a move to capture the hearts of young people."

Because Okuda implemented his plans in spite of opposition from leading figures of the Toyoda family like Eiji and Shoichiro Toyoda, there may be some truth in the rumors of a strained relationship.

Okuda has attempted to counter these rumors by saying, "It's unfortunate that people think we're fighting or something. I have a good relationship with the Toyoda family."

It is more than likely that Okuda believed that he had persuaded Eiji and Shoichiro Toyoda amicably to accept his decisions about the Formula One and the Fuji Speedway.

When Okuda promoted Shoichiro Toyoda's eldest son Akio Toyoda to the post of director, he declared, "I'm giving him a chance because he's from the Toyoda family. I'll make him a director, but after that he's on his own." On another occasion, he said, "We shouldn't depend on the Toyoda family forever. Blood thins out over time."

Here one can see Okuda's clear departure from the notion that Toyota belongs to the Toyoda family. For employees and executives in a new era whose watchwords are independence and self-reliance, centripetal management and a hereditary system centered on the Toyoda family is simply inappropriate. The idea is already foreign to most people, and it can be viewed as the last obstacle to Toyota's becoming more "open."

It is conceivable, in the future, that Akio or Shuhei Toyoda (Eiji Toyoda's third son) might accede to the company's presidency. But this will not be a return to imperial rule. It will have to be obvious to all that the president is the right man for the job. In 1967, media editorials implied that Eiji Toyoda had been named president "because he was a Toyoda." His rebuttal to this was "everybody would agree now that, at the time, Eiji was the right man for the job."

The Second Founding

Okuda has noted:

> We think of the controlling strategy of every era as the ultimate one, but the environment changes, thinking gets revised, and a new strategy triumphs. Then the environment starts to change again. We have to find new ways to grow and prosper in the 21st century.... With concern about environmental change on the rise, we are called upon to build a new paradigm for new reforms and products.... We can get off to a spectacular start in the 21st century if we act with the same boldness that Toyota's founders did. (Reingold, Edwin. 1999. *Toyota: People, Ideas, and the Challenge of the New.* London: Penguin Books.)

In recent years, Okuda has referred repeatedly to "a second founding" of Toyota. His building of one or two new dikes leads directly to this "second founding" and away from a centripetal focus on the original founding family. The time has come for "the same boldness" practiced by Toyota's founders.

BECOMING A LEADING COMPANY IN THE 21ST CENTURY

Toyota's *2001 Annual Report* to investors marked a striking departure from the past. Previous annual reports had concentrated on reporting business results. In the 2001 Report, though, Toyota's chairman, Hiroshi Okuda, and president, Fujio Cho, describe their management policies and strategies for the 21st century. In his preface to the *Annual Report*, Hiroshi Okuda states, "Toyota has taken every opportunity to make aggressive efforts to disclose and seek your understanding of what we think is valuable, what we do to achieve it, what we are about to do, and what the state of management is."

Cho takes the basic management policies Okuda refers to and discusses a concrete strategy for reforming Toyota. Toyota's *2001 Annual Report* is the first step toward Okuda's "aggressive disclosure."

In a variety of forums, Okuda and Cho have recently been active in issuing information concerning Toyota's policies and strategies. At the Tokyo International Automotive Conference sponsored by Nikkei BP and held on October 22 and 23, 2001, Fujio Cho gave a talk entitled "The Toyota Way in the Twenty-first Century: Things to Change and Things to Keep." At the International Automotive Roundtable sponsored by J. D. Power Asia Pacific and held on October 25, 2001, Hiroshi Okuda gave a talk entitled "Toyota Motor's Management Strategy—A Leading Company for the 21st Century."

Toyota's management strategy for becoming a leading company for the 21st century is structured as shown in Figure 6.1, which summarizes Okuda's and Cho's statements in the *2001 Annual Report*, the International Automotive Conference sponsored by Nikkei BP, and the Roundtable sponsored by J. D. Power.

Toyota's Vision for 2005

Toyota's 2005 Vision shown in Figure 6.1 was published in January 1996 and is based on the company's Basic Principles established in 1992 (see Table 2.2). In 1995, when Okuda was executive vice president, he directed the Management Planning Department to create this vision in order to give concrete shape to what Toyota would look like in ten years. Behind this vision lay ambitious quantitative goals for such things as consolidated sales growth, operating profits, and numbers of vehicle sales to be achieved by 2005, goals that kept sight of what was occurring at GM and Ford. "Some people call becoming number one in the world 'hegemony,'" said Okuda, "but the chairman (then Shoichiro Toyoda) and I share an underlying commitment to that goal."

Toyota had already become a giant corporation, one with a tremendous influence on society. A policy to expand even further necessitated staying in harmony with society. "From the 20th to the 21st centuries," Okuda predicted, "the new winds of world environmental issues, globalization, and the IT revolution have swept across the automotive industry.

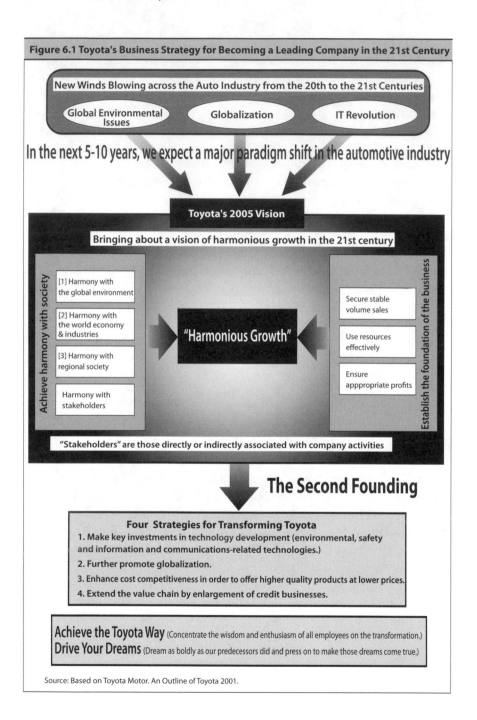

Figure 6.1 Toyota's Business Strategy for Becoming a Leading Company in the 21st Century

New Winds Blowing across the Auto Industry from the 20th to the 21st Centuries

Global Environmental Issues   Globalization   IT Revolution

In the next 5-10 years, we expect a major paradigm shift in the automotive industry

Toyota's 2005 Vision

Bringing about a vision of harmonious growth in the 21st century

Achieve harmony with society

[1] Harmony with the global environment

[2] Harmony with the world economy & industries

[3] Harmony with regional society

Harmony with stakeholders

"Harmonious Growth"

Secure stable volume sales

Use resources effectively

Ensure apppropriate profits

Establish the foundation of the business

"Stakeholders" are those directly or indirectly associated with company activities

The Second Founding

Four Strategies for Transforming Toyota
1. Make key investments in technology development (environmental, safety and information and communications-related technologies.)
2. Further promote globalization.
3. Enhance cost competitiveness in order to offer higher quality products at lower prices.
4. Extend the value chain by enlargement of credit businesses.

Achieve the Toyota Way (Concentrate the wisdom and enthusiasm of all employees on the transformation.)
Drive Your Dreams (Dream as boldly as our predecessors did and press on to make those dreams come true.)

Source: Based on Toyota Motor. An Outline of Toyota 2001.

Within five or ten years, there will be a major paradigm shift that will redefine the car industry and even cars themselves."

One of the issues raised by this sort of prediction or premonition is the achievement of "harmony with society," shown in Figure 6.1.

At the same time, achieving harmony with society requires managerial strength and this calls for the second pillar in Figure 6.1: "Secure a managerial base."

Combining these two pillars yields "harmonious growth."

At the Roundtable sponsored by J. D. Power Asia Pacific on October 25, 2001, Hiroshi Okuda referred to the ten years following the establishment of the 2005 vision in 1996 as Toyota's "second founding" and explained how reforms would be led by the integrative capabilities of the Toyota Group. The details were basically the same as the "four strategies for radical change at Toyota" that Fujio Cho described in the *Annual Report*.

Four Strategies for Radical Change at Toyota

Priority Investments in Technological Development

On this subject, Cho observed:

> There can be no doubt that the 21st century, too, will be a century of technological development for the automotive industry. What will be different from the 20th century, however, is the increasing importance, not of car technology per se, but of technologies at the interface of societies and individuals. As we can see in the case of fuel cells and ITS (intelligent transport systems), though, developing such technologies currently requires enormous investments of capital and time, as well as superior talent. It is vital that we continue to eliminate more waste and increase efficiency and productivity so that we can invest the resulting profits in protecting the global environment, contributing to the economy and to industry, and living in harmony with the local community. And we have to speed this development cycle up.

Toyota's development plans concerning the environment, safety technologies, and information technologies are described in detail on the company's Internet homepage. We will not repeat what can be found there, but it is important to note that Toyota's enthusiasm on these subjects is quite evident.

Driving Globalization Forward

International cooperation in environmental technologies is the first priority in dealing with future globalization. Environmental technologies require massive research and development capital. At the same time, environmental technologies are not an element of product competition; they are essential technologies with which cars must be equipped. For the industry as a whole, it is unwise for companies to make individual investments in basic technologies that are not grounds for competition. It is preferable for each company to build cooperative relationships to shoulder the mutual burden of development using the technologies in which each is strong.

Toyota has built cooperative relationships with automotive companies worldwide and is in the process of actively offering its pioneering hybrid technology and other technologies to GM, Ford, and other companies around the world. Even as it remains fiercely competitive as an automaker, in the field of environmental technology, Toyota is trying to cooperate to ensure that the entire industry survives.

Toyota's second globalization initiative involves the globalization of production. "Toyota's worldwide sales are roughly divided one-third each among Japan, North America, and then Europe and other regions," explains Cho. "But in order to become a truly global company, we are looking to grow as we contribute to the development of those areas through the most competitive and most appropriate sourcing and production."

The globalization of production aims at producing vehicles worldwide while achieving the following three: reducing the cost of finished vehicle exports (reported to cost ¥150,000 per vehicle), preventing trade frictions, and contributing to local economies.

When Okuda was president, he conducted a fierce assault on Toyota's lagging overseas advance, an issue he had raised when he took over the presidency. In August 1997, he announced a production joint venture with India. He made public the construction of a second plant in France in December of the same year and then made plans for expanding engine plants in the United Kingdom and the United States in January 1998. In April of the same year, he declared that Toyota would expand the production of passenger cars in the United States. Altogether, he announced nearly 300 billion yen in overseas investment in the span of barely a year. In July 2000, an ambition Hiroshi Okuda had had ever since becoming president was realized when the Tianjin Toyota Motor Company, Ltd., was established and began operations as a joint venture with the Tianjin

Automotive Group of China. The Tianjin Toyota Motor Company, Ltd., came into being soon after the start of joint passenger car engine production in 1998. "It was," said Okuda, "as though we were desperately rushing to catch the last bus."

In order to balance production and sales, Toyota began introducing world standard production equipment to allow for flexible production adjustments on a global scale. The company announced that in 2002 it would complete the conversion of all its volume production lines in the world to "global lines," flexible body welding lines on which a single fixture can accommodate eight different car models. (November 1, 2001. *Nikkei Sangyo Shimbun*).

Toyota's third globalization initiative is to give its managers and employees a feeling for the wider world. In 1996, the company set up an International Advisory Board so it could hear management-related advice from foreign experts. Composed of ten government and industry experts from Asia, Europe, and the United States—including, for example, former Federal Reserve Board chairman Paul Volker—the board holds meetings twice a year and exchanges views with Toyota management on global and local matters.

"We are confident," said Takashi Hata, the general manager of Toyota's Global Human Resources Division, "that we can groom the world's best operational managers in-house. But educating higher-level managers is difficult to do entirely inside the company." Because of this, Toyota began combining its know-how with that of universities, one of the results of which was a new educational system introduced in 1999 for executive staff candidates. Trainees picked from around the world hole up at the Wharton School of the University of Pennsylvania for two weeks of daily group discussions.

Enhancing Cost Competitiveness

Enhancing cost competitiveness is essential to triumphing in the unfolding global "mega-competition." Waste elimination is a sort of house specialty at Toyota, but lowering costs in the future will require new perspectives. We will be discussing strengthening cost competitiveness through radical changes in product development in a later section of this chapter; here we will focus on enhancing group unity, one of Toyota's cost competitiveness strengths.

"In order to keep coming out a winner among mightily shifting global alliances," Cho explains, "we will firm up our capacity to concentrate the wisdom and resources of the [Toyota] Group."

In fact, ever since the beginning of the Okuda regime, Toyota has been working to enhance the group's ability to concentrate resources. It acquired Daihatsu Motor. It increased its stake in Hino Motors and made Hino a Toyota subsidiary. And it sent staff-level employees into affiliated companies such as Denso, Toyoda Automatic Loom, and Aishin Seiki. Toyota drew public attention in April 2001 when it chose Tadaaki Jagawa, the powerful executive vice president and apparent successor to the Toyota presidency, as president of Hino Motors.

Enhancing the ability of the group to concentrate its forces does not stop at matters relating to capital or people, however. Toyota examined cost structures in Japan via cost competition with Volkswagen, with which it had a technical partnership, concluding that, while costs on the manufacturing shopfloor are low in Japan, the country has a high cost structure overall. It found the cause of this high cost structure to be redundant work occasioned by multilayered horizontal and vertical relationships between carmakers and parts suppliers. This led Toyota to take up the challenge of making mutual adjustments and enhancing the consolidation of products, parts, and technologies within the group, all with the aim of promoting parts commonization and reducing overlapping research, development, and design tasks.

Nineteen-ninety saw consolidation of the development functions of seven auto body manufacturers, with the functions of three companies in the east (Kanto Auto Works, Hino Auto Body, and Central Motor Company) going to Kanto Auto Works; the functions of four companies in the west (Toyota Auto Body Company, Daihatsu Auto Body, Toyoda Automatic Loom, and Araco) were concentrated at Toyota Auto Body.

For its parts suppliers, Toyota decided to revise the "multiple companies for one component" policy that had been the cause of different types of components coming from the same parts specification drawings. It did away with redundant parts among suppliers of such items as interior trim, brakes, ABS, steering wheels, and air bags, and it strengthened moves toward concentrating on one supplier for each item category. "We're going to take a bold new look at the business," announced president Takashi Matsuura of Toyota Gosei, a company that shared damping rubber and air bags with Toyo Rubber. "If we don't," he added, "we'll never be able to keep up with Toyota's CCC21 (see details in the section on reforming product development) cost improvement activities." (October 26, 2001. *Nikkan Kogyo Shimbun*).

In his 1997 book, *The Evolution of a Production System*,[1] Takahiro Fujimoto gives the percentages of automobile purchased parts that are market items, approved drawing parts, and loaned drawing parts, as well as an international comparison of the percentage of common parts.

Approved drawing parts are parts for which parts specifications are turned over to the local parts supplier, and detailed design and manufacturing are entrusted to the supplier (i.e., outsourcing both design and manufacturing). Loaned drawing parts are parts for which the carmaker produces detailed parts drawings, and only the manufacturing is left to the supplier (i.e., design insourcing and manufacturing outsourcing). Outsourcing generally means that suppliers are free to design parts, so that the percentage of approved print parts and the percentage of common parts are inversely proportional to one another, whereas loaned drawing parts and common parts are directly proportional. Market items are standard articles, so the percentage of market items and the percentage of commonized parts are proportional. These relationships are shown in Table 6.1.

Table 6.1 International Comparison of Product Development Performance & Organizational Capability (1980s vs. 1990s)

		Japan	U.S.	Europe	Mean
Percentage of purchased parts costs occupied by market goods	1980s	8	3	6	6
	1990s	6	12	12	10
Percentage of purchased parts costs occupied by approved drawing parts	1980s	62	16	29	40
	1990s	55	30	24	35
Percentage of purchased parts costs occupied by loan drawing parts	1980s	30	81	65	54
	1990s	39	58	64	55
Percentage of common parts	1980s	19	38	30	27
	1990s	28	25	32	29

Source: Fujimoto, Takahiro. 1997. The Evolution of a Production System, extract from Table 6.3

In Japan, the trend is shifting from a supplier-dependent model, in which design is outsourced, to a car manufacturer-centered model, in which plans are insourced and manufacturing is outsourced. Accompanying this shift is a rise in the percentage of common parts. It is probably fair to assume that the trend in Japan is influenced by moves at Japan's biggest automaker, Toyota.

The enhanced consolidation capabilities and reorganization of supplier responsibilities discussed above promote design insourcing and manufacturing outsourcing for the Toyota Group as a unit and seek to strengthen cost competitiveness by increasing the proportion of common parts.

In Japan in the 1980s, the proportion of approved drawing parts—i.e., the proportion of design outsourcing—was high. Outsourcing design meant that the work of product and parts research, development, and design partially overlapped between carmakers and their parts suppliers. In the case of drawings, this gave rise to three types of drawings managed by the manufacturer—the car manufacturer's specification drawings, the supplier's approval request drawings, and the carmaker's final approved drawings. Each of these overlapped the others by about 50 percent in terms of information content. Even when specifications drawings were the same, moreover, the detailed design would differ depending on the supplier to which it was issued. Different parts resulting from the arrangement were inevitable. Insourcing design and outsourcing manufacturing places a greater burden on the automaker, but it eliminates redundancy in research, development, and design work overall. A drawing becomes simply a kind of manufacturing print (loaned drawing), and drawing management costs fall by two-thirds. Even when the outsourcing company makes a change, there is no increase in the types of parts. The Japanese (Toyota) strategy in the 1990s of enhancing cost competitiveness can be viewed as a total group-oriented strategy of design insourcing and manufacturing outsourcing.

Table 6.1 further shows that trends in the United States were the diametric opposite of those in Japan. In fact, in 1995, GM broke off its internal parts division into a separate company, Delphi Automotive Systems. Ford followed, breaking off its internal parts division as Visteon in 1997. Both new companies did most of their business with their respective parent companies (in 2001, the figure for Delphi is 68 percent and for Visteon, it is 84 percent). When a parts division that has strong design capabilities and that used to be part of automobile development becomes a separate company, the proportion of market items and approved drawing parts naturally increases and the proportion of loaned drawing parts decreases. As a result, the proportion of common parts fell. In the past, it was widely accepted that the low proportion of common parts for Japanese manufacturers was due to lean production processes and fat design processes. Now design processes at Japanese manufacturers are becoming steadily "leaner."

It is interesting to speculate whether American companies split off their parts divisions because they attributed Japanese cost competitiveness to technically capable parts suppliers who actively participated in development and to a high proportion of approved drawing parts.

From the end of the 1980s to the beginning of the 1990s, European and U.S. car companies were greatly influenced by comparative studies of the Japanese and U.S. automobile industries published in numerous books and articles, including, for example, *Product Development Performance*, by Kim Clark and Takahiro Fujimoto (1991). Utilizing the 1980s data presented in Table 6.1, these two authors reported that technically capable Japanese parts suppliers are highly involved in development and that the proportion of approved drawings is high, a correlation that may explain why Japanese cost competitiveness is so strong.

In contrast, GM and Ford have left themselves with little parts-related data, information, and know-how. It is rumored that GM and Ford employees are no longer capable of visiting the now independent Delphi and Visteon, nor are they capable of reading the materials they find there.

This raises an additional interesting point. In contrast to Toyota, which has been consolidating and reorganizing the entire Toyota Group with an ultimate view to eliminating redundant functions, simplifying hierarchical structures, and promoting parts commonization, GM and Ford have moved ahead with outsourcing and organizational fragmentation. It will be very interesting to see which approach is better.

Enlarging the Value Chain

As shown in Figure 6.2, one element of Toyota's IT-based business strategy is vertical supply chain management (SCM) extending from parts suppliers to dealerships. SCM promises to be enormously effective when IT is woven into Toyota's robust system of just-in-time production.

Intersecting with vertical SCM, the "value chain" expands business along the horizontal axis. This is a strategy that pursues an economy of scope, both by pursuing a carmaker's economies of scale and by extending the value chain to new domains related to the automobile industry. It should strengthen Toyota's position as a comprehensive "mobility company" and works to put information technologies to broad use.

The five-part initiative is outlined below:

- *Gazoo.com*, a car-related e-commerce site
- ITS, targeting the building of business around next-generation traffic systems
- An information terminal business targeting the refinement of car navigation systems and increasing the value-added component of cars
- An electronic payment business using the TS3 (TS Cubic) Card
- And finally, a network business linking all four of the above.

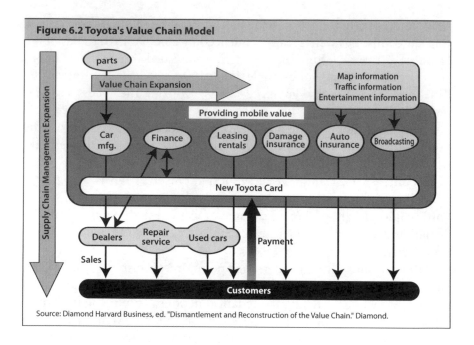

Figure 6.2 Toyota's Value Chain Model

Source: Diamond Harvard Business, ed. "Dismantlement and Reconstruction of the Value Chain." Diamond.

Toyota is concentrating its energies on the information and communications business on one hand and the credit business on the other. Toyota management believes that creating synergies among these will be increasingly important in the future. Details may be found in Toyota's *2001 Annual Report* and the *2001 Outline of Toyota*.

New Directions in Building People

Toyota's Crisis

In the new-year statement made at the beginning of 2001, at the start of the 21st century, Hiroshi Okuda told Toyota executives: "I want you to make a revolution with the idea that you are going to overthrow the old Toyota. Toyota's weaknesses will become apparent to you when you look at the company, not just from its own perspective, but from the standpoint of other firms. By overthrowing the old Toyota, you'll be able to get to the core of things."

At the Roundtable sponsored by J. D. Power Asia-Pacific on November 25, 2001, Okuda reiterated this idea: "A new Toyota will not develop unless we overthrow the old Toyota. The results we are achieving now don't come from management. I think they come from hard work on the shopfloor and because other companies haven't been doing so well. We need to break the old Toyota paradigms and build a new Toyota corporate culture."

Okuda rarely minced words but even so, these were extraordinary words. They exude Okuda's strong sense of crisis and focus on the work of Toyota employees.

For a long time now, Toyota leaders have repeatedly said that "building products means building people." The theory is eminently reasonable: Since people are the ones who build products, you have to build good people if you want to build good products. The way to build good people, according to Toyota philosophy, is to "work on their minds." Toyota executives and managers have been working on Toyota employees according to a theory of motivation that asks how to get people to *want* to do things.

In Taiichi Ohno's time, the method for motivating people was to make them uncomfortable. This technique was based on the premise that new ideas would come when people felt they had to do something to remove discomfort. It was the most effective method for an era in which many people went hungry. The fact that Toyota management continues to run its business with a sense of crisis stems from a vestigial underlying sense of hunger.

The world is a more prosperous place now, though; one can live without slaving away all the time. It is a global age, too, and diverse values now permeate society. As Okuda has observed, "The Japanese are losing their fighting instinct." At Toyota, which has long been viewed to have a winner-take-all philosophy, morale is starting to go slack in response to voices from both inside and outside the company.

This phenomenon creates a critical situation for Toyota, which has grown the way it has because of a kind of collective obsession with making work more rational. It is because Okuda feels this crisis that he uses radical language to castigate his own company. "We're stamping large elephants," he says. "We're at scenic Mikawa, but we're sitting in a guest room with an alcove. . . . Overthrow the old Toyota!"

It has been whispered since the start of the 1990s that the prime issue for Toyota in the 21st century would be to sustain its collective obsession with making work more rational. And, indeed, things at the company are reaching a critical point. Toyota's crisis now is that Toyota employees as a group are losing their fighting instinct and their creativity. No matter how extraordinary the talent may be in the upper reaches of management, it is the employees who shoulder the business. Implementing the 2005 vision requires many new people who can carry out the business of the second founding. A new theory is needed to draw out motivation in people, one that does not rely on the centripetal energy of the Toyoda family, one that is not based on a sense of hunger, and one that is compatible with a global world.

The Toyota Way 2001

In April 2001, Toyota compiled a booklet containing the most important slogans and phrases from the company culture that, from Toyota's perspective, must not change. These are shown in Figure 6.3: The Toyota Way 2001.

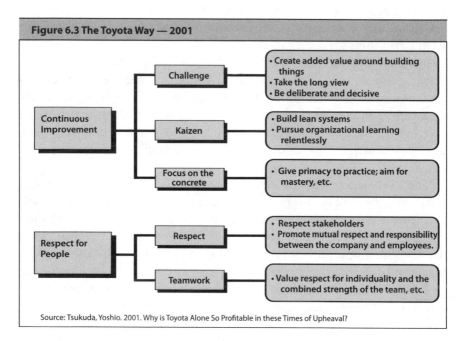

Figure 6.3 The Toyota Way — 2001

Continuous Improvement

- Challenge
  - Create added value around building things
  - Take the long view
  - Be deliberate and decisive
- Kaizen
  - Build lean systems
  - Pursue organizational learning relentlessly
- Focus on the concrete
  - Give primacy to practice; aim for mastery, etc.

Respect for People

- Respect
  - Respect stakeholders
  - Promote mutual respect and responsibility between the company and employees.
- Teamwork
  - Value respect for individuality and the combined strength of the team, etc.

Source: Tsukuda, Yoshio. 2001. Why is Toyota Alone So Profitable in these Times of Upheaval?

Toyota Way 2001 shows what sort of values people who work at Toyota share and how they should behave from the standpoint of how the Toyota Basic Principles manifest themselves in the activities of the company. The implication is that Toyota should be aggressive in changing everything else.

At the core of the Toyota Way are continuous improvement and respect for people. Respect for people means having each working individual fully demonstrate his abilities and receive commensurate evaluations and rewards. It means, conversely, not giving him work that is wasteful or does not add value.

The rest of Figure 6.3 needs no explanation. It is an extremely neat and logical system.

Drive Your Dreams

Figure 6.3 is overly theoretical, however, and not powerful enough to motivate people directly, to rouse their will to get things done. With this in mind, Toyota, in 2001, published a new corporate slogan for the start of the new century: "Drive Your Dreams." This expression conjures up the notion of new values-creation professionals who, from their own places and their own perspectives, all nourish dreams worthy of their predecessors and press forward to achieve those dreams.

At the Tokyo International Automotive Conference sponsored by Nikkei Business Publications and held on October 22 and 23, 2001, Honda senior managing director Takeo Fukui gave a talk entitled "Honda Brand Identity" and introduced the new Honda global brand slogan chosen in January 2001: "The Power of Dreams." Honda reportedly came up with the slogan after examining the unique nature of the company since it was founded.

At the same conference, Honda's president Hiroyuki Yoshino gave a speech entitled "The DNA of Honda." In the speech, he explained that Honda's DNA was the realization of dreams. New employees are encouraged to develop their own dreams—no matter how many years it takes—and to use the company to make those dreams come true.

Borrowed from the phrase "the American dream," Honda's slogan has been in use for many years. The general public has come to see the expression as being a characteristic of Honda. Inside Honda, too, if you look at what constitutes "Honda-ness," you end up with the idea of "dreams." This is Honda's centripetal force and the source of growth that, in barely half a century, has seen Honda surge through the principles of economies of scale and scope.

Toyota's "Drive Your Dreams" looks as though it has unintentionally appropriated some of Honda's stock. Toyota's slogan, however, is intended to dispel an image long colored by the company's traditional urgent "sense of crisis," an image that can no longer stir the affluent people of the current age. It is with the bright image of future dreams that Toyota people will work and demonstrate abilities beyond expectations. "Making dreams come true" is a key phrase for developing people in the 21st century.

INNOVATION IN PRODUCT DEVELOPMENT

From the end of the 20th and into the 21st centuries, the new winds of environmental issues, globalization, and an IT revolution have been sweeping across the automotive industry. As Figure 6.1 shows, Toyota has felt these new winds and has envisioned a major paradigm shift in cars and in the automotive industry over the next five to ten years. In response, Toyota is trying to get ahead of the times by bringing about a drastic change in the way it develops products.

Toyota's Strategy for Reforming Product Development in the 21st Century

The first tremors of a revolution in development at Toyota appeared in the shift to the Development Center system in September 1992. It is reasonable to assume that Toyota's aims in this shift encompassed the new development system concept shown in Figure 2.2.

In 1994, when Fujio Cho was president of TMM (Toyota Motor Manufacturing), the Toyota Motor plant in the United States, he visited the Ford factory in Atlanta—said to be the most productive plant in the United States—and was highly impressed. Toyota had a higher density of individual operations and was better at making use of people, but Ford had fewer parts and fewer operations, with the overall result that Ford used fewer people than Toyota. Until that time, the Toyota Production System had concentrated on the shopfloor and, if anything, had worked mightily to remove waste from shopfloor processes. Cho was convinced that the path toward the future would have to be one that integrated production and design. He was optimistic because Toyota was already moving in that direction (i.e., making the design work lean).

Akihiro Wada, who (in 1994) was a Toyota Motor senior managing director bringing together Development Centers One to Three, cited "earnest checking is necessary in advanced stages" as one factor in shortening development lead-times:

> *We can shrink lead-time if the components, suspension, body, and frame are finished before completing the exterior design. We can't cut the time, though, if several problems that hadn't emerged during the advanced stages come out after we get to full-blown prototype vehicles. We have to be able to do more conscientious checking at the earlier stages. This also means that we must not send vehicles to full-scale trials if they haven't been checked.*

From around 1995, Toyota began hammering out a rough strategy for serious reform of the development process for the 21st century. Figure 6.4 gives a comprehensive view of the product development revolution as it stands today.

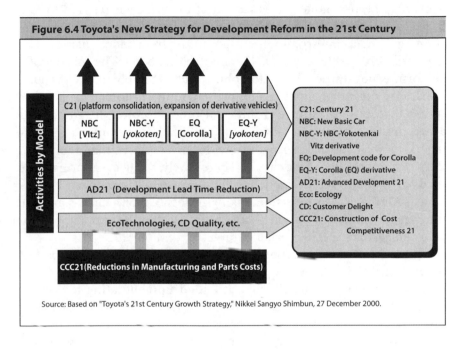

Figure 6.4 Toyota's New Strategy for Development Reform in the 21st Century

Activities by Model

C21 (platform consolidation, expansion of derivative vehicles)

| NBC [Vltz] | NBC-Y [yokoten] | EQ [Corolla] | EQ-Y [yokoten] |

AD21 (Development Lead Time Reduction)

EcoTechnologies, CD Quality, etc.

CCC21(Reductions in Manufacturing and Parts Costs)

C21: Century 21
NBC: New Basic Car
NBC-Y: NBC-Yokotenkai
 Vitz derivative
EQ: Development code for Corolla
EQ-Y: Corolla (EQ) derivative
AD21: Advanced Development 21
Eco: Ecology
CD: Customer Delight
CCC21: Construction of Cost
 Competitiveness 21

Source: Based on "Toyota's 21st Century Growth Strategy," Nikkei Sangyo Shimbun, 27 December 2000.

C21 is a strategy for expanding derivative vehicle models by consolidating platforms, AD21 is a strategy for shortening development leadtimes, and CCC21 involves cost-reduction activities by component. While C21, AD21, and Eco Technology strategy and CD Quality strategy activities are underway for individual models, CCC21—Toyota's strategy for revolutionizing 21st-century product development—cuts across all models. Each of these strategies is examined below.

Platform Consolidation and Expansion of Derivative Models

From 1993 to 1995, Toyota carried out activities focused on cost in order to rebuild its international competitiveness after the end of the economic bubble. In 1996 and 1997, it put its energies into product-power-enhancing VE activities with the aim of becoming the world's number one manufacturer. From 1998 onward, it decided to roll out C21 activities for this same purpose.

C21 involves two kinds of activities: (1) consolidating platforms and chasses and expanding product variations, and (2) unit and platform cost reductions.

A platform is a chassis on which certain functional units and components have been mounted. This section of the vehicle is referred to as a common base, or platform, because it can be carried over through generations of models and commonly used on different model names. The Japanese word for this is *shadai*, literally "vehicle base." The concept of a platform is not restricted to automobiles, but can apply to any product.

Because a platform isn't visually apparent to the customer, the idea has spread that, as long as there is sufficient product power, it can be used across multiple generations—without modification, by suitably increasing or diminishing chassis length or width or by substituting functional units or components on the chassis. Alternatively, a single platform can be used for multiple vehicle models as long as product power can be sustained. All this has the effect of making it possible for a chassis and the functional components on the chassis to be used and shared among specific models for a specific period of time.

This concept has long existed in both Japan and the United States, but because it was implemented on a case-by-case basis, there are many instances in which it failed when it ended up generating look-alike models. What is distinctive about recent moves is that, by implementing the idea in a planned fashion across the whole company and by providing for differentiation among products, Toyota has consolidated platforms and sustained Alfred Sloan's strategy of expanding product variations.

Having cut development costs by 30 percent with the *Vitz*, Toyota used the same New Basic Car (NBC) platform to expand (via *yokoten*) to derivative models such as the *Funcargo*. It then rolled out the *Corolla* in the same way, moving ahead with the technique of successively consolidating platforms while increasing the number of derivative models.

Outlined below are Toyota's plans for consolidating passenger vehicle platforms (excluding its RV models):

FF [Front-engine, Front-wheel Drive] Vehicles
1. NBC:
     Vitz, Funcargo, Platz, bB, Will Vi, Yaris (Europe)
2. Corolla Class:
     Prius, New Corolla, Corolla Fielder
3. Medium Class Vehicles with inline 4-cylinder, 2-liter engines and similar front suspensions:
     Vista, Corona, Carina, Ipsum

4. FF 3-Numbers:
    Camry, Windom, Avalon (all U.S.-produced)

FR [Front Engine, Rear-Wheel Drive] Vehicles
5. Inline 6-Cylinder Vehicles with similar front suspensions:
    Progrès, Altezza
6. FR Monocoque Medium High Class:
    Aristo, Crown, Mark II, Chaser, Cresta
7. High Class:
    Celsior

Toyota has created a Platform Committee to promote platform consolidation. With members drawn from chief engineers[2] and designing, production engineering, and marketing departments, the committee puts together a Platform Commonization Study Table for each platform component system. For each base vehicle's platform, common components and evolving components are examined and submitted to the committee, which then deliberates on their suitability.

Given lingering concerns about the wholesale carryover and sharing of components by platform, it may be that this system will be revised by combining it with the "modular design" approach described below.

Shortening the Development Cycle

Activities aimed at shortening development lead-times began in earnest at Toyota around 1995. Toyota gave the name AD21 to these activities and began standardizing them in 1998. The aim of what is usually referred to as shortening of the development cycle is to minimize product planning obsolescence by compressing the period between planning and market launch. Its major effect is the Clark-Fujimoto Rule described in Chapter 4: "Development resources are proportional to development time" (i.e., shortening development lead-time will diminish development resources). Toyota is trying to realize a momentous shortening of the development period, with the aim to drastically reduce development resources.

Shortening Lead-time Through Platform Consolidation

For the *Ipsum* and *Spacio*, which went on sale in 1995 and made use of the *Corolla* platform, and for the new model RV *Harrier*, which used the *Celsior* platform, the period of time between exterior design approval and volume production was cut to between fifteen and eighteen months, two-thirds of the previous timeframe.

The *Ipsum, Spacio,* and *Harrier* were not simply "tacked on" to *Corolla* and *Celsior* platforms. The *Corolla* and *Celsior* platforms had been developed to accommodate the subsequent derivation of the *Ipsum, Spacio,* and *Harrier.*

With these precedents and successes, Toyota launched AD21 activities in order to shorten development lead-times on a regular and rational basis.

A new standard process for the period between decision on the external design and volume production called for (1) eighteen months for a newly established or improved platform, with one advanced trial and one formal trial, (2) fifteen months for basic platform carryover, with just one formal trial and (3) twelve months for 100 percent platform carryover, with no trial. This was established as the standard development pattern.

Toyota has rolled out AD21 to all projects successively from the start of 1999. The first vehicle to which it was applied was the *Vitz,* which went on sale in 1999. Because the *Vitz* involved a newly established or improved platform, production began eighteen months after approval of the exterior design. As Figure 4.5 shows, the standard schedule in the past had been twenty-six months, meaning that AD21 lopped off eight months (or one-third of the total time) in a single stroke. For the *bB,* a *Vitz* platform carryover model that went on sale in February 2000, the standard for development was fifteen months and one formal trial because it involved basic platform carryover. Even the one formal trial was omitted in this case however, and the *bB* made it to volume production in thirteen months.

Shortening Lead-time by the Fujimoto Method

In his article *"Organizational Problem-solving in Support of Product Development,"*[3] published in the January 1998 issue of *Diamond Harvard Business,* Takahiro Fujimoto introduced a model of shortening lead-times by shifting the decision-making curve forward along with lead-time reduction policies and examples from a number of companies. In the second half of the article, Fujimoto refers to "the capacity for system emergence and evolution observable at Toyota," a reference that suggests that many of his insights came from Toyota. Indeed, the entire article can be viewed as the result of an analysis of Toyota policies and activities. Based on Fujimoto's model (and by taking into consideration additional information this author has acquired) we can represent the structure of Toyota's lead-time reduction activities as in Figure 6.5:

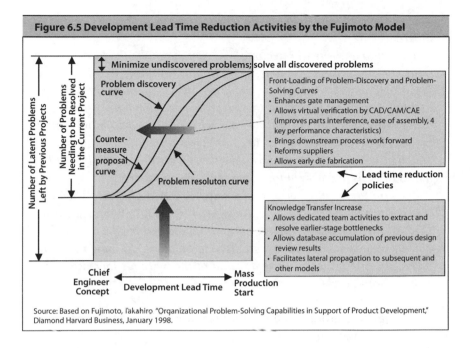

Figure 6.5 Development Lead Time Reduction Activities by the Fujimoto Model

Minimize undiscovered problems; solve all discovered problems

Number of Latent Problems Left by Previous Projects

Number of Problems Needing to be Resolved in the Current Project

Problem discovery curve

Countermeasure proposal curve

Problem resoluton curve

Front-Loading of Problem-Discovery and Problem-Solving Curves
• Enhances gate management
• Allows virtual verification by CAD/CAM/CAE (improves parts interference, ease of assembly, 4 key performance characteristics)
• Brings downstream process work forward
• Reforms suppliers
• Allows early die fabrication

Lead time reduction policies

Knowledge Transfer Increase
• Allows dedicated team activities to extract and resolve earlier-stage bottlenecks
• Allows database accumulation of previous design review results
• Facilitates lateral propagation to subsequent and other models

Chief Engineer Concept   Development Lead Time   Mass Production Start

Source: Based on Fujimoto, Takahiro "Organizational Problem-Solving Capabilities in Support of Product Development," Diamond Harvard Business, January 1998.

Shortening Lead-time Through V-comm

The trump card of lead-time reduction tools is an IT-based virtual development system, which is a cutting-edge, strategic IT technology for using computers to deal with every element of development (e.g., contour design; performance design; prototyping; assembly; experimentation; jig, die, gauge, and tool design; equipment design; and plant and process design). Although various systems, such as CAD/CAM (Computer Aided Design/Computer Aided Manufacturing), CAE (Computer Aided Engineering), CAT (Computer Aided Testing) and CAPP (Computer Aided Process Planning), have been used in this area in the past, a virtual development system synthesizes and applies all these as three-dimensional data.

In the September 10, 2001 issue of *Nikkei Business*, Kousuke Shiramizu, Toyota's executive vice president responsible for production technology, explained how Toyota has benefited from such technology:

> *[After external design approval,] we can move from design to assembly in twelve months for a new model Corolla-class vehicle. No company in Europe or the United States can match this. For them, the goal is to get the job done in less than 30 months. We're working on getting it*

down to ten months. In strategic terms, this constitutes an enormous difference.

But ten months is still too long. We want to make the lead-time so short it will astonish everyone. For example, building dies for a new Lexus used to take us seven months, and now we can build them in two months. Our current target is to do it inside of one month.

About 80 percent [of processes for which we used to build actual models have now been moved to computer screens]. It used to be that only highly skilled technicians could check places that were difficult for hands or tools to reach, but now we can use computers.

"[Computers] have been a big help [in cutting costs]. They are nearly entirely responsible for our no longer needing to build trial vehicles. In only ten years, the number of Toyota models has grown by about 50 percent. . . . where there used to be about 40, now there are about 60. And basically we've done all of this without increasing our research and development department staff.

For carmakers around the world, Shiramizu's revelations may seem more threatening than miraculous.

The computer system Toyota uses for these lead-time reductions is known as V-comm (Visual and Virtual Communications) and is basically the same as Mazda's MDI (Mazda Digital Innovation), described in detail in Osamu Imada's book, *Technology, Management, and Labor in Modern Automobile Companies.*[4] These systems carry out design, prototyping, experimentation, and trial production all by computer, reducing the number of advanced and formal trials and achieving simultaneous improvements in development lead-time, development costs, and product quality.

At the Manufacturing IT Forum 2001, sponsored by the Nihon Keizai Shimbunsha and held on November 19, 2001, Toyota managing director Akiyoshi Watanabe introduced Toyota's V-comm in a talk entitled "Using IT and Revolutionizing Development and Production Engineering Processes: Future Developments."

Watanabe said that V-comm is particularly effective in dealing with such issues as component interference problems in places like the engine room (where parts are densely packed together), operability problems in assembly, and appearance problems (such as gaps in exterior body panels), and distortion. He demonstrated production trials using a computer to build three-dimensional data on products, production equipment, and operators, and then simulated whether the product flowed smoothly, whether there was any interference with equipment, and whether excessive loads were being placed on operators. It was like seeing into the future. V-comm development began in 1996; since that time it is said to have cut the number of development stage design changes per model dramatically, from 10,000 to a current level of 400-500 (i.e., to one-twentieth of what it had been). Mazda worked out the concept of its MDI before Toyota developed its V-comm, but there is evidence to suggest that Toyota's concept has bounded ahead.

Cutting Manufacturing and Parts Costs with Modular Design

How CCC21 Was Launched

In July 2000, Toyota initiated cost-cutting activities it called CCC (Construction of Cost Competitiveness) 21, whose aim was to reduce costs by an average of 30 percent over three years, or by a total of 1 trillion yen. CCC21 activities aggressively pursue cost reductions at the most fundamental level, from concept development with suppliers through the rollout of integrated "concept-in" activities.

In the course of joint parts purchasing discussions that Toyota had held with Volkswagen since the end of the 1990s, the two companies decided to compare the costs of their respective parts purchases. Toyota's Procurement Department was brimming with self-assurance when it took up the challenge, but it was blindsided by the results. Many VW parts, it seemed, were less expensive than Toyota parts. A thorough investigation into Japan's high cost structure revealed that nearly all parts cost more in Japan, a realization that led to the birth of CCC21.

Below are excerpts from a *Nikkei Sangyo Shimbun* (December 27, 2000) report on CCC21:

> *"We were like the proverbial frog at the bottom of a well. It's quite frightening that we were unaware of the true state of affairs."* Then senior managing director Katsuaki Watanabe was in charge of procurement for Toyota Motor and he gulped when he saw the report his subordinates brought him. Chairman Hiroshi Okuda was the one who immediately sounded the alarm. *"Toyota has always been called a company with strong cost competitiveness. But we've been lulled into thinking we were the best in the world. Now the emperor has no clothes. I can't help but feel uneasy about whether Toyota really is better at making things than other companies are."*
>
> *"Toyota's overseas cost-cutting competition has come back to us like a boomerang,"* said senior managing director Ryuji Araki. When

Toyota learned that domestic and foreign rivals were cutting costs at an unexpectedly rapid pace, Toyota began preparing a counterattack. At the core was CCC21 (Construction of Cost Competitiveness), a cost-reduction program with the goal of slashing parts manufacturing costs by 30 percent in three years. Toyota set up 173 "absolute cost" items whose costs had to be reduced in order to beat the international competition. In addition, it used common parts as much as possible in its vehicle models and shifted to a philosophy of "component compatibility" for maximizing the mass production effect. "Instead of making parts to fit the car," said one Toyota executive, "we are making cars to fit the parts." They made a matrix of model compatibility on the vertical axis and component compatibility situated on the horizontal axis and set up a system for pursuing synergistic cost reduction effects (see Figure 6.4).

Each team then proceeded to take a radically new look at the items for which it was responsible, starting with the design step. They linked design simplification with reductions in the numbers of parts and other types of production streamlining, and finally, even with the consolidation of production functions and other kinds of cuts to fixed costs. From upstream to downstream, they used concurrent engineering (CE) to extend cost-reduction activities in synchrony and in parallel with one another. Watanabe's strategy was this: "We're not simply lowering the purchase prices of parts. We're working with suppliers to reduce the actual manufacturing cost of those parts."

The cost reduction target for the 173 items altogether comes to a total of 1 trillion yen. If CCC21 stays on track, Toyota manufacturing will once again achieve chairman Okuda's aim of occupying a position where it surpasses other companies.

The Modular Design, Aim of CCC21

The *Nikkei Sangyo Shimbun* article cited above suggests that the basic philosophy of CCC21 is probably "modular design," a phrase that Toyota has not widely used in public. As Figure 6.6 indicates, modular design is a technique for designing a variety of new products by combining a restricted number of component types.

Lego is a typical example of "modular design." By combining a limited number of block types, one can make a variety of products, such as cars, airplanes, or buildings. This analogy may seem silly, but, as Figure 6.7 illustrates, the Swedish truck and bus manufacturer Scania has been using *Lego*-like modular design for over fifty years. Because of recent

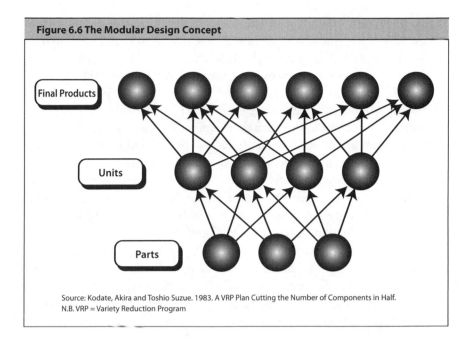

Figure 6.6 The Modular Design Concept

Final Products

Units

Parts

Source: Kodate, Akira and Toshio Suzue. 1983. A VRP Plan Cutting the Number of Components in Half.
N.B. VRP = Variety Reduction Program

industry interest in the concept, Scania is now conducting, jointly with Lego of the Netherlands, a worldwide caravan campaign to publicize modular design.

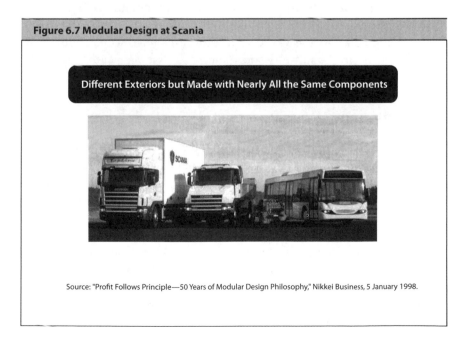

Figure 6.7 Modular Design at Scania

Different Exteriors but Made with Nearly All the Same Components

Source: "Profit Follows Principle—50 Years of Modular Design Philosophy," Nikkei Business, 5 January 1998.

In the section dealing with product diversification and component minimization in Chapter 4, we noted that part numbers per vehicle at Toyota (i.e., the modular design [MD] index) is a fraction of what it is for other carmakers. Even so, Toyota is still trying to lower its MD index.

In the January 1998 issue of *Diamond Harvard Business*, Kim Clark and Carliss Baldwin published an article entitled "Product Modularity for Next-generation Innovation"[5] [in which they explain the history and philosophy of modularization and some of its uses. They define modularization as "the provision of design modularity using small-scale subsystems, each of which can be designed independently from products or other components and which function in a unified way." In the sense that it encourages efficiency and innovation, they argue, "modularization (modular design) is particularly effective in such industries as automotive and finance."

In a dialogue with economist Masahiko Aoki, published in the Nikkei Sangyo Shimbun (July 31, 2001) as *Modularity behind Growth Spurs Leading-Edge Industrial Competition,*[6] Carliss Baldwin had this to say: "The concept of modularity is getting a lot of attention among economists. Some people even say it is one factor in the gap in economic growth between Japan and the United States. Once the rules of connecting modules to one another are established, individual modules can work together independently."

Applied to producer goods such as computers and machine tools, modular design brought about dramatic development and economic and industrial growth in the 20th century. In the 21st century, modular design is advancing through the world as a leading-edge concept about to be implemented for consumer goods, such as passenger cars, where the emphasis is on design and styling.

Modular Production and Modular Design

Modularization as generally discussed in the popular press is not the same as modular design; it is, in fact, something that can be more appropriately termed "modular production," which can be explained as "bundled delivery." In order to minimize the number of assembly processes at the finished goods maker, the supplier "bundles together" physically proximate parts for delivery, regardless of their functions or characteristics. For example, air conditioning system condensers and engine cooling system radiators (or sheet metal door systems and door functional components and plastic trim) are "bundled" and delivered as assemblies.

Modular production takes work that finished vehicle makers used to perform and shifts its management to parts suppliers. As may be expected, it lowers labor costs (due to the wage gap between the carmaker and suppliers), it reduces total assembly time, and it makes inspections between processes easier.

Because the production engineering concept here comprises assembling different functional parts, however, one concern is that this practice diminishes product engineering capabilities that require functional thinking.

The Research Institute of Economy, Trade, and Industry (RIETI) was an independent administrative agency and the forerunner of the Research Institute of International Trade and Industry within the Ministry of International Trade and Industry (MITI), now the Ministry of Economy, Trade, and Industry [METI]). At a RIETI-sponsored conference on "Modularization—A Shock to Japanese Industry" held on July 13, 2001, Nobuo Okubo, executive vice president of Nissan Motor—which was promoting modular production—said that Nissan predicted that modular production would lower costs by 5 percent and cut defects between processes to one-fifth of their previous level. At the same time, he said there was some fear that technology might become a black box and that influences on vehicle performance made painstaking decisions about the extent of modular production a point of concern.

At the Tokyo International Automotive Conference sponsored by Nikkei Business Publications and held on October 22, 2001, Majdi Abulaban of Delphi Automotive Systems stressed that in order to discover the advantages of modular production, other than the reduction of the labor cost, automakers must trust parts supplier and give them development responsibilities and authority. Abulaban's comments reflected the frustration of a parts supplier who wanted to expand business opportunities and was trying to explain the advantages of modular production to the manufacturer of finished vehicles.

Since modular production often involves a mega-supplier of bundled delivery units, some industry analysts suggest that cost advantages emerge in modular production in line with the progress of parts commonization and mass production. This leads to a kind of "putting a roof on a roof" effect, however, in which primary suppliers become secondary suppliers and secondary suppliers become tertiary suppliers. With a multilayered hierarchical structure being one of the factors contributing to Japan's high costs, this arrangement results in a high-cost structure overall. Moreover, as Okubo says, there is a concern that modular production can lead to technological black boxes. Its overall advantages have yet to be proven.

Modular design, a technique for designing various new products by combining a limited number of component types, is fundamentally different from modular production (bundled delivery). To begin with, the word "module" conveys the idea of combination, compatibility, and common use. "Bundled delivery" may convey the idea of assembly, but it does not suggest combination, compatibility, or common use. Thus, referring to bundled delivery as "modular production" is inaccurate. Ford and the Mazda Group still use the expression "full service supplier," a far more appropriate term. Nonetheless, since the tendency to use "bundled delivery" as "modular production" is currently prevalent, our discussion below follows suit.

Toyota's view of modular production is that it is partially effective and in some cases has no drawbacks, so it does not reject the concept across the board. Toyota does reject the idea of its wholesale use, however, because it diminishes the automaker's overall technical development capabilities. Rather than bundling components without regard for their functions, however, Toyota is more oriented toward "systemization," i.e., bundling components from the same functional family. In doing so, Toyota is applying the principles of modular design. Toyota's thinking is that, for example, an air conditioning system, is a system of components that belong to the same functional family. Thus, even though components such as the air conditioner unit, condenser, compressor, and evaporator are not physically close to one another, they should be bundled together, and parts suppliers and organizations involved in the production and assembly of these components should be rearranged accordingly. Components are sometimes delivered separately, as they always have been.

Modular production emphasizes production, whereas systemization emphasizes design. Toyota's orientation is to emphasize design. This is a reasonable choice since we are moving from an era in which production added value to one in which design adds value.

Furthermore, Toyota has declared that in the 21st century, the Toyota Group overall will grow as a system integrator that reorganizes work partially by modular units but overall by system units, and that becomes skilled at both modular production and systemization (modular design). Rather than being swept along by the fashion for modular production, Toyota has thought for itself and has devised its own unique and new approach.

Previous Examples of Modular Design at Toyota

Previous instances of modular design at Toyota (or, more properly, the Toyota Group) begin in the late 1970s at Toyota Motor's sworn ally, Nippon Denso (now Denso).

In 1981, Nippon Denso shocked radiator component suppliers around the world when it developed and marketed a revolutionary new type of radiator, the SR radiator. An article detailing the story of the new development appeared in the journal of the Japan Society of Mechanical Engineers in January 1985, and in 1985 the radiator won the JSME's Technology Award. A paper on the new radiator was subsequently presented in 1986 at the 29th National Meeting on Standardization and was later published in the journal of the JSME (April 1988).

These papers are valuable references for manufacturing industries and are recommended reading. The summary below comes principally from the paper by Kazuhiro Ohta and Mineo Hanai, which was published in the April 1988 issue of the JSME journal under the title "Flexible Automation and Design—An Example of Automobile Radiators."[7]

Nippon Denso's SR radiator was first put through a VE analysis resulting in both product diversification and component minimization, i.e., a smaller, lighter, higher performance product with fewer components. These apparently conflicting features were achieved by means of core diversification combinations shown in Figure 6.8.

Figure 6.8 A Response to Diversification

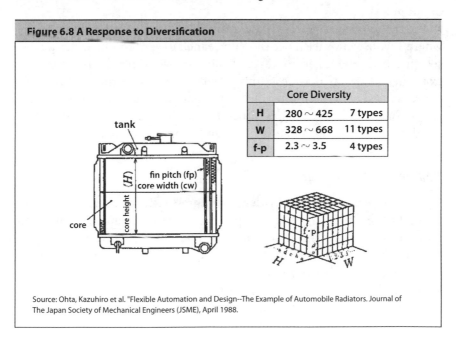

Core Diversity		
H	280 ~ 425	7 types
W	328 ~ 668	11 types
f-p	2.3 ~ 3.5	4 types

Source: Ohta, Kazuhiro et al. "Flexible Automation and Design--The Example of Automobile Radiators. Journal of The Japan Society of Mechanical Engineers (JSME), April 1988.

Nippon Denso had no special term for the method, but this was modular design. For the core in Figure 6.8, for example, a mere 28 types of fin tubes make it possible to build 7 × 11 × 4, or 308 core varieties. Standardizing the cores also minimized the types of components surrounding the core, including upper tanks, lower tanks, and side brackets.

In the past, designers would make fresh designs in response to carmaker demands. This meant that components varied infinitely and investment and maintenance costs for parts, equipment, and dies were enormous.

Modular design is a good concept, but the approach is difficult to adopt if no consideration is given to the carmaker that mounts the parts. Most carmakers send orders to suppliers after the design of the vehicle as a whole is completed, so sometimes the external portions of Nippon Denso's SR radiator would assume their characteristic shapes to conform to the shape of the vehicle. The external shapes of radiators mounted in Toyota vehicles, however, were all uniform, a reflection of Toyota's inclination to build the car around the components.

The basic requirements of modular design call for using fixed increment spacing (or module numbers) and standard product and component dimensions. In Figure 6.8, the module numbers are as follows: $(425 - 280) \div 7 » 20$mm spacing for height, $(668 - 328) \div 11 » 30$mm spacing for width and $(3.5 - 2.3) \div 4 = 0.3$mm spacing for fins (f. p., or fin pitch).

From the perspective of module numbers, we can glimpse instances where Toyota Motor itself occasionally leaned toward modular design. We see that care was taken to vary wheelbases by 80mm increments, for example, and that module numbers were applied to the leading-edge coordinates of combination switches in an attempt to standardize switch levers. Since modular design is difficult to apply piecemeal, however, Toyota did not venture into modular design beyond this level.

Approaches to Modular Design

In the 20th century, modular design progressed for producer goods for which little emphasis is placed on product appearance and styling (computers and industrial machinery, for example). In the 21st century, Toyota is revisiting modular design and applying its concepts to the totality of product design, component design, and related equipment design. Through the ensuing product diversification, component minimization, and the concentration of production functions, Toyota is lowering the cost of manufacturing itself.

Toyota Motor executive vice president Katsuaki Watanabe has this to say about component modularization: "When it comes to component modularization, Toyota focuses on how to change designs. We're moving ahead with modularization and systemization with an approach that asks what is a good design, what is good performance, what is good quality, and what is a good way to make things."

Clearly, when Watanabe says "component modularization" he is not talking about modular production, but about modular design predicated on systemization.

In response to predictable future changes, Hiroshi Okuda has cited the "cassette system" (simplification of frame construction) as a subject that deserves study (*Weekly Diamond, ed. Toyota Management and the Law of the Last Man Standing*).[8] This, too, may be seen as a reference to modular design.

Tadaaki Jagawa, who moved from an executive vice presidency at Toyota to become the president of Hino Motors in April 2001, says, "Toyota's Kyohokai [supplier group] is the focus of modular design for trucks." In real terms, this means that when it buys parts from Kyohokai suppliers, Toyota also covers development costs and certain types of new investments needed for driving modular design.

In March 2002, Hino Motors announced a business partnership with Scania, the Swedish truck and bus manufacturer which has been using modular design for over fifty years (see Figure 6.7). The official announcement cited "global complementarity" as the purpose of the partnership, but given Hino's sluggish performance, Jagawa's aim was probably an attempt (through modular design) to revive a truck and bus business whose sales showed little prospect of recovery.

The words and actions of men like Watanabe, Okuda, and Jagawa show that 21st-century Toyota is reinventing itself by seriously rethinking the idea of designing automobiles like Legos.

In the January 2002 issue of *Diamond Harvard Business*, Lee Fleming et al. published "Pitfalls of Faith in Modularization,"[9] an article warning against excessive modularization (modular design). The authors opine: "Many firms seem to be misusing the technology, destroying opportunities for breakthroughs and hollowing out the innovation process." One wonders what country they are talking about. In the United States, we see, modular design has advanced to the point where articles are coming out to warn against its shortcomings.

Modular design is all about high quality and low price, but it also carries within it the risk that products will look tired or overly simple. In driving modular design, it is critical, as Fleming et al. maintain, that "once modularization has progressed to a certain point, those in charge of research need to let developers 'play' with highly interdependent technologies in order to maximize the possibility of breakthroughs." Japan, as a whole, has not yet reached that level.

In the 20th century, modular design developed around producer goods for which exterior design was not particularly important. The reason that it did not spread to cars and other consumer goods where external design is important is that there were no universal procedures on the market for driving modular design. What is needed now is a general theory for applying modular design and for that theory to spread.

Reforming the Management of Product Information

One important issue in the design revolution is that of constructing a basic system for managing knowledge across the entire company—especially design department knowledge. Product development is a job that calls for total mobilization of company knowledge to increase the added value of product information while clarifying internal constraints. Two things are needed to perform this job efficiently.

1. Faster what-if analyses (i.e., asking what changes will cause what to change) by increasing the frequency per unit time of information exchange among departments
2. Obtaining new knowledge from this process and increasing the number of goal-seeking simulations (i.e., asking what is the shortest path to achieving the goal)

As we saw in Chapter 3 in the section on computer system management, making this possible requires the establishment of a company-wide product function structure to serve as a basic means for the unified management of design information and design knowledge. It then means creating the PDM (Product Data Management) system shown in Figure 3.15.

Toyota has probably begun resolving these issues already. If Toyota is going to cut development lead-time to an unprecedented 10 months and implement modular design as the ultimate form of product development, then it is going to have to establish PDM and make it possible to conduct what-if analyses and goal-seeking simulations.

In March 2002, Toyota announced that it was replacing *Caelum*, an in-house CAD system that it had already put on the market, and that it would use *CATIA* (made by Dassault in France) for interior and exterior contoured components and *Pro/Engineer* (made by Parametric Technology in the United States) for mechanical components. Both *CATIA* and *Pro/Engineer* are CAD systems with concurrent engineering functions that are well established in their respective fields. Best of all, they are each capable of performing integrated management of PDM information from CAD, CAE, component tables, and engineering information. The system integration described by Toyota's chief information officer and executive vice president Susumu Miyoshi (see Chapter 3, A Company-Wide Information System) has finally begun at the most basic level.

MANAGEMENT STANDARDS FROM TOYOTA

Hiroshi Okuda has said, "An important task for a manager is that he come to management with his own image of what kind of Japan he wants to build and what kind of company he want to make."

When he was appointed to the chairmanship of the Japan Federation of Employers' Associations (*Nikkeiren*) in May 1999, Okuda announced that during his tenure (of two terms and four years), he wanted to bring the national unemployment rate to 3 percent, or nearly full employment. Okuda's goal suggests a management standard that Japanese industries should aim for. Toyota, under Okuda's influence, began emerging as a "good company" willing to lend a hand to the economic recovery of Japan as a whole.

One tangible change appears in positive outside initiatives conducted by Toyota managers. Another is the standardization of the Toyota management system and its active transmission outside the company.

Outside Activities by Toyota Management

The year 2000 might well be said to mark the inauguration of Toyota's *extra-corporate* activities. As numerous Japanese companies adopted the Western system of outside directors, many companies invited important individuals at Toyota to join their boards. In response to these requests, several Toyota managers began to make contributions at other companies:

- May 2000. Sakura Bank. Shoichiro Toyoda and others become outside directors.
- September 2000. Consolidation of Sanwa Bank and two other banks. Toyota chairman Okuda joins as an outside director.
- November 2000. Aioi Insurance Company. Toyota president Cho joins as an outside director.
- November 2000. Nomura sets up a management consulting organ. Toyota chairman Okuda and four others become external advisors.
- January 2001. NEC Management Advisory Committee. Toyota president Cho and others join as external committee members.

At the end of July 2001, when NEC announced a management plan for broad restructuring, Cho, then on the Management Advisory Committee, called for a thorough investigation into the reasons for the delayed decision. "Why do you have to restructure so much production equipment and so many people now?" he asked. "Management needs to verify the situation again." NEC president Nishigaki stressed the utility of the Management Advisory Committee, saying, "We've heard about the production revolution at Toyota Motor and gotten many valuable suggestions." From this scenario alone, we get a glimpse of the enthusiasm Toyota managers showed for spreading Toyota-style management beyond Toyota.

Standardization and Transmission of the Toyota Management System

Standardizing Indexes for Assessing Management

In September 2001, a public-service corporation called the Central Japan Industries Association (CJIA, *Chubu Sangyo Renmei*) completed its Japan Management Standards (JMS) in cooperation with Toyota Motor and other companies representing Central Japan. In addition to Toyota, fifteen other companies, including Sony EMCS, Minokamo TEC, and Seiko Epson created the standards as a new management assessment system that could be applied to manufacturing firms in a variety of industries.

JMS divides the management of a manufacturing firm into two rubrics: functions (management functions) and processes (production processes). The functional rubric is divided into seven areas: management, human resources, quality assurance, cost, environment, safety, and financial returns. There are seven areas on the process side as well: development, production technology, purchasing and procurement management, shopfloor management and kaizen, equipment maintenance, manufacturing quality, and sales capability. Each of the fourteen areas undergoes a detailed evaluation of management methods and organizational systems, with some 395 diagnostic categories in all. Each category is rated on a four-point scale of 0, 2, 4, or 5. Midpoint rankings have been eliminated in order to avoid vague diagnoses. Figure 6.9 shows a portion of a JMS checksheet.

Central Japan Industries Association explains the JMS as follows:

The JMS makes it possible to grasp the management activities of a manufacturing firm in terms of the intersections of seven functional areas and seven process areas. Combined with a 0, 2, 4, or 5-point ranking, it shows the route needed to improve company performance as a three-dimensional matrix.

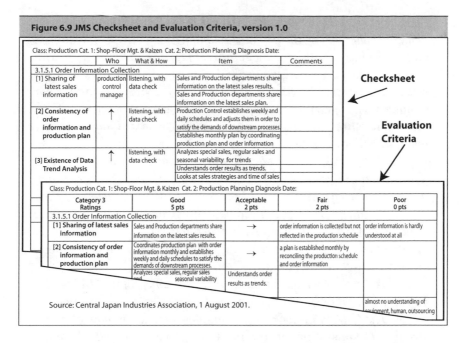

Figure 6.9 JMS Checksheet and Evaluation Criteria, version 1.0

Source: Central Japan Industries Association, 1 August 2001.

*The JMS involved constant on-site collection of actually imple-
mented management practices from fifteen top companies that have
shown continuous evolution and growth. These were studied exhaus-
tively over the course of two years in order to identify the most important categories common to manufacturing firms. For manufacturing
companies, then, these may be called management "genes of growth
and DNA of evolution." JMS checksheets are used consistently at each
phase, from **diagnosis** of the current situation to **improvement**
(kaizen) based on the results of that diagnosis, to later **evaluation**.
Finally, the Central Japan Industries Association provides recognition
to companies that have attained a certain level." (From the Central
Japan Industries Association homepage)*

Quite coincidentally, the shape the JMS takes, as intersections of seven
(management) function areas and seven (production) process areas,
resembles the structure of the Toyota Management System shown in Figure 3.1.

It was president Tadaaki Jagawa of Hino Motors who triggered the for-
mation of the JMS during his tenure as executive vice president at Toyota.
On September 14, 2001, Jagawa spoke about the origins and history of the
JMS at a reception during which completion of the JMS at the Central
Japan Industries Association was announced:

The decade (of the 1990s) caused us a lot of frustration. When we thought about reviving the Japanese manufacturing industry, we argued that we wanted to rediscover the sources of Japanese management. With the global economy entering our field of vision, three themes emerged when we considered how we might advance. The first was to take our comprehension of tacit knowledge and make it explicit. Next, this didn't mean qualitative transmission of knowledge. We needed a quantitative rollout. Third, we had to make it open.

As for the JMS, top managers, middle managers, and shopfloor management all need to have some things in common. Or rather, things get moving when they do. I think of the JMS as a means for that. When you diagnose and analyze your own company and you have some sort of what's often called a benchmark, then you need to get management plans and the true state of management to penetrate to every corner of the company.

I think it will be a truly encouraging endorsement if the JMS is used by companies that have in common the fact that they manufacture things. The CJIA's JMS looks at the management know-how of fifteen strong companies representing the Central region—well, there are other aspects as well—but to put it bluntly, I think they're about 70 to 80 percent similar to one another. If I had my way, I'd like to take this soon to Southeast Asia and elsewhere overseas so it could be of use to management around the world. And I'd like to move quickly to systematize it by including the thinking of various professors and not just business leaders. I'd like manufacturing to be in the spotlight again and I'd like a new, evolved Japanese management to be able to leap proudly out on the world stage again.

Toyota had had what might be called a Toyota version of the JMS some two years before this. When Tadaaki Jagawa suggested creating the CJIA's JMS on the basis of the Toyota version, certain people at Toyota opposed the suggestion at the implementation level, arguing that the know-how was Toyota property. Jagawa's view was that all companies have unique know-how and that the significance of this initiative lay in synthesizing Toyota's knowledge with that of other companies. Along with obtaining permission from then-president Okuda, Jagawa secured the participation of many people inside and outside Toyota and did everything he could to ensure the success of the CJIA's JMS. Jagawa, who left his position as executive vice president at Toyota and began serving as president of Hino Motors on April 13, 2001, was at one point a strong candidate for the presidency of Toyota. He had come up from the trenches of production engineering via procurement, personnel, and management planning, following an admirable career path that creates good managers. When Fujio Cho chose Jagawa to be president of Hino Motors Co., he told Hino he was sending them an ace. Jagawa is indeed a first-class manager with a broad vision, and under his direction, future trends at Hino Motors Co. will bear watching.

Japan Organization for Innovation in Manufacturing, Human Development, and Quality

May 23, 2001, saw the launch of the Japan Organization for Innovation in Manufacturing, Human Development, and Quality, *Nihon Monozukuri Hitozukuri Shitsu Kakushin Kiko*, usually called the *Nihon Monozukuri Kiko*, a management research organization that sought an ideal Japanese-type management model for "creating high added-value products and services." Since Toyota Motor emeritus chairman Shoichiro Toyoda was named honorary board chairman of the Nihon Monozukuri Kiko and former Toyota executive vice president and current Denso chairman Akira Takahashi became managing director, jokes are made about the organization being about standardizing Toyota management or relying on Toyota to rebuild quality. Takahashi doesn't deny the jokes.

> *"We'll be successful," Takahashi says, "if we can be a catalyst for Japan to generate a great business model in order to brink back its international competitiveness.*

> *"Japan has ISO 9000 and a variety of other business quality standards, but from a manager's perspective, these are merely fragmentary and, as might be expected of schemes made principally by academics, they have aspects that are difficult to understand. Even ISO 9000 is nothing more than a sort of passport for qualifying to do business. And as far as improving the quality of management is concerned, one can hardly say it's the real thing.*

> *"What's being demanded of companies now is that they build new business and improve the efficiency of existing business, in other words, that their management be quick-witted and good at change. Managers will probably find things easier to understand if we show ourselves to be heading in the general direction of building a business model in partnership with existing quality standards groups and industry, government, university, and other research organizations."*

The activities of the *Nihon Monozukuri Kiko* are based on three policies:

1. Instilling in employees and managers a sense that it is important that management increase trust, joy, and vitality.
2. Rebuilding and promulgating a Japanese management model in a form that is easy for managers to understand and that centers on self-assessment and *kaizen*.
3. Collaborating with existing organizations to develop a Japanese management model.

Based on these policies, the organization was to propose a sample new management model to industry in three years.

(The above is excerpted from "*Japan Organization for Innovation in Manufacturing, Human Development, and Quality Launched.*" June 19, 2001. *Nikkei Sangyo Shimbun*).[10]

The *Nihon Monozukuri Kiko* drew together a broad spectrum of business people and academics who hoped to rehabilitate Japanese manufacturing and formed them into eight working groups. Three years later, in April 2004, each working group announced its achievements to the public:

Working Group 1: New Product Development Working Group
1. *Report on the Activities of the New Product Development Working Group*
2. *Narrative New Product Development*

Working Group 2: Working Group for Business Process Innovation
1. *The Front Lines of Business Process Innovation*
2. *The Front Lines of Business Process Innovation, Digest Edition*

Working Group 3: Working Group for Customer Value Creation
1. *A Customer Value Creation System to Change Japan, from Manufacturing to Service and Agriculture*

Working Group 4: Working Group for the Development of Self-Diagnosis Methods for Management Systems
1. *Self-Diagnosis Methods for Management Systems*
2. *Appendix to Self-Diagnosis Methods for Management Systems: A Table of Self-Diagnosis Methods*

Working Group 5: Executive Development Working Group
1. *Proposal for a Development Program for Executives in Technical Fields*

Working Group 6: Working Group for the Development of Quality Experts
1. *A Proposal Concerning the Development of Quality Experts for the Revival of Manufacturing*
2. *Proposal: A Quality Expert Development Course for the Revival of Manufacturing*

**Working Group 7: Working Group for the Development of
    Shopfloor Personnel**
1. *Practical Notes on Developing Shopfloor Personnel*
2. *Bringing Dreams to the Shopfloor—Promoting Individual Growth*

**Working Group 8: Working Group for Improving the Quality of
    Health Care**
1. *Building a Healthcare Management Model Based on ISO 9000*

Even without going into the details of the above outcomes, surely we can see that this was a historical attempt to consolidate Japanese manufacturing wisdom. We can expect a resurgence of industrial prosperity as this wisdom spreads and is applied throughout Japanese industry.

It is a fine thing that busy and senior people like Shoichiro Toyoda and Akira Takahashi often take on activities of this sort that are tantamount to volunteer work. Probably they can do so because they are convinced that the Toyota Production System can be of help to the development of society and because they feel a sense of mission and want to contribute. What used to be jokingly referred to as an imperious "Mikawa Monroe Doctrine" is already a thing of the past.

Using Human Resources at Toyota

The Japanese economy was still sluggish when Okuda was named chairman of the Japan Federation of Employers' Associations (*Nikkeiren*) in May 1999. As previously noted, he announced that he wanted to bring Japan's unemployment rate to 3 percent. In July 2001, the unemployment rate topped 5 percent.

"We know what we have to do," said Okuda when he was selected to be a private-sector member of the [Prime Minister's] Council on Economic and Fiscal Policy. "All that's left is the implementation." At the first meeting of the council on January 6, 2001, Okuda declared, "It is vital that this council consider measures to rectify our country's high cost structure." Wherever one looks in the Japanese economy, one finds numerous jobs, systems and organizations that generate no added value. This amounts to wasteful consumption of the nation's energy.

The unemployment rate began to fall as the Japanese economy began to show signs of recovery in 2003. In the view of economics scholars and analysts, however, this was not the result of strength, but rather, of early "restructuring" effects of plant closings and personnel reductions. This would not close the gap and make Japan internationally competitive with the renascent nations of Europe and North America nor with the rapidly growing economic region of East Asia. Nor would it do to rely on stalled national policies of economic reform.

The Central Japan International Airport Company, Ltd., was founded in May 1998 with former Toyota executive Yukihisa Hirano as president. He applied rigorous Toyota-style management to the project, saving ¥60 billion, for example, by using a bidding system for landfill suppliers during airport construction. The overall savings for building the airport amounted to ¥124.9 billion. As a result, when the new airport opened in February 2005, the ¥655,700 landing fees for a jumbo jet were far lower than comparable fees at Narita Airport (¥948,000) and Kansai Airport (¥825,600), both of which are struggling with deficits. The use of a T-shaped terminal building to shorten flows and reduce connection times is another example, moreover, of prolific Toyota-style *kaizen* activities at the airport. Toyota has begun to step out and teach by example.

Starting around 2007, the first generation World War II baby boomers will reach retirement age in Japan and leave companies in large numbers. We have already seen the beginnings of this so-called 2007 Problem involving the loss of the valuable human resources that developed and sustained postwar Japanese manufacturing. Declaring that he wants to get "manufacturing seniors back to the plate," Takahiro Fujimoto of the University of Tokyo has established a course at the university to train "senior instructors in manufacturing" with a view to using these resources to raising the standard of Japanese technology.

Toyota will be no exception to the loss of the baby boomer generation. In order to continue using these valuable resources within the company, Toyota is taking the lead in the industry of applying to all employees a system of rehiring those who have reached the retirement age of 65. Not content to rely on national economic reforms, Toyota has also begun to teach Toyota-style reform by providing the society at large with "Toyota seniors" such as Hirano, who was trained within the Toyota system.

The "Leaning" of Industry on a Global Scale

The earth is in a bad way. There is a possibility that the planet may become uninhabitable by the end of the 21st century. The prime culprits are materials that burden the environment emitted by secondary manufacturing industries and by fossil fuel-powered products, such as the automobile, produced by those industries. At the rate we're going, our enjoyment of convenience will deprive our grandchildren of the right to exist. Unfortunately, people find it difficult to let go of any convenience they have once enjoyed.

The solution to this problem lies in lessening the burden on the earth as we maintain conveniences that we currently enjoy, in other words, in becoming "leaner." Becoming leaner means reducing wasteful energy use and increasing energy efficiencies. When energy is invested into achieving a given goal, that energy can be divided into energy used effectively and energy used wastefully. Energy efficiency is the proportion of energy used effectively. Reducing energy used wastefully increases energy efficiency. That is what becoming "lean" means.

Only 20 percent of the energy (fossil fuel) put into an automobile is used effectively. 80 percent of it is released into the air as carbon dioxide and heat energy. Hybrid vehicles raise energy efficiency to 30 percent and proportionately lower the release into the air of carbon dioxide and heat. This represents the "leaning" of a power device and a mechanism by which the burden on the earth can be reduced.

The Toyota Production System is called a "lean production system," and the situation on the production shopfloor is one in which production energy and production equipment operations are minimized with respect to the products of production. The fact that Toyota continues to lead Japanese industry in environmental management is not unrelated to Toyota's lean production system. A Toyota-style "leaning" of industry is needed on a global scale. And soon.

At the Nikkei BP-sponsored Tokyo International Automotive Conference in October 2001, Okuda gave a ten-minute speech outside the planned agenda. In it, he said the automobile industry faces three challenges as it looks toward the future:

1. Overcoming problems of exhaust emissions and waste products and making technical breakthroughs for sustainable development
2. Establishing an international system and rules of competition
3. Merging people and vehicles through information technology

A careful look at these three points reveals that each of them is connected to reducing the burden on the earth's environment:

1. In 1997, Toyota launched sales of the *Prius*, the world's first mass-produced hybrid vehicle. 2003 saw a full model change, with a further improvement in fuel consumption accompanied by significant improvements in running performance. Steady technical breakthroughs are proceeding.

   In recognition for the *Prius* launch, as well as for its construction of environmental management systems (including responses to ISO 14001) and its active disclosure of environmental information, Toyota received the "Global 500" award from the United Nations Environmental

Program (UNEP) in 1999. This prize is awarded to individuals and organizations for achievements in environmental protection and improvement for sustainable development. In cooperation with the Toyota Foundation, whose purpose is to subsidize research and citizen action, Toyota commemorated its receipt of this award in 2000 by setting up an assistance program to fulfill the ideals of the award.

2. On this point, Okuda has said that we need "technical and international consolidation and standardization of automobile functions." By "automobile functions," he means the "functional product components" we refer to in the computer system management section of Chapter 3 and in the section in the present chapter on revolutionizing the management of product information. He was proposing that functional product components be consolidated and standardized on an international basis.

   The basic functions of cars have not changed at all in the more than 100 years since the automobile came into being. Even if methods and performance have improved, the functions of engines, drive trains, steering wheels, brakes and suspensions, are the same as they were in automobiles 100 years ago, and consolidation and standardization across companies and countries is quite possible. Currently, each automaker creates and manages its own functional product components, so the waste is considerable.

   Consolidating and standardizing the functional components of automobiles would lead to substantial improvement in the flow of product and parts information for the entire automobile industry, including component suppliers. This is because functional product components provide basic coding systems for managing product and parts information. Having one standard for functional product components across the automobile industry and linking everything with IT would make the flow of product and parts information between automakers and component suppliers much smoother and make it possible to spread "lean" globally.

   At present, we see the spread of international CALS (commerce at light speed) standards for the common digital management of products throughout their entire life cycles. If functional product components are standardized, then a revolutionary new information age will be born and the economic effects will be incalculable.

   This idea is obviously not limited to the automotive industry. The basic functions of most of the products in the world have not changed since those products came into being. The concept, therefore, can be applied to nearly all products.

3. An automobile is a secondary living space, a space in which various kinds of information for living should be as accessible as they are in the primary living space. By providing an environment inside the vehicle in which one can gain access to information on such matters as traffic,

traffic jams, necessary products and business, the wasteful use of automobiles can be greatly reduced and the burden on the earth's environment lessened.

Toyota is beginning to deal in earnest with the protection of the earth's environment. In order to justify their own reasons for existence, industries worldwide in the 21st century should study Toyota's lean management—i.e., the Toyota Management System—and use it as a foundation for building their own strengths.

Endnotes

1. *Seisan Shisutemu no Shinkaron.*
2. *shusa.*
3. *Seihin Kaihatsu o Sasaeru Soshiki no Mondai-kaiketsuryoku.*
4. *Gendai Jidosha Kigyo no Gijutsu, Kanri, Rodo.*
5. *Jisedai no Inobeshon o umu Seihin no Mojuruka.*
6. *Seicho no Kage ni Mojuruka Ari, Sentan Sangyo de Kyoso Unagasu.*
7. *Furekushiburu Otomeshon to Sekkei—Jidoshayo Rajieta o Rei ni Shite.*
8. *Shukan Daiyamondo, ed. Toyota Keiei Hitorigachi no Hosoku.*
9. *"Mojuruka" Shinko no Otoshiana.*
10. *Nihon Monozukuri Kiko Hossoku.*

Index

About the Author

Born in 1945, Satoshi Hino earned a degree in engineering at Tohoku University and joined a major Japanese automotive manufacturer in 1968. He worked in research and development of engines until 1987. In 1988, he transferred to the administrative (staff) section of the R&D Department to take charge of activities focused on improving product development and management systems.

In 2001, Hino founded Integrated Management Intelligence Institute (IMAGINE). He authored the paper "Modular Design Approach for Wide Variation Products and Narrow Variation Parts," which received the Excellent Paper Award in 2001 sponsored by All Japan Management Efficiency Federation.

In 2004, Hino became a professor at Hiroshima University, in the Graduate School of Social Sciences, Department of Management Studies.

The author has spent more than 20 years researching the subject of this book.

- MAKE WORK FUN - CAME TO WORK ANXIOUS, GO HOME DESIRING TO TALK ABOUT IT -

  - GO TO MEETINGS PREPARED

  - TEACH PEOPLE TO WANT TO GROW

  - PERMANENT GROWTH COMES FROM ACCUMULATING KNOWLEDGE & PASSING IT ON

  - TAKING RISK IS MAKING A DECISION WHEN THE OUTCOME IS UNCERTAIN.

  ⊛ NEED TO TRAIN OUR CUSTOMERS + OUR SUPPLIER ABOUT WHAT WE KNOW!

  - ELEVATE VALUE OF PEOPLE THROUGH WORK

  - PLAY THROUGH WORK!

  - PROBLEM SOLVING PLANS

  - MUDA = WASTE.

  - FORESIGHT - SEE WHATS UP AHEAD